ARMS CONTROL

ARMS CONTROL

COOPERATIVE SECURITY IN A CHANGING ENVIRONMENT

EDITED BY
JEFFREY A. LARSEN

WITH A FOREWORD BY
THOMAS C. SCHELLING

LYNNE
RIENNER
PUBLISHERS

BOULDER
LONDON

Published in the United States of America in 2002 by
Lynne Rienner Publishers, Inc.
1800 30th Street, Boulder, Colorado 80301
www.rienner.com

and in the United Kingdom by
Lynne Rienner Publishers, Inc.
3 Henrietta Street, Covent Garden, London WC2E 8LU

Library of Congress Cataloging-in-Publication Data
Arms control : cooperative security in a changing environment / edited by
   Jeffrey A. Larsen.
     p. cm.
   Includes bibliographical references and index.
   ISBN 1-58826-013-5 (hc)—ISBN 1-58826-038-0 (pb)
   1. Arms control. I. Larsen, Jeffrey Arthur, 1954–
JZ5687 .A764   2002
327.1'74—dc21   2002069751

British Cataloguing in Publication Data
A Cataloguing in Publication record for this book
is available from the British Library.

Printed and bound in the United States of America

Contents

Part 3   Regional Perspectives

Part 4 Future Challenges for Arms Control

Foreword

Thomas C. Schelling

Beginning in the late 1950s the study and discussion of arms control were transformed from the rhetorical to the professional and the influential. All the chapters in this volume are professional; all will almost certainly be influential.

Some of us still remember the ideological disputes over the terms *arms control* and *disarmament*. Donald G. Brennan in his 1961 editor's preface to *Arms Control, Disarmament, and National Security* had to warn against the "false dichotomy" of "disarmament *versus* arms control." He said, "The point of view of this book . . . is that 'arms control' is a generic term that includes the possibility of literal 'disarmament' among other possible cases." He went on to say that a few writers held that "arms control" was a "distinctly wicked doctrine" and that those who advocated it in contrast to disarmament were made to appear as immoral proponents of the continuation of the arms race.[1]

Brennan was clearly smarting. He evidently felt that the "disarmers" occupied the moral high ground, and he needed to defend his own authors. I remember a number of occasions when accusations were vituperative, but the antagonism had already peaked by the time the book appeared. It was clearly "arms control" that successfully indoctrinated the John F. Kennedy administration, and Brennan's somewhat intemperate attack was probably unnecessary by the time the book was in print.

The dispute over terminology, like the dispute over substance, was not purely domestic. At that time, general and complete disarmament—or "GCD," as it was familiarly called—was every government's stated goal, especially the Soviet Union's. At a Pugwash conference held in Moscow in December 1960, the Soviet delegation refused to countenance the idea of "arms control," insisting it was a U.S. formulation intended to draw all attention to issues of arms inspection. There was actually introduced a resolution to the effect that anyone who did not subscribe to GCD should be asked to leave the conference and go home. The Americans, about 18 of us, met that evening in the hotel room of Leo Szilard, the acknowledged leader of our group. On the issue of GCD, Leo opined that it was a harmless resolution and we might as well go along with it. I vouchsafed that there were at least two in our group who did not believe in GCD. Leo, smiling, asked who the "other one" was. I said, "you." He thought a moment, smiled, and said he'd ask them to withdraw the resolution.

Three books appeared in 1961 that epitomized an emerging consensus on what strategic arms control should be about. Each was a group effort; each stimulated discussion while it was being composed. During the summer of 1960, Hedley Bull's manuscript for *The Control of the Arms Race* was circulated by the Institute for Strategic Studies in London in preparation for the institute's second annual conference. In the spring of 1960 Donald Brennan organized a conference on drafts prepared for an issue of the journal *Daedalus*—papers that eventually appeared in a 1961 book. And that same summer a study group, sponsored by the Twentieth Century Fund, met on the outskirts of Boston to explore arms control; out of it came a little book that Morton H. Halperin and I produced, reflecting what we took to be a consensus. An arms control seminar, jointly sponsored by Harvard and MIT, met monthly to critique chapters of the Twentieth Century Fund book.[2]

When President Kennedy put together his administration at the beginning of 1961, this new arms control consensus was thoroughly represented. Members of the Harvard-MIT seminar became the president's National Security Advisor and his White House science advisor, the general counsel of the Department of State, the assistant secretary of state for policy planning, and the deputy assistant secretary for arms control and deputy assistant secretary for Europe in the Defense Department. Eight years later, when Richard Nixon put together his administration, another member of that seminar became the president's National Security Advisor.

Meanwhile the military services, especially the air force and army, were sending senior officers to major universities and think tanks for a year, younger officers went to universities for doctorates in subjects that included arms control, and the war colleges were including arms control in their curricula.

This substantial convergence of academic and professional military interest in arms control reflected what I think was the most important characteristic of the "new" arms control thinking. It took for granted that nuclear deterrence was here to stay for the foreseeable future. The purpose of arms control was to help make certain that deterrence worked. There was a notable absence of antimilitary spirit. Indeed, many of the ideas that came to be identified as the arms control point of view were pertinent to the unilateral shaping of military forces. Most of the academics associated with arms control probably did not consider themselves arms controllers but rather analysts of foreign policy or national security policy. Most believed that there was no contradiction between an interest in military strategy and an interest in the possibility of collaborating with potential enemies to reduce the likelihood of a war that neither side wanted.

That is all now several decades behind us. But the legacy of that transformation is with us still in the professional quality of the thinking and in the expectation that, when professional work is produced, somebody will be listening. A difference is in the scope and diversity of the subject today. Back then, stabilizing mutual deterrence at the strategic nuclear level and avoiding any battlefield escalation into use of nuclear weapons were the overwhelmingly dominant arms control interests. (The test treaty of 1963 and the nonproliferation treaty of 1968 were mainly viewed as part of the same effort.) A quick glance at the table of contents of this book will illuminate how the subject has enlarged and matured. And a perusal of the brief biographies of the authors will illuminate the demographic breadth of the field.

*   *   *

In reviewing the chapters, I find missing only one historical development to which I would have given emphasis. It is that more than half a century has passed since the first, and so far the only, use of nuclear weapons in warfare. Who could have believed fifty years ago that a new century would arrive—a new millennium—without any nuclear weapons being fired at a target? In 1960 C. P. Snow delivered a lecture, reported on the front page of the *New York Times*, declaring that unless there were drastic changes in the international arms situation a thermonuclear holocaust within a decade was a "mathematical certainty." Yet even compounded over four decades, it still didn't happen. Nineteen sixty was the year that full-page advertisements appeared in major newspapers for fallout shelters, to be built in your backyard or basement. Nobody appeared to think that Snow's gloomy prediction was preposterous or even extravagant. Something quite unanticipated happened. Rather, something widely expected didn't happen.

The first time nuclear weapons might have been used was the first stage of the Korean War. The victorious landing at Inchon made moot the question of whether nuclear weapons might have been used, but at least the question had come up. I know of no evidence that an important consideration, in the U.S. government or among the U.S. public, was apprehension of the consequences of demonstrating that these weapons were "usable," of preempting the possibility of cultivating a tradition of nonuse.

Within a month of Dwight Eisenhower's assuming the presidency, Secretary of State John Foster Dulles, at a meeting of the National Security Council, "discussed the moral problem in the inhibitions on the use of the A-bomb. . . . It was his opinion that we should break down this false distinction." Eight months later Dulles said, "Somehow or other we must manage to remove the taboo from the use of these weapons." Just a few weeks later the president approved this statement: "In the event of hostilities, the United States will consider nuclear weapons to be as available for use as other munitions." And during the Quemoy crisis of 1955, Eisenhower said publicly, "In any combat where these things can be used on strictly military targets and for strictly military purposes, I see no reason why they shouldn't be used just exactly as you would use a bullet or anything else."[3]

The contrast with the John Kennedy–Lyndon Johnson attitudes was beautifully summarized in a public statement of Johnson's in September 1964. "Make no mistake. There is no such thing as a conventional nuclear weapon. For 19 peril-filled years no nation has loosed the atom against another. To do so now is a political decision of the highest order."[4] Contrast, "a political decision of the highest order" with "as available for use as other munitions." Johnson evidently felt the weight of those 19 peril-filled years.

Nuclear weapons went unused during the war in Vietnam. They went unused during the Yom Kippur War of 1973. Most impressively, the Soviets abstained in Afghanistan. I might have thought the "taboo," the abhorrence of nuclear weapons, would not be shared by the Soviet leadership. Their willingness to fight a disastrous war—and lose it—without introducing nuclear weapons is an impressive demonstration that the taboo cuts across cultures.

I call this *arms control*. The usual definition of arms control focuses on "not acquiring" and "not deploying." I include "not using."

Finally, something that deserves to be identified as arms control can come about informally and even without being recognized as arms control by the participants. This was shown in the apparent understanding that a war in Europe should be kept nonnuclear if possible and that reciprocated efforts should be made to ensure this. Secretary of Defense Robert McNamara began an aggressive campaign for building up conventional defenses in Europe on the grounds that nuclear weapons certainly should not be used and possibly would not be used. Throughout the 1960s the Soviet line was to deny the possibility that any engagement in Europe could be nonnuclear, even to deny that any nuclear war could be kept limited.

Yet the Soviets spent enormous amounts of money developing nonnuclear capabilities in Europe, especially aircraft capable of delivering conventional weapons. This capability was not only expensive but utterly useless in the event of any war that would be nuclear from the outset. It can only reflect a tacit Soviet acknowledgment that both sides might be capable of nonnuclear war and were vitally interested in keeping war nonnuclear.

If arms control includes expensive restraints on the potential use of weapons, as well as on their deployment, this reciprocated investment in nonnuclear capability has to be considered a remarkable instance of unacknowledged but reciprocated arms restraint.

The immediate question today is whether we can expect Indian and Pakistani leaders to be adequately in awe of the nuclear weapons they now both possess. There are two helpful possibilities. One is that they share the inhibition—appreciate the taboo—that I have been discussing. The other is that they will recognize, as the United States and the Soviet Union did, that the prospect of nuclear retaliation makes any initiation of nuclear war nearly unthinkable.

The instances of nonuse of nuclear weapons that I've discussed were, in every case, possible use against a nonpossessor. The nonuse by the United States and the Soviet Union was differently motivated: the prospect of nuclear retaliation made any initiation appear unwise except in the worst imaginable military emergency, and that kind of military emergency never offered the temptation.

The experience of the U.S.-Soviet confrontation may impress Indians and Pakistanis. The risk is that one or the other may confront the kind of military emergency that invites some limited experiment with the weapons, and there is no history to tell us, or them, what happens next.

We can hope that this book finds readers around the world, including the Indian subcontinent.

Notes

1. Donald G. Brennan, *Arms Control, Disarmament, and National Security* (New York: George Braziller, 1961).

2. Hedley Bull, *The Control of the Arms Race* (London: Bradbury Agnew Press, 1961), and Thomas C. Schelling and Morton H. Halperin, *Strategy and Arms Control* (New York: Twentieth Century Fund, 1961).

3. See McGeorge Bundy, *Danger and Survival: Choices About the Bomb in the First Fifty Years* (New York: Random House, 1988).

4. *New York Times*, 8 September 1964, p. 18.

Acknowledgments

In the fall of 2000 it was becoming clear that much had changed in the world of arms control and cooperative security in the six years since we first began writing the predecessor to this book, *Arms Control Toward the 21st Century*. The present volume is a logical extension, update, and improvement on that earlier text, reflecting the dramatically changed arms control environment. We held the first meeting of authors in Chicago in early 2001, with a second conference to present draft versions of our chapters in Washington that summer. I want to convey my appreciation to all the contributors for their diligence in meeting a series of stringent deadlines in order to finish this book so quickly; their skills and knowledge made it a reality.

The Air Force's National Security Policy Division (AF/XONP) provided the financial support that made our authors' meetings possible. A special thanks to Kurt Klingenberger and Donald Minner, XONP division chiefs, for their vision and support. Kurt also played a direct role in the project by helping to compile the treaty updates in Appendix 2. James Smith at the USAF Institute of National Security Studies (INSS) and Thomas Skrobala at the Navy Treaty Implementation Program also provided financial support. Brent Talbot and Diana Heerdt at INSS and Matthew Billingsley at Science Applications International Corporation helped organize the July conference. Diana also provided invaluable help preparing the manuscript for publication. The National Security Affairs Department at the Naval Postgraduate School, particularly its chairman, James Wirtz, and Elizabeth Skinner, managed the financial aspects of the project. Thomas Schelling, who graciously consented to write the foreword to this volume and who made many valuable contributions to our two-day session in Washington in July 2001, was especially generous with his time and insights. We all benefited from working with one of the founding fathers of arms control theory.

I dedicate this book to my four children: Heather, Peter, Andrew, and Carolyn. I hope that one day the blessings of peace in a world of controlled arms will allow them to recognize their father's interest in pushing this topic forward.

—Jeffrey A. Larsen

1

An Introduction to Arms Control

Jeffrey A. Larsen

The field of arms control is in the midst of an intellectual and operational sea-change. After some 40 years as the centerpiece of U.S. national security policy, arms control seems to be losing its luster. Some claim that arms control is not living up to its promises despite considerable optimism immediately following the end of the Cold War. To survive as a viable international security policy, they argue, arms control must adapt itself to new arenas and new approaches. Suggestions abound for enhancing the role of cooperative security measures as a supplement or complement to more traditional attempts to control arms. Yet official Washington seems to have lost interest in thinking about new arms control issues or dealing with the operational and funding aspects of existing treaties and agreements. These feelings grew stronger with the arrival of the George W. Bush administration in 2001. Wrote one expert, "The traditional arms control process of negotiating legally binding treaties that both codify numerical parity and contain extensive verification measures has reached an impasse and outlived its utility."[1] But do these widespread beliefs reflect reality?

Arms control can be defined as any agreement among states to regulate some aspect of their military capability or potential. The agreement may apply to the location, amount, readiness, and types of military forces, weapons, and facilities. Whatever their scope and terms, however, all plans for arms control have one common factor: they presuppose some form of cooperation or joint action among the participants regarding their military programs. The authors in this book assess the role, value, and purpose of arms control and cooperative security in the twenty-first century. They explore arms control theory, arms control's successes and failures during the Cold War, changes to the international security environment in recent years, and the likelihood of future cooperative security arrangements or arms control agreements in various issue areas and geographic regions. This book

1

takes the position that even though the negotiating methods, regions of concern, and weapons involved may have changed, the underlying principles and objectives of arms control remain relevant today. Arms control may not be as centrally important as it was during the Cold War and its immediate aftermath, but it still has a role to play in a globalizing world that has ongoing security concerns.

What Is Arms Control and Why Is It Important?

Arms control is but one of a series of alternative approaches to achieving international security through military strategies. As one early writer on the topic explained, arms control belongs to a group of closely related views whose common theme is "peace through the manipulation of force." One could conceivably achieve such an end state in multiple ways: by placing force in the hands of a central authority; by creating a system of collective security; by accepting a balance of power between the key actors in the system; by establishing a system of mutual deterrence; by abolishing or reducing force; and through restraints and limits on forces. The latter choice reflects what we generally call "arms control."[2]

In a system of sovereign states with the capability to build and maintain sizable armed forces, states cannot ensure that rival states will not attempt to achieve influence by pursuing military superiority. Trust often does not exist. States, therefore, interpret incoming information about the military capabilities of rival states in the worst light. Evidence of a new military program or spending by one state requires other states to respond in kind to prevent the other side from achieving superiority. This security dilemma can produce an arms race, thereby increasing political tension among states, raising the probability and severity of crises, and possibly causing war. Arms control tries to address the negative effects of this security dilemma.[3]

Early theorists defined arms control in the broadest sense to refer to all forms of military cooperation between potential enemies in the interest of ensuring international stability. As Hedley Bull put it, arms control is "cooperation between antagonistic pairs of states in the military field, whether this cooperation is founded upon interests that are exclusively those of the cooperating states themselves or on interests that are more widely shared."[4]

Arms control analysts of the early 1960s were in agreement that the objectives of arms control were threefold. For Thomas Schelling and Morton Halperin, they were reducing the likelihood of war, reducing the political and economic costs of preparing for war, and minimizing the scope and violence of war if it occurred.[5] Hedley Bull visualized similar objectives for arms control: to contribute to international security and stop the drift to war; to release economic resources otherwise squandered in armaments; and to preclude preparing for war, which is morally wrong.[6] Students and practitioners have debated which of these objectives should take priority, but most national security analysts agree that the prevention of war should be the foremost goal of arms control.

Until recently, political leaders and the media seemed to have a more limited definition. They generally confined arms control to that set of activities dealing with specific steps to control related weapon systems, codified in formal agreements or treaties. Many analysts and much of the general public during the Cold War focused on the bilateral arms control negotiations between the United States and the Soviet Union. They came to expect that arms control required a formal treaty, a system of inspections to ensure compliance, and an enforcement mechanism to compel compliance. But those three elements are not always necessary for arms control. Arms control is a process involving specific, declared steps by a state to enhance security through cooperation with other states. These steps can be unilateral, bilateral, or multilateral. Cooperation can be implicit as well as explicit.

Arms Control Versus Disarmament

There is a difference between conceiving of arms control as a means to achieve a larger goal and seeing arms control as an end unto itself.[7] The arms control process is intended to serve as a means to enhance a state's national security. Arms control is but one approach to achieve that goal. Arms control can even lead states to agree to increases in certain categories of armaments if such increases would contribute to crisis stability and thereby reduce the chance of war. This conception of arms control should be distinguished from general and complete disarmament. Proponents of disarmament see the goal as simply reducing the size of military forces, budgets, explosive power, and other aggregate measures. Their rationale is that armaments have been the major cause of international instability and conflict; only through reductions in the weaponry of all nations can the world achieve peace.

Disarmament has a longer legacy than arms control and was a common theme in international relations literature during the 1950s. In the early 1960s international security specialists began using the term *arms control* in place of the term *disarmament,* which they believed lacked precision and smacked of utopianism. The seminal books on arms control published in that era all referred to this semantic problem. They preferred *arms control* as a more comprehensive term.[8]

Of course, advocacy of disarmament as part of a state's arms control policy can also be part of a means-to-an-end approach. For example, the United States and other countries have negotiated global conventions that endeavor to rid the world of chemical and biological weapons. The United States decided in both cases that maintaining such weapons would not enhance its security, even if they were still possessed by other states. Efforts to rid the world of such weapons were perceived to enhance the security of all states. Similarly, the United States and Russia have agreed to eliminate certain classes of strategic arms.

Hedley Bull suggested that even though disarmament and arms control are not the same they nevertheless intersect. Disarmament is the reduction or abolition of armaments, whereas arms control is restraint internationally exercised upon armaments policy, addressing not only the number of weapons but also their character, development, and use.[9] Yet in the early 1960s many members of the prodisarmament crowd viewed Schelling and Halperin as traitors to the cause when they published *Strategy and Arms Control,* because their book abandoned the utopian goals of many disarmers. Those two authors believed that they were merely extending the breadth and reach of disarmament studies to make it more operationally relevant to military studies.[10]

Cooperative Security

This book places arms control under the rubric of cooperative security, a concept that has grown in popularity and use since the end of the Cold War. The term has been used to outline a more peaceful and idealistic approach to security. One commonly accepted definition of cooperative security is "a commitment to regulate the size, technical composition, investment patterns, and operational practices of all military forces by mutual consent for mutual benefit."[11] Thus the term *collective security* is slightly different in meaning than the terms *cooperative security* or *collective defense.* Collective security is "a political and legal obligation of member states to defend the integrity of individual states within a group of treaty signatories." Collective defense is more narrowly defined: "the commitment of all states to defend each other from outside aggression." By contrast, cooperative security can include the introduction of measures that reduce the risk of war, measures that are not necessarily directed against any specific state or coalition. International institutions such as the Organization of Security and Cooperation in Europe and the European Union (EU) certainly fall under the first definition, but groups such as the North Atlantic Treaty Organization (NATO) just as easily fall within the second. Such cooperation can take place among states that have little in common, but as the cases of NATO and the EU show, cooperative security can advance much farther when the states are like-minded liberal democratic market economies. In those cases the parties can use their shared liberal values to move beyond simple defense pacts, perhaps even achieving proactive efforts in the fields of collective diplomacy, economics, and military action outside their common space.[12]

The Development of Arms Control Theory

U.S. national security objectives include protecting and preserving fundamental freedoms and institutions by deterring and preventing attacks on U.S. national interests at home and abroad.[13] New threats have necessitated reordering the priorities among traditional U.S. national security objectives. Deterring nuclear attack is now less urgent than preventing or countering proliferation of weapons of mass destruction and terrorism, for example. Yet the grand strategic objectives of arms control as an instrument of national security remain virtually unchanged, at least in general terms.

Nevertheless, the conceptual problems facing defense planners and arms control policymakers at the operational level are fundamentally different today from those that confronted the founders of traditional arms control theory in the late 1950s and early 1960s.

Arms Control and National Security

The founding premise of traditional arms control theory—that arms control can be an important adjunct to national security strategy—has, in practice, not always been obvious or consistently observed because arms control is inherently a counterintuitive approach to enhancing security. As Kerry Kartchner has written, arms control makes national security dependent to some degree on the cooperation of prospective adversaries. It often involves setting lower levels of arms than would otherwise appear prudent based on a strict threat assessment. It mandates establishing a more or less interactive relationship with potential opponents and, in the case of mutual intrusive verification and data exchanges, exposes sensitive national security information and facilities to scrutiny by foreign powers. It requires seeking and institutionalizing cooperation where the potential for conflicts of interest seemingly far outweigh common objectives. It is fundamentally a high-stakes gamble, mortgaging national survival against little more than the collateral of trust and anticipated reciprocal restraint, often in a geopolitical context fraught with political hostility and tension. It is, in fact, a voluntary (and not always reversible) delimitation of national sovereignty. Viewed from this perspective, arms control is not obviously better than its alternative—unilaterally providing for one's own security.[14]

What compels the United States and other nations, then, to structure so much of their national security posture on an approach that seemingly contradicts a country's natural instincts toward self-sufficiency and self-preservation? An answer to this apparent paradox is that arms control allows security to be established by negotiation at levels of weapons lower than would be the case if these levels were determined unilaterally. The mere act of negotiating arms control also may lead to better communication, deepened understanding, and reduced hostility among adversaries.

Arms Control Theory

Arms control theory refers to the assumptions and premises of strategic analysts who first developed arms control as an adjunct to national security in the 1958–1962 time frame. Traditional arms control theory was the product of a unique confluence of factors and reflected the assumptions, analyses, and policy priorities of defense analysts and policymakers of that era.[15] The rethinking of arms control at that time was part of a general reevaluation of U.S. defense and foreign policy that was precipitated by dissatisfaction with the postwar diplomatic and arms control stalemate. Negotiations over armaments policy with one's potential adversary was not a novel concept. The United States had sought to establish through diplomatic means a variety of disarmament arrangements since 1945 (e.g., the Baruch Plan, Open Skies, and the Atoms for Peace proposal). Nevertheless, long negotiations and multiple proposals had yielded no tangible results, primarily because of Soviet objections to those verification regimes deemed essential by the West. In the mid-1950s policymakers began rethinking an approach that had emphasized general and complete disarmament and to consider instead limited partial measures that would gradually enhance confidence in cooperative security arrangements. Thus, more modest goals under the rubric of arms control came to replace the propaganda-laden disarmament efforts of the late 1940s and early 1950s.

Basic Tenets of Traditional Arms Control

The period that began with the 1958 Surprise Attack Conference and lasted through the 1962 publication of the proceedings of a Woods Hole Summer Study and the parallel studies at Oxford University produced the canons of modern arms control theory.[16] Out of the literature of this golden era of arms control emerged a virtual consensus on several key assumptions, which may be considered to be the basic tenets of traditional arms control theory.

First, arms control was conceived as a way to enhance national security. As Hedley Bull explained: "arms control or disarmament was not an end in itself but a means to an end and that end was first and foremost the enhancement of security, especially security against nuclear war."[17] Or as Schelling and Halperin stated near the end of their book: "the aims of arms control and the aims of a national military strategy should be substantially the same."[18] This principle established national security as the dominant goal of arms control, not the reduction of arms per se. In fact it was understood that not all reductions were necessarily useful. There was an explicit recognition that arms control could be harmful if not properly guided by overall national security strategy.

Second, the superpowers shared a common interest in avoiding nuclear war; this common interest could and should be the basis for effective arms control agreements. According to Bull, "The fact that the United States and the Soviet Union were locked in a political and ideological conflict, one moreover that sometimes took a military form, did not mean that they could not recognize common interests in avoiding a ruinous nuclear war, or cooperate to advance these common interests."[19] This assumption was one of the most important and controversial conceptual departures from past thinking promulgated by the new arms control theory. Previously, it was assumed that relaxation of political tensions had to precede the achievement of substantive arms control agreements. The founders of traditional arms control theory, in contrast, believed that the threat of global nuclear annihilation was so paramount that it transcended political and ideological differences. It was not necessary to fully resolve political conflicts before proceeding to negotiate arms control agreements; solutions to both could be advanced simultaneously.

Third, arms control and military strategy should work together to promote national security. The unity of strategy and arms control was a central tenet of traditional arms control theory. Such unity was essential if arms control and defense policy were to avoid working at cross-purposes. For example, if the implementation of U.S. defense strategy required deploying certain types of weapons that were restricted by arms control agreements, this could defeat the overall purpose of our national security posture and erode the legitimacy of both the arms control process and U.S. defense policy.

Finally, it was understood from the beginning that arms control regimes need not be limited to formal agreements but could also include informal, unilateral, and verbal agreements. The U.S.-Soviet presidential nuclear initiatives of 1991–1992 are among the most well known of these efforts.

The Objectives of Arms Control Theory

For arms control to be an effective instrument of national security, its objectives must be determined by, and be in close harmony with, the broader objectives of national security strategy.[20] At the most basic level of abstraction, three grand conceptual dilemmas dominated strategic thinking and the formulation of U.S. national security objectives during the Cold War: *What deters? How much is enough? What if deterrence fails?* Arms control was developed in an attempt to deal with these three questions.[21]

Traditional arms control theory was based on the premise that the superpowers inherently shared an area of common ground (avoiding nuclear war) and that this element of mutual interest could serve as the basis for limited cooperative arrangements involving reciprocal restraint in the acquisition of weapons of mass destruction. In defining the scope and application of arms control, they set forth three general objectives:

> We believe that arms control is a promising, but still only dimly perceived, enlargement of the scope of our military strategy. It rests essentially on the recognition that our military relation with potential enemies is not one of pure conflict and opposition, but involves strong elements of mutual interest in *the avoidance of a war that neither side wants, in minimizing the costs and risks of the arms competition,* and in *curtailing the scope and violence of war in the event it occurs.*[22]

Clearly, then, establishing the requirements of deterrence must precede and form the basis for creating policies that reduce the risk of nuclear war, while the goal of reducing defense spending must be informed by some notion of what constitutes sufficient levels of weapons. And any scheme for limiting damage should war occur presupposes at least some thought as to the nature of warfare and how forces are to be employed in combat. Thus, the primary objectives of traditional arms control theory—reducing the risk of war, reducing the costs of preparing for war, and reducing the damage should war occur—are necessarily determined by the three great dilemmas of military policy.

Reducing the risk of war. Arms control was seen as a prime means of setting limits on and restraining strategic arms race behavior. For early arms control theorists, restraining certain types of technology was practically synonymous with reducing the risk of war. The underlying premise was that war was most likely to begin with a surprise nuclear attack made possible by unrestrained competition in ballistic missile, guidance and control, and nuclear weapon technology. Therefore, those weapon systems employing technologies that in theory most contributed to the ability to execute a surprise nuclear attack against the nuclear retaliatory forces of the other side, or that undermined the ability of either side to hold deterrent targets at risk, became principal candidates for arms limitation agreements.

Reducing the cost of preparing for war. Arms control theorists believed that controls would release economic resources otherwise squandered on military spending. They believed that arms races were economically ruinous and that disarmament or arms control would make possible the diversion of resources toward worthier objectives.[23] If arms control succeeded in providing the same degree of security at lower levels of weapons than would otherwise be the case, it could lead to fielding fewer weapons and thus lower overall defense spending. Further, if certain types of technology were mutually outlawed, there would be fewer costs associated with defense research and development, weapons production, force deployment, operations, and maintenance. The savings thereby realized could be diverted to domestic economic priorities and promote overall prosperity.

Reducing the damage should war occur. If fewer weapons were fielded as a result of arms limitation agreements, and should war nevertheless occur, overall damage would be less than it would otherwise have been. But fielding fewer weapons is not the only way to reduce damage in the event of war. Damage also could be limited by developing certain types of active defense strategies and technologies, such as ballistic missile defenses.

In practice, the first of the three main objectives proposed by traditional arms control theory—reducing the risk of war or, more specifically, reducing the risk of surprise nuclear attack—came to eclipse and overshadow the other two. Achieving the first objective would also indirectly satisfy the other two. The process grew in complexity over the next four decades. It usually involved negotiations but was sometimes accomplished through unilateral decisions or reciprocated arrangements.

Arms control during the Cold War assumed a high priority on the national security agenda as a way of managing the superpower nuclear rivalry. The new importance of arms control was a reaction to the bipolar structure of the international system and the revolutionary nature of nuclear weapons. Generally, these negotiations were limited in scope and focused on increased strategic nuclear stability between the superpowers. The conduct of bilateral negotiations became very formal; agreements took years to reach. Every possible implication for the strategic balance was scrutinized, and increasingly complex provisions for verification became part of the process to guard against cheating. Even after a treaty was concluded, the benefits and pitfalls of arms control continued to be hotly debated.

Arms Control in the Post–Cold War Era

As the Cold War ended, the conception and execution of arms control began to change. The changes began with an increase in the number and types of bilateral arrangements between the superpowers. As *rapprochement* between the superpowers deepened, the forums and scope for other negotiations began to broaden. Regions beyond Europe also began to turn to arms control as a means to build security.

In the immediate aftermath of the Cold War, the West experienced a flush of optimism and activity regarding arms control. The early 1990s was truly the high-water mark for arms control, as formal agreements and cooperative measures were signed and entered into force with astounding speed. Many of these, in fact, were agreements reached years before but only now ratified. Arms control found a place in dealing with the new concerns of advanced weapons proliferation, regional instability, and economic and environmental security. The value of arms control appeared to be growing in the new world, as states attempted to implement treaties already in place, stem the illegal proliferation of weapons of mass destruction to rogue nations and groups, and meet their security needs in a more multipolar, interdependent world. In the 1996 edition of this book the editors expressed their belief that because of the broadening scope and complexity of negotiations and agreements, arms control might affect national security more than it had in the past. Like it or not, we argued, arms control was here to stay.

That may no longer be true. The early post–Cold War years now appear to have been an era of excessive optimism about new opportunities for arms control. In fact there is considerable debate over its future value—even with respect to existing treaties and agreements. The traditional role for arms control in the Cold War—to enhance stability and forego potentially devastating misunderstandings between the two superpowers—may no longer be of central concern within the international community or even achievable in some new fields. The United States must seriously consider what role arms control can play in enhancing its future national security considerations. These new roles might be different than in the past. Indeed, as one of our book's contributors put it in a recent article, "The place of arms control in U.S. national security strategy and its continued relevance to the evolving global strategic landscape cannot be taken for granted."[24] Two generations ago Hedley Bull wrote of strikingly familiar concerns: "The events of the last few years . . . raise the question . . . whether, if arms control is to remain relevant in the less polarized, more multilaterally ordered world into which we now appear to be moving, some fundamental rethinking of the subject must not take place."[25]

Arms control has changed to accommodate the new international security agenda. The very formal, structured approach to reaching agreement has been broadened to include more informal modes of cooperation. In particular the use of unilateral and reciprocal declarations has resulted in dramatic steps outside formally established negotiating procedures. Security negotiations between states have also developed an increasingly operational focus; they no longer simply pursue agreements to limit types and numbers of weapons. The growing interest in transparency is highlighted by the strict verification provisions written into treaties, as well as new agreements to share data. New international organizations have evolved to implement agreements.

New Approaches to Arms Control

Concern about the future of arms control may be misplaced; there still remains a vital role for this process to play. One way to consider how things have changed is to review the themes from the conclusion in the 1996 edition of this book. One would expect much of that conclusion to have been overcome by events. The surprise for many readers may be how much has *not* changed. Many of those earlier themes are still relevant today.[26]

Many in the United States no longer view Russia as much of a strategic threat, but it is still a spoiler in terms of arms control. This raises multiple questions: Should arms control be geared toward different problems? Should Russia now take a backseat to new concerns, such as an emerging China, troublesome relationships in South Asia, or the threat posed by global terrorism? Can Cold War arms control institutions work in terms of the new strategic relationship between the United States, Russia, China, and other nations? Are existing arms control institutions and treaties obsolete? Perhaps a new combination of unilateral approaches, nontraditional incentives, joint activities, and other imaginative collective security measures can supplant the reliance on classic treaty-based negotiations.

At the same time, the threat of the proliferation of weapons of mass destruction continues, particularly given the heightened threat from emboldened terrorist organizations (as was quite literally brought home to the United States on 11 September 2001). In the face of that threat, how can arms control address emerging security relationships and regional arms races?

As bipolarity fades, what new multilateral institutions are needed for arms control? What new kinds of arms control are necessary or possible? Since the mid-1990s attention has increasingly focused on several new topics of interest in the security realm that call out for means of control, including information war, landmines, space, and chemical and biological weapons. Will agreements to manage these areas call for new types of provisions, such as requiring states to criminalize certain activities, or requiring cooperation in the face of nonstate threats?

Efforts to reach agreement in many of these areas face great challenges if the traditional arms control focus on force structure levels and strict verification is the basis for evaluation. Nonstate actors have also become players by raising issues to the international agenda and creating momentum for agreements, such as the 1997 Mine Ban Treaty. We need to broaden the definition of the term *arms control* to encompass nonstate as well as state actors.

Overview of the Book

The book is divided into four sections, each successively addressing the conceptual and historical background of arms control, weapons-specific concerns and issues, regional considerations, and new topical areas in which arms control may have a role to play. Each chapter includes a list of suggested readings for the student who wishes to dig deeper into the best works on the subject.

Part 1, "Arms Control in Context," relates arms control to national security objectives. It also examines efforts by the Cold War superpowers and their allies to use arms control during that conflict to enhance their security, as well as the legacy of these efforts on the post–Cold War environment. These chapters establish the underlying concepts and principles that guide the conduct of arms control by reviewing the history of arms control efforts, the international and domestic contexts in which the process takes place, and the fundamental requirement for effective transparency, verification, and compliance measures.

In Part 2, "Preventing the Spread of Weapons," our authors discuss specific weapons types and efforts to control their proliferation and use. These include strategic nuclear systems, chemical and biological weapons, conventional forces, and the fissile components of nuclear weapons.

Part 3, "Regional Perspectives," looks at five global regions of particular interest to the United States and examines their perspectives on arms control, past and future. Each chapter—on Europe, Africa, the Middle East, South Asia, and East Asia—focuses on the perspectives regarding arms control in regions associated with potential major military contingencies of concern to the United States. The chapters address the strategic culture, geography, history, arms control experience, and the prospect for future success in each area.

Part 4, "Future Challenges for Arms Control," examines how arms control might prove useful in improving U.S. security in new, nontraditional areas of particular importance to the United States. We consider the asymmetries and vulnerabilities that face the international system and, in particular, the United States in the years ahead, including the new fields of strategic defenses as well as the offense-defense balance, information operations, and space arms control. We also project the long-term future for arms control. We are clearly in a period of transition: Where does arms control go from here?

Conclusion

Some of our Cold War institutions and agreements are showing signs of wear. The arms control momentum from the Cold War that infused our 1996 book has waned. With new arenas for arms control consideration, and new partners to deal with, the whole concept of arms control must be reconsidered—in much the same way as it must have appeared to the founders of this theory in the early 1960s.

We are at a crossroads today, with the future direction of arms control uncertain, but its past value indisputable. As Schelling and Halperin wrote in 1961,

Adjustments in military postures and doctrines that induce reciprocal adjustments by a potential opponent can be of mutual benefit if they reduce the danger of a war that neither side wants, or contain its violence, or otherwise serve the security of the nation. That is what we mean by arms control.[27]

Forty years later, those perspectives on the role and value of arms control as a tool of national security remain valid. As our authors show in the chapters that follow, these can be extrapolated to new fields of interest in international relations.

Notes

1. Richard D. Sokolsky, "Renovating U.S. Strategic Arms Control Policy," *Strategic Forum*, no. 178 (Washington, DC: National Defense University Institute for National Strategic Studies, February 2001), p. 1.

2. Hedley Bull, *The Control of the Arms Race: Disarmament and Arms Control in the Missile Age* (New York: Frederick A. Praeger Publishers, 1961), pp. 4–5.

3. Two classic works dealing with arms races are Samuel P. Huntington, "Arms Races Prerequisites and Results," in *Public Policy: Yearbook of the Graduate School of Public Administration* (Cambridge: Harvard University Press, 1958), and Colin Gray, "The Arms Race Phenomenon," *World Politics* (October 1971).

4. Bull, *The Control of the Arms Race*, p. xxxv.

5. Thomas C. Schelling and Morton H. Halperin, *Strategy and Arms Control* (Washington, DC: Pergamon-Brassey's, 1985 [orig. publ. 1961]), p. 3.

6. Bull, *The Control of the Arms Race*, pp. 3–4.

7. Some of the concepts in the following sections are expansions of ideas from the Introduction to the 1996 edition. See Gregory J. Rattray, "Introduction," in Jeffrey A. Larsen and Gregory J. Rattray, eds., *Arms Control Toward the 21st Century* (Boulder: Lynne Rienner Publishers, 1996), pp. 1–15.

8. For more on the background of these terms, see Richard Dean Burns, *Encyclopedia of Arms Control and Disarmament* (New York: Charles Scribner's Sons, 1993), pp. 2–3.

9. Bull, *The Control of the Arms Race*, p. vii.

10. Thomas Schelling, comments at the authors' conference for this book, McLean, VA, 12 July 2001; also remarks made by Schelling in a "Roundtable in Honor of Thomas Schelling" at the 97th annual meeting of the American Political Science Association, San Francisco, 31 August 2001.

11. Ashton B. Carter, William J. Perry, and John D. Steinbruner, *A New Concept of Cooperative Security* (Washington, DC: Brookings Institution, 1992), p. 6. Other good works on this subject include Janne Nolan, ed., *Global Engagement: Cooperation and Security in the 21st Century* (Washington, DC: Brookings Institution, 1994); Ashton B. Carter and William J. Perry, *Preventive Defense: A New Security Strategy for America* (Washington, DC: Brookings Institution, 1999); John D. Steinbruner, *Principles of Global Security* (Washington, DC: Brookings Institution, 2000); and Dan Caldwell, "Cooperative Security and Terrorism," paper presented to the annual meeting of the International Security Studies Section of the International Studies Association, Whittier, CA, 27 October 2001.

12. One can envision four rings of security that make up collective security writ large: individual security, collective security, collective defense, and promoting stability. For more on this argument, see Richard Cohen and Michael Mihalka, *Cooperative Security: New Horizons for International Order,* Marshall Center Papers No. 3 (Garmisch, Germany: George C. Marshall European Center for Security Studies, April 2001).

13. My thanks to Kerry Kartchner for providing much of the material in this section from his chapter in the 1996 edition of this book. See Kerry Kartchner, "The Objectives of Arms Control," in Larsen and Rattray, *Arms Control Toward the 21st Century,* pp. 19–34.

14. Kartchner, "The Objectives of Arms Control."

15. The term *traditional* is used here to denote something of historical origin that retains its vitality and relevance and captures the connotation that the objectives of traditional arms control theory remain cogent and compelling in the current era. See Hedley Bull, "The Traditional Approach to Arms Control Twenty Years After," in Uwe Nerlich, ed., *Soviet Power and Western Negotiating Policies,* vol. 2 (Cambridge, MA: Ballinger, 1983), pp. 21–30.

16. The three basic works on traditional arms control theory were all published in 1961: Schelling and Halperin, *Strategy and Arms Control;* Bull, *The Control of the Arms Race;* and Donald G. Brennan, ed., *Arms Control, Disarmament, and National Security* (New York: George Braziller), earlier published as a special issue devoted to arms control in *Daedalus: Proceedings of the American Academy of Arts and Sciences* (Fall 1960).

17. Bull, "The Traditional Approach to Arms Control Twenty Years After," p. 21.

18. Schelling and Halperin, *Strategy and Arms Control,* p. 142.

19. Bull, "The Traditional Approach to Arms Control Twenty Years After," p. 22.

20. In the introduction to their seminal book, Schelling and Halperin state: "There is hardly an objective of arms control to be described in this study that is not equally a continuing urgent objective of national military strategy—of our unilateral military plans and policies." *Strategy and Arms Control,* p. 3.

21. Throughout much of the Cold War these three dilemmas were elaborated mostly in nuclear terms: What deters nuclear war? How many nuclear weapons are enough? What if nuclear deterrence fails? But they are equally applicable to the full range of defense scenarios, including policies and threats involving conventional, chemical, biological, and other weapons.

22. Schelling and Halperin, *Strategy and Arms Control,* p. 1.

23. Bull, *The Control of the Arms Race,* p. 3.

24. Brad Roberts, "The Road Ahead for Arms Control," *Washington Quarterly* (Spring 2000): 231.

25. Bull, *The Control of the Arms Race,* p. xiv.

26. See "The Evolving Nature of Arms Control in the Post–Cold War World," in Larsen and Rattray, *Arms Control Toward the 21st Century,* pp. 285–292.

27. Schelling and Halperin, *Strategy and Arms Control,* p. 143.

Suggested Readings

"Arms Control: Thirty Years On." Special Edition of *Daedalus: Journal of the American Academy of Arts and Sciences* (Winter 1991).

Arms Control Association. *Arms Control and National Security: An Introduction.* Washington, DC: Arms Control Association, 1989.

Bull, Hedley. *The Control of the Arms Race: Disarmament and Arms Control in the Missile Age.* New York: Frederick A. Praeger, 1961.

Burns, Richard Dean, ed. *Encyclopedia of Arms Control and Disarmament.* 3 vols. New York: Charles Scribner's Sons, 1993.

Carter, Ashton B., William J. Perry, and John D. Steinbruner. *A New Concept of Cooperative Security.* Washington, DC: Brookings Institution, 1992.

"Is Arms Control Dead?" In Special Edition of *Washington Quarterly* (Spring 2000): 171-232.

Larsen, Jeffrey A., and Gregory J. Rattray, eds. *Arms Control Toward the 21st Century.* Boulder: Lynne Rienner Publishers, 1996.

Larsen, Jeffrey A., and James M. Smith. *Historical Dictionary of Arms Control and Disarmament.* Lanham, MD: Scarecrow Press, forthcoming.

Schelling, Thomas C., and Morton H. Halperin. *Strategy and Arms Control.* Washington, DC: Pergamon-Brassey's, 1985 [orig. publ. 1961].

PART 1

ARMS CONTROL IN CONTEXT

2

A History of Arms Control

Michael O. Wheeler

The history of arms control is as old as the history of war and preparations for war.[1] To put it another way, the urge to "smother war with diplomacy" (Eugene Rostow's memorable phrase) has deep roots in the Western experience. So does the disposition to create rule-based institutions to inject order into social relations. Seeking to stabilize the competition among potential adversaries (including the recently defeated) in the interest of reducing the likelihood of war, managing the costs of preparing for war, and limiting the scope and violence of war if it were to occur—these are at the heart of the modern arms control endeavor.

In their classic 1961 work on the subject, Thomas Schelling and Morton Halperin observed "that arms control is a promising, but still only dimly perceived, enlargement of the scope of our military strategy."[2] This perspective is important. It reminds us that the arms control process involves competitive as well as cooperative dimensions, as states engaging in arms control seek at a minimum to preserve, and ideally to improve, their security. Ensuring desirable outcomes requires vigilance by all parties to a negotiation. Thucydides gives the classic early example of the hidden agendas and maneuvering for advantage that an arms control negotiation can entail. In the fifth century B.C. Sparta sends its diplomats to Athens to seek agreement "not only to abstain from building walls for herself, but also to join . . . in throwing down the remaining walls of the cities outside the Peloponnesus."[3] The Spartans claimed they were directing this measure against invasions by barbarians. In fact they feared the growing power of Athens and sought to preserve Spartan advantages on land for the anticipated clash of arms. Athenian authorities realized this but wanted to buy time to complete their fortification programs. They neither accepted nor rejected the Spartan offer but delayed entering into talks while the population of Athens was mobilized in a frenzy of construction on the walls. A modern student of arms control, examining the cycles in the early nuclear testing talks, will find strong analogies to this story.

As for establishing norms, the history of arms control is replete with the lingering issue of double standards. In the twelfth century, for instance, the Catholic Church attempted to ban the use of crossbows—but only by Christians against Christians, not in wars with other civilizations. A student of modern arms control will recognize echoes of this in discussions in the United Nations (UN) First Committee or at the Conference on Disarmament.

The above examples are not chosen to deny the positive contributions that arms control can make to international relations, many of which will be explored in this chapter. Rather they remind us that in looking at history we need to be careful what lessons we take away. Examples can be found for almost any side of the debate on the value of arms control.

No survey chapter can do justice to the many streams in Western thought on war and peace that flow together into today's theory and practice of arms control, not to mention the nuanced history itself. What follows is one way to view the history, organized in a framework relevant to the other, more detailed chapters in this book.

Arms Control in the West
Prior to the Nuclear Age

The Hellenistic-Roman world lasted some 1,700 years, from the apogee of Mycenaean civilization to the disintegration of the Roman Empire. During this time, the earliest Western state systems emerged with institutions such as diplomacy, commercial relations, colonies, alliances, and—of course— war. As noted earlier, one finds evidence of arms control practices in the ancient Greek world. Roman writers such as Cicero (106–43 B.C.) and Tacitus (56–117 A.D.) addressed themes highly relevant to the modern study of arms control, such as how to create just peace after war. So did scholars in the Middle Ages—that long period lasting some 1,200 years following the collapse of the Roman Empire. *Just war doctrine,* which is central to modern thinking on war and peace issues, matured during this time. Transition to the modern era in international politics—the era of the sovereign nation-state—begins in the late fifteenth century. We still live in that system.

During the more than 3,000 years that spanned the age from the fall of Troy (c. 1250 B.C.) to the end of the Congress of Vienna (1815 A.D.), the theory and practice of arms control remained largely inchoate. That began to change after 1815. One of the oldest extant arms control instruments—the Rush-Bagot agreement that demilitarized the North American Great Lakes— was concluded in 1817. The nineteenth century had a passion for codification, often accomplished at large international gatherings. Beginning with the Geneva conference of 1864 and carried forward to the Hague conferences of 1899 and 1907, the laws of war were recorded in international covenants. This process was closely intertwined with what today we would recognize as arms control. In 1868, for example, the Saint Petersburg declaration prohibited the use in combat of explosive projectiles weighing less than 400 grams.

In August 1898, the imperial Russian court circulated a note from Nicholas II calling for an ambitious peace conference. Some scholars date the beginning of the modern era of arms control to the resulting Hague conferences.[4] Certainly these conferences were noteworthy because they included non-European powers and because of the scope of issues they addressed: limitation of armaments and war budgets; prohibitions on certain types of arms and military practices; revision and extension of the codified laws and customs of war; and creation of institutions for mediation, arbitration, and other methods for preventing war.

As arms control conferences, the Hague meetings were not terribly successful, and a third Hague conference was scheduled but never convened. Europe, after nearly a century of relatively peaceful relations among most of its major powers, slipped into World War I (1914–1918). Also known as the Great War, by historical standards it was brief, lasting only 51 months, but it changed the thrust and direction of world politics and of arms control, a process that continues to reverberate today. The victors who met in Paris in 1919 constructed a new order based on the Versailles Treaty, a vindictive instrument of peace that among other things attempted to disarm Germany permanently. "The coercive, unilateral disarmament of the German armed forces," Fred Tanner writes in a study commissioned after a similar effort was mounted almost a century later against Iraq, "left profound frustrations in the German population. The continued humiliation was epitomized by the uniforms of the foreign officers who had the right to conduct on-site inspections anytime, anywhere, without allowing the German authorities a right of refusal."[5] The international community had lost interest in enforcing disarmament on Germany by the time Adolf Hitler came to power.

The period between the two world wars was an era of renewed emphasis on arms control (broadly defined), pursued seriously but with limited results. Much of the activity was aimed at trying to control military technologies (battleships) that had figured prominently in the arms races before World War I. Naval conferences in Washington (1921–1922) and London (1930 and 1935–1936) took up this theme. Reacting to the use of gas by both sides in World War I, an international conference in Geneva produced a protocol (1925) that banned the first use of "asphyxiating, poisonous or other gases, or bacteriological methods of warfare." The fact that the major signatories imported into their statements of accession the right to respond in kind to use of chemical weapons by others effectively converted this into a first use ban.

Following six years of preparation, the 59-nation World Disarmament Conference convened in Geneva in 1932 under sponsorship of the League of Nations. The discussions were a year old and losing their momentum when Franklin Delano Roosevelt was elected president of the United States. One of Roosevelt's highest foreign policy priorities when he took office was to try to revive the moribund Disarmament Conference—a priority on par with talks on international finance and trade, because Roosevelt felt that limits on arms were inseparably linked to progress in the world political economy.[6] Roosevelt tried but failed to broker a compromise among the competing agendas at Geneva: demands for new security guarantees; attempts to craft disarmament formulas that achieved equitable outcomes; calls for limits on air, land, and naval forces; and the like. Along the way, Hitler first was evasive as to his intentions, but in October 1933 he abruptly announced that Germany was withdrawing from the Geneva talks and from the League of Nations. The World Disarmament Conference faded into history, and by the autumn of 1939 a new war in Europe was under way.

Harry Truman succeeded Roosevelt in April 1945. By this time Germany was on the brink of defeat, and U.S. military authorities were preparing to redeploy armed forces from Europe to the Pacific, where the war still was raging. Then on 16 July in the desert northwest of Alamogordo, New Mexico, the United States tested the first atomic bomb. A month later, the bomb was used in combat against the Japanese cities of Hiroshima and Nagasaki. The world had entered the nuclear age.

Arms Control During the Cold War

Nuclear arms control—dealing with nuclear arms races and with the instabilities inherent in a bipolar nuclear balance and in the proliferation of nuclear weapons to other powers—dominated much of the arms control agenda during the Cold War. The French scholar Raymond Aron spoke for many of the strategic analysts of his generation when he wrote in the early 1950s: "Attempts at disarmament in the past have always failed, but the attempt at atomic disarmament has even less chance of success because the nature of the weapons aroused additional obstacles to an agreement and even more to the supervision of such an agreement."[7] Devising arms control arrangements for the nuclear age was indeed a daunting challenge.

The Truman Years

The Truman administration set out to devise a grand strategy, including arms control, scripted for a new world order constructed around diplomatic, legal, political, and financial institutions that the United States championed: the United Nations system, the Bretton Woods framework, the Marshall

Plan, the Nuremberg and Tokyo tribunals, and an end to Europe's overseas colonial empires, to name some of the more prominent elements. In the autumn of 1945, after Japan had surrendered, many in the West hoped that collaboration with the Soviets could be extended from a wartime to a peacetime footing. It was clear to U.S. authorities—including the joint chiefs of staff—that U.S. security was threatened in an unprecedented way by the advent of nuclear weapons that over time could be delivered by a number of means against targets in the U.S. homeland by whomever the enemy might be. In October 1945 the joint chiefs advised the president:

> While the Joint Chiefs of Staff consider it imperative to retain technical secrets on atomic weapons for the present, they regard it as of great military importance that further steps of a political nature should be promptly and vigorously pressed during the probably limited period of American monopoly, in an effort to forestall a race in atomic weapons and to prevent the exposure of the United States to a form of attack against which present defenses are inadequate.[8]

This resonated with other advice that President Truman was receiving and with his consultations with U.S. partners in developing the atomic bomb (Great Britain and Canada). In January 1946 the newly created UN General Assembly, in its first resolution, established the UN Atomic Energy Commission (UNAEC) and charged it with four tasks: (1) to find a means to extend to all nations the exchange of basic scientific information for peaceful ends; (2) to find a means to control atomic energy that would allow its use for peaceful purposes; (3) to seek to eliminate from national armaments atomic weapons (and all other major weapons adaptable to mass destruction); and (4) to effectively safeguard, by way of inspection and other means, against the hazards of violations and evasions.[9] The resolution also specified that the work of the UNAEC should proceed by separate stages, the successful completion of each being necessary to develop confidence among all nations before the next stage was undertaken.

In June 1946 the UNAEC began its work. The United States presented a proposal (popularly known as the Baruch Plan) for international ownership and control of all phases of the nuclear cycle. Five days later, the Soviets presented a counterproposal. The two plans differed on issues such as whether all existing nuclear weapons would be destroyed before an international system of inspection was in place, and whether the veto in the UN Security Council would be suspended for purposes of enforcing the international nuclear control regime. The gulf between the two positions appeared unbridgeable. By the fall of 1946 the emerging East-West divide was clearly reflected in the stalemated discussions in the UNAEC.

Simultaneously, the UN was grappling with the question of how to enforce Security Council decisions, with one possible enforcement mechanism being armed forces vetted to the United Nations. These negotiations in the Military Staff Committee also stalemated along East-West lines. Although the separate UN Commission for Conventional Armaments (UNCCA) was created by the Security Council in February 1947, meetings of the UNAEC and the UNCCA became sterile propaganda exercises as the Cold War unfolded in 1947 and 1948. In early 1949 the West created the North Atlantic Treaty Organization (NATO), and in the fall of 1949 the Soviet Union tested a nuclear bomb, shortly before the communist forces prevailed in the civil war on the Chinese mainland. In 1950 the Korean War erupted. Both the United States and the Soviet Union were engaged in robust nuclear armament programs by this time, and the British edged closer to their first test of a nuclear weapon. The nuclear trajectories of the Cold War were largely in place.

In the fall of 1950 the Truman administration conducted a major review of its arms control policies. The result was National Security Council (NSC) Decision 112, a document that annunciated a set of principles approved by President Truman in July 1951—principles that extended into the early years of the Dwight Eisenhower administration and beyond.[10] Although NSC-112 is too detailed to summarize in this survey, it is worth noting the types of ideas that the document recorded: uncertainty about how much transparency is enough to build confidence; recognition of the inevitable shortfalls of verification regimes; and the notion of staged activities, where action at one stage is intended to build the confidence needed to proceed to another.

In the fall of 1951 the United Nations decided to establish a single disarmament commission as a successor to the UNAEC and UNCCA. To help prepare for this event and to elicit an external review of United States arms control policy, the Truman administration appointed a special panel chaired by J. Robert Oppenheimer, a key figure in the wartime Manhattan Project, which created the atomic bomb, and the chief author of the control mechanisms in the Baruch Plan. The Oppenheimer panel delivered its report in January 1953, after eight months of study, just as the Truman administration ended and the Eisenhower administration began.[11]

The Eisenhower Years

There is strong evidence that President Eisenhower wanted a much more ambitious arms control agenda than did many of his advisers.[12] Eisenhower was impressed by the arguments in the Oppenheimer report, not so much the pessimism about the prospects for early progress in arms control as the compelling argument Oppenheimer made that the public must be informed more accurately and comprehensively about the dangers and risks of the nuclear age—a point Oppenheimer expanded on in July 1953 in an article in *Foreign Affairs*.[13] Eisenhower asked all his major advisers to read the classified Oppenheimer report carefully and to be prepared to discuss it with him.

Joseph Stalin died unexpectedly in March 1953. With his advisers divided on the wisdom of launching a new arms control initiative in the early months after that event, Eisenhower looked for possible modest steps to engage Moscow in dialogue. His Atoms for Peace speech to the UN General Assembly in December 1953 grew out of that dynamic. Although the Soviets declined to engage in the substance of the proposal (which called upon each side to set aside part of its fissionable materials for peaceful uses by other states under international supervision), they did not block the creation of the International Atomic Energy Agency (IAEA) that flowed from Eisenhower's initial proposal. (The IAEA charter was adopted in October 1956.)

In March 1954 radioactive fallout from a U.S. thermonuclear test in the South Pacific blanketed a Japanese fishing trawler, with resulting fatalities. The international outcry for a suspension of nuclear testing began a process where the Eisenhower administration adjusted to the idea of nuclear test talks, with President Eisenhower himself strongly behind the idea. Nuclear weapons had become the central feature of the East-West competition by this time.

In May 1955 the Soviets first broached the proposition that conventional arms control agreements might be monitored by limited on-site inspections.[14] What they appeared to have in mind were international inspection teams at crossroads to monitor movements of equipment. The West did not see this as a serious concession. In Korea, in the months after the armistice of July 1953, the Chinese easily had circumvented such monitoring teams by simply rerouting their forces away from the monitors. In July 1955 at the Geneva summit—the first such meeting since the Potsdam conference at the end of World War II—Eisenhower unveiled a new verification and confidence-building scheme with his Open Skies proposal. When the Soviets failed to respond positively to that initiative, Eisenhower authorized the U-2 aerial reconnaissance program to proceed.

Meanwhile, nuclear proliferation was a slowly developing force below the visible surface of world politics. Britain had tested its first nuclear weapon in October 1952 and was proceeding methodically toward thermonuclear capability. The 1956 Suez crisis created a deep schism in the Western alliance and contributed to France's resolve to gain its own nuclear deterrent (the initial French test occurred in February 1960). The events surrounding the Suez crisis (especially the Soviet threats to the region) also contributed to the Israeli decision to pursue a covert nuclear weapon program.[15] The Taiwan Strait crisis of 1954–1955 apparently had contributed to similar Chinese resolve.[16]

Throughout this time, arms control discussions continued—with much public posturing—in the United Nations. Considerable effort was invested in attempting to devise formulas linking nuclear to conventional reductions. One of these was an Anglo-French proposal unveiled in April 1955 to begin the elimination of nuclear weapons when 75 percent of the agreed cuts in conventional arms had been accomplished, to be completed concurrently with the remaining conventional reductions. It was difficult in the 1950s (and still is today) to separate propaganda from serious efforts with respect to such initiatives as the Polish Rapacki plan, introduced in October 1957, for a nuclear weapon–free zone in Central Europe. The arms race entered a dangerous new phase in the fall of 1957 when the successful Soviet launch of the SPUTNIK satellite shocked the West. Much of the Cold War turned on subtle psychological maneuvers, and SPUTNIK directly challenged confidence in Western capitals of the West's ability to offset Soviet numerical advantages with superior technology. In March 1958 Moscow announced a nuclear test moratorium (having just completed a major nuclear test series), and a group of Soviet, British, and U.S. experts convened at Geneva in the summer of 1958 to discuss the prospects of monitoring a ban on nuclear testing. In October 1958 tripartite (U.S.-British-Soviet) nuclear test talks began. The same month, Ireland introduced the first in a series of resolutions in the United Nations, calling for exploration of an international regime to prevent nuclear proliferation. A surprise attack conference convened in the winter of 1958. As the decade ended in December 1959, one of the first Cold War arms control agreements—the Antarctic Treaty, which calls for demilitarization of the continent in perpetuity—was opened for signature.

For all the tensions and arms-racing during the 1950s, the decade can be seen as a preparatory phase in Cold War arms control. One of the tenets of arms control—respected in the West and apparently also at play in the East—was to ensure that any negotiation, if undertaken and concluded, would leave forces sufficient to carry out the national security strategy. This concept would later be called the "military sufficiency" principle in the U.S. arms control lexicon. Although it was possible that the national security strategy might be adjusted if and when confidence increased in the potential adversary's nonhostile intentions, this could not be taken for granted. The armed forces permitted by arms control also should be able to cope with surprises—especially surprises if the other side cheated on an agreement or, under cover of the agreement, covertly prepared to seize the advantage in a new arms race to follow sudden withdrawal from a treaty (concepts later called "militarily significant" violations and "breakout," respectively).

The record of discussions on nuclear arms control talks in the late 1950s clearly reflects these concerns. The 1950s also represented a transitional decade as the world entered the missile age. Theories of deterrence relevant to a world of slower delivery vehicles had to be adjusted. One of the elements needed for arms control to succeed was confidence in understanding the nature and direction of the other side's forces and programs.

Knowledge of the Soviet nuclear force posture was problematic for much of the period discussed thus far. U.S. understanding began to improve somewhat after U-2 flights began over the Soviet Union in the summer of 1956. These were risky endeavors, however, and the shootdown of a U-2 in the spring of 1960 led to a new chill in already cold relations. By the fall of 1960, the first U.S. satellite reconnaissance flights (part of the CORONA program) were returning data on Soviet forces. This went a long way toward providing the "national technical means" of verification that would be crucial to arms control initiatives in the 1960s.

The Kennedy and Johnson Years

John F. Kennedy came to office with a strong desire to integrate arms control more closely into U.S. security strategy. His first two years were consumed by crises—Congo, the Bay of Pigs, Laos, Berlin, the resumption of nuclear testing, the Cuban missile crisis, and a brief Sino-Indian border war. During 1961 his arms control agenda focused primarily on trying to rejuvenate the tripartite nuclear test talks that had stalled. His predecessor, Dwight Eisenhower, viewed his own failure to achieve a test ban as one of his greatest disappointments.[17] Kennedy, working with Congress, also moved quickly to create the new Arms Control and Disarmament Agency, a task that was guided largely by a specially appointed presidential adviser on disarmament, the senior statesman John McCloy. A unilateral but parallel moratorium on nuclear testing had been in place since 1958. Moscow abruptly resumed atmospheric nuclear testing in September 1961 and, in October, exploded a mammoth 30-megaton device. Kennedy authorized resumption of U.S. nuclear testing.

The declassified record of NSC meetings on nuclear testing shows Kennedy's obsession with the pending proliferation of nuclear weapons to China. After the shock of the Cuban missile crisis, a window opened for progress in arms control. In his American University speech in June 1963, President Kennedy called for a new focus "on a more practical, more attainable peace, based not on a sudden revolution in human nature but on a gradual evolution in human institutions—on a series of concrete actions and effective agreements which are in the interest of all concerned."[18] That same month, the United States concluded the first Hot Line agreement with the Soviets (providing direct communication between the heads of state) and, in August 1963, completed negotiations with the Soviets and British for the Limited Test Ban Treaty (LTBT) that restricted nuclear testing to underground. On the margins of the LTBT talks in Moscow, the United States tried unsuccessfully to engage the Soviets in a joint effort to launch a new initiative to prevent China from getting the bomb.

Kennedy was assassinated in November 1963, and Vice President Lyndon Johnson succeeded him. In January 1964 Johnson announced the U.S.

decision to cut back on production of fissile materials, a decision reached largely on domestic grounds but for which the United States sought leverage in new arms control initiatives.[19] During 1964 the United States edged closer to broadening its military commitment in Vietnam. In October of that year, Soviet Premier Nikita Khrushchev was ousted, and the Chinese conducted their first nuclear test. The United States had anticipated the test and responded with a diplomatic initiative that included a presidential address that appeared to offer a blanket security guarantee to any state threatened by Chinese nuclear weapons. The United States was on record opposing further nuclear proliferation, but the complicated debate was caught up with issues of NATO strategy and, specifically, West German access to nuclear weapons through mechanisms like the Multilateral Nuclear Force—a U.S. initiative that NATO had adopted. Johnson appointed a blue-ribbon commission headed by Roswell Gilpatrick, former U.S. deputy defense secretary, to study the problem and provide recommendations. The Gilpatrick commission delivered its report to Johnson in January 1965, unanimously recommending that he devote the prestige of his office to trying to negotiate a nonproliferation treaty (NPT).[20] By mid-1965, Johnson had assigned high priority to pursuing a nonproliferation treaty at the Eighteen-Nation Disarmament Conference (ENDC), which then served as the main UN multilateral negotiating forum. Also by this time, the United States had committed itself to a massive effort in the Vietnam War.

Since the early 1950s Washington and Moscow had pursued research-and-development programs for ballistic missile defenses, conducted in parallel to their efforts to develop and deploy long-range ballistic missiles. In early 1966, on the margins of ENDC discussions, U.S. and Soviet officials began informal exchanges on the possibility of bilateral negotiations on offensive and defensive strategic systems. Both sides approached the matter warily, and little progress was made in 1966. In January 1967 the two superpowers joined others in signing an Outer Space Treaty that banned placing in orbit weapons of mass destruction. At the Glassboro summit, in June 1967, the United States again raised the issue of limiting strategic systems but found Aleksei Kosygin, who succeeded Khrushchev as premier, unprepared for any serious discussions. In September 1967 President Johnson, in the face of divided counsel within his administration, decided to proceed to deploy a limited ballistic missile defense program code-named SENTINEL. As 1967 ended, NATO adopted the Harmel report.[21] This elevated "the search for progress towards a more stable relationship in which the underlying political issues can be solved" to be on a par with NATO's military activities. Arms control efforts were understood to be an important component of the dual-track process.

Reviewing the history of arms control in the Cold War reveals how closely the various strands of nuclear arms control—testing, nonproliferation, limits on strategic systems—have related to one another from the earliest days. After the Cuban missile crisis of 1963, several Latin American nations took the initiative to create a Latin America Nuclear Weapon Free Zone. The negotiations resulted in the Treaty of Tlatelolco, which was opened for signature in February 1967. The United States signed protocols to that treaty, which among other things legally committed it not to use or threaten to use nuclear weapons against non–nuclear weapon states party to, and in compliance with, the treaty. Such "negative security assurances," however, were not included in the multilateral NPT that was under negotiation at the same time, because they would undercut NATO strategy.[22] As the ENDC came to closure on the NPT, the Johnson administration pressed Moscow to set a date for strategic talks, arguing that the success of the NPT depended on evidence of bilateral progress toward curbing the strategic arms race. Moscow finally agreed, and when the NPT was opened for signature in July 1968, Washington and Moscow simultaneously announced their intent to begin strategic arms talks.

By this time Johnson—weary from the domestic backlash to the war in Vietnam—had announced that he would not seek another term as president. Washington and Moscow had privately agreed to open strategic arms talks when Johnson was scheduled to visit Moscow in early October 1968, but the Soviet invasion of Czechoslovakia in August made this politically impossible. It also delayed entry into force of the NPT until 1970.

The Nixon and Ford Years

Richard Nixon was inaugurated president in January 1969. Although his most pressing foreign affairs problem was to disengage the United States from Vietnam, he pursued it within a wider grand strategy combining elements of détente with the Soviet Union with rapprochement with China. The Nixon administration launched a number of strategic reviews under the supervision of Nixon's National Security Advisor, Henry Kissinger. The Soviets now were eager to begin the strategic arms talks, but the Nixon team delayed until its reviews were completed. The Strategic Arms Limitation Talks (SALT) began in November 1969 and, in May 1972, resulted in an interim agreement on strategic offensive arms (SALT I) as well as the Anti-Ballistic Missile (ABM) Treaty. SALT I set a ceiling on the number of long-range ballistic missile launchers (land- and sea-based) allowed by both sides. The ABM Treaty committed the sides not to deploy ABM systems for defense of their territories. Neither could they provide a base for such a defense.

Although strategic arms negotiations were considered most important, they were not the only dimension of arms control. In early 1969 the Soviet Union revived its earlier proposal for a conference on European security and cooperation. The Soviets appeared to be especially eager to revive détente in Europe after the Czech episode. In the fall of 1969, Willy Brandt was elected chancellor of West Germany and launched his policy of *Ostpolitik,* aiming at improving relations with the Soviet Union and its Eastern European allies, especially East Germany. In the United States, the Congress—weary of Vietnam—was talking of U.S. troop reductions in Europe. These strands converged in the commencement of a Conference on Security and Cooperation in Europe (CSCE) in 1973 and talks on Mutual and Balanced Force Reductions (MBFR). The genesis of the MBFR talks appeared to have been the European desire to prevent a decision in Washington for unilateral troop withdrawals, on the theory that the U.S. Congress would not undercut the negotiations.[23] Whatever the case, MBFR would continue inconclusively until it was superseded by the Conventional Forces in Europe (CFE) talks in 1989—talks conducted in a very different political climate with serious intent to reach agreement.

In November 1969 the United States, in service of its new détente policy, undertook a unilateral initiative, renouncing first use of lethal or incapacitating chemical agents and weapons and any use (even retaliatory) of biological weapons. This formed the basis for a bilateral treaty with the Soviets that entered into force and then became the basis for the multilateral Biological and Toxin Weapons Convention of 1972 (commonly known as the Biological Weapons Convention, or BWC). In 1975 the United States finally ratified the 1925 Geneva Protocol on chemical weapons. Other arms control agreements during this era included the Accidents Measures Agreement (1971), the Seabed Treaty and Incidents at Sea Agreement (1972), and the Prevention of Nuclear War Agreement (1973). In early 1974 talks came to closure on the Threshold Test Ban Treaty (TTBT), although that and its companion Peaceful Nuclear Explosions Treaty (PNET) of 1976 did not enter into force until December 1990, after the completion of verification protocols.

President Nixon had proclaimed an era of negotiations, and this succession of agreements appeared to substantiate his claim. The last year of Nixon's presidency was plagued by scandal, and after the public revelations in June 1973 concerning Nixon's complicity in the Watergate affair, policymaking in the Nixon administration tended to drift. Gerald Ford succeeded Nixon in the fall of 1974.

The reason that SALT I was an interim executive agreement instead of a treaty reflected the difficulty of the early negotiations in reaching consensus on how to control strategic nuclear arms in two military postures with different emphases, force priorities, and geostrategic circumstances. For instance, the two sides were still far apart on what to consider a "strategic" system—one of intercontinental range (the U.S. position), or one capable of striking the other's homeland (the Soviet preference). The Nixon administration had permitted the Soviets a numerical advantage in numbers of intercontinental ballistic missile (ICBM) launchers and submarine-launched ballistic missile launchers in SALT I because of offsetting U.S. advantages in bombers and in the technology of multiple independently targetable reentry vehicles (MIRVs). This came under heavy criticism in the United States by such important figures as Senator Henry Jackson. The SALT I interim agreement was set to expire in October 1977. Negotiations had commenced in 1972 on a more comprehensive treaty to replace it.

In November 1974, at a summit in Vladivostok, Ford and Soviet leader Leonid Brezhnev agreed on a formula for a new SALT II treaty that would set an aggregate ceiling of 2,400 launchers of strategic nuclear delivery vehicles and a subceiling of 1,320 launchers of MIRVed missiles. The United States would drop its insistence on reductions in heavy ICBMs, and in turn the Soviets would drop their demand for limits on forward-based systems (U.S. shorter-range nuclear forces deployed near Soviet territory, either in NATO, East Asia, or at sea). For the remainder of the Ford administration, Kissinger (now secretary of state) tried to cut a deal based on this formula. He did not succeed, largely because of the difficulty in resolving whether and how to limit nascent U.S. cruise missile programs (the Soviet concern) and how to treat development of the new Soviet Backfire bomber (the U.S. concern).

The Carter Years

Jimmy Carter took office in January 1977. The top foreign policy priorities of his administration at the outset were to conclude the SALT II negotiations, strengthen NATO, and restore momentum to earlier Middle East peace and Panama Canal negotiations. Normalizing relations with China was also considered important. In March 1977 Secretary of State Cyrus Vance went to Moscow with a new arms control proposal that departed from the Vladivostok formula to seek much lower limits and sublimits. The Soviets angrily rejected this departure, and after some initial discussions, negotiations were resumed on the basis of the Vladivostok framework. In June 1979 the SALT II treaty was signed in Vienna. This was a much longer and considerably more complicated document than SALT I.

What also was maturing during the Carter years was a highly polarized political debate in the United States and NATO on the merits of the emerging nuclear arms control regime. Critics of the SALT process argued that it was facilitating a shift in the strategic balance that would result in vulnerability of U.S. ICBM forces over time. Many of these critics also suspected that the Soviets were not complying with their arms control commitments. In NATO, there was growing unease that the eroding nuclear balance was decoupling the U.S. strategic deterrent from NATO strategy. This was exacerbated by the ongoing Soviet force modernization program for its theater conventional and nuclear forces. The mobile MIRVed Soviet SS-20 intermediate-range ballistic missile and the new Backfire bomber were at the center of that debate. Further, President Carter had canceled the B-1 bomber program in June 1977. The public explanation was that the preference was to modernize the aging B-52 force using cruise missiles. Unknown to the public at the time was the U.S. military's pursuit of revolutionary stealth technologies for a future generation of aircraft. Uncertainties about how cruise missiles—air-, sea-, and ground-launched, of a variety of ranges—would be dealt with in arms control further complicated the situation, as did the public controversy over the enhanced radiation weapons (neutron bomb) program. In October 1977, in a speech to the International Institute for Strategic Studies, West German chancellor Helmut Schmidt compellingly argued the European concern that further strategic limitations in SALT II with no constraints on the SS-20 would destabilize the so-called Eurostrategic balance of nuclear forces.

While these events were unfolding, the Carter administration was pursuing other arms control initiatives: talks on control of antisatellite systems and a new round of talks on a comprehensive nuclear test ban. These proceeded slowly and inconclusively. In June 1978, at the UN Special Session on Disarmament, Secretary of State Vance extended for the first time a U.S. negative security guarantee (albeit legally nonbinding) to non–nuclear weapon states party to the treaty. The Carter administration also pursued enhanced export controls on nuclear materials and adopted a stringent policy aimed at discouraging the use of plutonium to help fuel civilian power reactors. Nuclear anxieties were raised worldwide in March 1979 with the commercial nuclear incident at Three Mile Island in Pennsylvania.

In December 1979 two important events for the future of arms control took place. At a special meeting of foreign and defense ministers in Brussels, NATO decided to deploy a new generation of theater nuclear forces—Pershing II missiles and ground-launched cruise missiles—if anticipated theater nuclear arms talks did not constrain Soviet systems like the SS-20. This was known as the "two-track decision." The other event was the unexpected Soviet invasion of Afghanistan that led the Carter administration to withdraw SALT II from the U.S. Senate, where it was being considered for advice and consent. By this time, the Iranian revolution had proceeded to the point where U.S. hostages had been seized in Teheran—an issue that would preoccupy U.S. policy for the remainder of Carter's term in office.

Late in 1980 the theater nuclear force talks called for by NATO began between the U.S. and Soviet delegations in Geneva. These talks recessed when Carter lost the presidential election to Ronald Reagan.

The End of the Cold War

In the years 1975 to 1979, as governor of California and candidate for the presidency, Ronald Reagan wrote and spoke frequently on defense and arms control matters. His general views on arms control can be summarized in his radio broadcast of 11 September 1979: "Do arms limitation agreements—even good ones—really bring or preserve peace? History would seem to say 'no.'"[24] His scathing critique of SALT already was a matter of record: "No wonder [Soviet Foreign Minister Andrei] Gromyko describes [the SALT] negotiations as 'businesslike [and] useful.' Translated from the Russian that means '. . . Uncle Sam has been skinned again.'"[25] Many incoming members of the Reagan administration shared these sentiments.

In light of the above, how can one explain that during the 12 years of the Reagan and George Bush administrations (1981–1993) some of the most significant arms control agreements of the Cold War were concluded? Partly the explanation lies in the fact that the Reagan administration adjusted its policies in the face of allied and domestic public opinion in favor of arms control; the allies also held together on critical issues like the deployment of a new generation of theater missiles when it appeared that negotiations were stalemated. Partly it lies in the increased confidence the U.S. side had in itself as its military strength increased during the early Reagan years. But largely it is due to the change in Soviet attitudes. In 1981, a visibly feeble, aging Soviet leader—Leonid Brezhnev—was in power, having presided over Soviet policy since the ouster of Khrushchev in 1964. Brezhnev died in November 1982, to be succeeded by Yuri Andropov (who died in February 1984), and then Konstantin Chernenko (who died in March 1985). This finally brought a new generation of Soviet leaders to power under Mikhail Gorbachev, a man who saw arms control as an essential part of his agenda for stabilizing international relations in order to try to revive the Soviet system.

Within this process of cascading political change, we find a rapid succession of arms control agreements. In the nuclear arena, talks began in the fall of 1981 on Intermediate Nuclear Forces, resulting by the end of 1987 in a treaty that eliminated an entire class of missiles from the U.S. and Soviet inventories. In the fall of 1982 the Strategic Arms Reduction Treaty (START) negotiations began, resulting in two treaties: START I (signed in July 1991), and START II (signed in January 1993, after Gorbachev had resigned and the Soviet Union had been replaced by the Russian Federation). By the mid-1980s the U.S. and Soviet Union had begun drafting verification protocols to the earlier nuclear testing treaties—TTBT and PNET. With the conclusion of the protocols, those treaties finally entered into force in June 1990, over a decade after they had been signed. In the conventional arena, the CSCE process resulted in the Stockholm Confidence and Security Building Measures document, completed in September 1986. This had been under negotiation since 1983. As Gorbachev's reforms continued, NATO and the Warsaw Pact negotiated the CFE Treaty that was signed in November 1990. And on the margins of all this, Washington and Moscow concluded important bilateral agreements on issues such as chemical arms that would facilitate movement toward multilateral agreements.

A new U.S. administration took office in January 1989, led by President George H.W. Bush. In early 1989, there were virtually no experts in the West who anticipated how rapidly events would evolve later that year when the Soviet Empire begin to contract in an extraordinarily peaceful fashion. Along the way, in addition to the major negotiations cited above, a host of other confidence-building measures facilitated the adjustment of East-West relations, such as the expansion of the 1971 Accidents Measures agreement in 1986 to cover prior notification of missile launches, and the U.S.-Russia Dangerous Military Activities agreements of June 1989. The new arms control framework that was emerging involved an unprecedented degree of cooperative verification. It also was associated with a political process of signaling to Moscow that the West did not intend to take military advantage of the changes under way. Documents such as the Comprehensive Concept on Arms Control and Disarmament that was adopted by NATO at its summit in May 1989 were devised with this in mind, as were changes in the public statement of NATO nuclear doctrine.[26] The Berlin Wall fell in November 1989.

Gorbachev narrowly escaped a coup in August 1991. In September, responding in part to the need to signal further assurances quickly, President Bush announced the first of a series of unilateral nuclear initiatives. The U.S. and Russian nuclear initiatives of September and October 1991 and January 1992 may have appeared revolutionary at the time, but they had a sound basis in arms control theory and practice dating back to the 1950s and early 1960s. Schelling and Halperin had made it clear in their 1961 book that arms control could include "the less formal, less institutionalized, less 'negotiated' understandings and agreements."[27] The final years of the Cold War demonstrated how a host of formal and less formal cooperative measures that go under the general heading of "arms control" can interact in the appropriate circumstances to help achieve a desirable outcome.

Arms Control After the Cold War

As the Cold War was ending, a regional crisis many years in the making—Iraq's invasion of Kuwait in the summer of 1990—focused international attention on what was soon to become a defining feature of the post–Cold War arms control agenda: proliferation. Earlier we noted the Iranian revolution of 1979 that deposed the shah and brought a radical theocratic government to power in Iran. During the 1980s, Iraq and Iran fought a brutal nine-year war that involved, among other things, the use of chemical weapons (the creation of the Australia Group in June 1985 to attempt to control trade in the chemicals needed for chemical warfare stemmed from this fact). Iraq emerged from the war with its finances depleted, which in part appears to explain the Iraqi decision in August 1990 to invade Kuwait. The cooperative relationship that had emerged between Washington and Moscow facilitated action in the UN Security Council to oppose Iraqi aggression. In early 1991 the international coalition spearheaded by the United States ousted Iraq from Kuwait.

There was much discussion at the time that a new world order was being constructed, one in which great power cooperation would allow the Security Council to function as it was envisioned in 1945. Such discussion proved to be premature. As the early post–Cold War world unfolded, a number of new divides emerged: Western humanitarian intervention in the wars in the Balkans; the enlargement of NATO; disillusionment in Russia, accompanied by greater reliance on nuclear weapons; an acceleration in the proliferation of weapons of mass destruction and advanced delivery systems, facilitated by the revolution in world affairs that goes under the general heading of "globalization"; and the creation (for the first time since Nuremberg and Tokyo) of new international tribunals to try war crimes and crimes against humanity. These fissures intersected with lingering problems: the continuing crisis on the Korean Peninsula (made all the more dangerous by North Korea's pursuit of weapons of mass destruction and longer-range ballistic missiles); the India-Pakistan dispute over Kashmir (with the new factor that in 1998 India and Pakistan both openly tested nuclear weapons); and the unresolved status of Taiwan (against the backdrop of an increasingly assertive China emerging as a growing regional power). The war on terrorism that followed the September 2001 attacks on the World Trade Center and the Pentagon provided a new context for dealing with the lingering problem.

In this milieu, the post–Cold War arms control agenda took on a much more diffuse character. One of the most pressing problems was managing the breakup of the Soviet Empire, reflected in the series of agreements that determined succession rights to the Soviet nuclear arsenal and facilitated Ukraine, Belarus, and Kazakhstan joining the NPT as non–nuclear weapon states, and in the initiatives that followed the Nunn-Lugar legislation of 1991: Cooperative Threat Reduction; Material Protection, Control, and Accounting; and the Nuclear Cities initiative. In May 2001 President George W. Bush (the son of the man who presided over U.S. policy at the end of the Cold War) reiterated what he had said as a presidential candidate: "We must move beyond the constraints of the 30-year-old ABM Treaty."[28] He made good on this promise by announcing in December 2001 that the United States would withdraw from the ABM Treaty in order to develop a global missile defense system. In January 2002, the Bush administration unveiled the results of its Nuclear Posture Review. This provided context to President Bush's announcement preceding the Crawford summit in November 2001 that the United States would reduce its operationally deployed strategic nuclear warheads to a level between 1,700 and 2,200 over the next decade. Talks between the United States and the Russian Federation led to a treaty signed in Moscow on 24 May 2002 that codified U.S. and Russian strategic arms reductions and the substance of their respective commitments.

Resolving U.S.-Russia differences on strategic nuclear reductions and on the ABM Treaty may also affect the future of the Nuclear Nonproliferation Treaty. In 1995, at a contentious international conference, the NPT was extended indefinitely. A number of non–nuclear weapon states party to the NPT are openly critical of the slow pace of U.S.-Russian arms control, and this was further exacerbated when the U.S. Senate in 1999 refused to ratify the Comprehensive Test Ban Treaty that the United States had signed in 1996. Disputes such as these have prevented movement on the initiative to create a Fissile Materials Cutoff Treaty.

In the aftermath of the 1991 Gulf War, critics have openly questioned whether the NPT is enforceable through IAEA inspections and international sanctions. Although the UN Security Council initially mandated that Iraq dismantle its programs for weapons of mass destruction and for missile delivery systems, in December 1998 Iraq forced the UN Special Commission on Iraq (UNSCOM) to withdraw from its inspection activities. Although there is a successor organization—the UN Monitoring, Verification, and Inspection Commission (UNMOVIC)—and even though the IAEA's Iraq Action Team remains intact, Iraq refuses to cooperate, and thus far the Security Council refuses to force cooperation through pressure other than continuing sanctions (for which international support is eroding). Neither is it clear that the 1994 U.S.–North Korea Framework Agreement that addresses North Korea's nuclear programs will succeed. And notwithstanding the Missile Technology Control Regime of 1987, accelerated proliferation of missile technology continues, with North Korea as a major conduit and involving assistance from Russia and China. The ongoing effort to establish an International Code of Conduct Against Missile Proliferation reflects continued U.S. concern in this area.

In 1993 the new Chemical Weapons Convention (CWC) was opened for signature. This treaty, which entered into force in 1997, not only repeats the ban on use of chemical weapons derived from the 1925 Geneva Protocol but also prohibits the production or stockpiling of such munitions. Questions of compliance and enforcement linger in the background of the CWC, as they do for the BWC, where since 1994 an ad hoc group has attempted to devise a monitoring scheme that has yet to achieve international consensus and is opposed by the United States as an inadequate and potentially damaging initiative, at least as reflected in the draft protocol to the BWC.

A host of agreements for new nuclear weapon–free zones have been concluded (the treaties of Rarotonga [1985] for the South Pacific, Bangkok

[1995] for Southeast Asia, and Pelindaba [1996] for Africa), and several others are under discussion. Finally, one can note the new focus on other areas of arms control, such as the UN Register of Conventional Arms (1991), the Ottawa Convention to ban landmines (1997), a host of attempts to inject confidence-building measures into the Middle East and other areas where fighting continues, and a new international initiative to control traffic in light arms.

The two post–Cold War U.S. presidents—Bill Clinton (1993–2001) and George W. Bush (inaugurated January 2001)—have grappled with these issues. One of the greatest challenges for the United States is to create the framework that allows some form of ballistic missile defense to proceed (a goal both administrations shared, albeit with different interpretations of what that entailed) without seriously destabilizing international relations. Whether that can be accomplished remains unclear, but the United States is moving forward with its missile defense deployment plans following U.S. withdrawal from the ABM Treaty on 13 June 2002.

Conclusion

This chapter has surveyed the process of arms control as we know it today. It has evolved over thousands of years as world security structures have shifted. Seeking to manage war—and the causes and consequences of war—has led to our current arms control regime. If there is one lesson to be taken away from the history outlined in this chapter, it is that the urges behind what we understand as arms control are deep. Although arms control can take different forms at different times, it is a pervasive part of international relations and one of the mechanisms states have frequently turned to in order to reconcile short-term expediencies with the longer-term dream of a just and secure world order. It is premature to predict the death of arms control. It is not premature to anticipate its entering a new phase.

Notes

1. "The precise origin of the term *arms control* is unclear although what would now be termed arms control endeavors can be found throughout recorded history." Patrick M. Morgan, "Arms Control," *The Oxford Companion to Politics of the World* (New York: Oxford University Press, 1993), p. 50.

2. Thomas C. Schelling and Morton H. Halperin, *Strategy and Arms Control* (Washington, DC: Permagon-Brassey, 1985 [orig. publ. 1961]), p. 1.

3. Robert H. Strassler, ed., *The Landmark Thucydides* (New York: Free Press, 1996), pp. 49–50.

4. Detlev F. Vagts, "The Hague Convention and Arms Control," *American Journal of International Law* 94, no. 1 (January 2000): 321–341.

5. Fred Tanner, "Versailles: German Disarmament After World War I," in Fred Tanner, ed., *From Versailles to Baghdad: Post-War Armament Control of Defeated States* (New York: United Nations, 1992), p. 25.

6. Robert Dallek, *Franklin D. Roosevelt and American Foreign Policy, 1932–1945* (New York: Oxford University Press, 1979), p. 35.

7. Raymond Aron, *On War,* translated from *De la Guerre* by Terence Kilmartin (New York: University Press of America, 1985 [rpt. of the 1958 English ed.]), p. 16.

8. Memorandum for the President from Fleet Admiral Leahy for the Joint Chiefs of Staff, 23 October 1945. A declassified copy of this memorandum can be accessed at the Harry S. Truman Library, President's Secretary's Files, NSC, Box 199.

9. The text of the resolution can be found in Department of State, *Documents on Disarmament, 1945–1959,* vol. 1 (Washington, DC: U.S. Government Printing Office, 1960), pp. 6–7.

10. The text of NSC-112 can be found in Department of State, *Foreign Relations of the United States,* 1951, vol. 1 (Washington, DC: U.S. Government Printing Office, 1979), pp. 477–497. Hereafter, references to volumes in the Foreign Relations of the United States series will be abbreviated FRUS.

11. The text of the Oppenheimer report can be found in FRUS, 1952–1954, vol. 2, pp. 1056–1091.

12. Robert H. Bowie and Richard H. Immerman, *Waging Peace: How Eisenhower Shaped an Enduring Cold War Strategy* (New York: Oxford University Press, 1998), pp. 222–241. Robert Bowie was the first director of the Policy Planning Staff in the Eisenhower administration.

13. J. Robert Oppenheimer, "Atomic Weapons and American Policy," *Foreign Affairs* 31, no. 4 (July 1953): 525–535.

14. Michael R. Beschloss, *Mayday: The U-2 Affair* (New York: Harper and Row [Perennial Library ed.], 1987), p. 98.

15. Avner Cohen, *Israel and the Bomb* (New York: Columbia University Press, 1998), pp. 54–55.

16. John Wilson Lewis and Xue Litai, *China Builds the Bomb* (Stanford: Stanford University Press, 1988), p. 34.

17. In a discussion in spring 2001, Herb York, a distinguished American physicist whose involvement with nuclear arms control dates to the 1950s, shared with me his recollections of Eisenhower's deep commitment to the cause of controlling nuclear testing. For Eisenhower's own comments on the matter, see Dwight D. Eisenhower, *The White House Years: Waging Peace, 1956–1961* (Garden City, NY: Doubleday, 1965), p. 482.

18. The text of the American University speech can be found in the John F. Kennedy volume of *Public Papers of the President of the United States* (Washington, DC: U.S. Government Printing Office, 1964), pp. 459–464.

19. Glenn T. Seaborg with Benjamin S. Loeb, *Stemming the Tide: Arms Control in the Johnson Years* (Lexington, MA: D. C. Heath, 1987), pp. 33–41.

20. The text of the Gilpatrick report can be found in FRUS, 1964–1968, vol. 11, pp. 173–182.

21. The text of the Harmel report can be found in NATO Information Services, *Texts of Final Communiques of the North Atlantic Council, the Defence Planning Committee, and the Nuclear Planning Group,* vol. 1, 1949–1974 (Brussels: NATO), pp. 198–202.

22. For a discussion of the early development of U.S. policy on negative and positive security assurances, see Michael Wheeler, *Positive and Negative Security*

Assurances, Project on Rethinking Arms Control (PRAC) Paper No. 9 (College Park: Center for International Studies, University of Maryland, 1994).

23. Henry Kissinger, *White House Years* (Boston: Little, Brown, 1970), p. 400.

24. The radio addresses that Reagan wrote and edited are contained in Kiron K. Skinner, Annelise Anderson, and Martin Anderson, eds., *Reagan in His Own Hand* (New York: Free Press, 2001), p. 62.

25. Ibid., p. 76.

26. The text of the Comprehensive Concept of Arms Control and Disarmament can be found in NATO Information Service, *The North Atlantic Treaty Organization: Facts and Figures,* 11th ed. (Brussels: NATO, 1989), pp. 432–443.

27. Schelling and Halperin, *Strategy and Arms Control,* p. 5.

28. U.S. Department of State, International Information Programs, Text of Remarks by the President to the Students and Faculty at National Defense University, 1 May 2001, accessed at www.usinfo.state.gov.

Suggested Readings

Bull, Hedley. *Hedley Bull on Arms Control.* Selected and introduced by Robert O'Neill and David N. Schwartz. New York: St. Martin's, 1987.

Bunn, George. *Arms Control by Committee.* Stanford: Stanford University Press, 1992.

Rostow, Eugene V. *Toward Managed Peace.* New Haven: Yale University Press, 1993.

Schelling, Thomas C., and Morton H. Halperin. *Strategy and Arms Control.* Washington, DC: Pergamon-Brassey's Classic, 1985 [orig. publ. 1961].

3

The Changing International Context

Schuyler Foerster

States have often cooperated in regulating the conduct and instruments of warfare. Such efforts typically stemmed from a fear that warfare would unleash death and destruction on a scale and in forms widely considered unacceptable. These fears were usually genuine, arising from real advances in military technology, the effects of which were at least partly demonstrated in actual wars. Such fears increased following the terrorist attacks on the United States on 11 September 2001.

Cooperative efforts to regulate warfare have enjoyed a mixed record of success. Typically such efforts are successful only when the underlying international context is conducive to their success. This does not suggest that only friends cooperate, or that arms control succeeds only in benign relationships where they are not necessary. Success does require, however, relationships in which cooperation in certain defined security matters is valued, even if only to enable the broader political and strategic competition to proceed more safely. Conversely, cooperative security will fail when at least one sufficiently powerful state decides that competition—and perhaps even combat—is more important than cooperation in the pursuit of its own security.

Cooperative security can take many forms. First, states can come together to outlaw warfare, a strategy attempted by the international community in the 1920s with distinctly counterproductive results. Second, states can regulate the conduct of warfare through international laws of war, a strategy that enjoyed important success in the late nineteenth and early twentieth centuries but was little advanced during the Cold War. Third, states can negotiate disarmament agreements aimed at the elimination of weapons. This strategy often presumes that weapons themselves contribute to the causes of war. It was reflected in much of the rhetoric of the Cold War, especially in its early years, but there was—by design on the part of the major powers—little concrete result.

41

Finally, states can seek to regulate the number, deployment, and employment of certain weapons through arms control—as distinct from disarmament—agreements. In this context, arms control need not entail any reduction in armaments; indeed, it may even enable an increase in certain types of armaments within a controlled framework designed to achieve stability and predictability in an adversary relationship.[1] In the words of Thomas Schelling and Morton Halperin, this approach "is concerned less with reducing national *capabilities* for destruction in the event of war than in reducing *incentives* that may lead to war or that may cause war to be more destructive in the event it occurs."[2] This last form of cooperative security was the most successful form of cooperative security during the Cold War.

The thesis of this chapter is threefold: (1) Much of the historically unprecedented success of arms control during the Cold War is attributable to an international context that was especially—and perhaps uniquely—conducive to its success; (2) the years following the end of the Cold War have witnessed fundamental changes in the character of the international system—the nature of conflict, the forces at play, the technology of warfare, and actors and their roles; and (3) these changes have, in some circumstances, opened new possibilities for cooperative security, whereas in other circumstances they have rendered arms control virtually irrelevant.

The End of the U.S.-Soviet Adversary Relationship

For more than four decades, the Cold War conflict between the United States and the Soviet Union was the decisive characteristic of the international system. Beginning in the early 1960s that relationship gave rise to a series of arms control agreements that regulated in considerable detail the superpowers' respective nuclear arsenals: restrictions on weapons testing; prohibitions related to nuclear proliferation and to various deployment modes; and limits on the numbers and types of strategic weapons, both offensive and defensive. Ultimately, that relationship also gave rise to cooperative agreements on chemical and biological weapons, conventional forces, broader confidence-building measures, and more symbolic agreements on conflict prevention. Nonetheless, regulation of the superpowers' substantial nuclear arsenals and the desire to minimize the danger of cataclysmic nuclear war dominated this cooperative security framework.

Thus the Cold War arms control process was essentially bilateral, with each side viewing it as a way to manage the bipolar relationship. To be sure, several arms control regimes from the Cold War were multilateral. Yet the purpose of those regimes was ultimately to manage a two-sided relationship that included allies, particularly ones armed with nuclear weapons. Even in the case of the Nuclear Non-Proliferation Treaty (NPT), at least one of its principal purposes was to confine, as much as possible, the nuclear competition to the relatively familiar terrain of the U.S.-Soviet relationship.[3]

By the late 1980s, however, U.S.-Soviet relations had reached a point whereby each sought added security through cooperative measures aimed at redressing certain imbalances in their strategic relationship. For the United States, the Strategic Arms Reduction Talks (START) were pursued largely to eliminate what had long been viewed as the Soviet advantage in heavy missiles with multiple, hard-target kill warheads that posed a potentially destabilizing first-strike capability. On the conventional level, the Conventional Armed Forces in Europe (CFE) Treaty—a multilateral negotiation that was structured and negotiated as a bilateral, bloc-to-bloc enterprise—was similarly designed to codify asymmetric Soviet reductions in offensive conventional warfighting capability and to achieve the long-elusive bipolar balance in conventional forces in Central Europe.[4] Soviet motives for engaging in such a positive-sum game are complex and beyond the scope of this discussion; suffice it to say that Soviet leader Mikhail Gorbachev sought to stabilize a strategic relationship and free up resources to address pressing domestic issues, issues that ultimately caused the disintegration of the Soviet state.

Significantly, the end of the Cold War facilitated the conclusion of a range of arms control agreements on nuclear, chemical, and conventional forces, giving rise to even greater expectations for further progress in arms control. By the mid-1990s, however, it was clear that these agreements were the fruits of a dying Cold War relationship, not the beginning of a new period of U.S.-Russia strategic cooperation.

Since the mid-1990s the "traditional" agenda of Cold War arms control has largely stalled. The Russian Duma (parliament) finally ratified START II in 2000 only after the treaty's reduction deadlines were extended, the United States had made assurances regarding the scope of a START III negotiation, and it was clear to both sides that Russian force levels were going below the treaty's limits, with or without the treaty.[5] Likewise, the CFE Treaty was "adapted" in 1996—barely one year after its limits on armament holdings went into effect—to accommodate Russian concerns about the treaty's restrictiveness. To enable Russia to comply with the treaty's limits, the United States and its NATO allies endorsed "flexibility . . . in accordance with treaty terms" but nonetheless amended the regime sufficiently to require the U.S. Senate to give its advice and consent regarding the new terms.[6] Subsequently, conventional arms control negotiations in Europe devolved into a protracted discussion about updating the CFE Treaty, a process not likely to create further negotiated reductions. Instead this "updating" has focused on ways to restructure the regime so it no longer represents a bilateral treaty between opposing blocs.

The end of the U.S.-Soviet adversary relationship meant that near-term political conditions could enable substantial agreement on a traditional arms control agenda, which then promptly lost much of its relevance precisely because the adversary relationship had disappeared. Indeed, those who argued that arms control regimes had lost their relevance did so by citing the potential for the United States and Russia to be strategic partners in a post–Cold War world. Conversely, to argue that the regimes retained their importance in a post–Cold War environment was tantamount to suggesting that the adversary relationship persisted.

Without the clear hostility of the Cold War, arms control between the United States and Russia has become more a conversation about the character of their relationship than a substantive negotiation as to how they might regulate their military forces. The latter simply requires a mind-set that sees the other as at least a potential adversary, even if not a current one. When one is trying to define—or, indeed, shape—a new, more cooperative relationship, the latter can be especially counterproductive.

Localization of Conflict

If arms control in the Cold War was about reducing the chances of major war between two superpowers, a major security focus of the post–Cold War period has been how to deal with violent conflict on a local level, as well as to contain that violence if one cannot stop it or eliminate its causes. Much of the conflict since the early 1990s has been internal, pitting faction against faction within the sovereign borders of a state, fueled by ethnic, racial, religious, and/or national passions for political purposes. Most of the casualties have been civilians rather than combatants, often deliberately rather than accidentally.

In this environment cooperative security takes on an entirely different character than it had during the Cold War. Major powers are less likely to be the protagonists in conflict and more likely to be deciding whether to intervene to address it. The tools are more likely to be techniques of conflict management and resolution rather than bargaining about counting rules and reduction and verification schemes.

What was considered "soft" arms control in the Cold War, therefore, has become more relevant in dealing with local conflicts in the post–Cold War period. Institutions such as the Organization of Security and Cooperation in Europe have designed mechanisms to create greater transparency in a potential conflict situation. Regimes of information exchange and on-site inspection borne of consecutive Vienna Documents were designed not to control arms per se or to verify their reduction but to promote transparency and build mutual confidence. Originally applied to Central Europe as the Cold War was ending, these mechanisms became useful in breaking down some of the lingering distrust in Eastern and Southeastern Europe. They have also been adapted, albeit with no more than modest success, to other regional conflicts in the Middle East and Korea.

The intense local conflicts of the post–Cold War period have demonstrated the limits both of arms control and of confidence-building. In the absence of large arsenals of heavy weapons, regimes of arms limitation or reduction may be irrelevant. More fundamentally, what was true of the Cold War conflict remains true today: any form of cooperative security requires the willingness of the protagonists to engage in the process. Outside powers can coerce, cajole, and bribe the protagonists—even occupy their territory and impose regimes—but success will be elusive as long as those intent on conflict retain the ability to impose their will. Arms control is a policy tool. It can succeed in stabilizing potential conflict situations when the protagonists share an interest in stability; it has not been successful in eliminating conflict.

Globalization of Economic, Political, and Social Forces

There is a growing consensus that what we have long referred to as the "post–Cold War period"—a phrase testifying to our inability to describe the present—is best viewed as a period of globalization.[7] Fueled largely by rapid advances in information, communications, and transportation technologies, globalization has fostered a world of greater economic interdependence; more diffuse sets of political actors that at a minimum have eliminated any monopoly that states ever enjoyed as international actors; and an array of social forces that reach beyond national borders with a tendency to destabilize rather than stabilize.

These independent yet interlinked forces pull in different directions. On one level, the forces of globalization propel states to seek cooperation and more stable relations, based on a shared sense of a common future and in recognition of their inextricable interdependence. This more benign view of globalization presumes that the information age promotes democratization and liberates markets, two forces that strike directly at the causes of conflict rather than at its symptoms and tools. According to this view, cooperative security in the age of globalization gives rise to a broader theory of peacekeeping that begins with intervention to stop the violence, proceeds to physical enforcement of confidence-building mechanisms to block a return to violence, followed by the slow process of political and economic rehabilitation. Ultimately, according to this model, traditional arms control measures designed to regulate the means of conflict are ancillary to a broader strategy that looks to the growth of new relationships in civil society to neutralize the causes of conflict.

Whether this theory can succeed in practice remains to be seen, although efforts are discernible in various conflicts around the world. One difficulty, of course, is that the forces of globalization also operate on a level that encourages social and political disintegration. The benefits of globalization are hardly distributed evenly. Notwithstanding the macrobenefits of a global marketplace, people lose their jobs and livelihoods. Cultures are assaulted by external pressures that as often as not provoke reactionary sentiments. Fear and dislocation become political tools, waiting to be picked up by a demagogue promising an end to social chaos and a return to traditional values. The result is not democracy and market liberalization but populist authoritarianism, with its propensity for aggressive behavior, conflict, and even terrorism. As for the tools of peacekeeping and conflict resolution—external intervention, democracy, free markets—these are often discredited by rhetoric or experience.

Even before the attacks of 11 September 2001, terrorism itself had been transformed by the forces of globalization. Osama bin Laden directed a transnational network of terrorist organizations linked by information-age technologies and global business activities. Clearly one did not need advanced weaponry to inflict massive death and destruction. In the wake of those terrorist attacks, threats to security hardly seemed manageable through cooperative security—except that new and sometimes surprising coalitions emerged to fight a new common enemy.

Whether one views the forces of globalization as ultimately positive or negative, the focus in managing contemporary conflict has shifted from regulating weaponry in a stable but adversary relationship to searching for some formula that will address the volatile causes of conflict.

The Changing Technology of Warfare

The late Raymond Aron called the twentieth century the "century of total war." World War I produced an estimated 9 million casualties, which by some estimates is twice the total casualties of all wars during the previous 500 years. World War II produced an estimated 55 million casualties—six times higher than World War I. With the advent of the nuclear age, one could project that the second half of the twentieth century would see a continued exponential rise in the casualties of war. But such was not the case.

One dilemma of the nuclear age was how to limit the destructive power of modern weapons without negating the deterrent effect that weapons of mass destruction (WMD) could provide in the interests of preventing war. In the words of Michael Quinlan, "The absence of war between advanced states is a key success. We must seek to perpetuate it. Weapons are instrumental and secondary; the basic aim is to avoid war. Better a world with nuclear weapons but no major war than one with major war but no nuclear weapons."[8]

But what about a world with nuclear weapons *and* war, whether major or not? What about biological and chemical weapons? And what about high-tech information weapons (so-called cyberweapons) that wreak similarly indiscriminant and massive destruction of lives or at least livelihoods against civilian societies? It may be that weapons of mass destruction have lost their utility as instruments of warfare between major powers simply because major powers recognize that their use assures their own destruction. Such weapons remain, nonetheless, weapons of terror, which are distinctly usable by those who seek to terrorize, whether they be states or nonstate political actors. Thus in this new international environment, nonproliferation of weapons of mass destruction has become more important than arms control aimed at limiting existing arsenals of such weapons.

One major difficulty in stemming the proliferation of such weapons is that each employs technologies—nuclear, biological, chemical, informational—that are also peaceful and productive. Moreover, in the age of the Internet, technologies are more easily distributed not only among governments but also throughout the private sector. Thus the nonproliferation arms control agenda must increasingly address not only governments and their defense and research establishments but also private sectors and the technologies that many societies look to for future growth and prosperity.

Growing emphasis in the post–Cold War period on WMD, however, has raised further questions about what constitutes such weapons when the pace of technological change continues to rise exponentially. What, after all, constitutes a weapon of mass destruction? Is it the scale of destruction? Is it the inability to discriminate among combatants and civilians? Is it the manner of death and destruction that the weapons employ? The oft-cited WMD trio of nuclear/biological/chemical weapons may no longer be a sufficient or useful guide to policy. Should a radiological weapon, which disseminates radioactive material through use of a conventional explosive, be included even though it does not have the cataclysmic effect of a nuclear weapon? Should a massive fuel-air explosive, which does not result in radioactive fallout, be included? Should a cyberweapon that brings down a power grid or financial network without killing a single person or destroying a single structure be considered a weapon to be controlled? Or should that type of weapon be encouraged as an alternative to more traditional weapons that impose societal pain in the form of death and destruction?

These questions are never easy to answer, but they take on more significance in the international environment when security concerns go beyond well-regulated competition between two superpowers. For those who look to arms control as a mechanism to abolish weapons rather than to manage them, technological change imposes increasingly high hurdles.

It is no easier on the lower end of the technological spectrum. Much of today's warfare is not of the high-tech variety; indeed, U.S. defense planners increasingly worry more about so-called asymmetrical warfare rather than war that pits forces against similarly armed forces. Local conflicts are more likely to be fought with small arms—even machetes—in the possession of private individuals. Young, talented computer hackers with modest resources in faraway places—whether motivated by ideology or mischief—can pose as likely and potentially destructive a threat to U.S. interests as a ballistic missile.

The changing technology of warfare only serves to broaden the potential agenda for cooperative security. It also poses important challenges for governments as they seek to prioritize that agenda. How broad an agenda can the international community sustain? Are certain kinds of weapons unacceptable to the international community? Can they be controlled simply by negotiating their abolition? What mechanisms of verification and other assurances of security are necessary to proceed on that path? At what point does one accept the inevitability of certain weapons or their possession by certain states and seek to manage rather than abolish them? In comparison, the Cold War's U.S.-Soviet arms control agenda can seem simple.

New Actors and Roles

During the Cold War the principal actors in the arms control arena were the United States and the Soviet Union, with others playing important but inherently secondary roles. In the current international system, there are several new sets of actors playing important roles of their own. Some are states who find their own arsenals a potential focus of arms control regimes, whereas before they were essentially unaffected. Others are rogue actors—states and nonstates—who defy efforts to include them in cooperative regimes. There are individuals and nongovernmental organizations (NGOs) that assert their own influence in shaping cooperative security efforts. Finally, a variety of political institutions—multinational organizations and even courts—has emerged; increasingly they play roles once reserved to the state.

New States in the Game

As suggested earlier, nuclear arms control has largely been a bilateral game. For decades, there were five declared nuclear states—all of them recognized as such within the international system; but only two really mattered in this context. Arms limitations and reductions were the sole domain of the United States and the Soviet Union (later the Russian Federation), each of whom entered the START negotiations with some 12,000 deployed strategic nuclear warheads, not counting strategic reserve weapons in their stockpiles and some 20,000–30,000 nonstrategic nuclear weapons. France and the United Kingdom—each with a few hundred deployed strategic warheads—and China, with a relative handful of deployed strategic warheads, were never inclined to participate in nuclear arms limitation regimes as long as the superpowers' arsenals numbered in the many thousands. Beyond their political impact, moreover, the French, British, and Chinese nuclear arsenals were never viewed as significant in the overall nuclear balance.

In time that may change if U.S. and Russian deployed strategic arsenals continue to decline past the thresholds originally envisioned for START III (2,000–2,500 warheads), with corresponding reductions in the overall stockpile. (For its part, the United States has already eliminated some 90 percent of its nonstrategic weapons, with none operationally deployed.) Many observers suggest that further numerical reductions would cast in doubt the viability of maintaining traditional force structures and targeting strategies, such that levels below 1,000 warheads would be sufficient to maintain a general deterrent capability. In these circumstances, inclusion of other states' strategic nuclear forces would be necessary so as to preserve a stable deterrent posture among all the nuclear relationships. For Britain and France, reductions would raise questions as to the purpose for maintaining a nuclear posture at all; for China, reductions would raise questions regarding their ongoing strategic force modernization efforts and the ends to which that modernization is directed.

Following the Cold War, moreover, nuclear states other than the United States and Russia attracted attention. With pressure building on the post-Soviet states of Belarus, Kazakhstan, and Ukraine to rid themselves of residual Soviet nuclear weapons on their territory and join the NPT as non–nuclear weapon states, both France and China became NPT parties in 1992 and agreed to the treaty's indefinite extension.

The 1996 Comprehensive Test Ban Treaty further expanded pressures on states to adhere to a restrictive nuclear regime. This treaty required adherence by the five nuclear weapon states recognized by the NPT, as well as an additional 39 states who have nuclear weapons or the capability to acquire them. This includes India and Pakistan, each of whom had long possessed nuclear weapons but had not demonstrated that capability with nuclear tests until 1998. This also includes Israel, long suspected of having nuclear weapons but never admitting it. By requiring these states' accession before the regime can go into force, pressure can be brought to bear by those states who seek a broad-based norm within the international community on this or other issues.[9]

Rogue Players

States that defy cooperative security regimes are hardly unique to the post–Cold War period, but their significance is greater given the relative ease with which such states can acquire weapons of mass destruction.

These states, as well as nonstate terrorist groups and private individuals such as Osama bin Laden, are constant reminders that neither a norm of international conduct nor the existence of a legal regime is sufficient to restrict illegitimate and unwanted behavior. Iraq is a party to the NPT and the Biological Weapons Convention yet violated both, as demonstrated by United Nations inspectors following the Gulf War. North Korea is likewise a party to the NPT, yet concerns about a clandestine nuclear program prompted a crisis in 1994, from which emerged the U.S.–North Korea Framework Agreement. Nonetheless, inspectors cannot yet account for large amounts of fissile material that may have been associated with earlier North Korean weapon programs.

At the same time, the fact that Iraq and North Korea are parties to the NPT has at least provided an additional basis within international law for arms inspectors within those countries. The reality remains that a rogue state intent on defying the international community will not be persuaded by agreements but rather by calculated self-interest. Indeed, Iraq for years rejected UN inspectors, asserting sovereignty over the resolutions of the international community.

Private Actors

Thomas Friedman has highlighted the rise of "super-empowered individuals" who assert themselves on the world stage with a level of resources and influence that was traditionally the domain of politicians and government officials.[10] What is new about this phenomenon is not the appeal of the private individuals in question, but rather the wealth of resources available to such individuals—typically in excess of the gross domestic product of many nations in the world—and the information highways through which that influence can be transmitted. For example, the combination of Ted Turner's money and former U.S. Senator Sam Nunn's reputation enabled the launch of the private Nuclear Threat Initiative to address issues of nuclear material control and accountability in Russia. Turner also was a key in forging a compromise on U.S. payment of dues in arrears to the United Nations. And he and George Soros have both given substantial amounts of money to organizations operating in countries around the world, trying to build institutions of civil society as the ultimate prophylactic against internal conflict and civil war.

The other kind of super-empowered individuals are activists such as Jody Williams, who leveraged and energized a network of NGOs with links to governments to create momentum that ultimately resulted in the December 1997 Ottawa Convention banning landmines. Veterans of the famous Pugwash conferences that brought Soviet and Western scientists together decades ago to probe the implications of the nuclear age will undoubtedly note that Williams and others like her are hardly pioneers in transnational network-building. Yet the technology of the information age and the substantially freer movement of people and ideas today have led to quantum leaps in the impact these efforts can have. Of course, it is always worth recalling that such technology is simply a neutral transmission belt—the people and ideas being hurtled across borders are not always right, good, or conducive to the aims of cooperative security.

Multinational Organizations

The same forces of globalization that have prompted a greater sense of community beyond state boundaries have also propelled multinational organizations into new roles in the pursuit of arms control and cooperative security. On one level, as noted previously, the growth of localized conflicts that affect broader international interests has prompted greater engagement by the international community in intervening to stop the conflict as well as to lay the foundation for a more lasting peace in the area. In doing so, such organizations increasingly draw upon and are influenced by NGOs— corporations as well as service organizations—who are often on the front lines of the redevelopment and rehabilitation efforts.

The more striking change in the role of multinational organizations is their increased use in verifying international arms control regimes. Verification has always been a sensitive issue in arms control. It has two component parts: an objective activity—monitoring the activity of other parties to the treaty; and a political judgment—determining whether observed behavior constitutes noncompliance with the treaty. The former typically draws upon the sensitive intelligence resources of a state; the latter involves a political determination, often at the highest level of government regarding the behavior of another state, as well as the appropriate response to be taken as a result. During the Cold War, no state was willing to surrender the secrecy and the prerogatives associated with verification. Verification, it was repeatedly noted, is a national activity.

Today, however, the Chemical Weapons Convention has the multinational Organization for the Prohibition of Chemical Weapons in the Hague to manage inspections under the regime. In addition, the Comprehensive Test Ban Treaty called for a Comprehensive Test Ban Treaty Office, with provision for a preparatory commission that went into effect in Vienna shortly after signature of the treaty, despite the fact that the treaty's requirements for entry into force will not be met for any foreseeable future.

Skeptics will point to the fact a state believing that a regime affects its vital interests will not be content with the verification efforts of others, suggesting conversely that the existence of such multinational organizations is evidence of the weakness of the regime in question. Others, however, will note a growing recognition by many states that international security must be a collaborative venture, not one to which they should simply defer to the protection graces of the neighborhood superpower. Multinational organizations can impinge on the prerogatives of strong states with effective verification organizations that will do the heavy lifting. For most states, however, cooperation with a shared multinational resource may be their only hope for being able to shape their own destiny.

A Changing Agenda for Cooperative Security

The world has changed in fundamental ways. The relative simplicity of the Cold War has given way to a volatile world buffeted by the bewildering forces of globalization, and the implications for international security are enormous. To some this has created a more anarchic international system, in which self-help remains the ultimate protector of one's own security. To others it has compelled a more cooperative approach, in which high stakes and forces beyond the control of a single state demand new approaches to common security interests.

One complication is the vertical extension of the arms control agenda. Cooperative security efforts now seek to encompass the entire spectrum of weapons, from high-tech information weapons, to ballistic missiles, to landmines, down even to small arms.

We have also seen a form of horizontal integration in the arms control business. No longer is it sufficient in the nuclear realm, for example, to focus on delivery vehicles and deployed warheads according to a negotiated counting rule—a practice that never actually required the reduction of a nuclear weapon. The May 1997 Helsinki summit declaration suggesting the future directions of post–START II U.S.-Russia nuclear arms control anticipate inclusion of nondeployed warheads as a way of gaining transparency over the entire weapons stockpile. In addition, substantial negotiating and reciprocal monitoring work has focused on gaining greater control of fissile materials. Thus nuclear arms control now addresses the functional equivalents of the pistol, the bullets, and even the gunpowder in the bullets.

Finally, we have seen a widening array of actors raising serious questions regarding how much latitude (or even sovereignty) a state is prepared to relinquish in the interests of cooperative security. If one widens the aperture to encompass the full range of activities related to cooperative security, one would also have to add judicial forums such as the International Criminal Court and individual war crimes tribunals following conflicts in the former Yugoslavia and Rwanda.

A recurring theme of this discussion is that in each respect those who stress the primacy of Realpolitik will see little new in the post–Cold War world except illusion on the part of those who seek cooperation. Others, more optimistic about the prospects for international cooperation, tend to see greater potential for addressing the causes as well as the instruments of warfare.

Ultimately the search for security may be a problem of demand versus supply. If one seeks security through traditional arms control measures of negotiated limits, then the search for security tends to be a demand problem: one enters into negotiations in search of some particular solution to a security problem and demands certain measures from the negotiations as a result. The premise is that your negotiating protagonist has the means of improving your security but for some reason refuses to do so until the proper bargain is struck.

If, on the other hand, one views security as a collective good, with conflict arising from a sense of insecurity, then the search for security is essentially a supply problem. In this approach the preferred strategy for achieving greater security may in fact be to increase the security of those who can threaten your interests.

Today's arms control agenda reflects elements of both of these approaches, but the balance has shifted significantly toward the latter in comparison with the Cold War arms control agenda. The challenges relate more to seeking a common security foundation rather than bargaining over security desiderata in a structured negotiation. Even in the more traditional agenda of renegotiating limits on ballistic missile defense, in which the United States clearly wants a particular outcome from Russia, the discussions—at least on the rhetorical level—relate to how the collaborative pursuit of ballistic missile defense can serve all participants' national security on a positive-sum basis. Of course, on a practical level how specific policy is pursued—rhetoric notwithstanding—will have an important impact on the outcome. For the purpose of this book, it is sufficient to note that the international context of arms control has changed in ways that may enable cooperative approaches more easily.

To be sure, the international context of arms control and cooperative security has changed substantially, with important effects. The policy challenges are significant, posing difficult choices in a world with no easy answers. The following chapters will outline in more detail how these choices play out on specific issues.

Notes

1. Hedley Bull, *The Control of the Arms Race: Disarmament and Arms Control in the Missile Age*, 2nd ed. (New York: Praeger, 1965), pp. vii–viii.

2. Thomas C. Schelling and Morton H. Halperin, *Strategy and Arms Control* (New York: Pergamon Press, 1985 [orig. publ. 1961]), p. 3.

3. For a full discussion of U.S. arms control policies in the Cold War and in the context of alliance politics and broader strategies of détente, see Schuyler Foerster, *Détente and Alliance Politics in the Postwar Period: Strategic Dilemmas in U.S.–West German Relations*, unpubl. doctoral thesis, Oxford University, United Kingdom, 1982. Also, Schuyler Foerster, "Arms Control and Defense Policy: An Overview," in Schuyler Foerster and Edward N. Wright, eds., *American Defense Policy*, 6th ed. (Baltimore: Johns Hopkins University Press, 1990), pp. 333–348.

4. See Schuyler Foerster et al., *Defining Stability: Conventional Arms Control in a Changing Europe* (Boulder: Westview, 1999).

5. The framework for START III negotiations was agreed in the Helsinki summit meeting between Presidents Bill Clinton and Boris Yeltsin, May 1997.

6. Statement of Lynn Davis, Under Secretary of State for Arms Control and International Security Policy, testimony before the Senate Foreign Relations Committee, April 29, 1997. See also U.S. Arms Control and Disarmament Agency, *Fact Sheet on Adaptation of the CFE Treaty*, December 12, 1996.

7. Thomas Friedman, *The Lexus and the Olive Tree* (New York: Random House, 2000), remains the classic definition of this phenomenon, notwithstanding a continuing debate about whether globalization is good or bad or how policy ought to respond to the forces of globalization.

8. Michael Quinlan, "The Future of Nuclear Weapons in World Affairs," *Atlantic Council of the United States Bulletin* 7, no. 9 (November 20, 1996): 2.

9. As of this writing, 30 of the 44 states required for CTBT entry into force have deposited instruments of ratification. Department of State, Bureau of Arms Control, "Fact Sheet on Comprehensive Nuclear Test Ban Treaty Signatories/Ratifiers," 15 November 2000, www.state.gov/www/global/arms/factsheets/wmd/nuclear/ctbt/ctbtsigs.html. Neither India, nor Pakistan, nor Israel are party to the Nuclear Non-Proliferation Treaty, so none is recognized legally as either a nuclear or a nonnuclear weapon state.

10 Thomas Friedman, *Lexus and the Olive Tree*, pp. 10–14. I am grateful to Major Brent Talbot, deputy director, USAF Institute for National Security Studies, Colorado, for highlighting this dimension of the analysis. See his "Global Transformations and the International Politics of Arms Control," presentation at the annual International Studies Association conference, Chicago, 2001.

Suggested Readings

Art, Robert J., and Kenneth N. Waltz. *The Use of Force: Military Power and International Politics.* New York: Rowman and Littlefield, 1999.

Finel, Bernard, and Kristen Lord, eds. *Power and Conflict in the Age of Transparency.* New York: St. Martin's, 2000.

Goldstein, Avery. *Deterrence and Security in the 21st Century: China, Britain, France, and the Enduring Legacy of the Nuclear Revolution.* Stanford: Stanford University Press, 2000.

"Is Arms Control Dead?" *Washington Quarterly* (Spring 2000): 171–232.

Lodal, Jan. *The Price of Dominance: The New Weapons of Mass Destruction and Their Challenge to American Leadership.* New York: Council on Foreign Relations, 2001.

Schell, Jonathan. "The Folly of Arms Control," *Foreign Affairs* (September/October 2000): 22–46.

Schelling, Thomas C., and Morton H. Halperin. *Strategy and Arms Control.* New York: Twentieth Century Fund, 1961.

4

Domestic Factors in Arms Control: The U.S. Case

Jennifer E. Sims

While the international system shapes a state's sense of jeopardy, providing incentives for controlling the likelihood and destructiveness of war, domestic conditions affect how a state uses the arms control instrument and its effectiveness in doing so. The fact that internal politics affects external behavior is an observation that Thucydides made about Greek city-states; it is made less today as theories of interstate behavior focus on systemic forces and relationships of power.

This imbalance in how domestic factors are treated in the study of international relations may now be changing. The ingredients of international politics are increasingly transnational, involving the movements of goods, people, and ideas among societies. The rapidly expanding grassroots movement to control landmines, inspired and doggedly pursued by a few committed individuals, is evidence of this trend. But the escalation of terrorism during 2001 also revealed dark and threatening aspects to globalization.

A second reason for increased attention to the domestic factors driving international politics is the salience of one of the new century's central strategic questions: What will the United States do with its growing international prominence? This question raises the choice between pursuing cooperative security or selecting unilateral interests while protected by unassailable military capabilities. Because this will affect U.S. treaty obligations and defense budgets in significant ways, any decision will require public debate. Predicting the outcome requires analysis of the domestic ingredients of cooperative security in a generic sense as well as the U.S. case in a very particular sense.

Generic Issues in the
Domestic Context of Arms Control

As a government considers an arms control initiative, it assesses each party's ability to abide by the agreement, to implement it in a timely way, and to monitor the compliance of the other parties. Understanding domestic factors helps negotiators find a marketable middle ground for all parties. A minor concession for one might, in the domestic context of another, be a huge win leading to unexpected agreement and enhanced security for both. In order for negotiators and strategists to find non–zero sum solutions to national security dilemmas, they must be sensitive to the domestic context.[1]

Four domestic factors are of greatest importance in this context: strategic culture; the political and legal institutions for negotiating, concluding, and sustaining arms control agreements; prevailing economic and technological conditions; and the role of public opinion, particularly key interest groups.[2]

Strategic Culture

A nation's political culture is "that national soup of ideals, interests and propensities upon which decision-makers have been nourished as professionals and as citizens."[3] Strategic culture, a subset of political culture, embodies those national paradigms of greatest relevance to national security. Strategic culture helps to explain why particular arms control solutions win, why they sometimes fail to be accepted abroad, and why, even when discredited, they may nevertheless regularly reappear. The keys to unlocking any country's strategic culture are the ideas, myths, and national beliefs that are regularly recorded in academic literature, the speeches of politicians, and the press releases of policy advocates.

Assessing a nation's strategic culture requires sensitivity to the historical, the psychological, and the religious, including the impact of transcendent leaders and traumatic events. Strategic cultures are often shaped by geographic circumstance and the experience of repeated wars. The cultural effects, however, will differ and lead to different orientations toward negotiations and compromise. If policymakers are to rely on an appreciation of strategic culture in framing approaches to national security policy and arms control, two dangers must be avoided: oversimplification, and assumptions of immutability. Moreover, strategic cultures do change.[4]

The fact that strategic culture can change has prompted some analysts to raise the issue of arms control's political purposes. They note that the process of negotiation can influence the strategic cultures of other parties, leading not just to improved military balances but to stabilized political relations as well. Such analysts argue that this is exactly what the Anti-Ballistic Missile (ABM) Treaty accomplished among nuclear weapon states:

acceptance of a historically unprecedented vision of stability based on mutual vulnerability. For them, abolishing the ABM Treaty meant more than the loss of a particular accord; it meant the loss of the entire philosophical basis for agreed limits. Critics of the ABM Treaty are both unconvinced of a transformation in Russia and worried that the only shift in strategic culture may have been a U.S. one.[5] Calling the U.S. fixation on negotiated restraint and mutual vulnerability a new "civil religion," they urged a break with this deleterious past before it was too late.[6]

Political and Legal Institutions

The internal institutional framework of a state affects the way arms control is negotiated and the reliability of its implementation. Governments with strong executives tend toward greater flexibility and decisiveness in negotiations; those with effective legislatures offer enhanced confidence in the durability of agreements even as they may bring delays in their ratification and implementation. Similarly, states with civil societies shaped by strong traditions of legal process, including contract law, will tend to take international legal commitments more seriously than states with less well grounded legal institutions. For example, the U.S. public took the efforts to outlaw war between the two world wars quite seriously, an approach that aggressor nations arguably exploited.

When assessing the impact of political institutions on arms control processes, one must distinguish between real and what might be termed "Potemkin" structures.[7] What matters is not the formal structure so much as the informal one—the way things really work.

In assessing the impact of political and legal institutions on arms control, national security analysts must remain open to counterintuitive elements. For example, even though governments tend to think of an adversary's intelligence capability as a threat to its security, it is also a measure of that state's capacity to be a responsible arms control partner. One of the greatest dangers for leaders using the arms control instrument is the possibility of being duped (or of being perceived as being duped) by the other side. In fact arms control agreements can incorporate agreed procedures for data exchange while deliberately enhancing the capabilities and legitimacy of intelligence institutions among the parties concerned. During the Cold War, arms control agreements acknowledged "national technical means" for monitoring their terms. Stability was arguably enhanced by the confidence each side had in the other's intelligence capabilities. Thus, strong intelligence institutions protect governments from irrational decisionmaking. Similarly, stable and effective military institutions tend to enhance the viability of any accord, provided that they are part of the government's decisionmaking processes.

Economic and Technological Factors

Rapid technological change is not conducive to arms control, especially when it directly affects military capabilities. Although advances in weapon systems may foster fears of an arms race and heighten public interest in controls, negotiated restraint is often frustrated by the belief that a decisive technological advantage lies just around the corner for one or both parties.

The greater both sides' confidence that they can keep pace with the technological changes under way, the greater the likelihood that arms control proposals will be a cover for seeking unilateral advantage rather than serious initiatives. Washington's very public pursuit of disarmament during the 1950s seemed designed to counter the growing public interest in abolishing nuclear weapons by demonstrating Soviet ill-intent, noncooperation, and untrustworthiness. Formal disarmament initiatives during the early Cold War arguably satisfied a strong impulse in U.S. strategic culture to claim a moral high ground while allowing U.S. scientists and industrialists to lead the way in explosive technologies, warhead miniaturization, and ballistic missiles.

Economic conditions may mitigate the effects of technological change on arms control incentives. Certainly an economic downturn can make new military capabilities prohibitively costly, increasing the attractiveness of negotiated restraint. In fact some critics of arms control have argued that the negotiations pursuant to the Strategic Arms Limitation Talks (SALT) and Strategic Arms Reduction Talks (START) prolonged the economic viability of the Soviet regime by lowering the cost of competition while providing the prestige of so-called summit diplomacy. Arms control advocates respond that strategic nuclear stability—not lowered costs or economic destabilization—was the principal purpose of these negotiations. Indeed, most arms controllers argue that the leap from disarmament to arms control policies in the early 1960s involved the decision not to use nuclear negotiations, deployments, and doctrine as means for destabilizing or destroying the Soviet state. Strategic stability required reassurance, restraint, and confidence-building.

From this perspective, arms control objectives may actually be served by an adversary's improved economic conditions if that would lower the risk of preemptive attack, internal instabilities, or the forced export of destabilizing technologies.

Elites, Interest Groups, and Public Opinion

Arms control involves two parallel political processes: negotiations with one or more adversaries, and internal negotiations among competing domestic interest groups and bureaucracies. Of course, military dictatorships may have the easiest time dealing with this problem; they control the arms control process, the influence of advisers, and the reaction of the press (if it exists) by fiat.

In contrast, democracies with protected speech and independent media can be heavily affected by expressions of public interest.[8] The complicated politics and economics of arms control draw the attention of interest groups from all parts of the political spectrum and private industry.[9] Depending on the stakes involved and these groups' organizational skills and resources, a marketplace for ideas can emerge. Capitalist economies are particularly sensitive to limitations on production that could affect the nation's industrial base and future mobilization capacity in time of war.[10] If the affected firms' chief foreign competitors are not similarly constrained by the accord, the firms are doubly hurt. Arms control can thus have the indirect effect of sustaining inefficient foreign military-industrial sectors at the expense of the domestic economies of the parties. With jobs and local economies at stake, politicians may be strongly influenced by private-sector views on arms control.

Industry can also be a powerful supporter of arms control agreements. Inspection regimes expand the market for sensors and overhead reconnaissance satellites, which in turn generates new military requirements for stealth technologies or other forms of camouflage. Moreover, when the public interest in safety and damage limitation is high, industry can gain important public relations benefits from aligning itself with the national interest at the apparent expense of near-term profits.

The development of the Chemical Weapons Convention (CWC) is a good recent example of industry involvement in arms control. The accord was strongly supported by a powerful association of chemical and pharmaceutical companies that had participated intensively in the negotiation as well as the marketing of the draft agreement. Whereas some observers saw openness to industrial interests as evidence of a new, sophisticated approach by the U.S. government, others saw it as backdoor industrial policy. Small chemical producers believed the heavy hitters in the industry— the ones with the funds to sustain and lead the interest groups in Washington—were inadequately protecting them from the costs they would incur in implementing the inspection regime.

This example illustrates the value of examining the politics of arms control in the United States for insights into the relationship of domestic factors and policy outcomes. The United States has had a reasonably open policy process, a heavy national security burden since the early 1950s, and a rich record of arms control negotiations.

The U.S. Case

Although governments have practiced regulated war and weapons restraint for centuries, arms control may have never had as bold, vigorous, and enduring a champion as the post–World War II United States. After the defeat of Japan and Germany, the United States persistently advocated negotiated restraints. Arms control theory has permeated the literature on national security and been tested repeatedly by policymakers. U.S. policymakers have sustained an arms control process that has become an integral part of U.S. national security policy.

The intensity of America's fascination with arms control is explained in part by the public's midcentury discovery of nuclear fear. Yet in a polity gripped with nuclear fear, what kind of logic permitted decades of arms control accompanied by exponential growth, diversification, and proliferation of weapons arsenals? How have domestic forces contributed to a process at once both morally compelling and yet arcane and seemingly inconsequential in its outcomes? How has the U.S. public "done" arms control, and why have they done it for so long?

In the United States, as in most democracies, arms control outcomes are shaped by the four domestic factors discussed in the first section of this essay. As in most countries, the institutional setting has defined the players and the ratification process for past accords. Yet in the United States, the concept of cooperative military restraint has engaged a broader range of actors than those involved in the formal negotiation and ratification process alone. The United States has experienced a startling amount of "trickle-up" with respect to arms control ideas, energy, and initiative. Indeed, at least since the end of World War II, the engines of U.S. arms control have been public opinion, policy advocates, and the ideas around which they rally. The following case study will therefore focus principally on these factors.

Strategic Culture

U.S. strategic culture has had substantial impact on Washington's arms control policies. The dominance of the national security agenda throughout the Cold War has left a record of arms control ideas that is particularly rich. Understanding the most influential of these ideas and the political orientations from which they spring aids in unlocking America's arms control past as well as its future.

The tradition of unilateralism.   U.S. strategic culture rests on a mix of scientific rationalism, political realism, and unilateralist preferences—albeit often tied to concepts of U.S.-led internationalism. Interest in preserving the country's freedom of action, well understood since George Washington's Farewell Address, has biased the U.S. public against binding agreements with foreign powers. As President Woodrow Wilson discovered when he sought popular support for U.S. entry into the League of Nations after World War I, even liberals and progressives of an internationalist bent could blanch at the prospect of tying U.S. fortunes to those of other nations.[11]

It should thus not be surprising that, to the extent that arms control has involved binding U.S. defense policies to agreed and verifiable limits, it has often been a hard sell. The U.S. public has easily endorsed moral example (such as the 1925 Geneva convention against use of chemical weapons) but has not easily ratified treaties. Indeed, the first golden age of arms control, from the late 1950s to early 1960s, was built on an approach that denigrated formal agreements. Tacit agreements and signaling of defensive intentions became the tools of arms control policy; its objective—stability—required the maintenance of a bipolar equilibrium of power. Arms control became absorbed with maintaining each side's ability to obliterate the other with nuclear weapons and with preserving sufficient conventional capabilities so that lesser interests could be litigated without resort to nuclear war.[12]

Those formal agreements that were ratified were advocated as much for the military options they preserved as for those they foreclosed. The Limited Test Ban Treaty, for example, reduced environmental contamination but, in simply driving testing underground, hardly slowed U.S. efforts to develop new nuclear warheads. The 1968 Non-Proliferation Treaty slowed nuclear proliferation without significant enforceable constraints on the United States and other nuclear weapon states. SALT contained the bipolar strategic competition within certain stabilizing parameters but permitted both sides to expand their strategic nuclear weapon inventory and, significantly, to retain the technological option of pursuing multiple independently targetable reentry vehicles—the technology Washington believed would redress the strategic balance tilting dangerously in the Soviets' favor. Until the START negotiations of the late 1980s, few agreements had eliminated any options for the United States.

U.S. exceptionalism.   Closely tied to the U.S. public's preference for unilateralism has been an abiding faith in U.S. exceptionalism. This belief, based on confidence in the advantages of free enterprise and the American work ethic, has translated into expectations that U.S. technological development would guide the choices of others and, left unconstrained, would naturally prove superior. Such beliefs help explain the U.S. notion that the Soviets could be taught what a stabilizing force structure might look like and could be made to accept it by force of example as well as reason.

This belief in U.S. technological superiority was, however, repeatedly challenged throughout the Cold War. The first Soviet nuclear test in 1949, Soviet acquisition of thermonuclear weapons in 1953, and the SPUTNIK launch of 1957 fed a national paranoia that the Soviets must be stealing U.S. secrets (which history has demonstrated they often did). Later the Soviet challenge to U.S. scientific prowess was inspired by not only technological competition but also a certain respect for the adversary. The U.S. public went from regarding the Soviet system as crude and unsophisticated in the late 1940s to regarding it as almost invulnerable as it teetered on the verge of collapse in the 1980s.

National leaders who have framed national security programs compatible with the major elements of U.S. strategic culture—particularly the notion of U.S. exceptionalism—have found the public to be a powerful ally. For example, few modern arms control and defense proposals have more quickly captured the U.S. public's imagination than President Ronald Reagan's 1983 Strategic Defense Initiative. The can-do spirit in Reagan's pursuit of space-related technologies is again evident in the debate today over National Missile Defense. As in sending a man to the moon, conceiving a technology is, in the U.S. psyche, tantamount to acquiring it. This kind of perspective is awe-inspiring among allies; for the U.S. public it is simply motivational. In fact arms control has always fared best domestically when it has not prohibited the development of exciting technologies or ventures toward new frontiers. The United States likes to be first; it does not like to be told the finish line is unreachable.

Scientific rationalism.   The U.S. public has historically held reason and science in high regard. World War II accentuated this trend as nuclear triumph brought the influence of scientists to a peak. Since then the scientific community has had considerable influence on national security and arms control policies, but its impact has been neither monolithic nor uniform.

After World War II the U.S. scientific ethic, which incorporates principles of universalism and openness, became infused with a potent internationalism. Émigré scientists who had fled excessively authoritarian regimes in Europe held deep suspicions of the state system. After the first atom bomb to be used in combat was dropped on Hiroshima, some of these scientists, articulating an ever-deepening distrust of the government's use of science for augmenting national power, warned that the United States ought not to trust that its political or technological ingenuity could preserve nuclear peace. To these scientists, the nuclear era meant the end of exceptional states and the arrival of the imperative of world government and global disarmament.

Yet for others the postwar stature of science brought new faith in scientific and social engineering. Respected scientists joined an increasing number of their behavioralist colleagues in the social sciences in applying scientific principles to the art of changing international society and managing—not abolishing—the nuclear weapon establishment. These scientists believed that the state system ought not to be ignored or abolished but reorganized instead. Arms control would be the instrument of such reform.

David Lilienthal, chairman of the Tennessee Valley Authority in the 1940s and a chief architect of the first U.S. effort to control the atom, advocated a scientific methodology and functionalist approach to controls. His disarmament plan, based on rigorous study of the scientific facts, was later endorsed by Bernard Baruch when the latter pressed his adaptation—the Baruch Plan—on the international community.

By the mid-1960s social and hard-science scientists had coalesced in arms control advocacy and study groups under the auspices of organizations such as the American Academy of Arts and Sciences and Pugwash. These scientists' influence on arms control literature throughout the postwar period has been profound.

Although the special stature accorded scientific expertise was temporarily lost during the period of virulent anticommunism known as the McCarthy era, it reemerged during the later years of the Dwight Eisenhower administration with the establishment of the Presidential Science Advisory Committee. Such deference to experts has been so strong and long-lived that it may have contributed to public complacency as arms control became increasingly formulaic, expensive, and opaque to the general public during the 1970s and 1980s. By the time SALT II was negotiated and Ronald Reagan was elected president, the arcane business of planning stabilizing strategic limitations had become politically rootless. Indeed, the public's rapid endorsement of the Reagan administration's simpler proposals for strategic arms reductions, and of its extraordinary plan for strategic defense, was arguably a reflection of the nation's faith in scientific expertise under a new guise.

Realism.   The influence of science on politics following World War II triggered an intellectual revolt by the U.S. realist school that has been regularly reflected in postwar arms control debates. Realist theorists objected to scientific rationalism's excessive influence in Western political culture, as well as to the notion of exceptionalism so deeply ingrained in the U.S. strategic psyche.

Hans J. Morgenthau, a political scientist at the University of Chicago, cautioned against U.S. visions of sustainable superiority at the start of the Cold War. Morgenthau criticized excessive faith "in the power of science to solve all problems and, more particularly, all political problems which confront man in the modern age."[13] Morgenthau believed that the scientific community's universalistic, liberal bias had come to dominate and cause the decline of Western political thought since the eighteenth century. Indicative of this trend had been the rise of legalistic, ahistorically optimistic solutions to world order problems as epitomized by Wilson's League of Nations and evolving notions of "scientific disarmament."[14]

As postwar efforts to achieve internationalist solutions to the arms race collapsed in the late 1950s, it was the joining of realist balance-of-power principles with rationalist methodologies that created the most powerful and cohesive arms control school of modern times. This theoretical approach dominated arms control and general strategic thought in the United States for more than two decades. The approach treated strategic nuclear stability as the primary objective of arms control and based weapons management and controls on the principles of mutual assured destruction.[15]

Political and Legal Institutions

Knowledge of the intellectual backdrop to U.S. arms control helps explain the texture of the defense policy and arms control debates of the second half of the twentieth century. However, texture cannot necessarily describe or predict outcomes. Ideas are the tools wielded by advocates; political processes determine who will have the opportunities to influence arms control outcomes.

The United States is governed by a system of checks and balances that often seems designed for stalemate, particularly in the field of arms control. During the interwar period, U.S. presidents successfully negotiated agreements with foreign governments, only to be foiled in getting them ratified at home. Even initially popular treaties foundered in the absence of conscious efforts to rally domestic interest groups and, most important, the support of key members of Congress. Thus Wilson lost in his effort to secure U.S. participation in the League of Nations, and Calvin Coolidge failed to win ratification of the 1925 Geneva Protocol against chemical and bacteriological warfare, a U.S. initiative that 30 nations had already signed.

During the Cold War, as arms control became an institutionalized element of national security policy, intragovernmental negotiations over the formulation and ratification of arms control agreements became routinized. These bureaucratic interactions had a decisive impact on the shape of treaties, agreements, and the evolution of the defense establishment more generally.

The office of the president. The U.S. Constitution provides several instruments for concluding international arms control agreements: treaties, congressional-executive agreements, and presidential agreements. Of these, the first and second are of greatest weight because they are legally interchangeable and, once concluded, constitute the law of the land.[16] In Article II, section 2, the Constitution says the president "shall have the power, by and with the advice and consent of the Senate, to make treaties, provided two-thirds of the Senators present concur."[17] The president's constitutional power to negotiate allows the country all the flexibility, secrecy, speed, and surprise that the office can provide and that is so often necessary for the conclusion of agreements favorable to U.S. interests.

The president sets the overall pace and tone of an administration's arms control policy. Yet the manner in which he organizes his administration can affect the success of his program. Because negotiators must have leverage to win favorable terms in any draft accord, arms control policymakers rely heavily on good access to the president and strong bureaucratic staff work. The president generally has delegated authority to negotiate treaties to the secretary of state, who in turn has delegated these powers to specially appointed ambassadors, undersecretaries, and assistant secretaries. The president has also exercised his option to appoint special negotiators. This has at times caused tensions in the arms control community.

The State Department. Bureaucratic stature and access alone do not guarantee success for an arms control negotiator. Because national security policy involves a broad range of departments, successful policymaking requires consensus-building. Presidential guidance and bureaucratic power also matter. In the later years of the Eisenhower administration, a cabinet-level committee advised the president on arms control policy. However, the president's insistence on consensus decisions meant that policymaking became paralyzed whenever disagreements ran deep.

By the end of the Eisenhower administration, the weakness of arms control policymaking was widely acknowledged. Congress created the Arms Control and Disarmament Agency (ACDA) in 1961 in order to mend perceived flaws in the institutional infrastructure. ACDA was to be a quasi-independent agency attached to the State Department but with direct access to the president. The intent was to lend bureaucratic weight to arms control interests within the executive branch and to provide Congress better access to information on policy developments.[18] Although other departments, including the State Department, originally concurred with this development, official opinion was deeply divided.[19]

The bureaucratic influence of ACDA and its director waxed and waned over subsequent decades. ACDA's awkward position—being both within and outside the Department of State—created tensions with the latter that persisted through the SALT, START, and post–Cold War periods. Its substantive bureaus overlapped with those of the State Department. Without an authoritative voice on relevant foreign policy issues or comprehensive intelligence support, ACDA tended to be eclipsed by the larger department on matters outside the confines of highly structured negotiations. ACDA's direct access to the president never consistently compensated for the handicap of having to operate on a day-to-day basis at the subcabinet level. Neither did it compensate for exclusion from the deliberations of the National Security Council. Indeed, ACDA's longevity may have reflected the ease with which any president could effectively include or exclude it from inner policy circles.

In 1993 the State Department initiated a direct challenge to the existence of ACDA when the undersecretary for science and technology sought to subsume responsibility for arms control policy in a new bureau under her control. Congress quickly blocked the move. However, the growing impulse to cut the size and cost of the government led to an eventual merger between ACDA and the State Department in 1999. Although some analysts predicted the weakening of arms control's voice within government, such a result is not yet apparent. In fact the merger kept most ACDA functions intact, albeit subsumed within the State Department's structure. State now has four bureaus handling these issues: arms control, nonproliferation, verification and compliance, and political military affairs.

The intelligence community. The U.S. intelligence community plays a critical role at all stages of the arms control process. Apart from testifying before congressional committees on the government's ability to monitor compliance with any given accord, the intelligence community also must maintain adequate capabilities to support existing agreements, laws, and negotiations. It funds research, technological development, and deployment of collection capabilities for desired and anticipated arms control measures to maximize the prospects of successfully negotiating and ratifying them. Those who advocate arms control sometimes forget that the effectiveness of the agreements and laws they advocate depends on the intelligence community's ability to monitor them. Legislating new sanctions, controls, and regulations is meaningless without intelligence to help enforce them.

The critical support role that the intelligence community plays, however, can cause considerable friction with arms control policymakers. First, the intelligence community's assessments of monitoring capabilities with regard to a proposed treaty can undermine prospects for ratification. U.S. intelligence, which has traditionally embodied such core U.S. values as objectivity and balanced consideration of facts, wields a powerful voice in the rationalistic U.S. strategic culture. To guard against unforeseen monitoring issues arising at the treaty ratification stage, modern presidents have usually required intelligence officers to work closely with delegations negotiating accords. But conflicts can develop as policymakers, anxious to build a policy consensus on negotiating strategy, discover contrary intelligence community views. Charges of politicization have thus arisen both from supporters and opponents of arms control.[20]

Second, particularly in eras of budget downsizing, the intelligence community can make financial and budgetary decisions that affect prospects for an accord by underfunding research, development, and/or procurement of intelligence collection capabilities critical to monitoring it. Neither ACDA nor the Department of State has ever had significant influence in defense and intelligence-related budgets and programs. Cuts by separate working-level programmers may make independent sense yet collectively destroy a crucial monitoring capability. When negotiations or hearings begin, policymakers can be blindsided, on the one hand, or accused by Congress of being disingenuous on the other. State Department officials may also suspect that an accord opposed by the Department of Defense (DoD) has been deliberately if quietly sabotaged in this budgetary manner.[21]

Third, the intelligence community, in its efforts to fulfill its statutory obligations to protect sources and methods, can object to or delay the use of intelligence to démarche a foreign government suspected of being in violation of a law or treaty. It can also object to sharing intelligence with international organizations dedicated to implementing safeguards and monitoring a control regime.

Fourth, since the establishment of the congressional intelligence oversight committees, the intelligence community has tended to regard Congress as a legitimate consumer of its products. Executive-branch officials have often chafed at the willingness of intelligence officials to provide products and tailored briefings to individual members of Congress intent on building cases against administration arms control policies and appointments. This also risks disclosures from Capitol Hill; any opponent of policy can leak intelligence out of context in order to disrupt negotiations.

Despite these sources of friction, the policy community has generally developed a close, complex, and healthy relationship with the U.S. intelligence establishment. If problems occasionally arise, they are more than overshadowed by the strength of the mutual support and mutual dependence that characterize both communities' day-to-day business.

The military. The Department of Defense has been a major player in the U.S. arms control process ever since arms control was distinguished from disarmament and accepted as an integral aspect of national security policy. Although this new approach to arms control began in the early 1950s under Secretary of State Dean Acheson, it did not become institutionalized until the John F. Kennedy administration. By that time arms control thought had progressed to the point where substantial weapons restraint was believed possible through manipulation of force deployment and doctrine alone. Under Secretary of Defense Robert McNamara, DoD began using its annual statements on doctrine and budgets to signal to its adversary the U.S. government's interest in stabilizing deployments and force-sizing concepts. Even though that approach to self-restraint was later largely abandoned, the office of the secretary of defense has remained heavily involved in arms control policy.

The reasons behind DoD's involvement are several. In the first place, arms control strategy and policy can significantly affect force-sizing, deployment, and doctrine. Negotiating strategies can drive defense policies and spending priorities by accelerating or decelerating weapons building programs in order to create or deny "bargaining chips."[22] Second, arms control, regulatory, export, and security assistance policies can jeopardize the health of key industries in defense and high-tech commercial sectors. DoD has often weighed in strongly on Capitol Hill and in the executive branch to ensure that policymakers are aware when arms control policies may jeopardize technological capabilities in civilian and defense-related areas. To the extent that arms control infuses budgetary life into systems and technologies that DoD considers unnecessary, obsolete, and/or too costly, such congressional-industrial relationships work against DoD's interests. DoD also manages a substantial part of the arms control monitoring infrastructure, including the On-Site Inspection Agency and its associated overseas gateways, as well as the logistical infrastructure for providing access to foreign inspectors coming to the United States.[23] Therefore any increase in monitoring activities will have a direct impact on DoD budgets and personnel allocations.

Members of the joint chiefs of staff (JCS) testify separately on the military impact of treaties and are expected to give an unvarnished view. The JCS has, on occasion, opposed administration policies, almost always severely damaging the administration position by doing so.

The Congress.   Congress participates in the arms control process by shaping public opinion, ratifying treaties, regulating commerce (via export controls and sanctions), appropriating funds, and legislating changes in the organization of executive-branch departments and their statutory authorities.[24] Arguably Congress's greatest arms control powers lie in its role in amending and ratifying treaties and passing executive agreements. The Senate can also add unilateral statements, such as reservations and declarations, that modify the legal effect of the treaty for the United States. However, such steps can threaten to destroy the agreement if other parties to the treaty object. Unilateral declarations may clarify an understanding or interpretation that is shared among the parties. Once treaties are concluded, however, most legal opinion holds that they can be terminated only by the president or by the president and Senate acting together.

Although the Constitution specifies no particular role for the House of Representatives in the treaty-making process, the implementation of treaties often requires the passage of domestic laws or appropriations of funds that require the involvement of the House.[25] In practice, the Senate and House work closely together as the relevant committees consider the terms of treaties and the implementing legislation they require. The CWC, signed in 1993 and ratified by the Senate in 1995, is an excellent example of a treaty demanding coordinated consideration. Although it technically required only the concurrence of the Senate, implementing legislation necessarily involved multiple committees in both chambers. Senators and representatives considered the impact of the CWC's arrangements for international demand inspections of suspect facilities (which include private firms and house-holds) on constitutionally protected privacy rights. Moreover, appropriations for funding the large bureaucracy necessary for handling the convention's national reporting requirements and for creating the international secretariat to administer the convention required House approval.

Both houses of Congress are also involved in the regulation of commerce and the provision of military assistance and foreign aid. Congressionally authorized and funded security assistance programs and annual authorization and appropriations acts have proven to be particularly attractive tools for legislating the sanctioning of states that fail to abide by arms control norms.[26] The Arms Export Control Act, which authorizes the president to control the export of defense-related equipment and services, prohibits firms from marketing destabilizing and dangerous technologies and provides for punishment of those who do.

Treaty ratification involves the Senate Foreign Relations Committee, Senate Armed Services Committee, and Senate Select Committee on Intelligence. One of the more noteworthy developments in the domestic politics of modern arms control has been the weight and significance attached to the intelligence hearings and the detailed analysis of the prospects for monitoring and verifying any proposed accord.

When Congress acts on any of its authorities, it almost always uses formal hearings or briefings to establish a historical and legal record. Given the opportunities that hearings provide for shaping subsequent votes on the floors of the House and Senate, presidents have been wise to co-opt key senators, representatives, and even congressional staff members in positions to influence the hearing process. The executive may offer concessions on political appointments, give in on legislative matters, and, perhaps most effective, offer senators participation on delegations to the arms control talks. In return, senators may make public speeches of support and exert quiet influence through the process of selecting witnesses, timing hearings to the administration's advantage, and meeting with fence-sitting colleagues to trade favors and votes. Of course, a president who ignores Congress may have all these subtle efforts turned against him, resulting in a congressional momentum powerful enough to sink treaties once considered publicly popular. Such was the case with the Comprehensive Test Ban Treaty, which, though publicly popular, suffered a quick defeat in Congress.

Elites, Interest Groups, and Public Opinion

The formal and informal arms control policy process offers rich opportunities for citizens to engage. Because the U.S. public does not vote on arms control programs and agreements per se, its impact on particular arms control issues is primarily felt through activists and interest groups, many of whom have informal ties to government.

Think tanks. The arcane nature of modern weapons-related issues has meant that the most influential private-sector opinion leaders on arms control have generally been well-known scientific and technical experts. The better the ties these individuals have had within the government, the more influential their views.

Private research organizations increased dramatically in number during the Cold War, helping to frame often arcane and technical debates in lay terms. The impetus for their creation came from concerned citizenry (who formed groups such as Ground Zero and the Federation of American Scientists), military services interested in linking strategic concepts to force-planning (via studies done at research centers such as the RAND Corporation), and former bureaucrats turned policy advocates, waiting for their chance to return to the executive branch.

Some of these institutes were created specifically to support, or level focused opposition against, the arms control process. These issue-based advocates blanket Capitol Hill with leaflets and briefings designed to oppose particular accords. Other institutes have acted in quiet ways to prevent presidents from either intentionally or unintentionally killing treaties. For example, the prospects for timely ratification of the CWC were substantially improved by the role that the Washington, D.C.–based Stimson Center and other institutes played in informing congressional staff, thereby keeping the CWC alive between the George Bush and Bill Clinton administrations. The Stimson Center also provided a repository of expertise on the CWC that would have otherwise been lost when Democrats in the Clinton administration cleaned house after 12 years of Republican rule.

Industry. Industry has also been an active lobbyist on arms control issues in the United States. Most major private-sector firms have Washington-area offices that focus on courting congressional members and staff. They also keep in close contact with representatives from the districts and states that host their facilities. These senators and congressmen often weigh in with the executive branch if arms control policies threaten to hurt their companies or constituents.

The best industrial lobbying efforts equip politicians to shape decisions early and quietly. Arms control efforts are politically difficult to oppose or alter for parochial reasons once they come before the Congress as matters of national security policy. Lobbying techniques are often successful when used to shape the terms and timing of arms transfers, such as the 1991 sale of F-15 fighters to Saudi Arabia. McDonnell-Douglas, which faced a shutdown of its production line if the sale was successfully opposed, effectively lobbied Congress and the executive branch by assembling data on the geographic distribution of the new jobs that the contract would directly and indirectly create.

Of course, arms control has its industrial lobbyists, too. Monitoring technologies often involve some of the most important U.S. high-tech firms in multimillion-dollar projects. Many of the firms that gain from weapons sales also gain from an expanded need for monitoring equipment and technology. As a result, arms control negotiations have sometimes pitted firms against one another.

The general public is often unaware of the potential power of the industrial lobby because the extent of arms control's domestic economic impact is little appreciated. The CWC, for example, affects not only the entire chemical industry but also all firms who use chemicals. A comprehensive nuclear test ban has long been opposed by those who fear that without tests to perform the U.S. infrastructure for weapons research and development would whither as scientists looked for jobs elsewhere. Such economic fallout has been used as an argument for rejecting agreements with those adversaries who have command economies, which can ensure that industries are kept healthy despite controls placed on them or prohibition on their products.

The press and public opinion. In the United States, the primary facilitator—and sometimes important initiator—of intragovernmental negotiations on arms control is the press. The press in turn owes much of its power to its other role as educator of the people. In its formal role the press reports on developments in negotiations, characterizes the issues at stake, reports on the outcome of hearings, and publishes leaks. Informally the press helps powerbrokers make contact with one another.[27]

The press also shapes public attitudes to treaties. Although the U.S. public is sympathetic to arms control purposes, it can strongly oppose particular treaties if they are characterized as sacrificing a U.S. strategic advantage or are concluded by an administration that appears weak or untrustworthy on other grounds. The public's ambivalence on arms control allows politicians to use particular treaties to position themselves favorably at election time. Strong presidents interested in highlighting their roles as peacemakers often seek to push through arms control agreements before elections. Senators who have voted against defense spending or in favor of concessions on other national security matters under negotiation have sought to bolster their standing on national security by announcing their opposition to treaties they would have otherwise supported.

The United States in the Post–Cold War Era

The serious strategic threat that provided the backdrop for all post–World War II U.S. arms control debates disappeared in 1991. The United States is moving into an era in which domestic trends will shape arms control and national security policies in new ways. Three of the more salient trends include the new dominance of the U.S. unilateralist impulse; the revolutions in information, biogenetic, and manufacturing technologies; and the rise of the law enforcement community in the national security establishment.

Unilateralism

Recent U.S. foreign policy reflects a new preference for going it alone on matters of international importance. This approach has been evident in the George W. Bush administration's approach to global warming, the Balkans, National Missile Defense, and, arguably, its response to the terrorist attacks of 11 September 2001. To fight the war against global terrorism while preserving its freedom of action, Washington shaped a coalition of convenience rather than an international team as it did during the Gulf War. Although these policies have generated a fair amount of criticism in the press and overseas, they have also resonated to a significant degree with influential segments of the U.S. public. Europeans may regard missile defenses as an unwelcome reminder of the flipside of the U.S. unilateralist impulse—isolationism—but most NATO allies also seem supportive and grateful for U.S. willingness to go it alone on the front lines of the war against terrorism.

The return of the U.S. preference for independent action is not simply a reflection of a unipolar international system. It is a reaction to the advent of what might be an emerging international political culture that is sometimes at odds with U.S. preferences. The international institutions that Washington helped build after World War II have developed independence from U.S. control. Multilateral regimes in the areas of arms control, human rights, international law, trade, and environmental affairs have begun to generate transnational norms backed by international organizations with growing authority overseas. Other states, including traditional U.S. allies, are increasingly emboldened to levy judgments on U.S. preferences and actions that most Americans believe remain their sovereign business.

The implications of this trend for arms control are fairly clear, albeit controversial. To the extent that the political leadership in Washington ties its opposition to arms control treaties to the instinct to resist binding ties, it may succeed in gaining public support for overturning the old approach to formal arms control. Such a shift may not necessarily signal the end of cooperative security. U.S. preferences for reducing the costs of its military establishment may drive administrations to seek arms reductions through reciprocal unilateral measures. The chances of this shift occurring will increase if the political leadership successfully ascribes faith in the feasibility of reciprocal unilateralism to the public's faith in U.S. exceptionalism—that is, the certainty that in any unconstrained competition the United States can triumph by dint of pluck and skill.

If U.S. policy leaders do so, they may have to proceed without a well-mapped basis in deterrence theory. The academic disciplines that generated much of the deterrence theory of the 1960s—economics and social science—are refining and in some cases overturning models based on rational action.

Technological Change

The effects of the technological revolution under way are profound in multiple arenas, including information, bioengineering, and commercial space-based technologies and manufacturing.

Whereas the information revolution will likely have a neutral effect on arms control's prospects, advances in biotechnology are likely to increase the salience of bioterrorism in the arms controllers' pantheon of worries. This is not only because biological agents will be increasingly susceptible to tinkering in the labs. The problem is that the industries developing these technologies will also be at the cutting edge of advances in health, agriculture, and environmental protection. Arms control efforts to constrain the threat will be dealing with capabilities that are, more than ever before, tied to concepts of public good as opposed to militarism. And monitoring accords will involve civilian industries, not only defense-related ones.

This is not to say that controls on biological weapons will be infeasible. They will simply require unprecedented cooperation between civilian entities and the national security establishment. Such cooperation will be necessary, in any case. The steps that must be taken to defend against biological and chemical attacks will require massive overhaul of institutions largely regarded as civilian. Major efforts will be required in integrating defense and domestic policy. With the complexity of its health care system and its intolerance of any civilian loss of life, the U.S. government will find this arms control environment especially challenging.

Similarly the expansion of the Internet and related information technologies is creating new vulnerabilities for the United States even while it is improving prospects for monitoring the behavior of adversaries. With respect to the new vulnerabilities, literature on the asymmetric threat has blossomed, which created considerable momentum to revamp defense strategies and prompted efforts by the Clinton and George W. Bush administrations to protect critical infrastructures. National networks such as the nation's electrical grid, air traffic controls, border security, and communications have become computer-dependent. If the U.S. public and policymakers become convinced that the primary threats to U.S. security will be unconventional attacks against these vulnerable nodes and not traditional battlefields, classic arms control approaches may become, if not irrelevant, then something of a sideshow.

Yet in some respects the revolution in information and manufacturing technologies may improve the prospects for arms control. The Internet offers a new way to collect open-source (unclassified) information; computers are increasingly able to sort and store it for integration; and networks are increasingly able to protect and disseminate intelligence to users worldwide. Such advances can improve the capacity of governments and individuals to monitor and verify agreements. Advances in microengineering and nanotechnology may enormously increase the collection capabilities of the intelligence community.

These gains in collection, processing, and dissemination may make up for the losses expected in communications intelligence (the ability to intercept foreign telephones and computers) as a result of rapid advances in encryption. U.S. national security experts will have to hope such is the case. If the United States moves toward an approach to arms control that eschews treaties in favor of reciprocal unilateralism, the intelligence community will face a challenging requirement to monitor and verify tacit agreements. The absence of data exchanges and agreed provisions for verification will make the job of intelligence analysts considerably more difficult.

Perhaps the most interesting and challenging domain for arms control will be outer space. Here the natural alliance between arms controllers—whose interest is keeping space demilitarized—and commercial communications and reconnaissance firms—whose interests are to preserve a predictable operating environment in space—has yet to crystallize. In the meantime, the United States is posturing for dominance. The Rumsfeld commission's 2001 report on the future of space called for the country to focus on this new high ground as its next frontier.[28] In doing so it noted the importance of revisiting past arms control agreements that could constrain options not just for missile defense but for the defense of our increasingly vulnerable communications and surveillance satellites.

Law Enforcement

International terrorism, industrial espionage, international organized crime, and trafficking in women, children, and drugs through porous international borders has increased the role of domestic law enforcement agencies in national security affairs. Arms control initiatives that seek to regulate the trafficking of dual-use technologies and to protect proliferation-related and export-controlled technologies from transfer overseas will require the active involvement of federal law enforcement entities.

Arms control objectives could be significantly strengthened by increased involvement from the law enforcement community in the future. Closer cooperation between law enforcement and intelligence communities is already taking place. The growing influence of the Federal Bureau of Investigation overseas can be used to educate and train foreign police and customs officials to counter proliferation and the illicit export of sensitive technologies. Indeed, this trend is already evident as the number of legal attachés posted to embassies overseas grows.

Conclusion

Although international politics help to explain why states conclude arms control agreements, the particulars—including the content and timing of negotiations—turn on domestic politics and processes. In democracies great ideas do matter—particularly if they resonate with the popular political culture. The art of leadership in the national security domain involves more than a little salesmanship.

The foregoing discussion includes only some of the trends in domestic conditions that will challenge U.S. arms control and national security policymakers during the coming decades. Of course, other features may come again to the fore. An appreciation of how arms control policy is framed within any state requires analysis of generic factors, such as bureaucratic politics and economic drivers, as well as the unique, such as a nation's strategic culture. The weaving of these threads will produce, for every state, a fabric of strength, elasticity, or weakness in which basic patterns tend to repeat themselves and certain qualities seem dominant. The best negotiators are the ones who have a feel for not only the fabric of their enemy's polity but also their own.

Notes

This chapter is a revised version of chapter 3, "The Arms Control Process: The U.S. Domestic Context," in Jeffrey A. Larsen and Gregory J. Rattray, *Arms Control Toward the 21st Century* (Boulder: Lynne Rienner Publishers, 1996), pp. 55–76.

1. Arguably this careful balancing of needs was accomplished in the 1994 Agreed Framework between North Korea and the United States: The United States "won" a freeze and monitoring of Pyongyang's nuclear weapon program; North Korea "won" enhanced international standing and desperately needed domestic energy supplies. A conflict that seemed irresolvable gave way to a bargain that defined security needs broadly enough to take domestic factors into account.

2. These factors interact with each other in important ways. For example, a representative democracy with a legalistic strategic culture may take longer to ratify a treaty or to extract itself from prior commitments than will a dictatorship. The "stickiness" of arms control policies in legalistic democracies like the United States will be more apparent in a rapidly changing strategic environment than in a more static one. Whereas U.S. arms control critics are troubled by the resulting lags in military responsiveness to changing international conditions, advocates note that having institutionalized rules of the road can help in the management of what would otherwise be an unpredictable and potentially threatening strategic environment. Arguably the collapse of the Soviet Union would have been more destabilizing if

strategic arms control accords had not been in place, the monitoring of which indicated that the states of the former Soviet Union intended to abide by the Soviet Union's international commitments.

3. Jennifer E. Sims, *Icarus Restrained: An Intellectual History of Nuclear Arms Control, 1945–1960* (Boulder: Westview, 1990) p. 4.

4. For example, Dominique Moisi has written of the changing political culture in Europe brought about by an "alive, dynamic, and strong" civil society. Moisi, "The Real Crisis over the Atlantic," *Foreign Affairs* (July/August 2001): 149–153.

5. Critics of the notion of strategic conversion note that confidence in man's capacity to engineer the strategic environment through arms control is in itself a cultural trait—a statement of sociopolitical optimism hard for some in more fatalistic cultures to accept. They argue that if such cultures engage in arms control at all, their governments will tend to do so with deep suspicion and an emphasis more on the pursuit of unilateral advantage than on cooperative outcomes. Assuming an arms control partner is basically like oneself—an approach known as "mirror-imaging"—is not just simplistic; it can be terribly dangerous.

6. Malcolm Wallop and Angelo Codevilla, *The Arms Control Delusion* (San Francisco: ICS, 1987).

7. Grigori Aleksandrovich Potemkin (1739–1791) was a Russian statesman and field marshal who reportedly constructed fake building facades so that Catherine the Great would not see the poverty of the towns through which she was traveling.

8. For an important study of the impact of public opinion on arms control, see Jeffrey Knopf, *Domestic Society and International Cooperation: The Impact of Protest on U.S. Arms Control Policy* (Cambridge, UK: Cambridge University Press, 1998).

9. Reliance on experts is particularly marked when technological change is rapid or its military implications are unclear.

10. Ironically the firms best able to provide state-of-the-art military technologies to the government may become, through the procurement process, the most vulnerable to unpredictable production runs, cost increases, and export controls resulting from arms regulations and negotiated restraints. For example, firms building advanced fighter aircraft, cruise missiles, warhead components, and ballistic missiles may not be able to maintain open production lines and retain a skilled labor force if export controls narrow markets and increase the costs of production through intrusive inspection regimes.

11. William C. Widenor, "The League of Nations Component of the Versailles Treaty," in Michael Krepon and Dan Caldwell, eds., *The Politics of Arms Control Treaty Ratification* (New York: St. Martin's, 1991).

12. The guidelines for the U.S. strategic building program designed to assure U.S. deterrence at reasonable cost became, when projected onto a bipolar map, arms control's formula for strategic stability: mutual assured destruction.

13. Hans J. Morgenthau, *Scientific Man Versus Power Politics* (Chicago: University of Chicago Press, 1946), p. vi.

14. Sims, *Icarus Restrained*, p. 61. See also Hans J. Morgenthau, "The H-Bomb and After," *Bulletin of Atomic Scientists* (March 1950): 76–79.

15. Sims, *Icarus Restrained*, esp. pp 19–45. This approach is also summarized in Sims, "Arms Control: Thirty Years On," in *Daedalus* (Winter 1991): 251–272.

16. Unlike treaties, congressional-executive agreements may be ratified by majorities of both houses of Congress. The Supreme Court has found such agreements to have the same domestic legal authority as treaties. Presidential agreements, that are based on powers which inhere only in the executive, do not.

17. For excellent legal background on the treaty-making process and other matters of law related to arms control, see John Norton Moore, Frederick S. Tipson, and Robert E. Turner, *National Security Law* (Durham, NC: Carolina Academic Press, 1990).

18. The White House, citing executive privilege, had often denied Congress important information while the Departments of State and Defense have tended to relegate arms control to a second-order priority.

19. Former Secretary of Defense Robert Lovett announced that the agency would be "a Mecca for a wide variety of screwballs"; the joint chiefs of staff worried that the director's direct access to the president might undermine defense interests and national security policy; Senator Barry Goldwater opined that the United States was "developing a new mother-love type of agency." Duncan L. Clarke, *Politics of Arms Control: The Role and Effectiveness of the U.S. Arms Control and Disarmament Agency* (New York: Free Press, 1979), pp. 22–23.

20. Such charges were evident during the debate over whether to sanction Pakistan under the Symington amendment for having developed a nuclear explosive device. The intelligence community repeatedly stressed then, and on other occasions, that its job is to expose what is known but not to pass judgment on whether any given set of facts is sufficient for triggering sanctions.

21. This exclusion of the Department of State from resource decisionmaking in the intelligence community is changing. In 1999 the department created the Office for Intelligence Resources and Planning, run by a coordinator with departmentwide authorities. Working groups were established to monitor the funding levels for certain sensors deemed crucial for effective verification of strategic arms control treaties. In early 2001 Secretary of State Colin Powell announced his intention to strengthen this office and integrate it into a new planning directorate designed to work closely with other agencies with national security–related programs and operations.

22. *Bargaining chips* are assets brought to the negotiating table primarily to be used as items for trade during discussions with one's competitor.

23. Federal Bureau of Investigation and Defense Department counterintelligence operations are also engaged in protecting U.S. military and industrial secrets from foreign spies who might be participating in such inspections.

24. The role of Congress in this regard is not always altruistic; committees (and individual senators and representatives) have been known to redirect monies and programs from one agency to another, more in the interest of wresting legislative power from other, weaker committees than in the interest of broader national purpose.

25. Although legal opinions have varied on the subject, it is generally agreed that the House may not refuse to pass laws or appropriate funds for treaties signed by the president and ratified by the Senate. However, in practice the senators' close consultations with House colleagues have meant that controversial funding and legal provisions have been dealt with collegially and as part of the ratification process to avoid congressional division and abrogation of obligations. Moore, Tipson, and Turner, *National Security Law*, pp. 792–796.

26. *Security assistance* generally refers to programs associated with the Arms Export Control Act and part 2 of the Foreign Assistance Act (22 U.S.C. SS 2751-276c, 1982, and SS 2301-2349aa-b 1982). These programs have changed in scope, character, and geographic orientation since World War II. Although their scope has grown overall, grants have given way to sales on credit, and assistance has spread from Europe to East Asia and the Middle East. Michael John Matheson, "Arms Sales and Economic Assistance," in Moore, Tipson, and Turner, *National Security Law*, pp. 1111–1125.

27. Members of the press sometimes brought players in the SALT negotiations together for a backchannel reconciliation or joining of the issues, which occasionally led to resolutions. Strobe Talbott, *Master of the Game: Paul Nitze and the Nuclear Peace* (New York: Vintage, 1988), pp. 151, 353.

28. Report of the Commission to Assess United States National Security Space Management and Organization, pursuant to Public Law 106–65, January 11, 2001.

Suggested Readings

Arms Control Association and *Arms Control Today.* www.armscontrol.org.

Berkowitz, Bruce D., and Allen E. Goodman. *Strategic Intelligence for American National Security.* Princeton, NJ: Princeton University Press, 1989.

Clarke, Duncan L. *Politics of Arms Control: The Role and Effectiveness of the U.S. Arms Control and Disarmament Agency.* New York: Free Press, 1979.

Federation of American Scientists. www.fas.org.

Frei, Daniel. *Perceived Images: U.S. and Soviet Assumptions and Perceptions in Disarmament.* Totowa, NJ: Rowman and Littlefield, 1986.

Gilpin, Robert. *American Scientists and Nuclear Weapons Policy.* Princeton, NJ: Princeton University Press, 1962.

Graebner, Norman A. *Ideas and Diplomacy: Readings in the Intellectual Tradition of American Foreign Policy.* New York: Oxford University Press, 1964.

Henkin, Louis. "Nuclear Defense Policy: The Constitutional Framework." In Howard E. Schuman and Walter R. Thomas, eds. *The Constitution and National Security.* Washington, DC: National Defense University Press, 1990.

Institute for Defense and Disarmament Studies and *The Arms Control Reporter.* www.idds.org.

Kaplan, Fred. *The Wizards of Armageddon.* New York: Simon and Schuster, 1983.

Kegley, Charles W., and Eugene R. Wittkopf, eds. *The Domestic Sources of American Foreign Policy: Insights and Evidence.* New York: St. Martin's, 1988.

Knopf, Jeffrey W. *Domestic Society and International Cooperation: The Impact of Protest on U.S. Arms Control Policy.* Cambridge, UK: Cambridge University Press, 1998.

Moore, John Norton, Frederick S. Tipson, and Robert F. Turner, eds. *National Security Law.* Durham, NC: Carolina Academic Press, 1990.

Osgood, Robert E. *The Nuclear Dilemma in American Strategy and Arms Control.* 2nd ed. Elmsford, NY: Pergamon, 1985.

Sheehan, Michael J. *Arms Control: Theory and Practice.* New York: Basil Blackwell, 1988.

Sims, Jennifer E. *Icarus Restrained: An Intellectual History of Nuclear Arms Control 1945–1960.* Boulder: Westview, 1990.

Talbott, Strobe. *The Master of the Game: Paul Nitze and the Nuclear Peace.* New York: Alfred A. Knopf, 1988.

Waltz, Kenneth N. *Foreign Policy and Democratic Politics: The American and British Experience.* Boston: Little, Brown, 1967.

5

Verification and Transparency: Relics or Future Requirements?

Joseph F. Pilat

Arms control agreements have traditionally been assessed on the basis of three objectives: their ability to reduce the risks of war, limit damage should war occur, and reduce defense costs. Whether or not these objectives will have the same importance in the future, or whether they prove to be relics of the Cold War, the ability to meet them in a treaty, agreement, or other arrangement has, to date, depended on whether any terms are seen as being observed—in other words, on whether the parties are in compliance. Indeed, the entire arms control enterprise has often been judged on compliance grounds. So it should not be surprising that proposals to limit or eliminate weapons of mass destruction since 1945 have largely been perceived as acceptable or unacceptable not only on the basis of their potential impact on global power relations and domestic politics but also on their provisions for verification.

For the United States during this period, the capability to ensure that an arms control agreement was being implemented by the other party or parties was a critical criterion for entering into it. As a consequence, arms negotiations were limited in scope and number during the Cold War. Even before the fall of the Berlin Wall and the end of the Cold War, verification was becoming more important and intrusive, as attitudes in the Soviet Union changed, as the challenges of arms control became increasingly more complex, and as monitoring and verification technologies improved.

The end of the Cold War and the collapse of the Soviet Union fostered a productive period of arms control, bringing to conclusion negotiations begun before those landmark events. From the mid-1980s to the early 1990s, arms control flourished, with the conclusion of agreements on the elimination of intermediate- and shorter-range nuclear forces; the reduction of strategic nuclear forces; the limitation of conventional armed forces in Europe; the elimination of chemical weapons; and a host of lesser agreements regulating arms and promoting transparency and confidence in the U.S.-Soviet and European arenas.

Aside from the Comprehensive Test Ban Treaty (CTBT), however, little has been achieved in formal arms control since the early 1990s. The pursuit of transparency and confidence-building measures during Bill Clinton's administration has not delivered on its promise. The George W. Bush administration is skeptical about, and has shown limited interest in, this element of U.S. policy. Instead the president and his advisers have expressed a commitment to pursue some traditional arms control objectives, with a preference for unilateral means that offer, it is argued, the flexibility to respond to a dynamic international security environment. To date, the demands of the war on terrorism—the response to the terrorist attacks of 11 September 2001—do not appear to have fundamentally altered the administration's policy. However, we may see changes in priority or approach over time.

To assess the evolution of verification and transparency and to reveal areas of convergence and other interactions between them, this chapter provides conceptual clarifications, analyzes changing patterns over the last few decades, and speculates about future prospects in these areas.

Verification and Transparency in Arms Control

The meanings of the terms *transparency* and *verification* are not universally held, even within the arms control and nonproliferation communities. Verification involves monitoring treaty-limited items and activities, as well as assessing compliance on the basis of monitoring and other relevant information. As considered here, transparency measures, ultimately, involve obtaining information related to items or activities of interest or concern from an arms control perspective.

Transparency and verification, along with variants of both, can be viewed as instruments offering some level of confidence derived from information that is useful in determining compliance with arms control objectives. They differ in terms of their formality and the level of confidence they provide. Seen from this perspective, transparency and confidence-building are not identical, but they are both related to the objectives of verification. Transparency measures are designed to increase confidence or to provide warnings through access to information. Verification measures, viewed from this perspective, should in practice also achieve the objectives of confidence-building and early warning in the context of determining compliance and noncompliance with a treaty or other agreement. But even these considerations may be too simplistic to suggest the complex interactions of transparency and verification.

Verification can serve the objectives of increasing transparency and confidence by demonstrating compliance, offering assurances to others of a state's behavior, and the like. Some states may wish to use verification to demonstrate their bona fides to other parties of an agreement or to the international community, which may have an interest in compliance with agreements with which they are not directly involved.

Transparency measures, in contrast, presumably can increase confidence in a state's compliance with treaty obligations, although that may not happen with poorly crafted measures. And of course, transparency measures may reveal suspicious behavior within or outside the scope of a treaty's provisions that may affect judgments on verification. But transparency measures can also make verification more effective, more efficient, and, perhaps, easier and less expensive. In some cases transparency measures could also be put forward in place of verification, albeit not without significant risks. In broad terms, then, the differences between verification and transparency depend on the context and other case-specific factors; there may be areas where verification and transparency are in practice indistinguishable.

Verification, Intelligence, and Compliance: Issues and Assessments

The historical record suggests that arms control follows rather than leads changes in the political realm. It appears that some level of trust and some expectation of good faith on the part of the participants in arms control agreements are probably prerequisites for their being negotiated, but the stakes are usually too high to rely on such considerations alone. One could also presume that compliance with arms control and disarmament treaties and other agreements is based on clearly defined mutual interests, but even this has not been deemed sufficient in most cases (and has not always been realized in practice). The Outer Space Treaty, the Seabed Treaty, and the Biological and Toxin Weapons Convention (commonly called the Biological Weapons Convention, or BWC) are notable exceptions to these rules. These treaties do not have verification provisions, although there has been interest in establishing a verification protocol for the BWC in recent years. These cases aside, most agreements have some verification provisions, which provide a means for monitoring compliance.

Compliance is perhaps the critical issue in highly politicized debates on arms control and nonproliferation. In the 1980s U.S.–Soviet compliance disputes dominated the debate, but there were also concerns about Iraqi compliance with the Geneva Protocol on chemical weapons and the compliance of a number of states with the BWC.[1] Today it is likely that compliance with nonproliferation regimes (perhaps also including norms) will be the most contentious issues.

This prospect was revealed by the atmosphere of crisis during 1998 created by three situations: Iraq's refusal to comply with its obligations to disarm under United Nations (UN) Security Council Resolution 687 and its suspension of all cooperation with the UN Special Commission on Iraq (UNSCOM); the prospect of a North Korean violation of the Agreed Framework via underground nuclear activities; and the Indian and Pakistani nuclear tests.[2] Russian compliance with the full range of arms control treaties also remains a problem and may again be at the fore in the future, depending on the manner in which Russia develops over time and its ability to comply with treaty obligations.

The changing parameters of the debate over verification have not focused on the need to verify compliance—that requirement has become widely if not universally accepted—but rather on the degree to which the verification measures can be effective in ensuring compliance. Although this issue of "effectiveness" is important in itself, the debate has often masked a larger one about the value of arms control in general and of the specific treaty or agreement being considered. There is no means to ensure compliance at anything near 100 percent. Yet the inability to do so has not been seen by most observers as grounds for abandoning the arms control endeavor. Indeed, ensuring the practicability of agreements as well as their political acceptability has frequently meant forgoing the most intrusive verification means possible.

Measuring Verification Effectiveness

The measure for verification effectiveness must in the end be national security. As President Dwight Eisenhower recognized, all arms control involves some level of risk to national security, but that risk must be balanced against the benefits. The manner in which that risk has been discussed involves the military significance of noncompliance, or cheating. If an agreement involves a significant security risk from cheating, the verification standards must be higher; if it does not, the standards can in practice be relaxed. Drawing appropriate verification standards is difficult. However, in the end an agreement's verification provisions must be able to provide early warning of militarily significant noncompliance, with sufficient time to allow the appropriate diplomatic, military, or other response. In assessing verification requirements, such factors as the probability of cheating and the prospects of detecting noncompliance must be taken into account.

Progress in technologies, especially those deployed on satellites, has allowed these concerns to be addressed and has helped make possible far-reaching arms control agreements. Technologies have made it possible in the context of certain types of agreements to obtain good information without being physically intrusive or requiring a large contingent of human inspectors on the territory of the other parties to the agreement. National technical means (NTM)—advanced intelligence collection capabilities including photoreconnaissance, radar and electronic surveillance, and seismic and acoustic sensing—are critical to the monitoring on which verification depends. Technologies are also important to on-site inspections, which have become more important since the mid-1980s. However, there are limits to technologies that are grounded in physical principles and in the nature and footprint of the items and/or activities that are to be eliminated, reduced, or controlled in some fashion. These limits have become even more significant since the end of the Cold War, as political and other considerations have driven arms control in directions that are more difficult to verify (e.g., the interest in controlling smaller and more mobile arms).

Verification and Intelligence

In principle and practice, verification involves monitoring treaty-limited items and activities and assessing compliance on the basis of that monitoring and other relevant information. Aside from this declared purpose of verification, a common goal of verification provisions is to deter the parties from violations. This objective already presumes a reasonable level of effectiveness for the measures. But it is a difficult standard for verification. As in broader deterrence policies, where it is difficult to know with certainty what deters and under what conditions deterrence operates, verification raises similar questions: What risks is a party to a treaty willing to take? What is their sense of the benefits of cheating? What is their expectation of a significant response?

Treaties and agreements have frequently provided for enhanced verification measures such as on-site inspections, data exchanges, cooperative measures, bodies to address disputes, and noninterference with NTM. Whatever the specific verification provisions of treaties and agreements, however, all of the knowledge a party has about the other party or parties comes into play in the verification process. Intelligence is thus closely related to verification, and intelligence can guide verification by providing an alarm and/or triggering mechanism for, say, challenge inspections.[3] This means that verification is facilitated by open societies. The activities of closed authoritarian and totalitarian systems are intrinsically more difficult to verify. To the extent that we are witnessing democratic revolutions around the globe, formal verification standards may be eased. They will in any case certainly become less significant. Verification, by providing information related to forces and activities, can provide political benefits to a state's intelligence apparatus, whether or not related to the verified accord. For this reason alone, states without strong intelligence capabilities might in principle be expected to pursue more intrusive verification during treaty negotiations. Often, however, these states do not express greater interest in verification, and they may oppose measures where states with high-level intelligence capabilities are seen to have advantages.[4]

Assessing Compliance

A key question confronting the verification process is how to determine compliance and noncompliance. Ultimately this must be a matter of judgment. Because verification often involves sensitive intelligence, charges of noncompliance may be difficult to address and assess publicly. Indeed, the consequences of revealing intelligence sources may inhibit the public use of all available intelligence. This difficulty is compounded by the fact that arms control agreements may contain hundreds of pages of sometimes ambiguous and arcane language, leading to loopholes that one or the other side may exploit without technically being in violation of the letter of the agreement. Moreover, judgments may not be based on clear information but may themselves be ambiguous.[5]

One of the problems when encountering noncompliance is determining how to respond. International organizations, including the United Nations, have not always been able to act effectively, especially when the five permanent members of the Security Council (those holding veto authority) were involved. UN and other collective action, as provided for by treaties and agreements, can be more effective if the violator is a pariah state, a small power, or has been defeated in war. However, developments in Iraq since 1998 demonstrate that even in such cases the sustainability and end results of any collective action that might be agreed on are by no means certain.

If a violation is clear or probable, diplomacy will certainly attempt to rectify the problem, but its effects are uncertain. Embargoes, sanctions, and the threat or use of military force in response to violations could be significant in themselves if diplomatic solutions fail, and they may even have a deterrent effect. The problem is getting a consensus on action, whether domestically or internationally, which may be very difficult. Responses are in the hands of the party or parties that are affected by the cheating, a situation that may not provide the aggrieved party many good options, especially if it is a small or weak state. Of course, violations may be ignored by the parties, depending on how they assess their response options given the political and security context. A response may be equivalent to abrogating the agreement. Even publicly airing violations has risks, as it may politically undermine the agreement, particularly if no action is taken against the violator(s). These risks may or may not be acceptable, depending upon circumstances.

Violations cannot and should not be ignored, but dealing with them is by no means easy. Even if a violation is not significant, it may indicate a pattern of behavior or be a test of a party's resolve. If it is not responded to, the violating party might feel it has carte blanche to violate the agreement further, undermining the legal regime established by the agreement. And it may even lead to repudiation of the treaty or agreement. Violations brought before the public can bring domestic political forces and the international community into the picture and indicate to a violator the costs of its actions. Yet such publicity may undermine the agreement.

Changing Patterns of Verification

Even before the end of the Cold War, verification was changing in response to changes in politics and technology.[6] With the collapse of the Soviet Union, arms control flourished and new, more challenging avenues for arms control opened. Accordingly agreements of recent vintage, especially the major nuclear and conventional agreements of the 1990s, pose different challenges than agreements like the 1963 Limited Test Ban Treaty and the treaties resulting from the Strategic Arms Limitation Talks of the 1970s (SALT I, SALT II). The verification of those early arms accords was done primarily by national technical means, especially overhead surveillance. The new agreements require more intrusive verification measures going well beyond NTM, usually involving managed on-site access to sensitive facilities and activities.

In any event, verification efforts will for the foreseeable future be defined by these agreements—agreements on which negotiations began, or scope and objectives were decided, during the Cold War. These agreements, especially the Intermediate and Shorter-Range Nuclear Forces (INF) Treaty, the Strategic Arms Reduction Treaties (START I, START II), and the Conventional Armed Forces in Europe (CFE) Treaty, have elaborate verification systems that largely reflect Cold War concerns.[7] Post–Cold War uncertainties about the Russian Federation suggest the continuing importance of intrusive verification provisions for the United States and the West. But already these agreements and their verification provisions seem marginal to what are now seen as higher-priority concerns, including the fate of the old Soviet nuclear arsenal and special nuclear material stockpiles. These new concerns can at best be only marginally affected by existing arms accords and are being addressed today through ad hoc measures such as the Cooperative Threat Reduction program. The framework for START III agreed in Helsinki in 1997 would, if followed, bring at least some of these new issues into formal negotiations. However, there would be great difficulties in doing so, and in any event the George W. Bush administration does not appear particularly interested in formal arms control of this nature. Unless there is a downturn in the strategic environment, elaborate verification regimes can be expected to decline in significance over time and are not likely to be recreated in full in future efforts to restrain and reduce arms.

As we look to the future, it is important to recall that progress in technologies over the past decades allowed security concerns to be addressed and helped make practicable a number of arms control agreements. We may expect technology to improve in the future. However, even the evolutionary advances in verification technologies are unlikely to be able to fully meet the new challenges of arms control. As a consequence, transparency, confidence-building, and other cooperative measures may increasingly be used to augment or even replace verification.

In the emerging climate, then, we may expect to see hybrid verification-transparency regimes. Such regimes would have intrusive but much more limited verification provisions than Cold War accords, with extensive transparency provisions designed in part to augment the verification measures by filling in the gaps of the verification regime. These hybrid regimes could meet security concerns, be cost-effective, and be in line with developing U.S.-Russia and international relations. However, if international political relations—especially ties between the United States and Russia—take a turn for the worse, such regimes may prove to be very limited, hollow instruments.

Toward Multilateral Arms Control?

Multilateral agreements concluded during the Cold War, including the 1967 Outer Space Treaty, the 1972 Seabed Treaty, and the 1972 BWC, frequently had no verification provisions and were largely unverifiable except to the extent that NTM could play a role in assessing the activities of the states parties. A notable multilateral exception was the 1968 Treaty on the Nonproliferation of Nuclear Weapons.[8] Interest in multilateral arms control and nonproliferation accords has increased. The general sense of expectation about this approach has been high, but the prospects appear unlikely, as problems with the CTBT and the BWC protocol suggest.

New technologies, along with the collapse of the Soviet Union, furthered the old bilateral arms control process in the 1990s, although progress has apparently reached a stalemate. Neither the United States nor Russia nor any other Soviet successor state engaged in inherited arms control efforts has yet to permit international or neutral third-party verification of bilateral accords, and they are unlikely to do so in the future. A more limited international role in monitoring may be possible, although in the foreseeable future international and third-party verification is likely to be limited at best.

There do not appear to be many prospects beyond the 1993 Chemical Weapons Convention (CWC) for concluding a new international accord requiring international verification measures. The Fissile Material Cut-Off Treaty (FMCT) is one of the few new initiatives being discussed, but its prospects are not great at present. Although the fate of the CWC, the CTBT, the BWC protocol, and the FMCT are as yet undecided, these agreements would, if realized and implemented, require extensive international verification activity. Even if that should occur, the proponents of a greater international role expected far more. To date it has been primarily proliferation issues and counterterrorism that have spurred a consensus in the international community on an urgent need for action. But this consensus has not been fully realized in practice, and prospects will remain limited for the foreseeable future.

The experience in Iraq after the 1991 Gulf War, and in North Korea in the mid-1990s, demonstrated the limits of the international nuclear nonproliferation regime. Other areas of nonproliferation (e.g., missile technology) are less mature, so no grand new international regimes with significant formalized verification provisions appear likely. Efforts to improve the nonproliferation regimes will more likely occur through ad hoc, incremental initiatives. If the prospects for a dramatic expansion of nonproliferation verification appear unlikely in the near term, there is nonetheless considerable interest in the United Nations, the Conference on Disarmament, and elsewhere in pursuing outer space arms control, control of small arms and light weapons, restrictions on information operations, and other international initiatives.

Some of these initiatives remind us that certain arms activities may be intrinsically unverifiable. We are moving in the direction of incorporating into accords limits on systems that are more numerous, smaller and thus more mobile, and by nature dual-purpose. To the extent that such activities can be monitored at all, it depends on sharing knowledge of technologies and operations that can make systems vulnerable to countermeasures or, possibly, even preemptive attacks. But systems that are not sufficient to adequately monitor items limited or eliminated by arms accords may be effectively used to monitor a country's natural resources, from oil to gold. Although the long-term presence of NTM capabilities in the United States and Russia has reduced bilateral sensitivities in these areas in terms of space surveillance, the Open Skies negotiations revealed that air surveillance was, for the former Soviet Union, far more sensitive and controversial. Reflecting concerns about Open Skies being a "spy treaty," the Russian Duma (parliament) ratified the treaty in 2001, a decade after it was concluded; it finally entered into force in 2002.

Coercive Verification: The United Nations and Iraq

As we have seen, there are formidable obstacles to concluding and implementing verifiable multilateral and international arms control agreements. Changes in verification technologies will certainly change the way we look at these problems, but they may not be sufficient to resolve them. At the same time, we should not forget that fundamental changes in weapons-related technologies will require a watchful eye and continuous updating of verification regimes. The security and arms control environments will continue to be dynamic.

The inspections in Iraq after the Gulf War offer one vision of the shape of things to come, showing both the limits of and the prospects for short-notice, suspect-site inspections. UNSCOM was created in the aftermath of the Gulf War to eliminate Iraq's nuclear/biological/chemical (NBC) weapon and missile programs. UNSCOM reflected the post–Gulf War international consensus and the special interests of powerful states in dealing with Iraqi programs. From the beginning, Iraq has resisted full compliance with UNSCOM's mandate.

Despite the number of intrusive inspections, in which (after some initial difficulties) the inspectors largely had carte blanche to go and do what they wanted, we may never know exactly what level of capabilities the Iraqi programs achieved. In the nuclear sphere, further inspections as well as continuous monitoring are required for reasonable assurances about Iraq's denuclearization, but this may not be possible following the expulsion of inspectors from Iraq in the late 1990s. The UN Monitoring, Verification, and Inspection Commission, the successor to UNSCOM, is preparing for a resumption of inspections. Its prospects for success appear poor, although they may have improved somewhat due to the Bush administration's intensified interest in the context of the war on terrorism. Still, what was seen during the second UNSCOM inspection led ultimately to Iraq's admissions about its uranium enrichment programs. The Iraqi experience confirms what we have long known about both the value and the limits of on-site inspections.

The disclosures of Iraq's nuclear program led to efforts to strengthen the International Atomic Energy Agency's safeguards agreements, which are just now beginning to be implemented.[9] Beyond safeguards, the Iraqi experience could also help to promote certain technologies, techniques, and procedures, such as aerial inspection; if they can be dissociated with the ultimate failure of UNSCOM, their earlier successful use in Iraq may have established a rationale for their place in the new arms control panoply. Yet neither the inspections nor proposals for a continuous monitoring regime applied to Iraq are likely to have a place in future bilateral, regional, and international accords. Parties are not likely to accept instruments that treat them as defeated powers. The United States could not accept such an approach either constitutionally or as a matter of U.S. security policy. Moreover, as UNSCOM's failure suggests, the sustainability of such efforts is questionable.

Verification, Openness, Transparency, and Confidence-Building

Some of the problems surrounding verification derive from the fact that this requirement of arms control and disarmament emerged and developed its current meaning and significance during the Cold War. In particular, deal-ings with the closed Soviet Union drove verification requirements for the United States and the West. But the world is changing, and verification re-quirements are changing with it. Coercive verification, as we saw in the case of Iraq, may be a very limited instrument. Openness, transparency, and confidence-building measures, which also were forged during the Cold War, may have broader (albeit still limited) future applicability.

The objectives of openness and transparency measures coincide with the broader objectives proposed and pursued since the early 1990s. These include fostering formal arms control by breaking down barriers and obsta-cles; avoiding formal arms control measures and verification procedures; encouraging and reinforcing improved political relationships; lessening ten-sions and building confidence; reducing costs, difficulties, and the intru-siveness of monitoring compliance; obtaining information about military activities and deployments of other countries; obtaining insights into other countries' defense planning, thinking, and decisionmaking; and allowing more predictability in planning defense requirements.[10]

During the 1990s, openness and transparency appeared more attractive because of the new strategic environment, in which the certainties and sta-bilities of the Cold War were eroding. Cooperation with Russia in this sphere increased, but not as much as hoped. There may be scope for more transparency as formal negotiated arms controls appear to be giving way to less formal negotiated and nonnegotiated measures that are probably not verifiable with traditional tools (e.g., special nuclear material disposition). Interest in regional transparency should also grow, reflecting the rising im-portance of regional conflict and the proliferation of weapons of mass destruction.

Openness and transparency also have risks and limits, including the prospect that classified or proprietary information will be compromised or released, the possibility of information channels being used for misinfor-mation by the other parties, the creation of a false sense of confidence, and the questionable value of information obtained compared to intrusive veri-fication. But limited opportunities exist. Despite the disappointments of the 1990s, openness and transparency may yet make a genuine contribution.

Future Transparency

Transparency and openness had limited success during the Cold War.[11] Today the interest in and debate over transparency appear to be moving from a bilateral and Europe-centered matter to one with global dimensions, in part because of growing concerns about the security implications of the proliferation of NBC weapons. Such developments have already led the international community to revise verification or transparency measures for the Biological Weapons Convention and have raised broader questions about verification and its future role. The general sense of expectation in the immediate aftermath of the Cold War was reflected in a 1992 UN report on arms regulation and disarmament. The UN Secretary-General stated that transparency was no substitute for reductions in arms, but when properly applied it could promote confidence among states, alert the global community to excessive accumulations of armaments, increase the predictability of military behavior, provide reassurance to states of their rival's intentions, and offer early warning.[12] In this manner, it could serve as an additional instrument in facilitating nonproliferation efforts.

After a decade of initiatives in the realm of transparency that have had only limited successes, these expectations now appear wildly optimistic. A key question will be whether transparency can still play a role, albeit a more modest one than that envisioned a decade ago. If it is to have a major role, it may have to change fundamentally. The bilateral, regional, and global transparency agendas will be a critical aspect of arms control in the future and will, in some fashion, define the bounds of what is possible.

Bilateral Transparency

For several years there has been a discussion in the U.S. government and within the arms control community about the desirability of addressing warheads in a START III agreement. In the 1997 Helsinki summit statement on future nuclear force reductions, the U.S. and Russian presidents agreed to begin negotiations on a START III agreement. If realized, START III would reduce aggregate levels of strategic nuclear warheads to 2,000–2,500 for each party and include, among other things, "Measures related to the transparency of strategic nuclear warhead inventories and the destruction of strategic nuclear warhead inventories and any other jointly agreed technical and organizational measures, to promote the irreversibility of deep reductions including prevention of a rapid increase in the number of warheads."[13] There was also a commitment to consider confidence- and security-building measures related to the warheads of nonstrategic nuclear forces.[14]

Reflecting the difficulties of verifying warheads, perhaps, the Helsinki language referred to transparency measures. In addition to warheads, there is also a reference in the Helsinki joint statements to considering transparency of materials (presumably of weapon-origin) in START III.[15] If this were realized, it would likely occur in addition to a host of bilateral and multilateral initiatives in materials verification and/or transparency.

The challenges of this agenda are formidable. The Russians have been very hesitant to engage the United States in the area of transparency, and little progress was made on START III during the Clinton administration. There is now a possibility that some U.S. objectives can be met, albeit by other means. President George W. Bush's interest in unilateral cuts in arms, which would apparently anticipate reciprocal moves by Russia, may allow practical near-term results—such as the December 2001 U.S.-Russia agreement to cut their respective strategic arsenals at the Crawford summit.[16] But if proposals are to be successful in reducing the nuclear dangers associated with warheads and weapon-usable materials, effective transparency will be critical.

With what appears to be limited interest on Russia's part, transparency is also being pursued in a number of bilateral nuclear initiatives in place or under negotiation. The difficult negotiation on transparency measures for a storage facility being constructed with U.S. assistance at Mayak, Russia, is a case in point.

Exchanges between the United States and Russia concerning nonnuclear arms could also increase openness and transparency. Military-to-military contacts can increase transparency in areas of direct interest to the achievement of arms control objectives. Broader exchanges of information on defense budgets, doctrine and planning, and decisionmaking; on defense research and development; and on nonnuclear forces could also serve to promote predictability, mutual confidence, and other desired bilateral objectives that affect the arms control agenda.

Regional Transparency

Many regional transparency initiatives have been undertaken in Europe, including agreements on confidence- and security-building measures, as well as the Bosnian transparency measures agreed in Dayton in 1995. However, there is scope for additional initiatives, including information exchanges and technical assistance regarding military budgets, doctrines, and force structure. To the extent that such modest actions promote transparency and thereby reduce tensions and insecurities, they could be useful in reassuring Russia about expansion of the North Atlantic Treaty Organization (NATO), as well as in enhancing the security of the former Soviet bloc states not yet included in NATO's expansion plans. Such transparency measures, however, are by their very nature limited. If the goal is security and stability in Europe, then promoting transparency through multiple endeavors rather than further quantitative and qualitative limits on conventional forces appears to deserve the highest priority by policymakers.

Neither subregional issues, such as Cyprus, nor extraregional issues of special concern in Europe, including the Middle East and North Africa, appear susceptible to any but the most modest transparency measures in the foreseeable future, although even modest measures could be somewhat useful. But such issues remain divisive. Their persistence has long been a bane to achieving formal political and other agreements.

A host of confidence-building measures and unilateral actions (reciprocal and coordinated), including mere dialogue on intractable issues of conventional forces in Europe, are possible and would seem to be the best approach to the issues confronting European security. The CFE Treaty could benefit from transparency and related cooperative elements in addition to adjustments of weapons ceilings. The full implementation of Open Skies in the new climate will be difficult. Nonetheless, this transparency regime is now in force and holds the possibility of developing over time. At present, what is most critical is nurturing the political imperative for transparency that led to the conclusion of the Open Skies Treaty.

Confidence-building measures, including openness and transparency measures crafted to promote confidence, were widely perceived in the 1990s as offering an important means of dealing with regional conflict and tensions, including proliferation. Yet one specialist stated that "these unilateral, tacit or negotiated steps to improve cooperation or decrease tension were the forgotten stepchild of the Cold War, always taking the back seat to formal arms control negotiations." He continued: "Now with the end of the U.S.-Soviet rivalry, [confidence-building measures] are emerging from the shadows of strategic arms reductions to become the pre-eminent means of preventing accidental wars and unintended escalation in strife-ridden regions."[17]

Following the example of Europe, exchanges among the civilian and military officials of adversaries, declarations about military force levels, exercises, and the like are being pursued in other parts of the world. There have been discussions of expanding Open Skies, or at least the concept, to regional settings. Regional nuclear energy cooperation may also be influenced by European developments. Although the declared objectives of such proposals are not always clear, many seem designed primarily to promote transparency in nuclear-fuel cycles, particularly those that involve weapon-usable nuclear materials.

In addition to efforts to adapt European transparency and other measures designed to promote confidence to other regions, there have been other initiatives. In South Asia, for example, there are agreements such as nonattack on nuclear facilities, as well as proposals for the declaratory renunciation of nuclear weapons. Although such measures might, if realized, break impasses and lead to more formal and comprehensive measures when peace is on the horizon, they may be ill-suited to tense regions because of fears that they may be misused for the advantage of one or another of the participants. In the dangerous South Asia region, experience has demonstrated the problems with such approaches.

Global Transparency

Global transparency initiatives in the United Nations and elsewhere have not been particularly promising. Yet they do have a constituency and, where pursued, will need to be assessed in light of their cost, utility, and impact on regions. In similar fashion, efforts to use transparency measures to improve confidence in compliance with global treaties like the BWC will need to be carefully assessed in light of concerns with the protocol, notably those articulated by the United States.

Conclusion

Verification's importance has changed dramatically over time, although it has been in the forefront of U.S. perceptions about arms control since the end of World War II. The goals and measures of verification and the criteria for success have also changed with the times, reflecting such factors as the centrality of a prospective agreement to East-West relations during the Cold War, the state of relations between the United States and the Soviet Union, and the technologies available for monitoring.

Current verification challenges are quite formidable. Even without expansion of verifiable agreements, future challenges will grow. Monitoring capabilities have grown considerably, but further improvements are necessary. There are technologies derived from the U.S. nuclear weapon program and nuclear arms control verification experience that have been adapted to enhance verification in nonnuclear areas. Adapting current technologies to new problems will remain necessary. So will exploring new technologies specifically designed for areas in which arms control activity is now occurring and has captured the world's attention. But the limits and costs of verification raise serious questions about such endeavors.[18]

Prospects for the future role of verification will be, first and foremost, affected by the high costs of traditional arms control, especially those associated with requirements for verification. Moreover, the growing interest in informal and nonnegotiated arms control will have to address the issue of verification provisions, which are more difficult by the very nature of such types of arrangements. To the extent we see new multilateral agreements, their appearance may argue against highly intrusive verification measures, in part because of fears of promoting proliferation by opening sensitive facilities to inspectors from potential proliferant states.

As a result of such developments, it is more likely that openness, transparency, and confidence-building measures will achieve greater prominence, perhaps both as supplements to and substitutes for traditional verification. As the post–Cold War experience demonstrates, such measures are not panaceas and do not offer all that we came to expect from verification during the Cold War. However, such measures may be the best possible means to deal with current problems of arms reductions and restraints at acceptable levels of expenditure. Such measures may be more compatible with informal arms control, whether or not it is unilateral. The prospect of hybrid verification-transparency regimes could also be considered in this context. The limited outlook for transparency could improve with new models based on international financial openness and with commercialization of available enabling technologies. The expanded use of transparency measures (alone or in conjunction with verification measures) may or may not coincide with an end to formal arms control in the aftermath of the Cold War.

Notes

The views are the author's own and not those of the Los Alamos National Laboratory, the University of California, or the Department of Energy.

1. For a discussion of compliance in the U.S.–Soviet relationship at this time, see *Compliance and the Future of Arms Control: Report of a Project Sponsored by the Center for International Security and Arms Control, Stanford University, and Global Outlook*, Gloria Duffy, Project Director (Stanford: Stanford University Press, 1988).

2. The South Asian tests did not involve noncompliance per se because they were not prohibited by treaty obligations of the states involved. Neither India nor Pakistan signed or ratified the CTBT, which is in any event not yet in force.

3. *Challenge inspections* are prompt adversarial inspections called for by a party or parties to an agreement to prove or disprove a suspected treaty violation by another party or parties.

4. Additional sources of information may come into play when formal agreements or verification provisions cannot be agreed such as openness, transparency measures, and confidence-building measures. In practice such measures may facilitate meeting all of the goals of traditional arms control.

5. For the disputes over alleged Soviet violations of the threshold test ban treaty, see Warren Heckrotte, "Verification of Test Ban Treaties," in William C. Potter, ed., *Verification and Arms Control* (Lexington, MA: Lexington Books, 1985), pp. 70–71. For possible Soviet violations of the ABM treaty and the SALT II Treaty, see ibid., p. 246.

6. The earliest U.S. arms control initiatives after World War II, including the Baruch Plan and President Eisenhower's Atoms for Peace proposal, envisaged stringent on-site verification measures. The Soviet Union, by contrast, favored vague, unverifiable proposals that sought to capture the high moral ground and, irrespective of whether agreement was reached, offered political advantages. During the Cold War the U.S. position on the importance of verification remained largely unchanged, and the Soviets gradually came to accept the need for verification. Those Soviet moves toward the U.S. position were possible not only because U.S.-Soviet relations improved but also because new technologies for remote detection and monitoring lessened the need for physically intrusive verification measures, thereby reducing Soviet fears of possible U.S. intelligence benefits derived from treaties and agreements. Only after the launch of SPUTNIK in 1957 did a remotely sensing, mutually acceptable means of verification present itself. Space-based observation and sensing devices made possible many of the arms control achievements between the United States and the Soviet Union in the 1960s and 1970s.

The importance of space-based verification capabilities is evident in the areas of testing and strategic arms limitations. The United States simply did not have the means to verify compliance with a ban on underground testing in the early 1960s. Those technologies have since been developed, allowing U.S. and Soviet negotiators to conclude the Threshold Test Ban Treaty (TTBT) of 1974 and the Peaceful Nuclear Explosions Treaty (PNET) of 1976 and to enter into negotiations (1977–1980) on the Comprehensive Test Ban Treaty. The TTBT and PNET were not ratified until those specific concerns were remedied by protocols that allowed on-site inspections to limit the ambiguities of teleseismic detection and monitoring. The reopening of CTBT negotiations in the 1990s and the conclusion of a treaty in 1996 hinged on improved teleseismic methods, changes in the political climate after the Cold War, and the growing interest in pursuing a CTBT in the context of the extension of the NPT in 1995. The failure of the U.S. Senate to ratify the treaty reflected residual concerns about verification. See Glenn T. Seaborg, *Kennedy, Krushchev, and the Test Ban* (Berkeley: University of California Press, 1981).

7. The INF Treaty in 1987 contained unprecedented verification measures, including on-site inspections of the elimination of intermediate-range nuclear forces at special installations and missile sites, as well as of declared and formerly declared missile operating bases and missile support facilities; continuous on-site monitoring of the portals of designated missile production facilities; noninterference with NTM; and other cooperative measures. Verification measures for START I (and START II, which has not yet entered into force) are even more stringent than those of the INF Treaty. Verification of the ambitious CFE Treaty (1990), which involves significant arms reductions and geographical restraints on deployments, requires extensive data exchange, NTM, on-site inspections, and cooperative measures.

8. At the time of their origin, IAEA safeguards were an unprecedented on-site inspection measure. These same procedures subsequently were used to verify provisions of the NPT, as well as the Treaties of Tlatelolco, Rarotonga, and Pelindaba (which established nuclear weapon–free zones, respectively, in Latin America, the South Pacific, and Africa).

9. The process of strengthening IAEA safeguards following the revelations concerning Iraq's nuclear program in the aftermath of the Gulf War received a boost after the conclusion of the Additional Model Protocol (INFCIRC/540). The IAEA is now seeking to integrate, or harmonize, the measures of the protocol with those of traditional safeguards. The resultant integrated safeguards will contain new measures targeted at undeclared facilities and materials and old measures focused on declared materials.

10. See Lewis A. Dunn and Patricia McFate, *Transparency: Aspects, Prospects, and Implications,* briefing at Lawrence Livermore National Laboratory, Livermore, CA, 24 September 1992.

11. U.S. initiatives to make Soviet weapons activities more transparent were consistently rejected by the Soviet Union during this period. These included overflights by aircraft, envisioned in President Eisenhower's 1955 Open Skies proposal, along with on-site inspection proposals. The secrecy of the Soviet Union did not allow major breakthroughs except in areas like the presidential hot line and the Incidents at Sea Agreement.

12. Boutros Boutros-Ghali, *New Dimensions of Arms Regulation and Disarmament in the Post Cold War Era,* Report of the Secretary-General, United Nations A/C 1/47/7, 27 October 1992, pp. 18–19.

13. The White House, "Joint Statement on Parameters on Future Reductions in Nuclear Forces," Office of the White House Press Secretary, Helsinki, Finland, 21 March 1997.

14. Ibid.

15. Ibid.

16. See the address by President George W. Bush at the National Defense University on 1 May 2001, www.whitehouse.gov/news/releases/2001/05/20010501-10html.

17. Michael Krepon, "The Decade for Confidence-Building Measures," in Michael Krepon, Dominique M. McCoy, Matthew C. J. Rudolph, eds., *A Handbook of Confidence-Building Measures for Regional Security* (Washington, DC: Henry L. Stimson Center, September 1993), p. 1.

18. Verification regimes are expensive, and more and more they are seen as contributing only marginally to intelligence in the monitoring of agreements. This trend can be expected to continue to the extent that arms control agreements deal with items that are more challenging and difficult to monitor. Of course, on the basis of future budgetary decisions, verification may become far less important, and perhaps absent from some agreements. To the extent that societies become more open, this should not necessarily pose grave problems. Moreover, it may be the case that arms control negotiations and agreements will in the future be given less attention by presidents, parliaments, and publics than other issues. This will raise anew the question of the value of verification.

Suggested Readings

Arnett, Eric, ed. *Implementing the Comprehensive Test Ban: New Aspects of Definition, Organization, and Verification.* SIPRI Research Report No. 8. Oxford, UK: Oxford University Press, 1994.

Brown, James, ed. *Arms Control Issues for the Twenty-First Century.* Albuquerque, NM: Sandia National Laboratories, 1997.

Gallagher, Nancy W. *The Politics of Verification.* Baltimore: Johns Hopkins University Press, 1999.

Koulik, Sergey, and Richard Kokoski. *Conventional Arms Control: Perspectives on Verification.* Oxford, UK: Oxford University Press, 1995.

Krepon, Michael, ed. *A Handbook of Confidence-Building Measures for Regional Security,* 2nd ed. Washington, DC: Henry L. Stimson Center, January 1995.

Trapp, Ralf. *Verification Under the Chemical Weapons Convention: On-Site Inspection in Chemical Industry Facilities.* SIPRI Chemical and Biological Warfare Studies. Oxford, UK: Oxford University Press, 1993.

PART 2

PREVENTING THE SPREAD OF ARMS

6

Strategic Nuclear Arms Control

Forrest E. Waller Jr.

During the darkest days of the Seven Years' War (1756–1763), a young Scot at the University of Glasgow went to see his professor of moral philosophy to talk about the war. Great Britain was fighting in Europe, North America, India, Africa, the West Indies, and the seas between. The war's cost in treasure and blood was staggering, and the young student feared that the war would ruin the nation. But the professor, Adam Smith, understood how vast the moral and material resources of a nation were.[1] Trying to calm his student's fears, Smith said, "There is a great deal of ruin in a country." This remark summarized centuries of European experience. Wars came and went. Wars were won and lost. Nations and societies suffered, but they survived.

Almost two centuries later, at the end of another great world war, U.S. political leaders concluded that the nature of warfare had changed. Atom bombs, the wonder weapon of World War II, had the power to rain fatal ruin on even the most powerful civilization. They believed that it was essential to negotiate political controls between adversaries in order to manage the risk of nuclear war. Although U.S. leaders were pessimistic about negotiating nuclear arms control agreements with the emerging superpower rival, the Soviet Union, they attempted it anyway. For 50 years strategic nuclear arms control was the crown jewel of U.S. arms control efforts. The Cold War standoff between the United States and Soviet Union made arms control nearly impossible, but it also clarified why the effort was necessary. Eventually their perseverance paid off. Strategic nuclear arms control became one of the most successful arenas of U.S.-Soviet cooperation.

In this chapter I discuss the history and future of strategic nuclear arms control. I examine the contemporary argument against pursuing additional nuclear arms control arrangements with Moscow, as well as alternate futures for nuclear arms control. The purpose of such a forecast is analytic and didactic. Four futures describe the objectives, expected outcomes, and strengths and weaknesses of a spectrum of plausible arms control strategies. By understanding them, we can see an integrated picture of strategic nuclear arms control—past, present, future.

The Problem of Terminology

When discussing strategic nuclear arms control one faces the immediate problem of defining the relevant terms. This chapter uses two terms interchangeably—*strategic nuclear arms control* and *strategic offensive arms control.*

International arms control specialists cannot always agree on a precise definition for the terms *strategic nuclear arms* and *strategic offensive arms.*[2] So *strategic nuclear arms control* means different things to different people. For some, the word *nuclear* is the key to the definition. Explosive nuclear yield is the operative element describing the weapons that must be controlled. For others, the *delivery platform* is key. A *strategic nuclear arm* is an intercontinental delivery system equipped to carry nuclear weapons. For another group, the *target* is the operative element. A *strategic nuclear weapon* is one targeted to explode on one's homeland. For a final group, the term *offensive arms* is crucial. Those who build nuclear bombs fear that nuclear arms control negotiations inevitably will reveal sensitive information about nuclear weapon design. They prefer to avoid reference to nuclear arms altogether and list the weapon systems under political control (for example, B-52).

The U.S. government combines the second and fourth approaches to reach its definition (delivery platform and nature of the weapon). *Strategic offensive arms* are intercontinental delivery systems equipped to deliver nuclear weapons.[3] The United States identifies these systems by name (e.g., SS-18, Minuteman III). As used in this chapter, *strategic nuclear arms control* and *strategic offensive arms control* refer to the same thing: the imposition of political or legal constraints on the arms designated to carry out intercontinental nuclear attacks.

Historical Background

A U.S. undergraduate student at the beginning of the twenty-first century probably cannot recall a day during which the United States wasn't the most powerful nation on earth. This was not always so, and it is not likely to remain so forever. Beginning in the late 1940s, following the end of World War II, the United States and the Soviet Union became locked in the high-stakes Cold War. The evolution of U.S. strategic arms control policy from 1945 to 1991 reflected the intensity of the struggle between the two superpowers' political systems.

U.S. strategic arms control policy can be divided into two periods. From 1945 to 1967, the United States pursued a variety of multilateral efforts to control nuclear arms, including strategic nuclear arms.[4] From 1968 to the present, the United States has pursued bilateral nuclear arms control initiatives directly with the Soviet Union; some but not all of these involved strategic offensive arms. During each period, the United States struggled to balance its vital interest in controlling nuclear weapons with its urgent need to rely on nuclear weapons to deter Soviet aggression.

Multilateral Efforts to Control Nuclear Arms (1945-1967)

On 16 July 1945, the United States detonated the world's first nuclear explosive device at a test site near Alamogordo, New Mexico. The detonation, small by current standards, was the equivalent of 21,000 tons of high explosives. Among the handful of U.S. political, military, and scientific leaders who knew about the test, the atomic bomb caused grave concern about the future of U.S. national security. Most understood that the United States could not base its security indefinitely on its monopoly of atomic weapons. Eventually, other states would develop them and pose a threat to the United States, perhaps even to its survival as a nation.[5]

The Truman administration. In September 1945 Secretary of War Henry Stimson proposed to President Harry Truman that the United States discuss the control and limitation of atomic weapons with the Soviet Union. In March 1946 an interagency group met at Dumbarton Oaks in Washington, D.C., to develop the first U.S. nuclear arms control proposal, a plan for comprehensive nuclear disarmament. The major alternative to arms control was nuclear deterrence—peace through the threat of devastating nuclear retaliation. Deterrence had forceful advocates. In November 1945 U.S. Army General Henry H. "Hap" Arnold, an aviation pioneer who figured prominently in the eventual formation of the U.S. Air Force, provided Secretary of War Stimson an assessment of the atom bomb's impact on postwar national security.

> This country . . . must recognize that real security . . . in the visible future will rest on our ability to take immediate offensive action with overwhelming force. It must be apparent to a potential aggressor that an attack on the United States would be followed by an immensely devastating [nuclear] air attack on him.[6]

When confronted with the difficult choice between nuclear arms control and nuclear weapon programs for deterrence, Truman set a precedent that other presidents would follow for decades: he chose both options. In mid-1946 Truman approved the Dumbarton Oaks arms control proposal and, in early 1947, expressed shock when told how few atom bombs the United States actually had.[7] Truman ordered the largest nuclear weapon modernization effort in U.S. history.

The Baruch Plan. On 14 June 1946 U.S. Ambassador Barnard Baruch introduced the U.S. arms control proposal at the first session of the UN Atomic Energy Commission. Thereafter the proposal was known as the Baruch Plan. It called for the complete transfer of all U.S. atomic weapons, atomic power facilities, and atomic know-how to an international organization responsible for all aspects of the development and use of atomic energy. The plan denied the UN Security Council a veto right on matters of compliance with atomic energy restrictions. Most important, the plan gave the United Nations authority to compel national compliance, backed up by the use of force.[8]

The Soviets rejected the U.S. proposal immediately, calling it a transparent effort to monopolize nuclear weapon technology. The Soviets counterproposed that the United States disassemble its nuclear weapon infrastructure and completely disarm before an international agreement was negotiated. U.S. allies in Western Europe were equally unwilling to accept the Baruch Plan. By the end of 1946 the United States could convince only China to put the Baruch Plan to a test-vote. For 10 years, the United States negotiated its nuclear disarmament initiatives at the UN Disarmament Commission without success.

Low-hanging fruit. The failure of the Baruch Plan, and continued deterioration in U.S.-Soviet relations, led the United States to abandon its approach to nuclear arms control. Instead of comprehensive disarmament, the United States tried to negotiate multilateral agreements dealing with discrete arms control opportunities.[9] The United States was looking for arms control successes, so it selected the opportunities carefully. Most of the U.S. initiatives were noncontroversial and had low risk of failure. Many were based on the assumption that it was easier to ban a nuclear practice that had not yet appeared than it was to control a practice once it had begun.[10] It also helped the success of the negotiations that arms control opportunities prohibited nothing the United States or the Soviet Union desired. Three treaties prohibited nuclear weapon deployment in environments that were extremely inhospitable (Antarctica, outer space, and the ocean seabed). Deployments in any of those areas would have inflated program costs and would have raised nearly insurmountable problems for nuclear weapon maintenance and security.[11] The treaties represented successes, but their contributions to national security were modest.

The Limited Test Ban Treaty. Two multilateral treaties negotiated during this period were clear exceptions to this typology, that is, their contributions to national security were significant. The first was the Limited Test Ban Treaty (LTBT) of 1963. The LTBT forbade nuclear testing anywhere on earth except underground and under conditions prohibiting the spread of radioactive debris. The LTBT negotiations attracted and sustained considerable public and international interest due to the danger atmospheric nuclear testing posed (from radioactive fallout) to public health and the environment. However, the LTBT shared at least one commonality with the other three agreements. Ending atmospheric testing was uncontroversial. Neither the United States nor the Soviet Union wanted to poison the environment with their nuclear tests.

The Nuclear Non-Proliferation Treaty. The second exception was the Nuclear Non-Proliferation Treaty (NPT) of 1968. The NPT forbade providing nuclear weapons and nuclear weapon technology to other states. Neither the United States nor the Soviet Union wanted to see other states deploy nuclear weapons. Multiple nuclear adversaries added more uncertainty and unpredictability to nuclear relationships. By the mid-1960s three other states—the United Kingdom, France, and the People's Republic of China—had detonated nuclear devices. The United States and Soviet Union led the effort to produce the NPT. However, non–nuclear weapon states demanded that the five nuclear powers accept balanced obligations. In return for giving up the legal right to build nuclear weapons, non–nuclear weapon states insisted that the nuclear powers negotiate an end to the arms race and achieve disarmament under verifiable conditions. The five nuclear powers accepted the obligation, and the non–nuclear weapon states have never let them forget it.

Alliances. The period 1945–1967 was one of intense alliance-formation for the United States. The United States and its regional allies created the North Atlantic Treaty Organization, the Southeast Asia Treaty Organization, and the Central Treaty Organization to contain Soviet expansion. The United States also signed a series of mutual defense pacts with the same goal. These involved treaties with Australia, New Zealand, China (Taiwan), Japan, the Philippines, and the Republic of Korea (South Korea). To support these pacts, the United States sometimes threatened to use, or implied it would use, nuclear weapons to halt communist aggression and deter nuclear intimidation. Although not arms control per se, this "nuclear umbrella" allowed U.S. allies to avoid developing their own nuclear weapons. Thus, the security agreements had an effect similar to that sought in the NPT.

Bilateral Nuclear Arms Control (1968–2001)

In the late 1960s the United States abandoned its successful strategy of multilateral agreements to enter direct bilateral negotiations with the Soviet Union. Negotiations to limit strategic offensive arms had become a necessity for the United States due to Soviet deployment of hundreds of intercontinental ballistic missiles (ICBMs). This development was not a surprise. U.S. national security specialists had predicted nuclear stalemate for 20 years.[12] However, some in the United States began to wonder whether their counterparts in the Soviet Union had made the same prediction to Soviet leaders. Soviet strategic offensive arms modernization programs went beyond the quantitative requirement for equality. For the first time it appeared that the Soviet Union might deploy enough nuclear weapons of sufficient power to threaten the survivability of U.S. retaliatory forces. At roughly equal numbers, there was balance between the sides. However, if either side could eliminate the retaliatory forces of the other in a first strike, there might be an incentive to strike first in a crisis. U.S. analysts considered such a situation unstable and intolerable.

The Nixon administration. President Richard Nixon came into office in January 1969 hoping to restore U.S. nuclear supremacy by modernizing forces. However, once in office he understood there was no hope of deploying more forces than the Soviet Union. The Soviets were deploying 200 ICBMs per year.[13] Nixon turned to arms control for help. Although he had a reputation as a cold warrior, Nixon tried to change the atmosphere of tension and conflict between Washington and Moscow. In late 1971 Nixon and Soviet leader Leonid Brezhnev signed the Accident Measures Agreement. In it, both sides pledged to improve technical safeguards against accidental and unauthorized use of nuclear weapons, notify each other should the risk of nuclear war arise, and provide advance notification of missile launches into international airspace or waters. The Accident Measures Agreement also expanded the 1963 U.S.-Soviet memorandum establishing the "hot line" direct-communications system. In 1972 the United States and Soviet Union signed the Incidents at Sea Agreement, committing the U.S. and Soviet navies to follow safe practices when their warships were in close proximity.[14] In 1973 Nixon and Brezhnev signed the Prevention of Nuclear War Agreement. In it, both sides committed to avoid confrontations likely to lead to nuclear war and, if such crises arose anyway, to consult with each other on ways to solve differences peacefully.

During the Nixon administration arms control policy became a full partner in achieving U.S. national security objectives. The administration defined its security requirements in terms that facilitated arms control. Weapons system requirements and arms control planning were closely integrated.[15] The objective of U.S. strategic arms control policy was to ensure strategic stability by assuring the ability of the United States to destroy the Soviet Union. Although Nixon considered trying to reduce the vulnerability of the United States to Soviet strategic arms, there was nothing practical he could do about it. Many considered the resulting condition—mutual assured destruction (MAD), in which both societies were mutually vulnerable to annihilation—a good thing, because both sides had a powerful disincentive to go to war. Critics of MAD called it an immoral strategy. In practice, MAD was never an objective, doctrine, or strategy of the U.S. government. Mutual societal vulnerability was a simple fact that no administration could change.

The Nixon administration negotiated three strategic arms limitation agreements: the Anti-Ballistic Missile Treaty of 1972 and two agreements limiting strategic offensive arms; the forum for negotiating all three was the Strategic Arms Limitation Talks (SALT).[16] The first strategic offensive arms agreement (SALT I)[17] was a temporary agreement limiting the growth of strategic forces, whereas the more detailed second treaty (SALT II)[18] froze the level of deployed strategic weapons. SALT I froze each side's forces at unequal levels, placing the United States at a numerical disadvantage in deployed delivery systems. As the quality of Soviet ballistic missiles improved, the vulnerability of U.S. strategic nuclear forces to destruction in a preemptive strike became an urgent concern.[19]

The Carter administration.   The Jimmy Carter administration inherited the SALT II negotiations.[20] President Carter attempted to redefine the SALT II Treaty and push it toward more weapons reductions.[21] However, the Soviets refused to change the objective of the agreement so late in the game. The SALT II Treaty was supposed to help the U.S. force vulnerability problem, but conservative critics pointed out that the treaty did nothing to improve the survivability of U.S. retaliatory forces. They complained that SALT II made matters worse by granting the Soviets unilateral advantages in heavy ICBMs. They also questioned whether SALT II was verifiable. Liberal critics pointed out that SALT II did not limit deployed warheads, and they predicted that deployed nuclear weapons would grow in number as modern multiple-warhead ballistic missile systems replaced older single-warhead systems.

The critique of SALT II was bitter medicine for the Carter administration. The joint chiefs of staff testified in favor of the treaty, provided that U.S. strategic modernization went forward. Congress appeared willing to support both the treaty and modernization programs. However, in December 1979 the Soviets invaded Afghanistan. Understanding that the U.S. Senate would not ratify the SALT II Treaty, the administration withdrew the treaty from consideration.

The Reagan and Bush administrations. The critique of SALT II resonated with California governor Ronald Reagan. He considered SALT II fatally flawed and made arms control a major issue in his 1980 presidential campaign. When he became president in 1981, he refused to resubmit the SALT II Treaty to the Senate for advice and consent to ratification. Reagan proposed entirely new bilateral negotiations whose objective was the deep reduction of nuclear arms. He also initiated the Strategic Defense Initiative, a research and development program to provide the United States with a nationwide missile defense system. The complementary initiatives formed Reagan's overall strategy to end MAD. The U.S. nuclear arms control efforts begun during the Reagan years succeeded spectacularly. The 1987 Intermediate-Range Nuclear Forces Treaty (INF) eliminated an entire class of nuclear arms.[22] The INF Treaty also set new standards in verification, data exchange, and on-site inspection.

President George Bush inherited the Reagan arms control agenda and completed the greatest strategic offensive arms reduction treaties in history. The Strategic Arms Reduction Treaty (START) of 1991 reduced U.S. and Soviet strategic offensive forces by one-third, limiting both sides to no more than 1,600 deployed delivery systems and 6,000 deployed warheads. START built on the INF precedents in verification, establishing a regime for data exchange, open telemetry, and multiple kinds of on-site inspection. The START Treaty, at 400 pages, is the longest and most complex treaty of its kind. U.S. and Soviet delegations negotiated for nearly nine years to complete it. By the time START was finished the Cold War had ended, and the Soviet Union was on the verge of political and economic collapse.

As the START Treaty was being prepared for signature, the U.S. Department of Defense prepared a list of operational practices, nuclear systems, and nuclear modernization programs it no longer considered necessary. The department recommended to the White House that the United States secure parallel cuts in Soviet nuclear programs. The recommendation resulted in the Presidential Nuclear Initiatives of 1991–1992.[23] In September 1991 and January 1992 President Bush announced several unilateral U.S. steps to further reduce nuclear tensions and invited Moscow to match them. Soviet President Mikhail Gorbachev and Russian President Boris Yeltsin responded with unilateral initiatives of their own.[24] As a result of these initiatives, both sides withdrew substantial numbers of nonstrategic nuclear weapons from forward deployment sites, canceled a variety of nuclear force modernization programs (strategic and nonstrategic), and relaxed the alert posture of their respective strategic retaliatory forces.

The dissolution of the Soviet Union in December 1991 left the successor Russian Federation destitute. As the scope of Russia's economic plight became clear, the United States recognized that Moscow could not afford to deploy the number of strategic offensive arms permitted under the START

Treaty. Sensing an opportunity to reduce the threat posed by Russia's nuclear arsenal and to lessen the expense of U.S. strategic forces, the Bush administration proposed a second round of START. In January 1993, after six months of negotiation, the two sides signed the START II Treaty, which reduced the ceilings on strategic offensive warheads from 6,000 to 3,000–3,500.[25] President Bush submitted the treaty to the Senate for advice and consent to ratification on 20 January 1993, his last day in office.

The Clinton administration. When the Soviet Union collapsed at the end of 1991, U.S. Senators Sam Nunn and Richard Lugar feared that political turmoil there would lead to the spread of Soviet nuclear weapons to radical states and terrorist groups in the Near East. They sponsored legislation to help the Russian Federation secure its nuclear weapons and provide stable employment to scientists and technicians employed in Soviet nuclear weapon fabrication. Styled as "cooperative threat reduction," the Nunn-Lugar program formed the bulk of the Clinton administration's nuclear arms control effort. Building on the Bush-Gorbachev-Yeltsin nuclear initiatives, Clinton and Yeltsin agreed to detarget their ICBMs and submarine-launched ballistic missiles (SLBMs), that is, they agreed to aim their missiles routinely on open areas of the ocean, rather than on targets in Russia and the United States, to prevent a catastrophe from occurring by accident. They later agreed to establish the Joint Data Exchange Center in Moscow to share ballistic missile early warning data. The purpose of the center was to prevent a catastrophic misjudgment as Russia's system for detecting ballistic missile attack slowly decayed. In 1997 Clinton and Yeltsin set goals for deeper nuclear reductions, to levels of 2,000–2,500 deployed strategic warheads, in future START negotiations.[26] The timing of negotiations depended on entry into force of the START II Treaty.

Strategic Nuclear Arms Control Today

Strategic nuclear arms control after the Cold War began brilliantly, but in recent years it has faltered badly. George Bush and Mikhail Gorbachev signed the first START Treaty just prior to the collapse of the Soviet Union. Understandably the treaty was of much lower priority to Russians than sorting out the political and constitutional arrangements by which they would be governed. So START I entered into force much later than expected. Nonetheless, the parties implemented it successfully and met many treaty limits ahead of schedule. They completed START II negotiations with breathtaking speed. However, the agreement immediately ran into political trouble in Moscow. The agreement is admittedly generous to the United States.[27]

Eventually both sides ratified the START II Treaty. However, START II has yet to enter into force, and it is doubtful that it ever will. Russian ratification is conditioned on U.S. observance of the ABM Treaty, a requirement the administration of President George W. Bush and many Republican members of Congress find unacceptable.[28] Yet without START II entry into force, START III negotiations cannot begin. The strategic arms reduction process that began in the early 1980s—arguably history's most successful arms control initiative—ended at midnight on 31 December 2001 when the parties completed the implementation of the START I Treaty.

For some the end of formal strategic nuclear arms control negotiations is long overdue. Many national security experts consider it an anachronism for several reasons. First, the international security environment has changed dramatically. The Soviet Union is gone, its empire has crumbled, and Moscow is unlikely to ever be a superpower again. Second, the United States and Russia are not enemies. They cooperate on many fronts. War between them is unthinkable. Third, the security threat to the United States comes from rogue states (aggressive regional powers that hope to dominate their regions) and terrorist organizations associated with them. For some of these adversaries, the United States and its allies are the only real obstacle to their ambitions. The rogues are acquiring ballistic missiles and nuclear, biological, and chemical weapons to deter foreign (that is, U.S.) military intervention. Fourth, strategic offensive arms control contributes to an adversarial atmosphere between the United States and Russia. It perpetuates obsolete ideas like MAD. Some even claim that formal arms control actually interferes with unilateral arms reduction, because the United States and Russia hang on to weapons they don't need in order to trade them in some future arms control negotiation. Finally, formal strategic offensive arms control inhibits missile defense programs that U.S. security interests require.

These analysts conclude that the United States and Russia ought to proceed unilaterally to the strategic nuclear force levels that make sense for each. Parity of forces is not required for either. The implication for U.S. national security policy is that additional strategic offensive arms control is unnecessary and that some existing bilateral arms control agreements, like the ABM Treaty, should be changed or discarded. Formal strategic offensive arms control has come to an end because U.S. national security strategy during the Cold War worked. Cold War arms control played its part, but now its part is over. Different threats face the United States, and we need tools tailored to meet those threats.

For other national security analysts, the work of strategic offensive arms control is unfinished. Even though the likelihood of war between the United States and Russia is remote, there is always the risk that conflict could result from accident, miscalculation, misjudgment, or unauthorized use of nuclear weapons. There is persistent concern in the United States about the alert postures, safety, and security of nuclear weapons. Not even the most ardent believer in strategic arms control's success would claim that START has finished the job of nuclear weapon reduction. START requires the destruction of delivery systems, not warheads. Many hundreds of strategic warheads are in storage even though the delivery systems for them no longer exist. Thousands of nonstrategic nuclear weapons remain in the U.S. and Russian inventories. According to this school of thought, formal strategic nuclear arms control retains an urgent purpose.

Visions for the Future of Strategic Nuclear Arms Control

Given the divergence of views, what is the future of strategic nuclear arms control? This section examines the objectives, characteristics, strengths, and weaknesses of four alternate futures for strategic offensive arms control: (1) continuation of the current formal nuclear arms control approach; (2) abandonment of that approach without replacement; (3) reorganization of the entire nuclear arms control effort emphasizing key principles and objectives; and (4) transformation of strategic offensive arms control into a new kind of enterprise.[29]

Continuation of Formal Strategic Arms Control Policy

The reason for continuing the strategic arms reductions begun 20 years ago is to complete unfinished business. That business includes implementing the START II Treaty and negotiating, signing, and implementing START III. The START process is the most successful arms control process in history. Through it, both parties agree that their security requirements allow much deeper reductions. Both sides have agreed to solemnize their agreement in treaties.

The continuation of the current approach will involve formal negotiations, legal agreements, and legislative scrutiny under appropriate constitutional arrangements. Upon ratification, the process transforms to a period of implementation, routine evaluation of compliance issues, and efforts to improve the effectiveness and viability of the treaties. The expected outcome of continuing formal strategic nuclear arms control would be a reduction of Cold War strategic offensive arms levels by more than 90 percent from their peak levels, to 1,000–2,000 deployed warheads, and measures to ensure the irreversibility of those reductions. By any measure, these are important goals.

The reasons for continuing the current approach are the recognized strengths of the ritual arms control process. The process is deeply dignified.

It is cautious. It is respectful of the rights of state parties. It confers status on the participants. It reflects the prerogatives of legislative institutions and constitutional forms. It is observable to third parties, including the public. It is the most respected process for arms reduction.

The reasons for ending the strategic arms reduction process are to avoid its collateral consequences. Although it may be possible to deploy limited missile defenses while continuing START, for example, it is unlikely that the United States could avoid either stricter constraints on its defenses than supporters would like or unacceptable impact on the nonnuclear capabilities of U.S. strategic forces.[30] In May 2002, Presidents Bush and Putin signed the Treaty of Moscow setting ceilings on deployed strategic offensive arms (1,700–2,200 warheads for each party by 2012) comparable to those envisioned in START III. This treaty ends the START process, though not in a completely satisfactory manner. START II would have banned MIRVed ICBMs and all heavy ICBMs. START III would have taken steps to make sure that nuclear reductions were permanent, and to reduce the levels of tactical nuclear warheads. The Treaty of Moscow did none of these things.

Abandonment of Strategic Offensive Arms Control

The reasons for abandoning START are to eliminate artifacts of the Cold War: MAD and the notion that Russia is a U.S. equal. This approach requires one to believe that U.S.-Russia relations since the Cold War are irreversible, that Russian nuclear arms no longer form a reasonable threat to U.S. security no matter how many there are, and that addressing rogue states and terrorism is more important than continuing the START process.

This approach is distinguished by continued observance of existing nuclear arms control agreements; abandonment of START II, START III, and the ABM Treaty; the absence of formal negotiations whose purpose is a legally binding arms control agreement; and increased reliance on transparency and stability-building measures.

The strengths of this approach are its flexibility in arranging force structures. If the security environment deteriorates, Washington could build forces without serious constraint from arms control treaties. If the environment improves, it could go to lower levels without delay. The predictable outcome of such an approach would be a shift in U.S. resources from those formations that deter Russia to those appropriate for warfare with rogue states and terrorists.

The weaknesses of this approach are its unpredictability and reduced confidence. Absent negotiated arms control agreements, neither the United States nor Russia has an obligation to follow the other to lower levels of strategic nuclear arms or to provide the other insight into future plans. Unilateral arms reductions may not be appreciated or matched, causing the presumed unimportance of the nuclear balance to wear thin. Inevitably such an approach will cause both sides to behave more cautiously about reductions than they might have done with a treaty in place. Abandonment of the START process also is likely to disappoint third parties that look to Washington and Moscow to make permanent progress toward nuclear disarmament.

Reorganization Around Key Principles

The reason for reorganizing the START process is to focus on the issues that matter most. For two generations, U.S. policymakers have pursued strategic arms control for security, stability, and predictability.[31] During the Cold War all three objectives were judged equally important. Today that's no longer true.

The risk of premeditated nuclear war between the United States and Russia is low. New strategic offensive arms control initiatives might focus on other problems—for example, reducing the chance of accidental or unauthorized use of nuclear weapons; or making irreversible the nuclear reductions made thus far; or, if the security and safety of remaining weapons are of concern, exchanging intelligence information and/or cooperatively developing security technology. The principles around which the initiatives could form are open and flexible. They could involve any aspect of security, stability, or predictability. They could involve issues of political convenience. For example, if the United States determined that mutual reduction of U.S. and Russian strategic offensive arms to 1,000–2,000 warheads—without a formal treaty—was the priority, Washington could persuade Moscow to enter a negotiation with the objective of creating an executive agreement. The strength of the reorganized approach is its flexibility.

Transforming Strategic Offensive Arms Control

The reason for transforming strategic offensive arms control is to do something more ambitious than can be accomplished in START. This approach would apply a transformation paradigm to the arms control process applying new principles, defining new objectives, introducing new technologies, and/or creating new organizations. The strength of transforming the U.S. approach to arms control is that it is likely to lead to a renaissance of activity focused in those areas where arms control is best able to make a contribution. And where it is unable to make a contribution, it will wither and die. Transformation is a direct answer to the indictment aimed at U.S. arms control organizations by those who believe them to be out of step with the times. The weakness of the transformation paradigm is that government does not transform easily. Such strategies are difficult enough in business, where corporate officials have maximum authority to introduce change in organization, staff, and budget authority. In government, almost no one has exclusive authority to introduce change. Often there is no incentive to try.

New principles. Nuclear arms control has been a highly compartmented effort throughout its history. As the number of strategic offensive systems and warheads drops thanks to START, the START process covers an ever-smaller portion of the remaining nuclear inventories. A new principle for strategic nuclear arms control could be *inclusivity.* In addition to the traditional systems, a transformed approach might include all fields related to strategic offensive arms: nuclear testing, weapons fabrication, special nuclear materials production and disposition, and environmental protection. Another approach could be to include all nuclear weapons regardless of how they are delivered to their targets. This approach would begin to capture the tens of thousands of nonstrategic nuclear weapons.[32]

New objectives. Traditional strategic arms control concentrated on limiting the number of weapon systems and warheads. New objectives could include weapons safety, weapons security, and prevention of unauthorized or accidental use. The United States and Russia have taken the first steps in weapons security with the Cooperative Threat Reduction program and prevention of accidental use by agreeing to form the Joint Data Exchange Center in Moscow.[33]

New technologies. Efforts to share advanced technology to support arms control objectives have a checkered history. In START, the United States attempted to introduce a variety of technologies to support "tagging" of mobile ballistic missiles. The efforts were unsuccessful because there was no mutual advantage in applying technology for that purpose. There is mutual advantage, however, in technologies for disposing special nuclear material and supporting the finest security and safety systems for nuclear weapon storage. Technology exchange in these areas offers the prospect of significant progress toward U.S. and Russian arms control objectives.

New organizations. Evolution is the most difficult challenge facing any organization. The arms control community has undergone significant organizational change since the end of the Cold War.[34] However, none of these changes transformed any aspect of U.S. arms control, not even in the agencies affected by reorganization. Organizational transformation must lead to innovation, cultural change, and institutional rebirth.[35] This approach differs from reinventing government in that one expects some organizations to shut their doors permanently and new ones to emerge.

Conclusion

When one considers the 50-plus years of the U.S. strategic nuclear arms control experience, the contemporary international security environment, and the spectrum of plausible nuclear arms control futures, several connected themes emerge. First, arms control policies must be appropriate for their environment. They do not occur, and cannot succeed, in a vacuum. Arms control must address appropriate objects of concern with measures within reach of the politics of the day. For better or worse, contemporary political possibility in the United States portends a departure from past strategic offensive arms control practice, perhaps to a more unilateral approach. Today the United States is far less concerned about the thousands of Russian nuclear weapons than it is about a handful of weapons of mass destruction under the control of rogue states or even a single weapon in the hands of a terrorist. Ballistic missile defense will be a priority for the United States. To the degree that strategic nuclear arms control conflicts with missile defense, the United States appears ready to sacrifice nuclear arms control.

Second, the history of strategic nuclear arms control is one of abandonment. The United States abandons arms control initiatives when they fail. It abandons successful initiatives to achieve more ambitious ends. The current course of U.S. policy departs from previous U.S. arms control experience by abandoning a successful arms control venture to pursue arms control objectives that are less ambitious, are less predictable, and inspire less confidence.

Third, the international security environment radically changed for the United States on 11 September 2001, and it can change more. Russia's social and political order is weak. It may deteriorate further with dangerous consequences for the spread of Russian nuclear weapons among rogue states and terrorist groups. Therefore, the United States can ill-afford to ignore Russia's nuclear weapons, even if bilateral relations are good. Strategic nuclear arms control is a proven tool for shaping the threat environment so that—come what may—the United States can effectively manage the security risk posed by Russian nuclear weapons.

Fourth, strategic nuclear arms control isn't just for adversaries. When the United States and Soviet Union decided to negotiate bilateral nuclear arms control agreements in the late 1960s, multilateral nuclear arms control continued. Regional neighbors negotiated treaties that declared their regions to be nuclear weapon–free zones. Today most of the Southern Hemisphere is a nuclear weapon–free zone thanks to the overlap of such agreements.[36] The success of nuclear arms control among friendly states points to a fundamental weakness in arguments against formal nuclear arms control.

Strategic nuclear arms control is a hearty child. It survived bad times. It will survive good times. Cold War strategic nuclear arms control may be over, but strategic offensive arms control has a future. Some of those futures are exciting and useful. They have the potential to address real problems having real consequences for U.S. national security. Given vision and energy, U.S. strategic nuclear arms control efforts have more history to make.

Notes

1. Adam Smith authored *The Theory of Moral Sentiments* (1759) and *The Wealth of Nations* (1776).

2. The reasons for the lack of a definition are complicated. The United States did not want to define *strategic nuclear weapon* in a way that would include its theater nuclear weapons located in Europe and the Far East. In addition, the agency responsible for building U.S. nuclear weapons (first the Atomic Energy Commission, then the Department of Energy) never wanted to define what a *nuclear weapon* was for fear of revealing critical nuclear weapon design information.

3. Although it may seem paradoxical, there is no requirement that an intercontinental delivery system actually carry nuclear weapons for it to be captured under strategic offensive arms control treaties.

4. Multilateral arms control efforts involve several nations or more. In this period, most of the multilateral efforts occurred in the United Nations Committee on Disarmament.

5. Truman was at the Potsdam conference shortly after the Trinity test. When informed that the United States had developed a devastating new weapon, Josef Stalin and V. M. Molotov pretended not to know that Truman was talking about atomic weapons. The Soviets had had an atomic bomb development program since April 1943. Molotov wrote in his 1991 memoirs that the Soviets knew the United States had only one or two weapons.

6. *Final Report to the Secretary of War* (Washington, DC: War Department, November 1945).

7. It was fewer than fifteen, none of them an assembled weapon. Michael O. Wheeler, *Nuclear Weapons and the Korean War,* Lessons from Nuclear History Project (McLean, VA: Center for National Security Negotiations, November 1994), p. 54.

8. R. Joseph DeSutter. "Strategic Arms Control: Theory and Practice," in Schuyler Foerster and Edward Wright, eds., *American Defense Policy,* 6th ed. (Baltimore: Johns Hopkins University Press, 1993), p. 352.

9. During this 10-year period there were a series of international crises in Europe, the Middle East, and Far East that pitted the United States and its allies against the Soviet bloc or its clients: the communist coup in Czechoslovakia, a series of crises over Berlin, the Suez crisis, the Korean War, and the crisis over Quemoy and Matsu.

10. U.S. Arms Control and Disarmament Agency, *Arms Control and Disarmament Agreements: Texts and Histories of the Negotiation* (Washington, DC: Arms Control and Disarmament Agency, 1990), p. 20.

11. The agreements were the Antarctic Treaty, Outer Space Treaty, and Seabed Arms Control Treaty.

12. NSC-162/2, the analysis on which the doctrine of massive retaliation was based, had predicted the loss of U.S. nuclear superiority.

13. During the years that the United States and the Soviet Union negotiated SALT I, the Soviet ICBM force grew from 1,000 to 1,500 deployed missiles and the number of SLBM launchers quadrupled. The payload of some heavy Soviet ICBMs was so large that it threatened the survival of U.S. missiles based at heavily fortified hardened silos. During the same period, the U.S. nuclear force structure remained steady at 1,054 ICBMs and 656 SLBMs. These numbers are deceiving, however. The United States was deploying multiple independently targetable reentry vehicles (MIRVs) aboard its ICBMs and SLBMs. So in overall numbers of deployed ballistic missile warheads, the United States had the advantage.

14. During times of tension, U.S. and Soviet surface fleets often found themselves in close proximity. It was not unusual for ships to try to shoulder each other out of the way. These dangerous incidents exacerbated military tensions, and U.S. leaders were concerned that unsafe maritime practices between fleets would spark a war.

15. Jerome H. Kahan, *Security in the Nuclear Age* (Washington, DC: Brookings Institution, 1975), p. 171.

16. The SALT process established the relationship between strategic offensive and defensive forces that has existed ever since. The SALT negotiations also established mutual assured destruction (MAD) as the basis of the U.S.-Soviet nuclear relationship. Although three presidential administrations have tried to end MAD, it remains the underlying fact behind nuclear deterrence and the nuclear balance between the United States and Russia.

17. "Interim Agreement Between the United States of America and the Union of Soviet Socialist Republics on Certain Measures with Respect to the Limitation of Strategic Offensive Arms" (1972). The interim agreement was to last only five years. It allowed both sides to complete missile launchers under construction, but they could build no more afterward. The Soviets deployed more than 1,600 ICBMs whereas the United States deployed only 1,054. Moreover, the Soviets were permitted to deploy up to 950 SLBMs compared to 710 for the United States.

18. "Treaty Between the United States and Union of Soviet Socialist Republics on the Limitation of Strategic Offensive Arms." The objective of the United States in SALT II was to secure equal limits on the number of deployed strategic nuclear delivery vehicles. The parties set the limit at 2,400 delivery vehicles including ICBMs, SLBMs, and heavy bombers. They set a sublimit of 1,320 ballistic missiles with MIRVs. The treaty also banned the construction of new ICBM launchers and limited the number of new types of strategic nuclear delivery vehicles that the sides could deploy after entry into force of the treaty.

19. Qualitative improvements include the number of warheads aboard missiles, the yield of those warheads, and the accuracy of the missile.

20. The SALT II Treaty did not deal with deployed warheads. Both the United States and Soviet Union were deploying MIRVs aboard their ICBMs and SLBMs. So the number of deployed warheads was expanding geometrically in each nation's force.

21. SALT II required the Soviets to reduce their deployed strategic nuclear delivery vehicles by about 200 in order to meet the 2,400/1,320 ceilings.

22. The INF Treaty eliminated only guided missiles—ballistic and cruise—within a narrow spectrum of combat range. It did not eliminate aircraft systems in the same range category. The INF Treaty did not capture strategic offensive arms, because such systems were outside the definition of intermediate-range nuclear weapons.

23. In September 1991 and January 1992 the United States unilaterally promised to remove from alert status all ICBMs scheduled for deactivation under START, accelerate the elimination of such systems once START was ratified, terminate the mobile Peacekeeper program, cease production of Peacekeeper ICBMs, terminate the Small ICBM program, cease production of new warheads (W-88) for sea-based ballistic missiles, remove all U.S. strategic bombers from alert, cancel the SRAM II program, and halt purchase of the advanced cruise missile.

24. Soviet/Russian unilateral initiatives included removal of 503 ICBMs from alert, restrictions on rail-mobile ICBM production/operation/deployment, termination of a small mobile ICBM, elimination of 130 ICBM silos, retirement of three SSBNs (nuclear ballistic missile submarines) and dismantlement of six others,

reduction of SSBNs on patrol by 50 percent, removal of heavy bombers from alert, termination of a short-range nuclear missile, cessation of production of two heavy bomber types, limitation of heavy bomber exercises to include no more than 30 aircraft, and cessation of production of existing types of long-range air-launched cruise missiles.

25. START II reduces permitted warhead ceilings to 3,000–3,500 deployed warheads, ends heavy bomber discount rules, eliminates all heavy ICBMs and MIRVed ICBMs, and allows greater flexibility in structuring ballistic missile forces for single warhead missiles.

26. The START III framework sets the following goals: a ceiling of 2,000–2,500 deployed strategic offensive arms, steps to make the reduction of such arms irreversible (e.g., through warhead elimination), and measures to apply constraints to nonstrategic nuclear weapons.

27. Russian objections to START II read like U.S. objections to SALT II. Russians complain that the treaty was negotiated in haste, calls for unequal Russian reductions, is too expensive to implement, and grants the United States military advantages contributing to U.S. superiority.

28. On 13 December 2001 the United States announced that it would withdraw from the ABM Treaty in six months.

29. Jim Dator, "Futures Studies in Higher Education," *American Behavioral Scientist* (November/December 1998): 304–305.

30. Deeper warhead reductions must come disproportionately from heavy bomber forces. Since the early 1990s heavy bombers have been earmarked for both nuclear and nonnuclear missions. They have proven their value as precision nonnuclear delivery platforms. Deep reductions would require U.S. bombers to be eliminated or converted. Either approach is unacceptable to the U.S. Air Force.

31. *Security* means reducing the risk of war between adversaries by reducing force structure and limiting force modernization. *Stability* means controlling the arms race, ensuring crisis stability, and effective crisis management. Arms control contributes to these by controlling the qualitative characteristics of nuclear forces, particularly those that prompt use in a crisis. *Predictability* refers to verification, data exchange, inspections, and cooperative measures designed to increase confidence in the balance of strategic offensive forces permitted under a treaty.

32. See Jeffrey A. Larsen and Kurt J. Klingenberger, eds., *Controlling Non-Strategic Nuclear Weapons: Obstacles and Opportunities* (Colorado Springs, CO: USAF Institute for National Security Studies, 2001).

33. The Cooperative Threat Reduction program has provided Russia with security technology to protect nuclear weapons and special nuclear materials. Its largest effort has been the construction of a large storage facility for the highly enriched uranium and plutonium removed from dismantled nuclear weapons.

34. The Arms Control and Disarmament Agency merged with the State Department in 2000. The Defense Department merged three defense agencies with arms control responsibilities into the Defense Threat Reduction Agency in 1998.

35. One way to do this is to create an "ambidextrous" organization, a small independent unit responsible for identifying and pursuing innovation. The upstart exists in parallel with traditional organizations. If the small unit succeeds, it draws resources from the traditional organization until, potentially, nothing is left of the traditional institution.

36. The treaties of Tlatelolco (Latin America), Rarotonga (South Pacific), Bangkok (Southeast Asia), and Pelindaba (Africa).

Suggested Readings

U.S. Arms Control and Disarmament Agency, *Arms Control and Disarmament Agreements: Texts and Histories of Negotiations*. Washington, DC: U.S. Government Printing Office, 1996.

Cirincione, J., ed. *Repairing the Regime: Preventing the Spread of Weapons of Mass Destruction*. New York: Routledge, 2000.

Newhouse, John. *Cold Dawn: The Story of SALT*. New York: Holt, Rinehart, and Winston, 1973.

Payne, Keith. *The Fallacies of Cold War Deterrence and a New Direction*. Lexington, KY: University Press of Kentucky, 2001.

7

Nuclear Proliferation

Leonard Spector

Since the early 1990s two contrasting views of nuclear proliferation—that is, the spread of nuclear weapons to additional states—have emerged among U.S. policymakers and specialists. One view perceives nuclear proliferation as fundamentally a political issue, a danger to global stability that is driven by the fears and ambitions of specific countries in specific circumstances. Proponents of this viewpoint argue that diplomatic measures, such as treaties, agreements, sanctions, incentives, and political engagement, although not completely successful, have been effective in limiting the spread of nuclear weapons in the past.[1] They believe that these tools are the key to managing—and potentially halting—nuclear proliferation in the future.

The second view sees nuclear proliferation most importantly as a growing and inevitable military threat to the United States and its allies. Proponents of this viewpoint note that during the 1990s diplomatic measures—despite very active efforts by the United States and other concerned states—were unable to restrain proliferation in a number of cases. They call for the United States to meet the increasing challenges in this area through heightened military preparedness—enhancing deterrence, developing preemptive countermeasures, and building defensive capabilities.[2]

Thoughtful advocates of each school realize that a combination of both approaches would be best, yet they will differ on the relative weight to be given diplomatic and military initiatives.[3] My intent in this chapter is to help readers judge the best course of action along this continuum, providing an understanding of the current state of nuclear proliferation (including some relevant history), a review of existing constraints on the further spread of nuclear arms, and an assessment of evolving trends that are likely to influence nuclear proliferation in the years ahead.

119

The Map of Nuclear Proliferation

Eight countries are known or believed to possess nuclear weapons. In order of their acquisition of nuclear arms, they are: the United States (1945), the Soviet Union (now the Russian Federation, 1949), the United Kingdom (1952), France (1960), China (1964), Israel (1967?), India (1974), and Pakistan (1989). In addition, North Korea may have become the ninth nuclear nation in 1994. South Africa acquired nuclear weapons in 1979 but eliminated its nuclear arsenal in 1991.[4] Only a handful of additional states are thought to be actively pursuing nuclear weapons, most notably Iran, Iraq, and possibly North Korea.[5] Given the central role of these weapons in international affairs, it is surprising that they have spread so slowly (see Figure 7.1).

In terms of scale, the United States and Russia each deploy roughly 6,000 nuclear warheads on strategic (long-range) systems and retain, according to one unclassified estimate, several thousand tactical nuclear weapons (deployed on shorter-range delivery systems or available for rapid deployment on them).[6] The arsenals of the other three long-recognized nuclear powers—Great Britain, France, and China—number in the hundreds. The Israeli, Indian, and Pakistani capabilities are considerably smaller; North Korean capabilities are minute. Even if U.S. and Russian arsenals were reduced to 1,700–2,200 deployed strategic warheads, as agreed by Russia and the United States in the May 2002 Moscow Treaty, the overall destructive power of those forces would continue to eclipse that of the other nuclear states for the foreseeable future.

Nonetheless, some regional powers may believe that even a handful of nuclear weapons might be enough to deter the United States from intervening

Figure 7.1 Nuclear-Weapon States Since 1945, Total Listed by Date Acquired

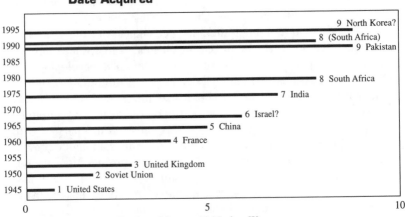

Number of States with Nuclear Weapons

militarily against them. They see small nuclear arsenals as providing the capability to intimidate nonnuclear neighbors, dominate regional power balances, and bolster national standing in the international community. Pronouncements by U.S. officials and in official U.S. analyses beginning late in President Bill Clinton's administration have recognized the potency of even small nuclear arsenals in the hands of adversaries. This has led to increased U.S. interest in developing ballistic missile defenses to counter this asymmetric nuclear threat.[7]

From Openness to Ambiguity

The first five nuclear weapon states announced their arrival as members of the nuclear club unambiguously, either with the combat use of nuclear weapons (the United States in 1945) or with atmospheric nuclear tests (all others), which left no doubt about their capabilities.[8]

The situation was far more complex for the other nuclear weapon states, however. By the time these states achieved the ability to deploy nuclear weapons, U.S. and international concerns about nuclear proliferation had intensified to the point that it was advantageous for those states to avoid outright acknowledgement of their nuclear weapons status.

Israel, for example, whose existence has been repeatedly threatened by its neighbors, has never acknowledged possessing nuclear weapons. However, so much information has leaked out about its nuclear program, and it has dropped so many hints about its capabilities, that most countries accept Israel's status as a nuclear weapon state to be a military reality.[9] Still, to this day no one is sure precisely when Israel crossed the nuclear weapon threshold.

India, similarly, conducted a nuclear test in 1974—partly in response to external challenges, partly for domestic political reasons.[10] It claimed, however, that the detonation was a peaceful nuclear explosion of the type the United States and Soviet Union were then exploring to excavate harbors and to fracture geologic strata to facilitate oil and natural gas production. India did not declare itself to be a nuclear power until it conducted a second series of nuclear tests in May 1998. The latter tests were apparently motivated by its desire to develop warheads for a missile-based deterrent against China before mounting pressures for India to join the Comprehensive Test Ban Treaty (CTBT) made testing politically infeasible. No one doubted, however, that India could deploy nuclear weapons after 1974.

Apartheid-era South Africa, fearful of a Soviet-backed onslaught from neighboring black-ruled states, secretly built a handful of nuclear weapons beginning in 1979. In 1990, when the Soviet threat collapsed and white rule in South Africa was in decline, Pretoria dismantled these weapons. In 1991 it joined the Nuclear Non-Proliferation Treaty (NPT) and, in 1993, acknowledged the previous existence of the program and placed all of its nuclear activities under International Atomic Energy Agency (IAEA) inspection, as the NPT requires.[11]

Pakistan, perceiving itself under continuing threat from the larger and more powerful India, apparently assembled its first nuclear weapon in 1989.[12] Pakistan did not declare itself a nuclear weapon state until 1998, when it conducted a series of nuclear tests to match India's.

North Korea's nuclear status is uncertain. It denies that it has used its nuclear facilities to produce nuclear weapons. The U.S. government, however, has stated that North Korea possesses sufficient nuclear weapon material (in this case, plutonium) for one to two nuclear devices, presumably acquired to intimidate U.S.-backed South Korea and to compensate for its loss of Soviet support after the end of the Cold War.[13] If, over the course of the 1990s, North Korea formed this plutonium into nuclear weapons, then North Korea needs to be counted as a member of the nuclear club. Under a 1994 understanding with the United States, known as the Agreed Framework, North Korea has frozen the most sensitive parts of its nuclear program.[14] Thus, if North Korea is in fact a nuclear weapon state, its arsenal is quite small.

Although the circumstances differ, this history makes clear that after the first five nuclear powers arrived the international environment had changed sufficiently to lead new nuclear countries to adopt a more cautious approach in crossing the nuclear threshold.

Deliberate Abstinence

Understanding the current state of nuclear proliferation also requires an appreciation that since 1945 a surprisingly large number of countries have actively explored developing nuclear weapons but in the end decided not to pursue them. This group includes a number of advanced Western countries that considered nuclear weapons in the 1950s and 1960s (Australia, Canada, Sweden, and Switzerland); Romania, Spain, and Yugoslavia, which explored nuclear-arming in the 1970s; two regional nations at considerable risk, Taiwan and South Korea, which halted nuclear weapon programs in the 1970s after U.S. diplomatic intervention; and Argentina and Brazil, which, as their political systems became more open and as nationalistic tendencies eased, backed away from fledgling nuclear weapon programs and accepted comprehensive nuclear inspections in the 1980s.[15]

Belarus, Kazakhstan, and Ukraine are another cluster of states that could have acquired nuclear weapons but did not. When the Soviet Union broke apart in 1991, many nuclear-tipped Soviet missiles remained on their territories. All agreed to transfer the weapons to Russia and to join the NPT, thereby renouncing nuclear weapons and agreeing to comprehensive inspections of their nuclear activities. All nuclear weapons on their territories were returned to Russia by 1996.[16]

West Germany and Japan, among the most advanced Western countries, took several years before deciding, in the mid-1970s, to renounce nuclear weapons permanently by joining the NPT. They decided that on balance retaining non–nuclear weapon status while protected by the U.S. nuclear deterrent was the most advantageous course.

Eastern European states were under Soviet domination during the Cold War. Moscow gave them no opportunity to develop nuclear programs that might lead to nuclear arms and required them to join the NPT. After the end of Soviet control, however, the Czech Republic, Hungary, and Poland—all prime candidates for achieving nuclear weapon status given their histories of subjugation by outside powers—voluntarily remained within the NPT, in part to pave the way for membership in the North Atlantic Treaty Organization (NATO), for which this was a precondition.

Coercive Nonproliferation

If Iraqi leader Saddam Hussein had not invaded Kuwait in 1990—a step that ultimately led to Iraq's defeat at the hands of the U.S.-led coalition in the 1991 Gulf War—Iraq might very well have nuclear weapons today. However, that defeat, coupled with comprehensive United Nations (UN) inspections from 1991 to 1998, exposed Iraq's nuclear weapon effort and rendered it harmless. Since Iraq expelled those inspectors in 1998, however, it has undoubtedly sought to rebuild its program, though probably with only limited progress. If UN inspections can be restored, it is likely that Iraqi nuclear ambitions can be contained in the coming years.[17]

The Slowing Pace of Proliferation

Finally, it is important to recognize, as illustrated in Figure 7.1, that since 1989 the total number of nuclear weapon states has remained constant (if one assumes that North Korea is a member of the nuclear club). If it is believed that North Korea has not been able to transform its nuclear weapon capability into actual nuclear arms, then the number has declined since 1989—from nine to eight—and there has been no increase in the total number of nuclear weapon states since 1979. This suggests that the *rate* of nuclear proliferation may be slowing, although future developments in Iran and Iraq leave this matter in doubt.[18]

Incentives and Constraints

Broadly speaking, every country that has considered the acquisition of nuclear arms has had to weigh the potential benefits of acquisition against the economic and political costs. For some countries, the imperatives of national security, prestige, and/or ambition have been so powerful that they have outweighed the costs. But the calculus has come out the other way for most countries. The circumstances of each state are different, but in general states that are at peace with their neighbors (like those in Latin America and Southeast Asia), that are protected by reliable nuclear-armed allies (such as the members of NATO as well as Australia, Japan, and South Korea), that do not aspire to regional or global leadership, or that are impoverished or technologically backward are less likely to pursue nuclear weapons in the face of the powerful constraints on their acquisition.[19] These constraints include significant technological obstacles, a network of international treaties and export control agreements aimed at limiting nuclear proliferation, and targeted diplomatic initiatives, usually led by the United States, to curb the spread of nuclear arms.

Technological Obstacles

Nuclear weapons are very difficult to manufacture.[20] Most significantly, they require fissile material for their explosive cores. Fissile materials are materials in which atoms can be made to fission, or split, at an exponentially increasing rate, creating a chain reaction in which each fission contributes energy that results in enormous explosive force. The two types of fissile material used in nuclear explosives are highly enriched uranium (HEU) and plutonium. Neither of these materials occurs naturally, and they must be produced, starting with the mining of uranium, by means of an elaborate chain of facilities, many of which are highly complex and very costly. International regulations assume that a nuclear device could be made from 25 kilograms (55 pounds) of HEU or from 8 kilograms (17.6 pounds) of plutonium.[21]

In brief, HEU is produced by increasing the concentration of one isotope of uranium that is particularly unstable, uranium-235 (U-235), from its naturally occurring rate in U-238 of 0.07 percent to 90 percent or more, a process referred to as "enrichment." The principal techniques are gaseous diffusion, electromagnetic separation, gas centrifuge, and laser isotope separation.[22] The first two were used in the U.S. nuclear weapon program of the 1940s, the Manhattan Project. Gas centrifuges were developed in the 1950s and 1960s, laser isotope separation in the 1970s.

Plutonium is produced by irradiating U-238 in a nuclear reactor. For the reactor to operate, however, it must use uranium fuel that has been enriched to 3 percent U-235 or more surrounded by so-called light water (i.e., ordinary water). Or the reactor can use natural uranium surrounded by heavy water (i.e., water in which the concentration of molecules containing deuterium, a relatively rare isotope of hydrogen, has been concentrated). Both alternatives are technologically complex. The major nuclear weapon states have designed reactors specifically for this purpose, known as production reactors, usually of the heavy-water type. A country could also use a large research reactor or a nuclear power plant to produce plutonium. After the uranium fuel has been irradiated it must be processed in a reprocessing plant, where the plutonium is chemically separated from other constituents of the spent uranium fuel.

In addition to acquiring fissile material, a nation must design its nuclear device—not an easy task, even though much information on this subject has been disseminated over the years. It is generally believed that if a country conducted extensive tests on components and took advantage of computer modeling, then it would not need to conduct the test of a complete nuclear device to develop a reliable fission weapon (an atomic bomb) of the type that destroyed Hiroshima and Nagasaki. Testing is generally considered important, however, for a country to develop more complex and potentially much more powerful thermonuclear weapons (hydrogen bombs).

The key point here is that in the past the process of developing even simple fission weapons has been extremely costly and time-consuming (usually requiring five to ten years), has required highly trained nuclear physicists and engineers, and has entailed the development of many facilities that may be difficult to conceal, potentially permitting outside states to disrupt nuclear weapon development activities before a first nuclear weapon can be produced.[23]

The constraint posed by the technological barriers to proliferation is significantly strengthened by the agreement of the key nuclear supplier states to impose strict controls on the transfer of equipment, technology, and materials relevant to the production of nuclear weapons. In effect, this requires would-be proliferators to manufacture these items themselves or to resort to smuggling, significantly prolonging the time needed to develop nuclear arms. These controls are implemented by each supplier country, through its domestic laws, and are coordinated internationally through two informal organizations, the Non-Proliferation Treaty Exporters Committee and the Nuclear Suppliers Group.

The potential erosion of constraints. Two developments could erode the long-standing technological barrier to proliferation. The first is the risk of leakage of nuclear weapon material from the states of the former Soviet Union, especially Russia. With the collapse of the Soviet police state and the severe economic decline in Russia and the other successor states, controls over nuclear materials were greatly weakened and incentives for unauthorized diversion of the materials for sale to proliferant states greatly increased. Russia possesses hundreds of tons of these materials outside of existing nuclear weapons, enough for thousands of additional nuclear devices. If even a small percentage of this material were to be acquired by a country of proliferation concern, that country would be able to avoid the need to produce the material itself, bypassing the greatest obstacle to manufacturing nuclear weapons.

To address this danger, the United States has funded a series of large-scale cooperative programs with Russia and several former Soviet countries to improve nuclear material protection, control, and accounting at sites where such materials are stored or processed. In addition, the United States is implementing an agreement with Russia to purchase 500 tons of Russian weapons-grade HEU. The material is blended down to non–weapons usable low-enriched uranium and sold commercially as nuclear power plant fuel. Other U.S. programs include constructing a secure plutonium storage facility at a Russian reprocessing site, helping to end the production of additional weapons plutonium, and working to eliminate 34 tons of this material by burning it in Russian nuclear power plants.[24] The United States has also launched cooperative programs with Russia and other former Soviet countries to provide jobs for impoverished nuclear weapon scientists to reduce incentives for them to sell their expertise to proliferant states. Although very small amounts of weapon-usable materials apparently leaked from Russia in the mid-1990s, there have been no reports of major diversions of Soviet-origin nuclear weapon material to states of proliferation concern.[25]

A second development that threatens to erode the value of technological barriers to proliferation is the advent of uranium enrichment by means of lasers. The technology is several decades old and is not known to have been used in existing nuclear weapon programs because of its technical complexity. However, many observers fear that it could become more accessible in future years, as advanced laser and computer technology in general spread around the globe. A particular concern is that the facilities required for laser enrichment of uranium are far smaller in scale—and therefore far easier to build and far more difficult to detect—than those used for other, less advanced enrichment methods. Reportedly, Iran has sought this technology.[26]

The Nuclear Non-Proliferation Treaty

Multilateral treaties and agreements to limit the spread of nuclear arms are a second major constraint on proliferation. By far the most important today is the Nuclear Non-Proliferation Treaty, which was opened for signature in 1968 and entered into force in 1970.

The treaty divided its parties into two categories: nuclear weapon states, and non–nuclear weapon states. Because the treaty was trying to halt the *further* spread of nuclear weapons, it used a special, legal definition of *nuclear weapon states*. It defined them as the countries that had detonated a nuclear explosive prior to 1 January 1967: the United States, the Soviet

Union (Russia), Great Britain, France, and China. All other countries are *non–nuclear weapon states* for the purposes of the treaty (even India, Israel, and Pakistan, which acquired nuclear weapons after the treaty definition was drafted).

Under the treaty, non–nuclear weapon state parties agree not to manufacture or otherwise possess or acquire nuclear explosives. They also agree to accept inspections and audits ("safeguards") implemented by the Vienna-based IAEA on all of their peaceful nuclear activities. The NPT nuclear weapon states parties are not subject to these conditions. They are permitted to retain their nuclear weapons and are not required to accept IAEA safeguards on any nuclear facilities, including those used for the production of nuclear arms.[27] The nuclear weapon states agree not to transfer nuclear explosives to non–nuclear weapon states or assist those states in the manufacture of such explosives. In addition, as part of the bargain embodied in the treaty between the nuclear weapon states and non–nuclear weapon states, all states, including the former, are bound to "pursue negotiations in good faith on effective measures relating to cessation of the nuclear arms race and to nuclear disarmament."[28] Under the treaty, all parties are also required to ensure that any exports to non–nuclear weapon states of nuclear materials and equipment especially designed or prepared for the processing or production of nuclear materials will be placed under IAEA safeguards by the importing country. (This reinforces the requirement that non–nuclear weapon states place all of their nuclear activities under such IAEA monitoring.) Finally, all parties agree to facilitate the sharing of nuclear technology for peaceful purposes under IAEA safeguards.

Significantly, the treaty permits non–nuclear weapon states to produce and separate plutonium and/or to enrich uranium to HEU, as long as these activities are subject to IAEA monitoring. Some observers fear that this would enable a country to develop a stockpile of nuclear weapon material under IAEA monitoring while secretly developing other nonnuclear components for nuclear weapons. If the country then abrogated or withdrew from the NPT, the country could rapidly produce nuclear weapons, perhaps in a matter of weeks. To reduce these risks, the United States and other nuclear supplier countries have restricted the export of reprocessing and enrichment technologies. In addition, the United States has opposed reprocessing and enrichment in regions of tension.[29]

The NPT currently has 187 parties, including the NPT nuclear weapon states. India, Israel, Pakistan, and Cuba are the significant nonparties.[30] On 11 May 1995 the members of the treaty agreed to extend its initial 25-year term indefinitely.[31]

Export control organizations.   The NPT is reinforced by two multilateral nuclear export control organizations. The first is the NPT Exporters

Committee (also known as the Zangger Committee), formed in 1974 to develop a list of nuclear equipment and material exports that would trigger the application of IAEA safeguards in recipient states, as required by the NPT. The second is the Nuclear Suppliers Group, formed in 1976, which has adopted a parallel "trigger list."[32] The latter organization, which included some supplier states that were not NPT parties at the time of the group's formation, has adopted more extensive export controls than those required by the NPT itself. In particular, Nuclear Suppliers Group members have agreed to restrict exports of sensitive technology, including uranium enrichment and reprocessing, and in 1992 the group adopted the rule that members would make nuclear exports to non–nuclear weapon states only if the recipient had accepted IAEA inspections on *all* of its nuclear facilities ("full-scope safeguards"), a rule that in effect banned nuclear exports to India, Israel, and Pakistan.[33]

Noncompliance.   Two NPT parties are considered to have violated the treaty: Iraq and North Korea. Under IAEA practice through the 1980s, the agency limited its inspections in NPT member countries to those nuclear facilities and materials declared by those states. During the 1980s Iraq developed a sizeable nuclear weapon program using a number of clandestine nuclear installations that it did not declare to the IAEA. These were discovered by highly intrusive UN-mandated inspections after Iraq's defeat in the 1991 Gulf War. Iraq's expulsion of the UN inspectors in 1998, and the inability of the UN Security Council to agree on terms for demanding their return, presumably allowed Iraq to resume its clandestine nuclear program.[34]

Responding to the need to strengthen its inspection system, the IAEA declared it would begin to exercise previously unused authority to conduct special inspections at locations suspected of housing undeclared nuclear activities in NPT non–nuclear weapon states. The first test of the IAEA's authority to conduct such inspections took place in North Korea. That country had joined the NPT in 1985 but was able to delay the start of IAEA inspections until 1992. In the course of those inspections, the IAEA concluded that North Korea had separated a quantity of plutonium from spent fuel irradiated in its reactor at Yongbyon. North Korea had not declared this plutonium to the agency, and the United States believed it might be enough for one or two nuclear weapons.[35] The IAEA then sought a special inspection at a suspected nuclear waste site, hoping to find further evidence of plutonium separation. North Korea refused. When under U.S. urging the UN Security Council appeared ready to impose economic sanctions to enforce the IAEA's inspection rights, North Korea stated it would consider the action an act of war. In response, the United States sent additional military forces into the region to support South Korea in the event of conflict. Adding to U.S. concerns was North Korea's construction of a larger plutonium production reactor at Yongbyon, potentially capable of producing enough plutonium annually for 10–12 weapons. An additional, still larger reactor was also under construction at Taechon.

The crisis ended in October 1994 when North Korea agreed to freeze operation of the Yongbyon reactor and associated reprocessing plant, as well as to halt construction of the second reactor at that site and the reactor at Taechon. In return, the United States agreed to provide North Korea two proliferation-resistant commercial nuclear power plants and an interim supply of heavy fuel oil for electricity production. This understanding, embodied in the document known as the Agreed Framework, also provided for comprehensive IAEA inspections in North Korea prior to its receipt of nuclear components for the two commercial reactors and, as the first of the new nuclear power plants was completed, for the removal from North Korea of the remaining plutonium-bearing spent fuel from the Yongbyon reactor.[36] The IAEA is currently monitoring the freeze—which North Korea is implementing—but because of delays in implementing the Agreed Framework, the agency has not yet conducted the full-scale inspections in North Korea called for in that document. This leaves North Korea in continuing noncompliance with its IAEA safeguards obligations under the NPT. The United States remains concerned, moreover, that North Korea might develop additional, clandestine nuclear facilities undeclared to the agency.[37]

The cases of Iraq and North Korea create uncertainty about the future effectiveness of the NPT in restraining other determined proliferators. Proponents of the treaty point out that the obligation of non–nuclear weapon state NPT parties to accept IAEA inspections on all of their nuclear activities, backed up by intelligence that the agency may receive from interested states, places a significant constraint on would-be proliferators that attempt to develop clandestine nuclear facilities. Under new authority that the agency is seeking from non–nuclear weapon state NPT parties, moreover, it would have the right to visit undeclared buildings at declared sites and to use advanced sampling techniques.[38] NPT proponents also point out that the UN Security Council supported IAEA inspectors and staunchly backed the NPT when challenged by North Korea. These developments, proponents argue, have overcome the flaws in the treaty observed in the case of Iraq. Critics argue, however, that the IAEA's authority remains insufficient to track down clandestine nuclear facilities and point out that the current stalemate in the UN Security Council over the reintroduction of UN inspectors into Iraq raises questions about that body's commitment to enforcing international nuclear controls.

The Comprehensive Test Ban Treaty

A second multilateral treaty that seeks to constrain proliferation is the Comprehensive Test Ban Treaty. Long sought by the world's non–nuclear weapon states as a means for restricting the ability of the nuclear powers to develop more advanced nuclear armaments, the CTBT is also a mechanism for constraining the capabilities of emerging nuclear states, because testing is important for the development of thermonuclear weapons and to provide confidence in the performance of smaller nuclear weapons used for missile warheads. After lengthy negotiations, the CTBT was opened for signature at the United Nations in 1996.

The CTBT prohibits any nuclear test explosions in any environment.[39] The treaty also establishes the extensive International Monitoring System of seismic and other sensors to detect prohibited detonations; provides authority for countries that suspect others of cheating to perform challenge inspections to determine whether such cheating has occurred; and creates a new international body to implement these verification provisions, the Comprehensive Test Ban Treaty Organization, based in Vienna.

The CTBT will enter into force after ratification by the 44 nations that in 1996 possessed research or power reactors—a group that includes all states known or suspected of possessing nuclear weapons and all of today's nuclear weapon aspirants, including Iran and Iraq.[40] Of this group, the most important states that have not ratified the treaty are China, India, Israel, North Korea, Pakistan, and the United States.

In October 1999 the U.S. Senate voted against giving its advice and consent to ratification of the CTBT. Opponents argued that the treaty's permanent restrictions on nuclear testing could lead to questions about the reliability and safety of the U.S. nuclear deterrent. They also questioned the effectiveness of the treaty's verification procedures in detecting prohibited low-level nuclear tests, a flaw that might enable Russia, China, and possibly others to cheat and maintain their weapon stockpiles more effectively than the United States. Opponents also questioned the value of the treaty as a nonproliferation measure, arguing that testing is not essential for developing reliable fission weapons.

Those favoring ratification responded that progress already made on the U.S. Stockpile Stewardship Program—for maintaining the stockpile without testing—demonstrated that it would be effective, that the United States would be at an advantage if it could freeze testing because it had already conducted more tests than any other country, and that secret low-level tests by others would not provide them a militarily significant advantage. They also stressed the importance of the CTBT in restraining advanced nuclear proliferation.

Although the Clinton administration strongly supported the CTBT, believing that the treaty successfully addressed all of the foregoing critiques, the George W. Bush administration firmly opposed the pact.[41] Nevertheless, it continued to support the global moratorium on nuclear testing, which has been in place since June 1998.[42] In its FY 2003 budget, however, the Bush administration requested $5.87 billion for the Stockpile

Stewardship program,[43] an 8 percent increase over the previous year's final appropriation. And during a January 2002 briefing on the Nuclear Posture Review, the administration indicated that it plans to accelerate its nuclear test readiness program from a two-to-three year period to a substantially shorter time period.[44]

In view of growing concerns about the spread of weapons of mass destruction to Iran, Iraq, Libya, North Korea, and Syria, among other states, Bush administration officials have become increasingly interested in the potential utility of low-yield, earth penetrating nuclear weapons for destroying underground bunkers that might house stocks of such WMD or their production facilities.

The Fissile Material Cut-Off Treaty

The United States has sought to negotiate a third international treaty to slow proliferation, the Fissile Material Cut-Off Treaty (FMCT). The FMCT would prohibit the further production of fissile materials for nuclear weapons. Any such material produced after the treaty entered into force would be placed under IAEA safeguards to ensure it was used only for civilian research and nuclear energy production and not for nuclear explosives. In practice this would mean placing IAEA inspections on uranium enrichment plants and spent fuel reprocessing plants not currently under such monitoring. Like the CTBT, all parties would be subject to this rule. Under the treaty as envisioned by the United States and many other countries, states possessing nuclear weapons would not be exempted. However, they would be able to retain their nuclear armaments because they would not be required to place existing stocks of fissile material (including that contained in nuclear arms) under IAEA safeguards. Thus, under this approach to the FMCT, the treaty would cap the amount of fissile material available for weapons and thus limit the size of nuclear arsenals, but it would not, by itself, require reductions in existing nuclear forces. Special verification procedures, perhaps including challenge inspections, would be needed to prevent countries from cheating by producing additional fissile material for weapons clandestinely at undeclared facilities.

The FMCT combined with the CTBT would place important constraints on India, Israel, and Pakistan and would complement the NPT. The original five nuclear weapon states currently possess more fissile material than they need for their nuclear forces, however, so an FMCT that exempted existing stocks of fissile material would have little impact on them.

Negotiations on the FMCT will be conducted at the Conference on Disarmament, a UN body in Geneva. Negotiations have not started, however, because of disputes concerning the overall agenda of that body.[45]

Targeted Diplomacy

The NPT, the CTBT, IAEA safeguards, and the export control groups noted above represent the core elements of the nuclear nonproliferation regime. That regime reinforces the international norm against nuclear proliferation and often forms the backdrop for more targeted diplomatic efforts, usually led by the United States, directed at slowing nuclear proliferation in particular countries.

U.S. diplomatic action in the case of North Korea, using the threat of UN sanctions and the offer of incentives in the Agreed Framework, was predicated on North Korea's status as a non–nuclear weapon state NPT party and the associated requirement that it accept IAEA inspections on the entirety of its nuclear program. The United States has intervened diplomatically many times in past decades in other cases, seeking to curb proliferation in Algeria, Argentina, Brazil, India, Israel, Pakistan, South Africa, South Korea, and Taiwan, through offers of military and economic assistance, peaceful nuclear cooperation, strengthened alliance ties (including pledges to use nuclear arms to defend the target state), and increased integration into the Western economic sphere.[46] To press its case, Washington has also used threats to reduce such links, often under the strictures of U.S. laws imposing sanctions for certain proliferating activities, such as nuclear detonations by states treated as a non–nuclear weapon state under the NPT.[47] The United States has also sought to constrain Iranian nuclear ambitions by actively pressing Russia to halt sensitive nuclear exports to that country.[48] The United States has been most effective in cases where it has unusually strong leverage, such as with countries heavily dependent on the United States for their defense, or where the motivation for acquiring nuclear arms is weaker.

Another U.S. diplomatic strategy is to engage countries of proliferation concern so as to reduce tensions with them. These tensions are sometimes an important factor contributing to the desire of these states to develop nuclear weapons. And if they develop such weapons, the tensions add to the military threat they pose to the United States. Political openings leading to improved relations often depend on the advent of more moderate leaders in the target country.

Counterproliferation

The foregoing discussion has concentrated on diplomatic approaches to retarding nuclear proliferation. During the 1990s, however, the United States began to focus more actively on the challenge posed by cases in which nonproliferation efforts are unsuccessful and new nuclear states emerge. The new focus was spurred by evidence that traditional diplomatic tools had failed to unmask and halt the Iraqi and North Korean nuclear programs and had not succeeded in stemming the growth of longer-range missiles and chemical and biological weapon programs in a number of regional powers, most of them hostile to the United States.

Military measures include strengthening deterrence, developing the capability to disrupt nuclear programs before they produce nuclear arms, destroying such weapons and/or their delivery systems before they can be used, and developing defenses against nuclear-armed missiles.[49] A number of these issues are treated in depth elsewhere in this volume, but it is valuable to review their application to nuclear proliferation specifically.

Deterrence long served as the cornerstone of U.S. strategy to address the massive nuclear threat posed by the Soviet Union, and deterrence is likely to prove a crucial tool for dealing with regional nuclear adversaries should they emerge. As one example, few would question that North Korea's recognition of U.S. military might contributed to its decision to end the confrontation of 1994 and accept the Agreed Framework. Several U.S. strategists have suggested that the credibility of U.S. nuclear deterrence against regional nuclear powers would be reinforced by the deployment of smaller nuclear weapons, thereby avoiding the need to deter regional adversaries with much larger nuclear weapons that the United States might be reluctant to use.[50]

Acting militarily to disrupt nascent regional nuclear weapon programs through preventive attacks would carry substantial risks, because the most likely target countries (Iran, Iraq, and North Korea) possess other weapons of mass destruction and missiles that could be used to retaliate against U.S. regional allies. The United States might be able to deter such retaliation by the threat of further intervention, but in effect a preventive strike would inevitably entail the risk of war. Moreover, target states are likely to hide key nuclear facilities, following the example of Iraq after Israel's 1981 attack on the Tuwaitha reactor. This would create uncertainty about the ultimate effectiveness of future preventive attacks. Preemptive attacks in time of war raise fewer problems of escalation, but they would be no easier to execute successfully.

Active defenses against nuclear-armed missiles are, by definition, a last-resort capability to be used when nonproliferation and deterrence fail. There is broad consensus on the desirability and practicality of defenses against theater-range missiles, but there is also continuing debate over the merits of such defenses to protect the U.S. homeland.[51]

Given the complexity of proliferation by new regional powers and the fact that several of them already possess chemical or biological weapons and missiles for delivering them, military measures are an essential component of U.S. strategy for meeting the proliferation challenge.

The Continuing Debate

Is further nuclear proliferation inevitable? Given North Korea's desperate economic situation and political isolation, it is quite possible that political accommodation on the Korean Peninsula and effective implementation of the Agreed Framework may halt proliferation there. In the Middle East, the proliferation challenge posed by Iran and Iraq may be more daunting. Both have strong compulsions for acquiring nuclear arms, including their mutual hostility, their enmity toward Israel, their quest for leadership in the Persian Gulf, and their respective desires to prevent future U.S. military intervention in the region. Nonetheless, a restoration of UN inspections in Iraq, as well as political moderation in Iran that led to a strategy of nuclear fuel cycle development (including a capability to produce plutonium or HEU) under IAEA inspection without the actual production of fissile material for nuclear arms, remain part of a feasible, if not probable, scenario that could slow proliferation in this region. The challenge of halting proliferation in all three countries will be compounded by the overhang of poorly secured nuclear materials in Russia, which will continue for at least a decade, and by the global spread of relevant technological capabilities, in particular laser enrichment of uranium.

How should the United States integrate diplomatic and military measures in addressing nuclear proliferation? Given the overall record of diplomatic efforts, there is good reason to continue employing them vigorously, especially because some important military options cannot be made available for a number of years. But diplomatic initiatives are far from perfect, and they face particular challenges in containing determined proliferators. Thus military preparedness is also needed to address the possible—some would argue probable—contingency that nuclear weapons will spread to additional regional powers hostile to the United States and its allies. In practical terms, the United States has adopted this dual-track policy. As it refines its deterrent strategy and advances the development of missile defenses, it is also pursuing near-term diplomatic efforts for restraining nuclear proliferation. Observers will need to evaluate whether it has struck the right balance as events unfold.

Conclusion

The terrorist attacks of 11 September 2001 have introduced several new dimensions to the issue of nuclear proliferation. Perhaps the most grave threat to the United States and its allies will not be from nuclear-armed states but rather from the possession of nuclear weapons by a terrorist organization with no homeland and no restraints on its desire to cause harm. These events also highlight the possibility that the recognized government of a nuclear-armed state, such as Pakistan, might lose control of its nuclear weapons because of internal political turmoil or a coup d'état by disaffected members of the military. Nevertheless, widespread international support for the U.S. war on terrorism may open the door to a mediating role for the United States between India and Pakistan, to the consolidation of power by moderates in Iran less bent on arming the country with nuclear weapons, and to solidarity in the UN Security Council that leads to the restoration of inspections in Iraq.

The challenge of restraining nuclear proliferation and dealing with its consequences, already an urgent priority, is now of even greater importance to U.S. and international security.

Notes

1. For a report on this approach, see President Bill Clinton, "Letter to Congressional Leaders Reporting on Proliferation of Weapons of Mass Destruction," *Weekly Compilation of Presidential Documents,* 9 November 2000, p. 2842.

2. See Ambassador Robert G. Joseph, "The National Security Importance of the Non-Proliferation Regime," testimony before the Senate Foreign Relations Committee, 21 March 2000, www.ndu.edu/ndu/centercounter/21MAR00.doc.

3. President George W. Bush in his first major address on proliferation in May 2001 embraced such a comprehensive approach but made clear that his near-term emphasis would be on military measures to address emerging threats by regional powers. White House Press Office, "Remarks by the President to Students and Faculty at the National Defense University," 1 May 2001, www.whitehouse.gov/news/releases/2001/05/20010501–10.html. Academics may debate whether the spread of nuclear weapons to additional countries will enhance international stability. However, the international community and, in particular, the United States have firmly rejected this view and have worked vigorously to slow the spread of these weapons. See Scott D. Sagan and Kenneth N. Waltz, *The Spread of Nuclear Weapons: A Debate* (New York: W. W. Norton, 1995).

4. See Richard Rhodes, *The Making of the Atomic Bomb* (New York: Simon and Schuster, 1986); Richard Rhodes, *Dark Sun: The Making of the Hydrogen Bomb* (New York: Simon and Schuster, 1996); John Wilson Lewis and Xue Litai, *China Builds the Bomb* (Stanford: Stanford University Press, 1988); and Rodney W. Jones and Mark G. McDonough, *Tracking Nuclear Nonproliferation: A Guide in Maps and Charts, 1998* (Washington, DC: Carnegie Endowment for International Peace, 1998), www.ceip.org/files/Publications/trackingTOC.asp?p=8.

5. Libya is sometimes added to the list of countries seeking nuclear weapons but is considered much farther away from this goal. Director of Central Intelligence, *Unclassified Report to Congress on the Acquisition of Technology Relating to Weapons of Mass Destruction and Advanced Conventional Munitions: 1 January Through 30 June 2000,* www.cia.gov/cia/publications/bian/bian_feb_2001.htm; Office of the Secretary of Defense, *Proliferation Threat and Response* (Washington, DC, U.S. Department of Defense, January 2001); Statement of Director of CIA George Tenet to Congress, "Worldwide Threat 2001: National Security in a Changing World,"

www.cia.gov/cia/public_affairs/speeches/UNCLASWWT_02072001.html; Vice Admiral Thomas Wilson, "Global Threats and Challenges Through 2015," www. usinfo.state.gov/topical/pol/terror/01020712.htm; Michael Barletta, *WMD Threats 2001: Critical Choices for the Bush Administration,* www.cns.miis.edu/pubs/opapers/op6/index.htm; and President William Clinton, Letter to Congressional Leaders Reporting on Proliferation of Weapons of Mass Destruction.

6. "NRDC Nuclear Notebook: Russian Nuclear Forces, 2001," *Bulletin of the Atomic Scientists* (May/June 2001): 78–79.

7. In introducing the Department of Defense's widely read report, *Proliferation: Threat and Response,* Clinton administration Secretary of Defense William Cohen stated, "At the dawn of the 21st Century, the United States now faces what could be called a Super Power Paradox. Our unrivaled supremacy in the conventional military arena is prompting adversaries to seek unconventional, asymmetric means to strike what they perceive as our Achilles' heel." Office of the Secretary of Defense, *Proliferation: Threat and Response* (Washington, DC: U.S. Department of Defense, January 2001). Another official statement underscoring U.S. anxieties about proliferation, albeit concerned with missiles rather than nuclear weapons, is contained in National Intelligence Council, *Foreign Missile Developments and the Ballistic Missile Threat to the United States Through 2015* (Washington, DC: U.S. Central Intelligence Agency, September 1999), preface, www.cia.gov/cia/publications/nie/nie99msl.html.

8. The United States secretly tested the world's first nuclear weapon in July 1945. It used one weapon against the Japanese city of Hiroshima and one against Nagasaki in August 1945, the only occasions in which nuclear weapons have been used in conflict. Russia's first nuclear test took place in 1949, Great Britain's in 1952, France's in 1960, and China's in 1964. These were all fission, or atomic, weapons. The United States tested its first thermonuclear, or hydrogen, device in 1952. The four other states' first tests of thermonuclear devices were as follows: the Soviet Union, 1955; Great Britain, 1957; China, 1967, France, 1968.

9. "Revealed: The Secrets of Israel's Nuclear Arsenal," *London Sunday Times,* 5 October 1986; Pierre Pean, *Les Deux Bombes* (Paris: Feyard, 1982); and Avner Cohen, *Israel and the Bomb* (New York: Columbia University Press, 1998), and statements by Israeli leaders quoted therein. Israel hid its nuclear program from the United States during the 1960s, a time when the United States was becoming increasingly important to Israel as a military patron. Disclosure might also have provoked Israeli adversaries in the Arab world to seek nuclear weapons of their own.

10. On the Indian nuclear program, see George R. Perkovich III, *India's Nuclear Bomb* (Berkeley: University of California Press, 1999).

11. Waldo Stumpf, "South Africa's Nuclear Weapons Program: From Deterrence to Dismantlement," *Arms Control Today* (December–January 1995–1996): 3–8; and J. W. de Villiers, Roger Jardine, and Mitchell Reiss, "Why South Africa Gave up the Bomb," *Foreign Affairs* (November/December 1993): 98–109.

12. Under a 1985 U.S. law known as the Pressler amendment to the Foreign Assistance Act, U.S. military aid for Pakistan was conditioned upon the president certifying that Pakistan "does not possess a nuclear explosive device." Foreign Assistance Act of 1961, section 620E(e). At the time, Pakistan was known to be close to producing the essential materials for a nuclear weapon. After making this certification for several years, President George Bush in January 1990 declared that he could no longer make this finding.

13. Larry Niksch, *North Korea's Nuclear Weapons Program* (Washington, DC: Congressional Research Service, 21 February 2001), www.ceip.org/files/projects/npp/pdf/norkornuclear.pdf.

14. October 1994 Agreed Framework Between the United States of America and the Democratic People's Republic of Korea, www.kedo.org/Agreements/agreedframework.htm.

15. A starting point for learning about states that considered developing nuclear weapons but ended these activities can be accessed at www.isis-online.org/mapproject/introduction.html.

16. Jon Brook Wolfsthal, Cristina Chuen, and Emily Ewell Daughtry, eds., *Status Report: Nuclear Weapons, Fissile Material, and Export Controls in the Former Soviet Union* (Monterey, CA, and Washington, DC: Monterey Institute of International Studies and Carnegie Endowment for International Peace, 2001), www.cns.miis.edu/pubs/print/nsr.htm.

17. For a review of efforts to restore UN inspections and establish the successor to the UN Special Commission on Iraq, the United Nations Monitoring, Verification, and Inspection Commission (UNMOVIC), see David Albright and Kevin O'Neill, "The Iraqi Maze: Finding a Solution," *Nonproliferation Review* (Fall 2001). See also the UNMOVIC website, www.un.org/Depts/unmovic/index.htm.

18. Another measure of the rate of proliferation is to examine the trend by decade. From 1945 to 1955, three states acquired nuclear weapons: the United States, the Soviet Union, and Great Britain. From 1955 to 1965, two achieved this status: France and China. From 1965 to 1975, two states became nuclear powers: Israel and India. From 1975–1985, only one new state developed nuclear arms: South Africa. From 1985 to 1995, Pakistan and possibly North Korea became nuclear powers, but South Africa renounced this status.

19. Much has been written on the subject of why states refrain from developing nuclear weapons. See, for example, Mitchell Reiss, *Bridled Ambitions: Why Countries Restrain Their Nuclear Capabilities* (Baltimore: John Hopkins University Press, 1995).

20. For a detailed review of the technological requirements for producing nuclear weapons, see Office of Technology Assessment, *Technologies Underlying Weapons of Mass Destruction,* OTA-BP-ISC-115 (December 1993), www.fas.org/spp/starwars/ota/9344.html.

21. IAEA, *IAEA Safeguards Glossary,* IAEA/SG/INF/1 (Vienna, Austria: IAEA, 1980), p. 22.

22. Gaseous diffusion forces uranium in gaseous form through a selective superfine filter or barrier. Electromagnetic separation uses large electromagnets to bend a stream of ionized uranium atoms in a pattern that allows the U-235–rich product to be culled out. High-speed centrifuges (in the form of large vertical rotating cylinders) spin uranium in gaseous form to create a differentiated stream of U-235–rich product that can be culled out. Laser isotope separation uses lasers to differentially excite U-235 atoms from other uranium isotopes, allowing them to be gathered.

23. Israel's destruction of Iraq's large research reactor at Tuwaitha in 1981 is the best-known example of military intervention to slow a potential nuclear weapon program. Iraq responded by disguising and dispersing the next phase of its nuclear weapon effort, which remained undiscovered until Iraq's defeat in the 1991 Gulf War.

24. These programs, administered by the U.S. Departments of Defense, Energy, and State, are commonly referred to as "cooperative threat reduction" programs, although only the Department of Defense uses this term in the names of its programs and organizational elements. See websites for the Department of Defense (www.dtra.mil), Department of Energy (www.energy.gov/security/index.thml), and Department of State (www.state.gov/t/np).

25. William C. Potter, "Nuclear Leakage from the Post Soviet States," Presentation to the Permanent Subcommittee on Investigations, Committee on Governmental Affairs, U.S. Senate, 13 March 1996, www.cns.miis.edu/pubs/reports/senoral. htm; also, U.S. Department of Energy, National Nuclear Security Administration, *Material Protection, Control, and Accounting Program Strategic Plan 2001* (Washington, DC: U.S. Department of Energy, July 2001), p. 2.

26. Alex Wagner, "Moscow Puts Hold on Transfer of Laser Isotope Separator to Iran," *Arms Control Today* (October 2000), p. 28.

27. All of the nuclear weapon states have voluntarily accepted some IAEA monitoring, either on certain civilian nuclear installations or on material or equipment imported from other NPT states.

28. Text of the Treaty on the Non-Proliferation of Nuclear Weapons, Article VI.

29. During the 1970s the United States intervened diplomatically to curtail efforts by Taiwan and South Korea to initiate reprocessing activities. Germany and Japan, it may be noted, pursued enrichment and reprocessing under IAEA inspection and accumulated large quantities of plutonium for civilian use. Neither is considered a proliferation risk. For many years the international nuclear power industry advocated recycling plutonium as fuel in conventional power reactors, a step that would be followed by the use of plutonium to fuel breeder reactors. Breeder reactors would ultimately produce more plutonium than they burned, creating a virtually inexhaustible energy supply. The economics of this approach proved unattractive, however, and only France and Japan have significant plutonium recycling programs today.

30. Because India, Israel, and Pakistan did not detonate nuclear explosions before 1 January 1967, they are not considered nuclear weapon states under the treaty and, if they joined, would be obliged to accept the conditions applying to non–nuclear weapon states, i.e., to renounce nuclear weapons in the manner of South Africa. Cuba possesses a very modest civilian nuclear program, all elements of which are subject to IAEA monitoring.

31. For additional background on the NPT, its text, and a current list of parties to the treaty, see www.state.gov/www/global/arms/treaties/npt1.html.

32. As of April 2002 the Nuclear Suppliers Group had 39 members: Argentina, Australia, Austria, Belarus, Belgium, Brazil, Bulgaria, Canada, Cyprus, the Czech Republic, Denmark, Finland, France, Germany, Greece, Hungary, Ireland, Italy, Japan, Latvia, Luxembourg, Netherlands, New Zealand, Norway, Poland, Portugal, Republic of Korea, Romania, Russian Federation, Slovak Republic, Slovenia, South Africa, Spain, Sweden, Switzerland, Turkey, Ukraine, United Kingdom, and the United States. The NPT Exporters Committee had 35 members. All members of the Nuclear Suppliers Group are members of the NPT Exporters Committee except for Belarus, Brazil, Cyprus, Latvia, and New Zealand. China is a member of the latter group but not a member of the Nuclear Suppliers Group, largely because it does not endorse the group's rule restricting nuclear exports to states with full-scope safeguards, a rule that would prevent Chinese exports to Pakistan's nuclear power program.

33. In the late 1990s Russia announced plans to supply India with two, and possibly four, nuclear power reactors. Russia has argued that because the sale is based on a 1988 contract it is permitted under an exemption to the group's guidelines allowing transactions to proceed that predate the group's adoption of the full-scope safeguards rule. In addition, in 2000 Russia agreed to sell India fuel for the Tarapur nuclear power station (units originally supplied by the United States but for which the United States has refused to supply fuel, as required by the restrictions in the Atomic Energy Act). The Russian fuel will be subject to inspection by the International Atomic Energy Agency. The Clinton administration objected to Russia's

expansive reading of the guidelines' grandfather clause and strongly opposed the Russian claim that the fuel sale could be justified on safety grounds. At its April 2001 plenary session, the Nuclear Suppliers Group indirectly expressed its concern over the Russian transactions by reaffirming its commitment to making full-scope safeguards a condition for nuclear exports. U.S. law buttresses the multilateral export control regimes by imposing sanctions on states that disregard their rules. Under the 1994 Glenn amendment to the Arms Export Control Act, for example, states that export enrichment or reprocessing technology to countries deemed non–nuclear weapon states under the NPT are subject to the termination of certain U.S. economic and military assistance. See Arms Export Control Act, sec. 101 (1994).

34. The United Nations is monitoring imports into Iraq, but Iraq is known to be engaging in extensive smuggling activities with neighboring states, opening the possibility that these unmonitored channels could be used to support clandestine nuclear activities.

35. Niksch, *North Korea's Nuclear Weapons Program*, p. 3.

36. The Agreed Framework also established a new international organization, the Korean Peninsula Energy Development Agency, to finance and construct the two nuclear power plants; see www.kedo.org/news.htm. Members as of mid-2002 were Argentina, Australia, Canada, Chile, the Czech Republic, the European Atomic Energy Community, Indonesia, Japan, New Zealand, Poland, South Korea, the United States, and Uzbekistan. The reactors will be financed principally by South Korea and Japan.

37. In 2000 concerns that North Korea might be constructing a secret underground nuclear facility at Kumchamg-ri led the United States to request an inspection at the site. North Korea permitted the inspection, which was conducted by a team of U.S. specialists, but the underground site was empty and found not to be suitable for the type of nuclear installation the United States had feared might have been built there. Niksch, *North Korea's Nuclear Weapons Program.*

38. This new inspection authority is contained in an additional protocol to supplement IAEA agreements with NPT non–nuclear weapon state parties. The additional protocol is deemed to be an amendment to these agreements that requires ratification by NPT parties. Arms Control Association, "Fact Sheet: The IAEA 1997Additional Safeguards Protocol," www.armscontrol.org/factsheets/93_2fact.asp. The text of the model protocol agreement and a list of states that have ratified the instrument can be accessed at www.iaea.or.at/worldatom/Programmes/Safeguards/sg_protocol.shtml. Iran, Iraq, Libya, and North Korea were among the states that had not ratified additional protocols to their IAEA safeguards agreements as of mid-2002.

39. The 1963 Partial Test Ban Treaty banned nuclear tests in the atmosphere, underwater, and in outer space. It did not prohibit underground nuclear testing, however. The Comprehensive Test Ban Treaty bans nuclear tests in all environments, including underground.

40. The 44 countries whose ratification is needed to bring the CTBT into force are: Algeria, Argentina, Australia, Austria, Bangladesh, Belgium, Brazil, Bulgaria, Canada, Chile, China, Colombia, North Korea, Egypt, Finland, France, Germany, Hungary, India, Indonesia, Iran, Israel, Italy, Japan, Mexico, Netherlands, Norway, Pakistan, Peru, Poland, Romania, South Korea, Russian Federation, Slovakia, South Africa, Spain, Sweden, Switzerland, Turkey, Ukraine, United Kingdom, United States, Vietnam, and Zaire. See the website of the Comprehensive Test Ban Treaty Organization at www.pws.ctbto.org.

41. Because it has signed the CTBT and because President George W. Bush has not withdrawn it from consideration by the Senate, under customary international

law the United States is bound not to act in a manner that would undermine the basic objectives of the treaty.

42. The five NPT nuclear weapon states had previously adopted a de facto nuclear testing moratorium. The last test by each of these countries was as follows: Russia, 1990; United Kingdom, 1991; United States, 1992; France, 1996; China, 1996.

43. See Jonathan Medalia, *Nuclear Weapons: Comprehensive Test Ban Treaty* (Washington, DC: Congressional Research Service, 19 February 2002).

44. U.S. Department of Defense, News Transcript, 9 January 2002, "Special Briefing on the Nuclear Posture Review," at www.defenselink.mil/news/Jan2002/t01092002_t0109npr.html.

45. See Tariq Rauf, Mary Beth Nikitin, and Jenni Rissanen, *Inventory of International Nonproliferation Organizations and Regimes* (Monterey, CA: Center for Nonproliferation Studies, 2000), pp. 25–26, www.cns.miis.edu/pubs/inven/inven2k.pdf.

46. Jones and McDonough, *Tracking Nuclear Proliferation*.

47. Arms Export Control Act, 22 U.S.C. 2799aa, secs. 101 and 102.

48. See A. Norman Schindler, Deputy Director, DCI Nonproliferation Center, "Iran's Weapons of Mass Destruction Programs," Statement to the Senate Governmental Affairs Committee, 21 September 2000: "Russian entities are interacting with Iranian nuclear research centers on a wide variety of activities beyond the Bushehr project. Many of these projects have direct application to the production of weapons-grade fissile material." Available at www.cia.gov/cia/public_affairs/speeches/archives/2000/schindler_WMD_092200.htm. Also see Michael Dobbs, "U.S., Russia at Odds on Iranian Deal," *Washington Post*, 15 June 2001.

49. The U.S. counterproliferation program also addresses the threats posed by chemical and biological weapons. In this setting another important dimension of the program is the deployment of passive defenses—for example, protective clothing, detectors, and vaccines. Passive defenses are obviously less relevant to the nuclear threat.

50. Such smaller weapons might be available by adapting existing U.S. nuclear weapons without the need for nuclear testing, an approach that would preserve the nuclear testing moratorium and avoid acting in derogation of the CTBT. C. Paul Robinson, *Pursuing a New Nuclear Weapons Policy in the 21st Century* (Albuquerque, NM: Sandia National Laboratories, March 22, 2001).

51. See James J. Wirtz and Jeffrey A. Larsen, eds., *Rockets' Red Glare: Missile Defenses and the Future of World Politics* (Boulder: Westview, 2001).

Suggested Readings

Hays, Peter L., Vincent J. Jodoin, and Alan R. Van Tassel, eds. *Countering the Proliferation and Use of Weapons of Mass Destruction.* New York: McGraw-Hill, 1998.

Jones, Rodney W., and Mark G. McDohough. *Tracking Nuclear Proliferation, 1998: A Guide in Maps and Charts.* Washington, DC: Carnegie Endowment for International Peace, June 1998.

Lavoy, Peter R., Scott D. Sagan, and James J. Wirtz, eds. *Planning the Unthinkable: How New Powers Will Use Nuclear, Biological, and Chemical Weapons.* Ithaca: Cornell University Press, 2000.

Office of the Secretary of Defense. *Proliferation: Threat and Response.* Washington, DC: U.S. Department of Defense, January 2001.

Paul, T. V. *Power Versus Prudence: Why Nations Forgo Nuclear Weapons.* Montreal, Canada: McGill University Press, 2000.

Sagan, Scott D., and Kenneth N. Waltz. *The Spread of Nuclear Weapons: A Debate.* New York: W. W. Norton, 1995.

Wilkening, Dean, and Kenneth Watman. *Nuclear Deterrence in a Regional Context.* Santa Monica, CA: RAND, 1995.

8

Chemical and Biological Weapons

Marie Isabelle Chevrier

Chemical, biological, and nuclear weapons represent the trio of weapons of mass destruction. The destructive power of nuclear weapons is well known; that of chemical and biological weapons less so. If effectively produced and disseminated, chemical weapons have the potential to kill tens of thousands of people, biological weapons hundreds of thousands. Chemical and biological weapons (CBW) could also be targeted against animals or agriculture, causing severe economic and/or ecological damage. One of the guiding principles of arms control—to limit the destructiveness of violent international conflicts—leads inevitably to the exploration of the means to suppress CBW as instruments of warfare. This search predates modern arms control: the Hague Conventions of 1899 and 1907, for example, formalized normative prohibitions against the use of poison weapons. Yet effective means to eliminate CBW from world arsenals are only now, perhaps, within the grasp of the international community.[1]

The Chemical Weapons Convention (CWC) of 1993 was hailed as a treaty that "broke the arms control mold."[2] As the first post–Cold War arms control treaty, its intrusive multilateral verification provisions set a new standard for inspection procedures and heralded a new era in arms control—one in which cooperation among governments, private industry, and a substantial international inspectorate is necessary to achieve success. Regarding biological weapons, the end of the Cold War was thought to create the opportunity to adopt a protocol modeled, with appropriate changes, after the CWC to strengthen the weak 1972 Biological and Toxin Weapons Convention (commonly cited as the Biological Weapons Convention, or BWC). That treaty outlawed the possession and development of biological weapons but contained no monitoring provisions or on-site measures to investigate alleged treaty violations.

Thus, the mid-1990s were a time of unprecedented but guarded optimism regarding CBW arms control. That optimism has given way to considerable

143

frustration with the implementation and management of the verification and monitoring activities of the CWC and a mixture of cynicism and despair over stalemated progress of the BWC protocol negotiations. In this chapter I examine chemical and biological weapons and the modern instruments that have been developed for their control. I emphasize the ways in which CBW arms control differs from nuclear arms control and the reasoning behind the different approaches to control their proliferation and use. I also examine the major problems with implementation of the CWC and stumbling blocks to achieving agreement on a protocol to strengthen the BWC.

Background

Biological weapons are living organisms, most commonly bacteria and viruses, deliberately disseminated to cause death or disease in humans, animals, and/or plants. Chemical weapons are nonliving substances that cause death or incapacitation by their chemical action when dispersed to cause such an effect. CBW are considered weapons of mass destruction because they have the potential to destroy life on a scale surpassed only by nuclear weapons. They could also be used for smaller-scale effect and in clandestine operations.

The spectrum of CBW ranges from the classic chemical weapons agents used in World War I—chlorine and mustard gas—to more modern nerve agents; to toxins, which are poisons of biological origin; and finally to bacteria, viruses, and other living biological agents.[3] The weapons generally become more deadly on a per-weight basis as one moves along this spectrum. Scientific advances, particularly in the area of biotechnology, have contributed new entries to the list of potential threat agents and added impetus to arms control negotiations.[4]

CBW share certain military characteristics. First and most important, CBW affect only living matter. Although the weapons could be used to restrict access to airstrips, for example, and thus inhibit the ability to transport troops and materiel, they do not have the ability to destroy an opponent's weapons. In contrast to nuclear and conventional weapons, the use of CBW would not significantly retard the retaliatory capacity of the victim nation, except insofar as it incapacitated key personnel and military forces. Second, gas masks and chemical suits can protect troops against both chemical and biological agents. A crucial caveat is that troops must put on the suits and masks before exposure. Thus a detector or warning must alert troops to the necessity of donning the oftentimes clumsy and uncomfortable gear. In addition to these characteristics, which limit but do not eliminate the military utility of CBW, the use of such weapons also carries the contradistinction of being "condemned by the general opinion of the civilized world."[5]

Efforts to constrain the use of chemicals and biological agents as instruments of war have a long history. The extensive use of chemical weapons in World War I gave impetus to modern arms control efforts. The 1925 Geneva Protocol prohibited the use of CBW in warfare.[6] The 1972 Biological Weapons Convention and the 1993 Chemical Weapons Convention went further, prohibiting the development and possession of biological and chemical weapons, respectively.

Objectives of CBW Arms Control

The objectives of CBW arms control overlap with the objectives of nuclear arms control in some respects but markedly differ in others. CBW arms control primarily serves to reduce the horror of war should it occur; reducing the risk of war is not its key purpose. An additional goal of CBW arms control is to influence the behavior of nonstate actors as well as that of sovereign states. CBW arms control hopes to reduce the probability of terrorist acquisition and use of these weapons, as well as to reduce the horror of terrorism and the likelihood of mass-casualty terrorism. A third objective is to avoid the accidental release of dangerous pathogens.[7] Finally, in contrast to nuclear arms control, CBW arms control is less likely to lower defense costs. Because disarmament is harder to verify and terrorist development or acquisition is possible, security demands robust, but not necessarily secret, defenses.

The Principal Instruments of CBW Arms Control

Throughout the twentieth century countries concerned about the use and proliferation of CBW have crafted a detailed fabric of agreements and practices that outlaw the use and possession of these weapons, as well as means to slow their proliferation and to respond to proliferation if it occurs. The path the United States took to formal CBW arms control agreements also differed considerably from the nuclear and conventional fields. In both the chemical and biological arenas, the United States unilaterally decided to dismantle and/or destroy its offensive capability before negotiating limits on other states' possession of them. Thus, by the time the two multilateral treaties were completed, CBW fell into the category described by Thomas Schelling as a dominant negative preference: "not having the weapon is preferred *irrespective* of whether the other side has it."[8] The dominant negative preference for biological weapons can be seen in U.S. biological weapons policy under President Richard Nixon. Long-term proliferation, he believed, would be dampened by unilateral U.S. renunciation of possession.[9] Following the dissolution of the Warsaw Pact, the declining threat to

Western Europe from the collapsing Soviet Union, and the Gulf War, the United States made the decision to get rid of its chemical weapon arsenal as well.[10]

Although chemical and biological weapons share some important characteristics and are often thought of in concert, since the early 1970s different agreements have developed to control their spread. The Biological and Toxin Weapons Convention and the Chemical Weapons Convention are both disarmament treaties. Each requires that parties renounce the possession, development, and transfer of these weapons and to destroy any such weapons in their possession. Each contains a *general-purpose criterion* that outlaws the possession of toxic chemicals and biological agents unless justified by a peaceful purpose. Both treaties codify long-held norms against these weapons. Moreover, toxins are an area of overlap between the treaties. Although all toxins are covered under the earlier BWC, two toxins—ricin and saxitoxin—are listed in the CWC schedules of chemicals. The appearance of the two toxins in the CWC underscores the profound difference between the treaties: CWC negotiators recognized that the extensive on-site provisions to verify the destruction of weapons, munitions, and weapon production facilities and to monitor a county's commercial chemical industry contained in the CWC would prevent the acquisition of these toxins as weapons more effectively than the BWC, which has no corresponding provisions. It relies on very weak mechanisms, including consultations among parties and complaints to the United Nations (UN) Security Council, to resolve treaty implementation problems.

In addition to the formal multilateral treaties, other national and multilateral instruments add to the prohibitions. The Australia Group, for example, is an informal group of 34 countries that share information on CBW proliferation concerns and coordinate their export policies to prevent trade in chemicals, biological agents, and equipment to make CBW. The Australia Group was established after Iraq had used chemical weapons against Iran in the 1980s and the extent of Western trade with Iraq in establishing its chemical weapon program became known.[11] In addition, both the BWC and the CWC require parties to enact domestic legislation complementing the international treaty to allow criminal prosecution of individuals who violate the treaties' prohibitions.

The *trilateral process* is yet another plurilateral instrument established to deal with a known biological weapon proliferation problem. In the 1990s scientists from the Soviet Union's biological weapon program confirmed Western suspicions of an extensive offensive biological weapon program inside the country. After the collapse of the Soviet Union the three depositaries to the BWC—the United States, the United Kingdom, and the Russian Federation—engaged in reciprocal on-site inspections of biological facilities to increase confidence that their activities were consistent with peaceful aims. Unfortunately, the process was not public, and few open source documents describe its activities. Moreover, the process stalled when the Russians purportedly refused entry to facilities under control of the Ministry of Defense.[12]

Finally, the efforts to eliminate Iraq's CBW arsenal, as well as its nuclear weapon program, were conducted through the UN Special Commission on Iraq (UNSCOM). These can be seen as a tailored and specific response to CBW acquisition and use. A detailed examination of UNSCOM's efforts and findings demonstrates the difficulty of coercing compliance with international agreements and norms. It also demonstrates the difficulty of sustaining international commitments to counterproliferation efforts in the face of other international priorities.[13]

Despite the many threads that make up the fabric of CBW arms control, there are weaknesses in the weaving that are readily apparent. They include a host of problems in implementing the CWC, a breakdown in the decades-long effort to strengthen the BWC, and disagreement about how to respond to CBW proliferation.

Managing the Implementation of the CWC

Amy Smithson noted in 1996 that "getting the CWC successfully off the ground will, in and of itself, be a monumental task."[14] Today the world has made progress toward that goal. Requisite ratifications have been secured, implementing legislation has been passed, national authorities have been established, and the Organization for the Prohibition of Chemical Weapons (OPCW) is up and running.

A list of the accomplishments since the CWC entered into force in 1997 is indeed laudable. The treaty has 143 state parties;[15] four states have declared possession of chemical weapons and their stockpiles have been inventoried;[16] three of the four states possessing chemical weapons have met the first timeline for destroying stockpiles;[17] half of the declared chemical weapon production capacity in 11 countries worldwide has been destroyed or converted to peaceful purposes; and the OPCW has conducted hundreds of inspections worldwide under CWC article 6, including most facilities producing dangerous chemicals. OPCW inspectors have experience in conducting more than 1,000 inspections at military and industrial facilities and plant sites in 49 state parties, and 140 of the 143 parties have submitted initial declarations.[18] The establishment of the technical secretariat and the respect that its inspectors have earned throughout the world is particularly impressive.[19] Moreover, considerable obstacles were strewn in the path of the OPCW.[20] These achievements of the CWC and the OPCW should not be discounted as we turn to the regime's outstanding issues.

As the CWC entered its fifth year of operation in May 2001 it faced problems that, in the words of the director-general of the OPCW, "threaten . . . even the very survival of the OPCW."[21] The major problems can be summarized as: universality, particularly in the Middle East; Russian destruction; allegations of noncompliance without using the framework of the CWC to address them; budget and financial issues; differing national interpretations of the CWC's declaration requirements; failure of the regime to monitor trade in scheduled chemicals; lack of policy guidance on international cooperation; and abuse of confidentiality provisions.

Universality

Nearly five years after entry into force, the CWC had 145 state parties. Nevertheless, 29 states signed the CWC but have never ratified it, and an additional 20 have not signed or acceded to the treaty.[22] Although treaty holdouts are found all over the globe, the Middle East is an area of particular concern. Egypt, Iraq, Lebanon, and Syria have not signed the CWC; Israel signed but has not ratified.

On the positive side, Jordan, Saudi Arabia, Iran, Oman, Qatar, Kuwait, Yemen, and the United Arab Emirates have all ratified the treaty.[23] Outside the Middle East, neither North Korea nor Libya has signed it. Experience with the Nuclear Non-Proliferation Treaty indicates that states can be convinced to join multilateral arms control regimes if the correct mix of incentives, political persuasion, and will are applied. Ratifications and accessions to the CWC have been steadily increasing since its entry into force, and it is too early to tell if that trend will drop off. Nevertheless, as long as Israel possesses nuclear weapons other states in the region are likely to link their denunciation of chemical weapons to Israeli nuclear disarmament.

Russian Destruction

The United States, India, and South Korea have met time lines to destroy their stockpiles of weapons and munitions. The Russian Federation has not done so. Russia received a two-year extension of the initial deadline to destroy 1 percent of its stockpile. Russia's ability to comply with future deadlines is in jeopardy. In an unusually forthright statement, the OPCW director-general asserted that "it is by now clear that Russia will not be in a position to meet this second timeline either. And, frankly, it is simply unrealistic to expect that it will be able to destroy all of its chemical weapons by 2007."[24]

Russian arms control expert Alexander Pikayev attributes Russia's failure to meet the initial deadline to a mix of factors: "a lack of funding from domestic and international sources, political and bureaucratic instability, disagreements between federal authorities and regional leaders and public concerns about the environmental consequences of [chemical weapon] destruction."[25] Pikayev is cautiously optimistic that the Russian destruction program is on its way to being back on track.[26] OPCW Director-General José M. Bustani, however, has warned Russia that the "patience of the international community may be approaching its limits" and admonished Russia that lack of financial support from the international community to assist the Russian destruction efforts "can not be used as a pretext for continuing delays by the responsible authorities in Moscow."[27]

The failure of Russia to meet its destruction obligations under the CWC strikes at the heart of the chemical weapons regime. If other treaty parties view Russia's attitude toward destruction as cavalier or, worse yet, as deliberate foot-dragging, grave consequences could ensue. Some state parties could use Russia's compliance record as an excuse to delay or ignore their own obligations to make declarations, permit inspections, or make financial contributions to the OPCW. These consequences are not inevitable, however. Concerted political pressure on Russia to demonstrate progress on destruction could bear fruit. States should continue to provide sufficient financial assistance to enable it to do so. Russia, nevertheless, also needs to show its commitment to destruction.

Allegations of Noncompliance and Challenge Inspections

The United States has come under criticism for openly accusing Iran, China, and Russia of substantive violations of the CWC while refusing to make use of measures under the treaty—namely, challenge inspections—to address the compliance concerns.[28] U.S. officials have alleged that Iran and China possess undeclared stocks of chemical weapons and that Russia may be developing new chemical agents.[29] The U.S. government has not been explicit as to why it has not called for any challenge inspections in suspect nations. One possibility is that it is not yet fully prepared to host a challenge inspection if one were successfully launched in response to a U.S. request for a challenge. This theory suggests that it is only a matter of time and that the United States will seek a challenge when it has its own house in order. Other explanations are possible. It is not known, for example, whether officials within the U.S. State Department concerned with arms control compliance have recommended that the United States seek a challenge inspection yet have not received the requisite support at higher political levels. Furthermore, any state that requests a challenge inspection must take into account the full range of the condition of its relations with the country accused and assess the effect of a challenge inspection on that relationship. Regrettably, chemical weapons concerns may not be high on the priority list of issues that the United States faces with Iran, China, and Russia. Making suspicions of noncompliance public while failing to make use of available remedies is likely to seriously erode confidence in the effectiveness of the CWC. In addition, other states with suspicions may be unwilling to take the political heat that a challenge inspection is sure to generate.[30]

On another level, a tug-of-war is going on between those countries that see challenge inspections as a necessary and workable tool to address suspicious activities, and those that view challenge inspections as an extreme measure that should be used only after other methods to attain clarification have failed.[31] Some states would like to require consultations between state parties before allowing a request for a challenge inspection to move forward. Others want challenge inspections that fail to uncover violations to be defined as abusive.[32] Such interpretations would make states even more reluctant to call for challenge inspections and lead to even less confidence in the effectiveness of the regime.

Budget and Financial Issues

Budgetary and financial problems have been brewing since before the CWC entered into force. Several interrelated issues have contributed to the financial problems. Growth in the OPCW budget has been held below requests, making it difficult for the OPCW to fulfill its approved work program.[33] In 2001, for example, only 60 percent of the projected and approved inspections could be carried out.

To make matters worse, since the inception of the OPCW a significant number of member states have not paid their assessed contributions to the budget.[34] Cumulatively, states owe more than 5 million euros to the OPCW.[35] Although there are penalties for failure to pay OPCW assessments, that may not be a sufficient inducement to pay assessed dues. At the end of December 2001, 30 states were more than two full years behind in payments, up from 23 states in May 2000.[36] As a consequence these states—20 percent of the CWC state parties—have lost their right to vote in the OPCW.[37]

Third, states with chemical stockpiles and chemical weapon production facilities are responsible for the costs of verifying destruction of same. Yet only four of the nine pertinent countries have fully reimbursed the OPCW. The states with the largest chemical weapon stockpiles—Russia and the United States—have each tried to minimize their reimbursements to OPCW.[38]

Interpretations of the CWC's Declaration Requirements

A document as massive as the CWC could certainly be the cause of good-faith interpretations that differ across state parties. Nevertheless, some interpretations of the language of the CWC are not regarded by others as in good faith and have resulted in unequal treatment of members. An example is the U.S. interpretation of the requirement to declare facilities that produce dual-use chemicals.[39] The treaty exempts facilities that produce mixtures of chemicals with a low concentration of the dangerous chemical from declarations. The common interpretation of "low concentration" is 30 percent or less of a mixture. The United States, however, interprets it to be 80 percent or less of a mixture. Understandably, other countries have a difficult time agreeing that a mixture with 80 percent of a dangerous chemical is a low concentration and that the United States chose this interpretation in good faith. As a result, the United States does not declare many facilities that would be declared by other countries, thereby severely tilting the level playing field created by the drafters of the CWC.

Monitoring Trade in Scheduled Chemicals and International Cooperation

The CWC sets out procedures to monitor the transfer of scheduled chemicals. Different rules apply to chemicals on three schedules, categorized according to their relevance to chemical weapons, with the most stringent rules reserved for chemicals on Schedule 1.[40] Thus far the OPCW has failed to effectively monitor relevant transfers.[41] Partly because of this failure the members of the Australia Group have maintained their national export controls on chemicals and equipment—much to the dismay of countries that are party to the CWC and also subject to Australia Group restrictions.[42] Those countries believed that national restrictions on trade in chemicals would be replaced by the monitoring regime under OPCW.[43]

Similarly the implementation of CWC article 11, which includes international cooperation, has been called "unacceptable."[44] Article 11 requires states to cooperate in the exchange of chemicals, equipment, and information relating to the use of chemistry for peaceful purposes. Michael Moodie has noted that establishing programs for international cooperation should have been secondary to the other aspects of the treaty, including declarations and inspections.[45] Nevertheless, many state parties may have different priorities.

Transparency

An effective and robust arms control regime must have the support of the populations of its member states.[46] The "abuse" of confidentiality provisions in the CWC by member states has led to a situation where "it is practically impossible for an outsider to understand what the Organization is actually doing, whether all Member States are implementing their obligations in full, and what their compliance status is."[47] The public audience, including academics and nongovernmental organizations (NGOs), need to have sufficient information about the workings of arms control to form a judgment independent of their official government pronouncements. Worse yet, the abuse of confidentiality provisions means that even state parties to the CWC do not always have access to all the information needed to form national judgments on, for example, the effectiveness of the verification activities conducted by the OPCW.[48]

The problems of implementing the CWC are synergistic. The budgetary and financial problems make it more difficult to implement international cooperation programs. The failure to effectively implement international cooperation could reduce incentives for states outside the OPCW to ratify or accede to the CWC, adding to the universality problem. Weak international cooperation could also lead states to continue to neglect their financial obligations because they fail to realize benefits from the regime. At the same time, progress in one area would have positive spillover effects in other areas. Problems with the implementation of the CWC, moreover, have had a negative impact in the negotiations to strengthen the BWC.

Strengthening the Biological and Toxin Weapons Convention

A 1979 outbreak of anthrax in the Soviet city of Sverdlovsk (now Ekaterinburg) highlighted the weakness of the BWC and its lack of on-site measures to address allegations of noncompliance. The Soviets denied that the disease was connected with clandestine biological warfare activities. The only way to resolve issues of noncompliance through the BWC for state parties is to consult with one another or to take concerns to the UN Security Council, where a veto by any one of the five permanent members would block any action.[49]

Every review conference of the treaty has discussed steps to rectify the treaty's weaknesses. Politically binding confidence-building measures were initiated in 1986 and augmented in 1991. Treaty parties recognized, however, that confidence-building measures alone would be inadequate to address the treaty's weaknesses.[50] Consequently, they identified and evaluated possible verification measures for the BWC from a scientific and technical standpoint—an exercise entitled VEREX—which concluded that some of the measures would make the treaty a more effective instrument.[51] At a 1994 special conference to discuss the VEREX findings, the state parties created a mandate for an ad hoc group to draft proposals for a legally binding protocol to strengthen the effectiveness and improve the implementation of the BWC.[52]

A Protocol to Strengthen and Improve the BWC

From January 1995 through February 2001 the ad hoc group produced a lengthy rolling text.[53] In April 2001 the group's chairman, Ambassador Tibor Toth of Hungary, presented a composite text that demonstrated his view of how to resolve the outstanding disagreements among the drafting nations. Like the CWC, the composite text of a BWC protocol would require declaration of relevant facilities, establish an organization to observe activities at declared facilities, and allow state parties to call for on-site investigations of alleged violations of the treaty. The protocol would facilitate international cooperation in the peaceful uses of biology and biotechnology and monitor transfers of biological agents, toxins, and relevant equipment.[54]

The text garnered a groundswell of support from European countries, Canada, Australia, and key members of the Non-Aligned and Eastern European groups, including South Africa, Brazil, Peru, Poland, and Croatia. Nevertheless, in July 2001 the United States firmly rejected the composite text and the very approach taken by the ad hoc group to fulfill its mandate.[55] Ten years of scientific, technical, and diplomatic efforts came to a standstill. Although the U.S. rejection of the composite text came as no surprise to close observers of the process, many delegations in Geneva and NGOs were bitterly disappointed in the U.S. decision.[56] The U.S. government followed its rejection of the protocol with a demand that the ad hoc group's mandate be withdrawn. The U.S. demand took place on what was to be the final day of the fifth review conference of the BWC in December 2001. The ensuing uproar, including a refusal to meet with the United States by its European allies, led to a one-year suspension of the review conference.

The U.S. rejection of the ad hoc group's efforts and mandate came after a policy review by the incoming George W. Bush administration. Protecting the secrecy of U.S. biodefense programs and distaste for commitments that are viewed as eroding the sovereignty of the United States were at the root of the U.S. rejection. Long-standing disagreements exist within the U.S. government regarding the extent to which multilateral cooperative instruments such as the BWC protocol further U.S. interests or hinder the government's ability to take unilateral steps that may be in violation of such agreements. Nevertheless, U.S. declaratory statements of its reasons for rejection are first and foremost that a protocol would have exposed secret portions of the U.S. biodefense program to unacceptable disclosures. In September 2001 the *New York Times* disclosed details of U.S. activities that would be viewed as highly suspicious by the United States if undertaken by other countries and that could be regarded as a U.S. violation of its obligations under the BWC.[57] Moreover, the United States kept its programs under wraps in spite of obligations to the contrary. Other secret activities remain a concern as well. A U.S. Defense Department spokesperson denied that the *New York Times* revelations would harm U.S. biodefense efforts.[58]

In rejecting the composite text the United States pledged to "develop other ideas and different approaches" to strengthening the effectiveness of the BWC.[59] Those ideas and approaches center on four areas. The first is domestic penal legislation to enhance bilateral extradition agreements and make it a criminal offense for individuals to engage in activities prohibited by the BWC. The second area is a set of recommendations to improve national control over pathogens, including strict national standards, mandatory international reporting of releases, and oversight of high-risk experiments. The third area is meant to address compliance concerns. This includes a mechanism for international investigations of suspicious disease outbreaks and/or alleged biological weapons incidents upon a determination by the UN Secretary-General and a voluntary cooperative mechanism for clarifying and resolving compliance concerns. Finally, the United States calls on countries to adopt and implement strict biosafety procedures, based on World Health Organization (WHO) or equivalent national guidelines, and to support WHO's global disease surveillance programs.[60] The fate of the U.S. proposals and those contained in the composite text of the BWC protocol will likely entail many more years of consultations and negotiations.

Evaluating Competing Proposals

Recent criticism of the BWC composite text notes that the protocol is not strong enough either to detect violations with certainty or to deter biological weapons acquisition because of its weak on-site system to monitor legitimate biological activity.[61] The criticism rarely acknowledges that several of the weaknesses contained therein have come at the insistence of the U.S. government and could be strengthened if the United States followed the lead of its Western allies. Criticism that the protocol does not render the BWC verifiable is not useful because verification is not, and never has been, the purpose of the protocol.[62] In judging the chairman's text from a U.S. perspective, the appropriate question is whether it incorporates U.S. interests as the delegation has presented them.[63] The answer to that question is yes. From an international perspective the appropriate comparison concerns the mandate. Would implementation of the composite text strengthen the effectiveness and improve the implementation of the BWC? Although many U.S. allies would have preferred a stronger protocol, and some states—Pakistan, Iran, India, and China—preferred a weaker regime, all countries who participated in the negotiations, except for the United States, wanted to proceed with negotiations on the basis of the composite text and the rolling text from which it was taken.

The U.S. proposals are considerably weaker than the proposed protocol. The ability to investigate the alleged use of biological weapons would be stronger if undertaken through legally binding access requirements contained in the composite text of the protocol rather than through the UN Secretary-General. The Secretary-General already has the authority to investigate the possible use of CBW, but states could more easily deny access based on principles of sovereignty when their obligations have not been previously negotiated. One of the most glaring weaknesses of the U.S. proposal is its emphasis on investigating biological weapons use while rejecting on-site investigations at facilities that might be producing those same weapons. Preventing the ability of a state to wage biological warfare, rather than punishing one who does, requires more sustained attention to international procedures. Such attention and discipline seems a worthwhile investment given the stakes. At the same time, strengthening the ability of the United Nations to investigate alleged use in countries that are not parties to the BWC has great merit for reinforcing the norm of nonuse of biological weapons.

The U.S. proposals rely on export controls in lieu of inspections. Export controls in addition to those currently imposed by the Australia Group may be desirable. Yet the natural occurrence of disease, the international public health consequences of restricting some equipment, and the widespread know-how to reproduce pathogens and toxins render export controls a relatively weak tool to fight biological weapon proliferation and control. Domestic legislation to punish those who acquire biological agents for hostile purposes is already a requirement of BWC article 4. Article 4 certainly needs more widespread implementation and, perhaps, assistance to countries that have not yet drafted the requisite criminal statutes. International surveillance of disease is important and valuable. Yet worldwide cooperation is more likely to be effective if the World Health Organization or NGOs undertook the task.

CBW Arms Control and Cooperative Security

If the twenty-first century is to be an era of cooperative security, it follows in the path of decisions and practices firmly established in the twentieth. As John Ruggie argues, from Presidents Woodrow Wilson to Bill Clinton "the American vision as to what constitutes a desirable world order has been clear and consistent, and it embodies certain key multilateral principles."[64] The CWC and the BWC with its proposed protocol are a realization of those principles: "greater openness, greater non-discrimination of treatment, and more extensive opportunities to realize joint gains."[65] Moreover, to the extent the United States has come to embrace cooperative security, it has done so not because of what critics term "misguided idealism" but because the United States needs the cooperation of other states in order to realize its own interests. The interest of the United States in preventing the acquisition, proliferation, and use of CBW requires the cooperation of others. Because the technology to produce CBW is widely known and available, the United States could not successfully pursue this goal on its own. National measures, and limited international efforts such as the trilateral process to address Soviet noncompliance with the BWC, though not complete failures, have not been sufficient to protect U.S. interests in promoting compliance and halting proliferation. The United States and most of its allies have decided to dismantle or forego their offensive chemical and biological weapon programs. Therefore, attempting to bind other states to the norm of nonpossession of CBW does not carry with it the same consequences for the West as nuclear disarmament would. Effective CBW arms control is a necessary but insufficient component in addressing the CBW threat, which in turn is but one component in a cooperative security environment.[66]

How, then, does one judge the effectiveness of CBW arms control? In essence the CWC and BWC have three arms control purposes: to disarm nations, to preclude acquisition or rearmament by states, and to prevent proliferation to nonstate actors. The existence of structures within the CWC and the BWC that address noncompliance with the regime's prescribed norms "make it difficult for the international community of nations not to take action against transgressors of the norms and provide the nucleus around which such international action can crystallize."[67] The control of chemical weapons, a process that faces serious problems, is nonetheless firmly on the path of cooperation, whereas the control of biological weapons awaits closure by the governments that have engaged in the ad hoc group. Opponents of cooperative, multilateral approaches argue that such approaches constrain U.S. options to take action on a unilateral basis. The flipside is that dismissing cooperative paths to security, such as those embodied in the CWC and proposed for the BWC, foreclose options to act in concert with friends and allies or limit the likelihood of their success. The success of CBW arms control will be determined in large measure by governmental and public evaluation of the value of cooperative security.

Conclusion

Following the 11 September 2001 attacks, the United States is paying renewed attention to the necessity of international cooperation to defeat terrorist groups and their supporters and sponsors. Will the benefits of international cooperation in managing cumbersome multilateral arms control arrangements to curb the proliferation and use of CBW continue to command attention and necessary resources? This question is likely to remain a critical and continuing arms control theme in the twenty-first century.

Notes

1. John Ellis van Courtland Moon, "Lessons from the History of Biological and Toxin Warfare," in Erhard Geissler and John Ellis van Courtland Moon, eds., *Biological and Toxin Weapons: Research, Development, and Use from the Middle Ages to 1945*, SIPRI Chemical and Biological Warfare Studies No. 18 (Oxford, UK: Oxford University Press, 1999), p. 256.

2. Amy Smithson describes the CWC as "breaking the arms control mold." Marie Isabelle Chevrier and Amy E. Smithson, "Preventing the Spread of Arms: Chemical and Biological Weapons," in Jeffrey A. Larsen and Gregory J. Rattray, eds., *Arms Control Toward the 21st Century* (Boulder: Lynne Rienner Publishers, 1996), p. 202.

3. Graham S. Pearson, "Biological Weapons: The British View," in Brad Roberts, ed., *Biological Weapons: Weapons of the Future?* Significant Issues Series 15, no. 1 (Washington, DC: Center for Strategic and International Studies, 1993), pp. 10–11.

4. Malcolm Dando, "The Impact of the Development of Modern Biology and Medicine on the Evolution of Offensive Biological Warfare Programs in the Twentieth Century," *Defense Analysis* 15, no. 1 (1999): 43–62; and Malcolm Dando, *The New Biological Weapons: Threat, Proliferation, and Control* (Boulder: Lynne Rienner Publishers, 2001).

5. "Convention on the Prohibition of the Development, Production, Stockpiling and Use of Chemical Agents and on Their Destruction" (corrected version), 8 August 1994. "Convention on the Prohibition of the Development, Production, and Stockpiling of Bacteriological (Biological) and Toxin Weapons" (1972). The full texts of both conventions are available at the official website of the Organization for the Prevention of Chemical Weapons, www.opcw.org.

6. Many countries entered reservations to the protocol reserving the right to retaliate with chemical or biological weapons or both if the weapons were used first by an opponent in war. Thus, for many countries, the Geneva Protocol became essentially a no-first-use agreement.

7. For an account of the 1979 outbreak of anthrax in the Soviet city of Sverdlovsk, see Jeanne Guillemin, *Anthrax: The Investigation of a Deadly Outbreak* (Berkeley: University of California Press, 1999).

8. Thomas C. Schelling, *Choice and Consequence: Perspectives of an Errant Economist* (Cambridge: Harvard University Press, 1984), p. 244, emphasis in original.

9. Chevrier and Smithson, "Preventing the Spread of Arms, " p. 212.

10. Ibid., pp. 205 and 223, n. 13. For a discussion of the role of the Gulf War in demonstrating the limited military utility of chemical weapons, see Ambassador Dr. Adolf von Wagner, "Lessons Learned," *Synthesis 2000: The Year in Review*, publication of the Organization for the Prohibition of Chemical Weapons, p. 13, www.opcw.org/synthesis/synthesis_four/htm/.

11. See the Australia Group website for current and historical information about the group; www.australiagroup.net.

12. Iris Hunger and Marie Chevrier, "Questions of Compliance: The Case of Biological and Toxin Weapons Control Regime," Geneva Centre for Security Studies, 1999–2000 Arms Control Cluster Papers, www.gcsp.ch/e/index.htm.

13. The most comprehensive source for all publicly released documents and reports of the United Nations Special Commission (UNSCOM) is the website for Iraq Watch at www.iraqwatch.org. For a concise secondary account of UNSCOM activities,

see Tim Trevan, *Saddam's Secrets: The Hunt for Iraq's Hidden Weapons* (London: HarperCollins, 1999).

14. Chevrier and Smithson, "Preventing the Spread of Arms," p. 208.

15. The Nuclear Non-Proliferation Treaty, which entered into force in 1970, has 187 state parties. The BWC, which entered into force in 1975, has 144. See SIPRI-Bradford Joint Chemical and Biological Warfare Project for an up-to-date listing of parties to the BWC, www.projects.sipri.se/cbw/cbw-sipri-bradford.html.

16. Russia and the United States were the only states openly admitting their possession of chemical weapons when the CWC entered into force. India has since acknowledged its chemical weapon arsenal, as has another state party, which is officially anonymous, but commonly known to be South Korea. See, for example, Alexander Kelle, "Overview of the First Your Years," in Jonathan B. Tucker, ed., *The Chemical Weapons Convention: Implementation Challenges and Solutions* (Monterey, CA: Monterey Institute of International Studies, April 2001), p. 11; and Amy E. Smithson, *Rudderless: The Chemical Weapons Convention at 1-1/2,* Report No. 25 (Washington, DC: Henry L. Stimson Center, September 1988).

17. The United States, for example, has destroyed one-fifth of its stockpile.

18. Opening statement by the director-general to the executive council of the Organization for the Prevention of Chemical Weapons at its twenty-fourth session, The Hague, 3 April 2001. Full text can be accessed at the OPCW's website, www.opcw.org.

19. Robert J. Matthews, "Chemical Disarmament: Advent and Performance of the OPCW," *VERTIC Verification Yearbook 2000* (London: VERTIC, 2001), p. 75.

20. Amy E. Smithson, "U.S. Implementation of the CWC," in Jonathan B. Tucker, ed., *The Chemical Weapons Convention: Implementation Challenges and Solutions* (Monterey, CA: Center for Nonproliferation Studies, Monterey Institute of International Studies, 2001); and Alexander A. Pikayev, "Russian Implementation of the CWC," in ibid.

21. Opening statement by the director-general at the OPCW's sixth session, The Hague, Netherlands, 14 May 2001.

22. Under international law treaty signatories are bound not to take action that is in fundamental conflict with the precepts of the treaty; thus the 31 signatories are obligated not to produce chemical weapons.

23. For an up-to-date list of all CWC state parties and signatories, see the OPCW website, www.opcw.org.

24. Opening statement by the director-general at the OPCW's sixth session. In late 2001, Russia submitted a revised program for destruction of its chemical weapon stockpile, requesting an extension until 2012. See "Developments in the Organization for the Prohibition of Chemical Weapons," "Progress in The Hague, Quarterly Review No. 36," *CBW Conventions Bulletin,* no. 54 (December 2001): 3.

25. Pikayev, "Russian Implementation of the CWC," p. 31.

26. Ibid., p. 37.

27. Opening statement by the director-general at the OPCW's sixth session.

28. For a more detailed discussion of compliance issues and policy recommendations, see Amy Sands and Jason Pate, "CWC Compliance Issues," in Tucker, ed., *The Chemical Weapons Convention,* pp. 17–22.

29. Office of the Secretary of Defense, *Proliferation Threat and Response* (Washington, DC: Department of Defense, January 2001), pp. 15, 36, and 57, www. defenselink.mil/pubs/ptr20010110.pdf.

30. Sands and Pate, "CWC Compliance Issues," p. 17.

31. Papers from a seminar on challenge inspections cohosted by the United Kingdom and the OPCW, published in *Synthesis* (May 2000): 14–27. Articles contributed

by Cuba, Canada, China, India, Iran, Pakistan, Russia, South Africa, and the United Kingdom.

32. Author interview with a U.S. government official, May 2001.

33. "Developments in the Organization for the Prohibition of Chemical Weapons," p. 3. Continued deficit budgeting, according to Bustani, "will sound the death knell for the Organization." Opening statement by the director-general to the executive council at OPCW's twenty-fourth session, The Hague, 3 April 2001.

34. See Kelle, "Overview of the First Your Years," p. 11.

35. As of 1 December 2001, state parties owed 2.6 million euros in assessed contributions and 1.85 million euros for the cost of inspections under articles 4 and 5. "Developments in the Organization for the Prohibition of Chemical Weapons," p. 7.

36. The May 2000 figures are taken from OPCW Document C-V/DG.10, 12 May 2000. The 2001 figures are taken from "Developments in the Organization for the Prohibition of Chemical Weapons," p. 7.

37. Ibid.

38. Kelle, "Overview of the First Four Years," p. 11.

39. *Dual-use chemicals* are those that have been used as weapons, or precursors to weapons, and are produced in large quantities for commercial purposes.

40. In general all scheduled chemicals have been produced, used, or stockpiled as chemical weapons or their precursors in the past or have a high level of toxicity or ability to incapacitate. Chemicals on Schedule 1 have no purposes other than as weapons; those on Schedule 2 are not produced in large commercial quantities (but may have some commercial uses); chemicals on Schedule 3 are produced in large quantities for commercial or other peaceful purposes. See the Chemical Weapons Convention, Annex on Chemicals, pp. 35–41.

41. According to Bustani, "The regime that has been established to monitor trade in scheduled chemicals, and to identify or prevent possible proliferation attempts has, quite frankly, failed thus far." Opening statement by the director-general to the executive council at OPCW's twenty-fourth session, The Hague, 3 April 2001.

42. When the U.S. Senate considered the CWC, it attached twenty-eight conditions to ratification. One of those conditions required that the president certify that the United States maintain its national export controls and that the president has received assurance that Australia Group members would not weaken their national export controls. See "Summary of the Senate Resolution of Ratification to the Chemical Weapons Convention," *Arms Control Today* (April 1997): 29.

43. Daniel Feakes, "Export Controls, Chemical Trade, and the CWC," in Tucker, ed., *The Chemical Weapons Convention*, p. 46.

44. Opening statement by the director-general at OPCW's twenty-fourth session, The Hague, 3 April 2001.

45. Michael L. Moodie, "Issues for the First Review Conference," in Tucker, ed., *The Chemical Weapons Convention*, p. 63.

46. Alexander Kelle, "The Chemical and Biological Weapons Control Regimes Under Stress—Old Wine in New Bottles or Result of the New Inequalities?" Paper presented at the International Studies Association Conference, Chicago, February 2001.

47. Opening statement by the director-general at OPCW's twenty-fourth session, The Hague, 3 April 2001. According to the Confidentiality Annex of the CWC, the organization may not publish or release any information without the express consent of the state party from which it was obtained.

48. Tom Inch, "The Chemical Weapons Convention: A Viewpoint from the Chairman of the Advisory Committee to the UK National Authority," in *CBW Conventions*

Bulletin (December 2000): 3–5; Moodie, "Issues for the First Review Conference," p. 59.

49. The first and second review conferences of the BWC established the right of state parties to call a multilateral consultative meeting and the obligation to do so.

50. Marie Isabelle Chevrier and Iris Hunger, "Confidence Building Measures for the BTWC: Performance and Potential," *Nonproliferation Review* (Fall/Winter 2000).

51. United Nations, *Summary Report, Ad Hoc Group of Governmental Experts to Identify and Examine Potential Verification Measures from a Scientific and Technical Standpoint*, Fourth Session, Geneva, BWC/CONF.III/VEREX/8, 13–24 September 1993, pp. 1–20.

52. For a more detailed discussion, see Marie Isabelle Chevrier, "A Necessary Compromise," *Arms Control Today* (May 2001).

53. A *rolling text* is a negotiating text that includes proposed and alternate language for controversial sections. Text that is not agreed is placed in square brackets to reflect disagreement.

54. See "Executive Summary of the Chairman's Text," *Arms Control Today* (May 2001) for a more detailed description of the measures contained in the compromise text.

55. "Statement by Ambassador Donald A. Mahley, United States Negotiator for Chemical and Biological Arms Control Issues," United States Delegation to the Ad Hoc Group of the Convention on the Prohibition of the Development, Production, and Stockpiling of Bacterial (Biological) and Toxin Weapons and on Their Destruction, Geneva, 25 July 2001.

56. See, for example, Graham S. Pearson, Malcolm R. Dando, and Nicholas A. Sims, "The U.S. Rejection of the Composite Protocol: A Huge Mistake Based on Illogical Assessments," Bradford Evaluation Paper No. 22 (Bradford, UK: Department of Peace Studies, University of Bradford, August 2001).

57. Judith Miller, "When Is a Bomb Not a Bomb? Germ Experts Confront U.S.," *New York Times*, 5 September 2001.

58. United States Department of Defense, News Briefing, Victoria Clarke, ASD(PA), 4 September 2001.

59. Statement by Ambassador Donald A. Mahley, 25 July 2001.

60. Statement of the Honorable John R. Bolton, Undersecretary of State for Arms Control and International Security, U.S. Department of State, to the fifth review conference of the BWC, Geneva, Switzerland, 19 November 2001, found at www.usinfo.state.gov.

61. Moodie, for example, criticizes the draft protocol because it "specifies so few total visits annually and such a limited number of visits for any one country or facility that it may, in fact, be difficult to develop the 'mosaic' that serves as the baseline from which unusual behavior can be distinguished . . . visited facilities are under the total control of the visited party." "Building on Faulty Assumptions," p. 20. The U.S. government promoted both of those provisions.

62. O. J. Sheaks, Assistant Secretary of State for Verification and Compliance, testimony before the U.S. House of Representatives, Committee on Government Reform, 5 June 2001; Edward J. Lacey, Principal Deputy Assistant Secretary of State for Verification and Compliance, testimony before the Subcommittee on National Security, Veterans Affairs and International Relations, Committee on Government Reform, U.S. House of Representatives, 10 July 2001; and Chevrier and Smithson, "Preventing the Spread of Arms,"p. 226, n. 43. Indeed, a 1951 report to President Harry Truman noted that "it would be practically impossible to detect biological

warfare activities by an inspection scheme." Frederick Aandahl et al., eds., "Formulation of a United States Position with Respect to the Regulation, Limitation, and Balanced Reduction of Armed Forces and Armaments, July 6, 1951," *Foreign Relations of the United States, 1951,* vol. 1 (Washington, DC: U.S. Government Printing Office, 1979), NSC-112, p. 489.

63. See Chevrier, "A Necessary Compromise," for a more detailed description of the ways in which the composite text incorporates U.S. interests.

64. John Gerard Ruggie, "Third Try at World Order? America and Multilateralism After the Cold War," *Political Science Quarterly* (Fall 1994): 560.

65. Ibid.

66. Charles A. Kupchan, "The Case for Collective Security," in George Downs, ed., *Collective Security Beyond the Cold War* (Ann Arbor: University of Michigan Press, 1994).

67. Julian Perry Robinson, Memorandum [on the effectiveness of the 1972 Biological and the 1993 Chemical Weapons Conventions], in Appendix 29, House of Commons Foreign Affairs Committee, Session 1999–2000, Eighth Report: "Weapons of Mass Destruction" (London: TSO, 2000), p. 204.

Suggested Readings

Dando, Michael. *The New Biological Weapons: Threat, Proliferation, and Control.* Boulder: Lynne Rienner Publishers, 2000.

Lederberg, Joshua, ed. *Biological Weapons: Limiting the Threat.* Cambridge: MIT Press, 1999.

Price, Richard M. *The Chemical Weapons Taboo.* Ithaca: Cornell University Press, 1997.

Roberts, Brad, ed. *Hype or Reality: The New Terrorism and Mass Casualty Attacks.* Alexandria, VA: Chemical and Biological Arms Control Institute, 2000.

Robinson, Julian P. Perry, ed. *Health Aspects of Biological and Chemical Weapons.* Geneva: World Health Organization, 2001.

Tucker, Jonathan B., ed. *Toxic Terror: Assessing Terrorist Use of Chemical and Biological Weapons.* Cambridge: MIT Press, 2000.

———. *The Chemical Weapons Convention: Implementation Challenges and Solutions.* Monterey, CA: Monterey Institute of International Studies, April 2001.

Zilinskas, Raymond A., ed. *Biological Warfare: Modern Offense and Defense.* Boulder: Lynne Rienner Publishers, 2000.

9

Conventional Weapons

Jo L. Husbands

As the transformation of the international system from the Cold War continues to unfold, the struggle to limit violence presents one of the twenty-first century's primary security challenges. Curbing the spread of conventional weapons is considered an essential part of this effort, where the classic goals of arms control—to reduce the risks of war, to reduce the costs of preparing for war, and to reduce the damage should war occur—remain relevant. Today's wars are being fought almost entirely with imported conventional weapons. The conventional weapons that could be used to deliver weapons of mass destruction (WMD) are a significant component of the proliferation problem. Nonstate actors are readily able to acquire large stocks of a disturbingly wide variety of weapons, a matter of greatly increased concern in the aftermath of 11 September 2001. Arms are not a direct cause of conflict, but they can enable combat to continue, and on occasion particular weapons can significantly influence the tide of battle. Weapons can also make the conflict more intense and more deadly to both combatants and civilians, and their continued presence after combat ends can seriously inhibit efforts at relief and recovery.

This chapter is divided into two sections. In the first I review the current state of international arms transfers (sales and aid). In particular, I try to sort out longer-term trends from the continuing legacies of the Cold War in order to provide a context for discussing approaches to control. In the second section I explore efforts to curb the spread of particular kinds of weapons in order to illustrate the range of options to control or limit arms transfers.

Arms Trade Fundamentals

The Size of the Market

The international arms market, at least for major military equipment, is significantly smaller than it was during the Cold War. After it reached its

163

all-time high in the mid-1980s, developing and developed countries have spent less in real terms on their militaries in the 1990s, both for imports of major weapons as well as for overall defense expenditures.[1] All arms trade statistics need to be treated with great caution, as the quality of the data varies widely and because, in many cases, statistics are not available except as expert judgments and estimates.

The size of the arms market, which reflects primarily the trade in advanced conventional weapons, is not the best guide to its impact on conflict and violence, however. First, with obvious and important exceptions, most of the 130-plus wars since World War II have been fought with relatively unsophisticated and inexpensive weapons. The arms trade in sub-Saharan Africa, for example, is relatively small in terms of dollars but has had a devastating impact on the region. Second, the spread of democracy in regions such as Latin America and Central Europe, which many believe will reduce conflict between nations, is not well reflected in arms trade statistics. Latin America was never a significant component of the trade in major weapons, and in Central Europe the painful economic transitions would make new arms purchases difficult for any government. What weapons are available to whom and from whom means more to the future of conflict than the sheer volume or relative dollar value of sales. The smaller market nonetheless has important implications for suppliers and recipients and for hopes of curbing the spread of conventional weapons.

The Shape of the Market

The supply and demand sides of the arms market have always been highly concentrated. Among recipients, a few nations and regions account for most of the weapons imported into the third world. Arms transfers to the third world were negligible in the 1950s, as most U.S. military assistance went for the reconstruction of Europe, and the Soviet Union did not begin a military assistance program to the third world until late in that decade. In the 1960s most transfers went to Asia, especially to Southeast Asia during the war in Indochina. Since the mid-1970s between 60 and 75 percent of all arms exports to the third world, and the vast bulk of the most sophisticated arms, has ended up somewhere between North Africa and South Asia. A number of East Asian states also purchased significant amounts of weaponry. On the supply side, the five permanent members of the UN Security Council account for 80 percent or more of the arms exported to the third world.

More than weapons are being transferred; technology and production capabilities are spreading steadily from the developed to the developing world. How much actual knowledge is being transferred varies widely, as some of the arrangements involve little more than assembling finished components.

But such cooperative arrangements helped create a number of new third world arms exporters such as Israel, Brazil, and China. The new producers sought their own military industries for reasons of national pride, self-reliance, independence from the major suppliers, and in some cases as part of a strategy of national economic development. Their role and impact is the subject of debate, but at present they are all having a hard time competing with the bigger suppliers.

In addition to the open trade, the arms market includes significant gray and black components. The *gray market* means equipment and components that are sold for ostensibly civilian purposes but then used by the military. The *black market* is clandestine and includes weapons supplied by governments as part of covert assistance programs. Not surprisingly, no solid estimate exists of the size of these markets. Most of the supplies to nonstate actors come through these channels, as does much of the technology for developing biological, chemical, and nuclear weapon capabilities. This trade, along with the open trade in so-called light arms (discussed below), has recently attracted long overdue attention from those concerned with preventing or controlling civil and ethnic violence.

The Implications of Technological Diffusion

The spread of advanced weapons technology has a number of apparently contradictory effects. Most of the 30–50 million casualties from the conflicts fought since the end of World War II were not caused by sophisticated weapons. The impact of sophisticated weaponry on combat in the third world is uncertain. For example, exports of advanced fighter aircraft sales often spark controversy, but few of them are ever actually used in combat. And with the exception of the Arab-Israeli conflicts, those aircraft that have seen combat generally performed below their advertised capabilities.

Nonetheless, as already mentioned, the introduction of particular technologies may have an important impact on the tide of battle or the outcome of a war. And technological sophistication and its impact are relative. Allied airpower completely dominated the Gulf War in 1991, yet the much-maligned Iraqi air force was later able to turn its helicopter gunships on its own rebellious citizens with devastating effect. The Stinger missiles covertly supplied by the United States to the Afghan mujahideen in the early 1980s helped to turn the tide of the Soviet invasion of Afghanistan.

Three Cold War Legacies

During the Cold War, the United States and the Soviet Union used arms transfers as essential tools in their competition for influence, especially in the third world. Today the legacies of that competition still have a significant impact on international arms transfers.

The single greatest effect of the end of the Cold War was the end of the political rivalry between the United States and the Soviet Union, which influenced almost every aspect of arms transfers in the post–World War II period. Taken together, the legacies point up the importance that economic factors have now assumed in shaping supplier policies. They color the prospects for achieving meaningful controls on transfers of conventional weapons.

The Prominence of Economic Factors

An ironic peace dividend from the Cold War was the substantial overcapacity of the military industries in peacetime in the West and the East as military forces were restructured and procurement budgets cut. No major nation, including the United States, can sustain its defense industries in peacetime solely through purchases for its own forces. Reduced military budgets also mean less trade among the developed states and fewer large new weapons programs. The military spending cuts came in conjunction with and accelerated other important trends in the defense sector. In particular, the trend continues in the United States and Europe toward fewer major firms and greater transnational ownership and cooperation. Some of this trend reflects the general trend toward larger, globalized industries, but more is the result of conscious policy choices. In particular, in the early 1990s the U.S. Defense Department deliberately encouraged U.S. firms to merge. European firms have followed suit, although more slowly and unevenly given the varied patterns across the continent of state versus private ownership and of commitment to maintaining some sort of national arms industry. In general, however, major weapon systems such as fighter aircraft, large naval vessels, and main battle tanks are being produced in smaller numbers by a small number of firms.

The result is that all the major arms-producing states face potent economic pressures to export weapons to sustain what remains of their defense industries. In principle this smaller group of suppliers could more easily agree to control the export of advanced weapon systems and platforms, but so far the economic pressures to export have proved too strong. It is much too soon to say whether the major increases planned in U.S. military spending will reduce the export pressures on U.S. firms, but that did not happen during the last major surge in procurement spending under the Ronald Reagan administration.

The nature of defense production is changing in other ways as well. A key trend is the increasing dual-use nature of military technology, with many innovations coming from the civilian sector to the military. Information and communication technologies are the leading examples. Major components may be purchased commercially off the shelf rather than specially designed to military specifications. In the future, with the exception of complete weapon systems, it may become virtually impossible to distinguish between civilian and military goods in a number of important areas.

These trends have sparked efforts to find new patterns for export controls. Some experts argue that the trends make export controls futile. Others argue that in the future controls will have to be based on significant international cooperation—on transparency and shared information rather than on denial.[2]

The Dominance of the United States

The United States has emerged from the Cold War as the largest arms supplier in the world. Since the early 1990s it has accounted for at least half of all the world's arms sales. In 2000 U.S. arms sales agreements worth $18.6 billion represented more than 50 percent of all agreements worldwide.[3] The United States also maintains the only remaining military assistance program of any significance—and that program is growing as part of the war on terrorism. No state is likely to be able to challenge that primacy for at least a decade and probably longer. How the United States conducts its arms transfers and whether it seeks and supports multilateral cooperation and restraints thus has an immense impact.

In the executive branch and Congress, discussions of arms export policy are dominated by concerns for U.S. jobs and the U.S. defense industrial base. During the 1992 presidential campaign incumbent President George Bush announced a sale of F-16s to Taiwan at the factory where the fighters would be produced. The Clinton administration gave nonproliferation a high priority, but this concern was primarily confined to WMD and ballistic missiles. Promoting arms transfers as a means of retaining economic competitiveness was an important U.S. policy goal. Such economic considerations seem likely to remain under the George W. Bush administration as it sets its own arms transfer goals, in tandem with the desire to use arms exports to sustain a global antiterrorism coalition in the wake of the terrorist attacks of 11 September 2001.

The Disappearance of the Soviet Union

Until the end of the Cold War the Soviet Union was the world's largest arms supplier. But in 1993 Russian sales agreements with the third world totaled $1.8 billion, a far cry from the record high of $27 billion in 1987.[4] The virtual disappearance of the military assistance that sustained much of the former Soviet Union's arms transfers explains why exports declined so sharply, eliminating countries such as Cuba, Angola, and Vietnam from the ranks of major arms importers. The second key reason was loss of the huge imposed market in the Warsaw Pact countries.

By the end of the 1990s, however, Russian arms transfers had revived, with Russia finishing second to the United States in arms sales agreements with developing countries during the last half of the decade.[5] Russia's primary customers are China, India, and Iran, and Russia has undertaken major technology transfer arrangements as part of its arms sales agreements. Unfortunately, China and Iran are significant sources of security and proliferation concerns for the United States. Particular sales, such as that of *Kilo*-class submarines to Iran and advanced combat aircraft to China, have sparked sharp diplomatic exchanges. Russia's refusal to limit its sales to these countries remains a major irritant in U.S.-Russia relations.

The New Security Environment

Recent reports by the World Bank and others paint a grim picture of the security environment in many parts of the world.

More than 50 countries have experienced significant periods of conflict since 1980. Fifteen of the world's 20 poorest countries experienced a major conflict between 1992 and 1997. In a number of cases conflicts led to a complete breakdown of the state. Thirty countries have had more than 10 percent of their populations displaced by conflict, either internally or as refugees in other countries. In 10 of those countries, more than 40 percent were displaced. An estimated 4 million people have been killed in conflicts since the fall of the Berlin Wall. Civilians accounted for at least 90 percent of these casualties.

In 1995 peacekeeping operations cost the international community an estimated $3 billion. The proportion of official development assistance devoted to relief rose from 2 percent in 1989 to more than 10 percent in 1994 while overall spending for long-term development assistance declined.[6] The humanitarian workers delivering this relief are increasingly at risk. The United Nations reported, for example, that 180 of its workers have been killed since 1992; in 1998, for the first time, more civilian aid workers were killed than military peacekeepers. Even after conflicts ostensibly end, violence continues in many societies where weak governments cannot provide basic security for their people.

Most of the conflicts causing this devastation are civil conflicts, and most are being fought with vast quantities of cheap, durable, and increasingly deadly light weapons.[7] Much of the world is awash in these weapons. In 1995 UN Secretary-General Boutros Boutros-Ghali called attention to the toll these weapons were taking. He proposed a new focus on micro-disarmament: "practical disarmament in the context of the conflicts the

United Nations is actually dealing with and of the weapons, most of them light weapons, that are actually killing people in the hundreds of thousands."[8]

The information available about the volume and values of light weapons transfers and stocks is limited, piecemeal, and sometimes suspect. No country systematically reports either its imports or exports of light weapons. A significant portion of the trade in light weapons is illegal, and governments continue covert transfers of arms to other governments or to insurgent groups. Huge surplus stocks left over from the Cold War and enormous quantities of weapons already in circulation further complicate efforts to accumulate reliable estimates. Depending on what is included, estimates of the value of the legal trade in light weapons range from $3 billion to $6 billion, with the illegal trade adding perhaps another $2–10 billion. Estimates of the number of legal and illegal military and civilian-style firearms currently in circulation worldwide range from 500 million to more than 1 billion.[9]

Reports from researchers and journalists in the field have added significantly to our understanding of the light weapons problem. The durability of these weapons means that automatic rifles left behind by U.S. forces in Vietnam have found their way to conflicts in Central America and the Middle East. In Africa and elsewhere, as one conflict ends weapons frequently flow across porous borders to be used in others. And arms are a standard part of the inventories of global organized crime syndicates, with insurgent groups or governments under international embargoes sometimes allying themselves with the syndicates to trade commodities from areas under their control for weapons.

In the case of light weapons, the economic pressures are a less significant barrier to control efforts. Instead, the sheer volume of the trade, the multiple and often illegal trade routes, and the weakness of the governments most affected by the light weapons and the violence they enable represent the more significant hurdles that must be overcome.

Controlling Arms Transfers: Arguments and Examples

The debate over the feasibility and desirability of attempting to control conventional arms transfers has gone on for decades.

The Pros and Cons of Arms Trade Controls

For most nations, access to conventional weapons is directly tied to fundamental issues of national sovereignty and the right of national self-defense enshrined in the United Nations Charter. North-South issues of access to technology and developing countries' resentment of the tendency of industrialized nations to believe they know what is right for the developing world are inextricably linked to arms transfers. Yet many nations, both developed and developing, are uneasy about the steady proliferation of weapons and weapons technology, as well as the impact that arms flows can have on particular conflicts. The urge to control arms transfers is part of a broader wish to find ways to control and ameliorate conflict. But it runs up against an equally strong desire to aid—or at least permit—friends and allies to acquire the weapons they believe are needed to ensure their national security.

These tensions are reflected in the continuing arguments over U.S. policy. In 1976 President Jimmy Carter made limits on U.S. arms exports a theme of his presidential campaign. In 1977 the White House announced a restraint policy, listing 11 purposes that limiting arms sales would serve.[10] Four years later the Reagan administration put a different emphasis on arms transfers, reflecting its concern with the East-West conflict and the support that arms transfers could provide to third world allies in that struggle. The 1981 White House statement gave seven other reasons for using arms transfers as a foreign policy tool.[11] The Clinton administration gave economic considerations greater emphasis; for the first time one of the five goals of its policy was "to enhance the ability of the U.S. defense industrial base to meet U.S. defense requirements and maintain long-term military technological superiority at lower costs."[12] Prior to 11 September, the George W. Bush administration was still seeking a balance among these tensions; now the security benefits of arms transfers for counterterrorism are receiving significant attention.

In addition, discussions of the merits or fallacies of arms transfers restraint always face questions of feasibility. Achieving significant controls can appear to be an overwhelming task, particularly as one goes down the ladder of technological sophistication from the high-performance weapons, such as fighter aircraft and main battle tanks, that are still produced by only a few suppliers, toward the light weapons that are responsible for most deaths. On some level, every nation in the world participates in the arms trade. Unilateral export restraint, even by the United States, may prove ineffective if former customers can find new suppliers. The record to date for multilateral restraint is not encouraging. Yet modest successes have occurred in spite of the daunting challenges, and there is a wide variety of potential means to try to control arms transfers.

Examples of Efforts to Control Arms Transfers

In the remainder of this chapter I examine several cases of attempts to curb the proliferation of conventional weapons that illustrate part of the range of available approaches.

Fostering transparency through the UN register. The UN Register of Conventional Arms is one of a growing number of international and regional efforts to foster transparency and openness about military spending, arms production, and arms imports and exports. Transparency is not control; instead the hope is that greater openness and knowledge will build trust and encourage restraint. The work of the Organization for Security and Cooperation in Europe is perhaps the best example of creating a web of confidence-building measures as part of a regional security strategy.

The idea for an international register to report arms imports and exports emerged in the late 1980s. In 1988 the UN General Assembly passed a resolution to create a group of governmental experts to study ways to promote transparency and openness about conventional arms transfers. The end of the Cold War and the revelations after the Gulf War about Iraq's arms programs increased interest in preventing weapons proliferation, and advocates thought increased transparency would support international nonproliferation efforts. The expert group's report formed the basis for a UN General Assembly resolution in December 1991 to create a register.

The UN register is a limited exercise, requiring countries to report their arms imports and exports for the preceding year in seven major categories: battle tanks, armored combat vehicles, large-caliber artillery systems, combat aircraft, attack helicopters, warships, and missiles and missile launchers. Its creators hoped the information would encourage governments to cooperate and coordinate their policies and provide knowledge to the public so that citizens would become more active in urging their governments to limit imports or exports.

The UN register receives mixed reviews. About half of the total General Assembly membership submitted reports the first year of its operation (1992), but the numbers have declined over the years. Some important countries—Saudi Arabia, Syria, and Iran, for example—do not submit reports. For some areas, in particular sub-Saharan Africa, the kinds of weapons reported in the register are irrelevant to the arms trade in their region. And the data provided by exporters and importers do not always match. Nonetheless, the register has so far succeeded in tentatively establishing a norm of transparency about international arms transfers and has provided useful data for arms trade experts. Moreover, a number of countries also submit additional information about their arms export policies or more detailed information about their purchases than required.

The issue now is the future of the register, especially efforts to expand its scope to include other categories of weapons. Many fear that the register must grow or die, but there is only limited consensus on what the growth should be. Another problem is simply getting key nations to submit reports.

It is not clear how much the information that the register provides genuinely enhances attention to arms transfers as a security issue. But getting the UN General Assembly to address arms transfers at all was a significant achievement. For many years developing countries had charged that any mention of the issue was an attempt by the developed states, and especially the nuclear powers, to divert attention from the far greater problems posed by WMD. If, as intended, the register is coupled with other UN initiatives to promote regional and cooperative security, it could be part of important efforts to address the problems of arms transfers.

The Missile Technology Control Regime. Other chapters in this volume describe the growing number of countries that have achieved or are pursuing ballistic and cruise missile programs and the proposals to respond to them with active defenses. Of all the advanced conventional weapons that are spreading throughout the third world, ballistic missile proliferation has received by far the greatest attention from policymakers. If one's concern is the potential threat to the U.S. homeland and forward-deployed U.S. forces, then the attention to missiles is understandable. From the broader perspective of the proliferation of weapons that are most likely to be used in conflict and to cause the most casualties, however, the intense focus on ballistic missiles is less easy to accept.

Most experts emphasize three reasons for singling out ballistic missiles as a threat. The first is the lack of effective defenses. Of all the potential delivery vehicles, only ballistic missiles face no effective defenses at present. Second, ballistic missiles are significantly faster than other delivery vehicles, especially over middle- and long-range distances. This offers the possibility of surprise and diminishes the chances that an adversary could mount an effective civil defense. The latter is important for reducing the potential casualties from an attack using WMD. Third, missiles promise significant psychological and political effects. Ever since the German V-1 cruise missile and V-2 ballistic missile attacks in World War II, missiles have carried a special psychological power, sometimes exceeding their actual military impact.

The United States launched the Missile Technology Control Regime (MTCR) in 1987 in an attempt to curb the spread of ballistic missiles and missile technology. Modeled on other suppliers' arrangements to govern exports related to nuclear, biological, and chemical weapon proliferation, the MTCR focuses on controlling exports of missiles and missile technology for systems with payloads over 500 kilograms and ranges over 300 kilometers. The MTCR has grown from its initial seven members—the United States, Canada, France, West Germany, Italy, Japan, and Great Britain—to 33 full members.

The MTCR has been controversial from the beginning. First, in conception and initial operation the MTCR was a classic export control regime based on denial by suppliers. As such it was subject to the same dual criticisms that all such regimes confront: discrimination, on the one hand, and insufficient scope and effectiveness on the other. In addition, with the United States and some other industrialized countries increasingly interested in defenses against ballistic missiles, some critics charge the MTCR is an effort to improve the chances that those defenses will be effective. This is the kind of arms control, they contend, that is designed primarily to make it safer and easier for the industrialized states to intervene in the developing world.

Other arguments over MTCR concern its effectiveness, particularly in response to the threat of WMD. Concentrating on missiles could give a false sense of security that one is doing something significant about WMD, especially if there is no comparable effort to address other potential delivery means.

The other critique of the MTCR's effectiveness centers on whether it can seriously inhibit the spread of missile technology. Some analysts argue that it has successfully dampened countries' efforts, particularly those indigenous production programs that depend heavily on imported technology. They cite successes such as the suppression of the joint Argentine, Egyptian, and Iraqi Condor II ballistic missile program and of South African and Central European missile activities. Others respond that delay is the best that can be achieved, citing continuing programs by Iran, North Korea, and Iraq.

Finally, even if the MTCR works, critics question whether it is worth the strain it puts on relations among suppliers and between suppliers and recipients. Over the years the MTCR has caused tension in U.S. relations with a number of its European allies and with the former Soviet Union and China. As part of its efforts to counter U.S. proposals for national missile defenses, for example, Russia has proposed the Global Control System outside the MTCR. Others, however, regard MTCR as the prototype of new arms control approaches based on cooperative responses to emerging threats. Much of one's view toward the MTCR depends on whether one sees the effort as serving general international goals or U.S. national security interests, as well as what one thinks about the efficacy of nonproliferation efforts more generally.

Landmines.   Even if war seems uncontrolled and uncontrollable, people have sought ways to limit its effects through the creation of a body of norms and international law: the laws of war, or international humanitarian law. Controlling and proscribing the use of certain weapons that are considered too indiscriminate and unnecessarily injurious is part of this effort. In 1868 the St. Petersburg declaration outlawed the use of a newly invented bullet designed to explode and shatter on contact with a soft surface, such as the human body. The Hague conventions of the early 1900s went on to ban other weapons. The Chemical Weapons Convention and the Biological Weapons Convention can be seen as other examples of this approach.

In the 1990s the primary focus of these efforts was finding a way to cope with the millions of antipersonnel landmines (APLs) sown in the course of conflicts around the world. The U.S. State Department has estimated that perhaps 60–70 million landmines are still in the ground in countries such as Angola, Afghanistan, Cambodia, Nicaragua, and Somalia.[13] Parts of some countries are genuinely infested with mines, which are increasingly used as weapons of terror to make territory uninhabitable or to enforce ethnic cleansing. Cheap to buy and easy to emplace, they are dangerous and expensive to clear and make it far more difficult for countries to rebuild and return to a normal life once conflicts are over. Returning refugees to their homes may become impossible if villages, roads, and fields are too dangerous to inhabit. Those who survive landmine explosions often lose limbs, placing additional burdens on already overloaded health care systems.

The Convention on Certain Conventional Weapons (CCCW) was the first international treaty to attempt to regulate the use of landmines in its protocol. A review of the CCCW in 1996 led to an amended protocol, which among other things distinguished between the use of antipersonnel and antitank mines and restricted the uses of all APLs. The United States has signed and ratified the CCCW, including the amended protocol. Further measures to limit landmines' use or ameliorate their effects are part of the regular process of periodic review conferences.

A number of nongovernmental organizations (NGOs) have sought more ambitious restraints on landmines. In an effort that ultimately earned them the Nobel Prize, a group of NGOs banded together in the early 1990s to form the International Campaign to Ban Landmines. This was the first example of the growing importance of NGOs in affecting national and international policy.[14] The campaign, joined over time by a growing number of international organizations and governments, led to the Convention on the Prohibition of the Use, Stockpiling, Production, and Transfer of Antipersonnel Mines and on Their Destruction (the Ottawa Convention). Signed by 122 countries in Ottawa, Canada, on 3 December 1997, the convention entered into force in March 1999. As of spring 2002, 142 nations had signed or acceded to the convention, including all NATO member states (except the United States and Turkey) and all European Union (EU) member states (except Finland).

The Ottawa Convention bans the use of all antipersonnel landmines (APL), including those that are self-destructing and self-deactivating, whether alone or in mixed systems with antitank mines. Signatories are prohibited from developing, producing, acquiring, and stockpiling APL; they also must not assist, encourage, or induce anyone else to undertake these actions. All APL held by signatories must be destroyed within four years of becoming a full member of the convention.

Despite early support for an APL ban and continuing leadership in efforts to ameliorate the residual effects of APLs, the United States has not joined the Ottawa Convention. President Clinton stated in September 1997 that the United States would not sign the treaty until alternative technologies that could provide similar capabilities to APLs had been identified and fielded. He announced an active research-and-development program to seek such alternatives. Clinton also established as presidential policy that after 2003 the United States would no longer use APLs outside of Korea, where, the Department of Defense has argued, landmines play a particularly important role. If alternatives for Korea and for mixed systems could be found by 2006, the United States would sign the Ottawa Convention. In the meantime, the United States has destroyed 3 million non–self-destructing and non–self-deactivating mines. That policy is under review by the George W. Bush administration, but the possibility of a decision to sign the convention is considered remote.

The light weapons problem.   Increasing attention to the issue of light weapons brought proposals for control from many quarters. Initially, considerable attention focused on measures that put light weapons in the context of the conflicts in which they were used and sought to identify policies suitable to a conflict's different phases. This perspective remains important, particularly for the implementation of peace settlements. Over time, however, two other perspectives have gained prominence. The social devastation created by the culture of violence in many countries, facilitated by the ready availability of light weapons, led to a broader concern with curbing illicit arms transfers and to other efforts to restore basic security to citizens. The focus on illicit arms also reflects growing concern with the power and global reach of terrorism and organized crime networks. A third approach, growing out of the practical problems for relief and reconstruction that incited UN attention, emphasizes measures to affect the demand side for these weapons. All the approaches are linked, and the distinctions among them often blur, especially on the ground in conflict-ridden countries. But they do represent different basic motivations for wanting to address the light weapons problem, and they bring different constituencies into the process of developing and implementing policy.

Conflict process measures.   Measures to stem the proliferation of light weapons can be divided into those that apply before a conflict or in its early stages, those that apply while conflict is raging, and those that apply once a conflict ends. For example, tracking flows of weapons could offer early warning of potential outbreaks of violence and the opportunity for preventive action. This would require significantly better information and more systematic analysis, as well as some expectation that the warning would be heeded. In addition to initiatives for improved intelligence-gathering and information-sharing among governments, there are also proposals to utilize NGOs working on the ground in conflict-prone countries.

While conflicts are under way, limits or outright embargoes on arms supplies are the obvious control mechanisms. Access to supplies of weapons can be a significant factor in sustaining adversaries' abilities to continue to fight. Suppliers have long used controls on the resupply of weapons to affect the outcome of war, even to force an early halt to fighting. Embargoes are controversial, however, because they may have only limited effectiveness and convey a significant advantage to one side.

More research and experience have accumulated regarding the weapons left over when a conflict ostensibly ends. Postwar arms control measures seek to reinforce peace settlements as well as to prevent weapons used in one conflict from flowing to another. Here the measures include formal disarmament provisions that may be part of peace settlements, disarmament measures that may be part of the demobilization and reintegration of former combatants, and the collection of surplus weapons. It also can include programs to buy guns back from the civilian populations of war-torn societies.

Combating illicit arms trafficking.   This area has seen perhaps the greatest activity because of its links to closely related law enforcement measures addressing the drug trade and organized crime. The Organization of American States (OAS) has undertaken two efforts. The first, under the auspices of the OAS Inter-American Drug Abuse Control Commission, used an experts group to create the Model Regulations to Control the Movement of Firearms, Ammunition, and Firearms Parts and Components. This set of regulations, adopted in November 1997, encourages regulation and licensing of firearms transfers by all OAS member states and seeks to standardize practices throughout the Western Hemisphere. Second, at the initiative of the Mexican government, the OAS Permanent Council completed the Inter-American Convention Against the Illicit Manufacturing and Trafficking in Firearms, Ammunition, Explosives, and Other Related Materials.

Also in 1997, the European Union adopted the Programme for Preventing and Combating Illicit Trafficking in Conventional Arms. This program makes explicit links between peace and security and economic development and reconstruction, important connections that development assistance agencies have frequently avoided acknowledging. It seeks to combat illicit trafficking on or through EU territories and to develop measures to reduce the number of weapons in circulation. Most of the EU effort is focused on Africa.

On the international level, in May 2001 the UN General Assembly added a firearms protocol to the 2000 Convention Against Transnational Organized Crime, declaring criminal such offenses as illicit manufacturing and trafficking in firearms, their parts, components, and ammunition, as well as falsifying and altering the markings on firearms. The purpose of the new instrument is to strengthen cooperation among state parties in order to prevent, combat, and eradicate illicit activities involving firearms and ammunition. Supporters argue that the new instrument creates a global standard for the transnational movement to prevent theft and diversion of firearms while providing law enforcement officials with tools to effectively detect, investigate, and prosecute illicit manufacturing and trafficking offenses.

Affecting the demand side. The international development community has been forced in recent years to confront the inextricable links between the need for basic human security and the hopes for long-term development. The dilemmas facing relief and aid workers that drove UN Secretary-General Boutros-Ghali to call for microdisarmament has led an increasing number of donor countries and international financial institutions to address security issues. The initiatives most commonly tackle post-conflict reconstruction. In 1997 the World Bank created a special unit devoted to these problems. Its Conflict Prevention and Reconstruction Unit has funded research as well as operational programs on the ground. Much of its work has been with demobilization and reintegration of combatants, an area that fits quite comfortably within the World Bank's mandate.[15] In addition, a number of the major donor countries, including Canada, Belgium, Sweden, and Norway, have become more directly engaged in the light weapons issue, in part through supporting the activities of NGOs.

The continuing role of the United Nations. The United Nations has demonstrated significant leadership in tackling the problem of light weapons. This reflects a new willingness by the affected developing countries to acknowledge the problem and seek either regional solutions or international action. Much of the UN attention has been confined to illegal and illicit transfers, in part because of reluctance by the United States to address the domestically difficult question of limits on legal transfers. In July 2001 the UN Special Session on the Illicit Trade in Small Arms and Light Weapons in All Its Aspects almost foundered when the United States took strong positions against restrictions on civilian gun ownership and a ban on transfers to nonstate actors. Many of the NGOs who had worked for months in preparation for the special session expressed strong disappointment. Nonetheless, the program of action at the end of the conference did call for a review conference in 2006, thus further legitimating continued UN engagement on the issue. And in late August 2001 the UN Security Council made clear its continuing concern with the burdens that the light weapons problem pose for carrying out its essential peace and security missions.

Conclusion

To date the record of attempts to control the spread of conventional weapons is mixed at best. Arms transfers are intimately tied to international, regional, and national politics; thus overcoming one barrier to limits leaves many others to be faced. The economic pressures to export remain so strong for producers today that it is hard to envision who would undertake the initiative for supplier restraint. And an argument can be made that in an anarchic world, where nations remain ultimately responsible for the security of their citizens, arms transfers serve the cause of peace and stability. If the resources of governments to pursue nonproliferation are limited, do conventional weapons deserve much attention?

In reality the choices are not so stark. An international effort by suppliers to put significant restraints on their exports is unlikely to happen very soon unless some shock forces a substantial change in priorities. But individual suppliers will continue to regulate their exports to ensure that they meet national goals. In addition, there may be continuing efforts like the MTCR to restrain the spread of particular technologies. Regional efforts have not yielded much in the past, but recent years have seen significant effort from within regions, including those where many would have argued indigenous peace efforts were impossible. Transparency measures like the UN Arms Register may increase the amount of attention arms transfers receive.

Taken together, these various individual efforts will not satisfy those for whom the arms trade is immoral and who want sweeping international controls and reductions. But arms control and collective security goals remain relevant to arms transfer problems, will almost certainly be part of any systematic effort to address weapons proliferation, and are an increasingly important part of new efforts by new constituencies to address the links between conventional weapons and their primary concerns.

Notes

This chapter represents the views of the author as an individual and does not represent conclusions or official positions of the National Academy of Sciences. Portions of this chapter are updated from the author's original contribution to Jeffrey A. Larsen and Gregory J. Rattray, eds., *Arms Control Toward the 21st Century* (Boulder: Lynne Rienner Publishers, 1996).

1. The primary source for arms transfers data is now the yearbook of the Stockholm International Peace Research Institute (SIPRI); the most recent is *SIPRI Yearbook 2000: World Armaments and Disarmament* (New York: Oxford University Press, 2000). With the elimination of the U.S. Arms Control and Disarmament Agency, publication of its annual *World Military Expenditures and Arms Transfers* has ceased. This makes the annual report compiled by Richard Grimmett from the Congressional Research Service, which uses the same data as the Arms Control and

Disarmament Agency reports once did, the best source of official U.S. statistics. The 2001 report, *Conventional Arms Transfers to Developing Nations, 1993–2000*, can be accessed at www.fas.org/asmp/resources/govtdocs.htm#Congress.

2. See, for example, the Henry L. Stimson Center and the Center for Strategic and International Studies, *Study Group on Enhancing Multilateral Export Controls for U.S. National Security: Final Report*. (Washington, DC: Henry L. Stimson Center, April 2001).

3. Grimmett, *Conventional Arms Transfers*, p. 3. Arms sales can fluctuate significantly from year to year, especially in a smaller market. A few large sales can significantly affect rankings among suppliers and also annual totals.

4. Ibid., p. 50.

5. Ibid., p. 39.

6. The statistics cited above are all taken from World Bank, *Post-Conflict Reconstruction: The Role of the World Bank* (Washington, DC: International Bank for Reconstruction and Development, 1998), p. 2.

7. One leading expert defines *light weapons* as "all those conventional munitions that can be carried by an individual combatant or by a light vehicle operating on back-country roads." Michael T. Klare, "The Global Trade in Light Weapons and the International System in the Post–Cold War Era," in Jeffrey Boutwell, Michael T. Klare, and Laura W. Reed, eds., *Lethal Commerce: The Global Trade in Small Arms and Light Weapons* (Cambridge: American Academy of Arts and Sciences, 1995), p. 33.

8. United Nations, *Supplement to an Agenda for Peace*, A/50/60-S/1995/1, 1995.

9. These figures are cited in Michael Renner, "Arms Control Orphans," *Bulletin of the Atomic Scientists* (January/February 1999): 24–26.

10. *Arms Transfer Policy*, Report to the Congress, United States Senate (Washington, DC: U.S. Government Printing Office), 1977, pp. 12–13.

11. Congressional Research Service, *Changing Perspectives on U.S. Arms Transfer Policy*, Report Prepared for the Subcommittee on International Security and Scientific Affairs of the Committee on Foreign Affairs, U.S. House of Representatives (Washington, DC: U.S. Government Printing Office, 1981), p. 127.

12. White House, *Fact Sheet: Conventional Arms Transfers Policy*, February 17, 1995.

13. U.S. Department of State, *Hidden Killers 1998: The Global Landmine Crisis* (Washington, DC: U.S. Department of State, September 1998).

14. Ann M. Florini, ed., *The Third Force: The Rise of Transnational Civil Society* (Washington, DC: Carnegie Endowment for International Peace and Japan Center for International Exchange, 2000).

15. Returning former soldiers to productive economic activity is considered an appropriate activity for the World Bank. In a similar way, all of its funding for humanitarian demining must be for returning land to productive use.

Suggested Readings

Boutwell, Jeffrey, and Michael T. Klare, eds. *Light Weapons and Civil Conflict*. New York: Rowman and Littlefield, 1999.

Lumpe, Lora, ed. *Running Guns: The Global Black Market in Small Arms*. New York: St. Martin's, 2000.

Markusen, Ann R., and Sean S. Costigan, eds. *Arming the Future: A Defense Industry for the 21st Century.* New York: Council on Foreign Relations, 1999.
Pierre, Andrew J., ed. *Cascade of Arms: Managing Conventional Weapons Proliferation.* Washington, DC: Brookings Institution, 1997.

10

Cooperative Security Measures

Guy B. Roberts

> The most urgent unmet national security threat to the United States today is the danger that weapons of mass destruction or weapon-usable material in Russia could be stolen and sold to terrorists or hostile nation states and used against American troops abroad or citizens at home. The threat is a clear and present danger to the international community as well as to American lives and liberties.
> —2001 U.S. Department of Energy Russia Task Force[1]

The end of the Cold War brought twin promises: ending the prospect of global annihilation, and ending the increased danger of nuclear weapons proliferation. With the dissolution of the Soviet Union into the Russian Federation and a set of newly independent states (NIS), the federation laid claim to the former empire's nuclear arsenal and other weapons of mass destruction (WMD); the NIS, in turn, quickly foreswore WMD and their means of delivery.[2] Ominously, as the Soviet Union deconstructed, so too did the infrastructure that supported its massive nuclear weapon program. That program had produced more than 40,000 nuclear weapons and over 1,000 tons of fissile materials,[3] was spread over 11 time zones, and involved dozens of production facilities and research institutes.[4]

With the ensuing political, economic, and social turmoil in the former Soviet states, the world is now faced with an unprecedented crisis on the supply side of nuclear proliferation. Never before has the world dealt with the phenomenon of the breakup, rapid political and economic transformation, and internal disarray in a nuclear superpower with tens of thousands of nuclear weapons and hundreds of tons of weapon-usable fissile material. Nuclear material security systems that once relied on the Iron Curtain and the iron hand of the KGB (the Soviet intelligence agency) are now grossly inadequate or nonexistent. Consequently, the international community now faces a common threat: the possibility that fissile materials could be stolen or diverted for terrorism purposes.

These materials are the essential ingredients of nuclear weapons. And if even a small amount of this material gets into the wrong hands, a state or terrorist group could come to possess one of the essential ingredients for building a nuclear weapon. Experts believe that the former Soviet Union produced more than 1,200 tons of highly enriched uranium (HEU) and 150 tons of plutonium; however, no one, not even the Russians, knows for sure.[5] Simply put, no national accounting system for nuclear materials in the Soviet Union existed. No one in Russia knows exactly how much plutonium and HEU was produced, and at most sites no one would know if any material was in fact missing. It is not unusual for facilities to discover stashes of HEU, for example, that they did not know existed.

More than half of this material resides in assembled nuclear weapons. Pursuant to the first and second treaties under the Strategic Arms Reduction Talks (START I, START II), as well as unilateral pledges made by U.S. President George Bush and Soviet Presidents Mikhail Gorbachev and Boris Yeltsin, and follow-on agreements by Presidents George W. Bush and Vladimir Putin, many thousands of U.S. and Russian nuclear weapons were retired at the end of 2001 with thousands more headed for irreversible retirement within the next decade.[6] As a result, on each side some 50-plus metric tons of plutonium, along with hundreds of tons of HEU, are now surplus to military needs. Despite this, Russia continues to produce approximately 2.5 metric tons of plutonium per year from reactors that cannot be shut down because they are the only source of power in the regions they service. Fortunately, because assembled nuclear weapons are strictly accounted for, difficult to transport, and heavily guarded within secure military installations, they are considered to be much less vulnerable to theft and diversion than weapon-usable nuclear materials in other forms.

The greatest proliferation threat is the approximately 650 metric tons of fissile material existing in forms such as metals, oxides, solutions, and scrap. These materials, enough to produce more than 40,000 nuclear bombs, are spread among eight countries. They are in use or stored at more than 50 sites across Russia, the NIS, and the Baltic states. In addition to nuclear weapon complexes, substantial quantities of fissile materials were held at civilian facilities. Some are controlled by the Russian Atomic Energy Agency (MINATOM), the rest by a variety of other organizations, which typically have only minimal physical protection.[7]

The security system that protected this material during the Soviet period has totally collapsed. Nuclear scientists and other employees of the nuclear weapons industry, once at the pinnacle of Soviet society, now go months without pay. A recently released study by the Carnegie Endowment for International Peace on the living and working conditions in so-called nuclear cities and missile enterprises reported that more than 62 percent of Russian nuclear and missile experts make less than $50 per month; 89

percent report a decline in living conditions since 1992; and 20 percent said they would be willing to work outside of Russia.[8] Budget cuts have decreased the number and effectiveness of guard-force personnel, security system maintenance, and operational readiness. Many nuclear workers now live under difficult conditions because they have not received wages for long periods of time and because the quality of available food, housing, and medical care has declined. These circumstances, coupled with low morale, increase the chances that insiders will steal nuclear material and/or share weapon information for financial gain.

Pessimistically, a United Nations report has claimed that more than 100 terrorist organizations have the capability of acquiring, or have actually acquired, the key elements for constructing a nuclear weapon.[9] The worldwide smuggling of fissile materials has doubled since 1996, and the International Atomic Energy Agency (IAEA) has recorded more than 550 confirmed incidents of nuclear trafficking since 1993.[10] There are almost weekly reports of smugglers being intercepted in Russia or elsewhere trying to sell fissile materials.

Given this extraordinary threat—and the concern it engendered in the United States—several cooperative initiatives have been undertaken since the early 1990s. Although not intended to be exhaustive, the discussion below details the cooperative measures initiated by the United States and other countries.[11] Such initiatives have focused on four main efforts: (1) providing technical and economic assistance in accelerating strategic arms reductions in accordance with previously negotiated arms control agreements; (2) securing and accounting for fissile materials; (3) properly disposing of excess fissile materials; and (4) preventing so-called brain-drain of weaponmakers.

The Cooperative Threat Reduction Program

Cooperative efforts to prevent the illicit transfers of weapons, materials, and technology from Russia, Ukraine, Belarus, and Kazakhstan were proposed in March 1992 and supported by funds made available by Congress through the Soviet Nuclear Threat Reduction Act of 1991—also known as the Nunn-Lugar act after its leading sponsors (Senators San Nunn and Richard Lugar).[12] This legislation is the cornerstone of all United States cooperative funding efforts. The act, renamed the Cooperative Threat Reduction (CTR) program in 1993, was initially designed to help the countries of the former Soviet Union destroy their WMD and associated infrastructure and establish verifiable safeguards against proliferation of those weapons in order to prevent their transfer to rogue nations and terrorist organizations. Since its inception, the program has spent $3.6 billion and has made significant progress in substantially reducing the threat of WMD in the former Soviet Union. For example, U.S. nuclear weapons elimination assistance resulted in Kazakhstan becoming nuclear weapon–free in 1995, with Ukraine and Belarus following in 1996.

Although the threat of the illicit transfer of fissile materials remains urgent, since 1992 significant programs have been instituted to begin the process of fully securing, safeguarding, and accounting for these materials and technologies. The CTR program remains the primary vehicle for addressing our proliferation concerns with the former Soviet Union and the funding source for many of the cooperative measures currently being implemented.

Dismantling and Securing Strategic Nuclear Weapons

The United States first negotiated umbrella agreements for CTR assistance, designating the Department of Defense (DoD) as the executive agent, with Russia (1992), Ukraine (1993), Kazakhstan (1993), Moldova (1994), Georgia (1997), and Uzbekistan (2001). Once these agreements were in place, DoD negotiated and concluded a total of 38 implementing agreements,[13] which provided a comprehensive legal framework for CTR activities.[14] However, in 1995 several CTR initiatives were transferred to the Department of Energy (DOE) and the Department of State, although the DoD remained responsible for implementing the weapon elimination programs.[15] These DoD-run CTR projects were designed to enhance the security of weapon storage sites and provide secure transportation to sites where warheads would be dismantled.[16]

Since 1992 DoD has spent more than $1 billion to assist in the elimination of hundreds of submarine-launched ballistic missile (SLBM) launchers and associated submarines, intercontinental ballistic missile (ICBM) silos, and heavy bombers. In addition, since 1992 DoD has provided security at weapon storage sites, designed comprehensive security upgrades and inventory control systems, developed transportation security measures for movement and storage of nuclear weapons, and funded and helped build a fissile material storage facility in Mayak designed to store the fissile material from more than 6,000 dismantled warheads (up to 50 metric tons of plutonium and 200 metric tons of HEU).

DoD has also provided funding and technical assistance for sealing nuclear test tunnels and holes; eliminating ICBM liquid propellant facilities, strategic air base infrastructure, and weapon storage facilities; and destroying mobile missile launchers and long-range air-launched cruise missiles. More than 1,900 nuclear warheads were returned to Russia from the Ukraine, and 54 ICBMs were returned to Russia from Belarus. In summary, by 2007, barring schedule disruptions, the CTR initiative will have funded or otherwise supported the deactivation of more than 9,800 warheads; the elimination of 1,037 ICBMs, 661 SLBMs, 93 bombers, and 250 mobile ICBM launchers; and the destruction of 565 ICBM silos.[17]

In tandem with these initiatives, DoD has encouraged a wide range of military reductions and reforms to further reduce proliferation threats from the former Soviet Union. These have included participation in joint exercises with Russian and other NIS forces, as well as a military-to-military contact program. Interestingly, the CTR program is the primary funding source for the bulk of defense and military contacts, such as exercises and defense personnel exchanges with the seven CTR-eligible states of the former Soviet Union (Russia, Ukraine, Moldova, Georgia, Kazakhstan, Kyrgyzstan, and Uzbekistan).

These efforts have been prone to occasional schedule and cost overruns, often the result of Russian economic woes, slowing the pace of and cooperation for weapons elimination. Nonetheless, the program has proven to be an extraordinary and unprecedented accomplishment, ensuring the elimination of thousands of potential nuclear weapons, enhancing the safe storage of WMD and related materials, and reducing opportunities for illicit acquisition of nuclear weapons, materials, and related systems and technology.

At the program implementation level, the biggest challenges (and a recurring theme to all these CTR initiatives) have been transparency and access. The Russians, despite their desire to achieve the program objectives, have been understandably reluctant to give visibility to sensitive military processes and facilities. One example of this is the ongoing discussion over whether to include a measure to ensure the material originates from a weapon, as well as a complete transparency regime for the U.S.-funded Mayak storage facility. These transparency measures are critically important, not only to conduct agreed activities but also to conduct the necessary audits and examinations that reassure Congress that CTR resources are being used for their intended purposes.

Threat Reduction: Fissile Material
Protection Control and Accounting Initiatives

Amazingly, the Soviet Union never instituted a national material protection, control, and accounting (MPC&A) system as required by the IAEA safeguards regime. The KGB and other national security forces effectively prevented the movement of those persons who might have the wherewithal to smuggle or illicitly transfer fissile materials. That, of course, changed dramatically when the physical security system collapsed along with the rest of the Soviet Union. The danger of stolen nuclear material being diverted for blackmail or worse purposes underscores the importance of rigorous national and international efforts to improve nuclear MPC&A and to prevent nuclear material from entering the smuggling pipeline, where it is difficult if not impossible to retrieve.

Partly as a result of Cold War resentment, embarrassment, and bureaucratic inertia, initial offers of assistance by the United States and others were met with reluctance on the part of the Russians; the other former Soviet states were slightly more enthusiastic. Consequently, serious negotiations over joint MPC&A projects did not begin until mid-1994. After overcoming their initial hesitancy, the Russians have agreed to an accelerated support effort, and it is now a critical component of the CTR effort.

Modern, well-designed nuclear MPC&A systems provide a cost-effective and reliable way for securing nuclear material from insider as well as outsider threats. MPC&A improvements provide the first line of defense against nuclear smuggling. Nearly all countries possessing nuclear materials have established MPC&A systems that are consistent with guidelines developed by the IAEA. In addition to traditional physical protection systems (guards, fences, alarms, etc.), material control systems are designed to limit access and use of nuclear material and to detect promptly the theft and diversion of the material should it occur. These systems can include portal monitors and other devices to control egress from storage sites. Material control is also achieved through the use of secure containers for nuclear material, seals, identification codes that make it possible to easily verify the location and condition of nuclear material, and material use and storage rules and procedures.

Reducing Proliferation Dangers by Securing Nuclear Materials

The United States, Russia, the NIS, and the Baltic states are now working together for nuclear material security, relying on technology-based MPC&A systems. Nuclear experts from these countries are cooperating to adopt effective MPC&A methods and technologies, as well as to develop comprehensive and self-sustaining MPC&A systems consistent with international standards. Significant progress has been made since this historic cooperation began. This new era of trust has manifested itself in recently signed agreements between DOE and MINATOM (October 1999) and the Russian navy (August 2000) to cooperatively secure vulnerable stocks of HEU and plutonium.

Since 1994 the United States has completed several significant MPC&A initiatives. These have included:

- Security upgrades for 750 metric tons of at-risk HEU and plutonium (enough material for roughly 45,000 nuclear bombs);
- Conversion of more than 1.6 metric tons of Russian nuclear weapon materials to lower proliferation risks;

- MPC&A upgrades for all plutonium and HEU in the NIS;
- Monitoring security upgrades through site inspections and training support; and
- Improving Russia's ability to detect and interdict nuclear smuggling by installing radiation detection equipment at key border crossings, including three seaports and one airport under the Second Line of Defense initiative (see below).

Although no donor country has established a program of comparable size as the United States, MPC&A programs in Japan, France, and the United Kingdom are valued in the tens of millions of dollars. Germany, Italy, Canada, Norway, and Sweden, among others, have smaller programs.

This program enjoys substantial bipartisan support in the United States and is considered the first line of defense against unwanted proliferation events. And yet after years of effort, only about 75 percent of the estimated 750 metric tons of fissile material considered at risk for theft and diversion have been secured through new MPC&A systems. DOE plans call for safeguarding 60 percent of the material by 2006 and the rest within 10–15 years after that. However, these MPC&A systems offer little defense against organized crime syndicates conspiring with well-placed insiders able to circumvent alarm systems, bribe guards, and falsify paperwork. Given these realities, site and fissile materials security will continue to be a grave proliferation concern for some time to come.

The laboratory-to-laboratory initiative. In 1994 DOE initiated and funded a second approach to joint MPC&A cooperation with Russia that encouraged U.S. national laboratories to cooperate directly with the Russian Federation's nuclear institutes to improve MPC&A. This effort was designed to complement the original government-to-government approach and achieve more rapid joint progress on MPC&A.

Under this initiative, technical experts from DOE national laboratories work directly with their counterparts in Russia, the NIS, and the Baltic states and have primary responsibility for designing and installing upgraded MPC&A systems and leading training activities. In addition, DOE national laboratory teams play a major role in providing assistance for the development of national nuclear regulatory systems. These programs are implemented by institutes and enterprises in Russia, the NIS, and the Baltic states, using U.S. as well as local equipment and methods.

The second line of defense initiative. Russia has more than 20,000 kilometers of border contiguous to 14 countries. Along with numerous poorly guarded fissile material storage facilities, this fact provides ample opportunity for smugglers to use multiple pathways from Russia to countries of proliferation concern. Although this has been an acknowledged threat for some time, only limited assistance from the United States and other countries has been provided to facilitate border controls over fissile material smuggling. Russia, the NIS, and the Baltic states are faced with the inherited task of securing fissile materials without the infrastructure and centrally maintained controls of the Soviet era.

This is the first U.S.-Russia cooperative program to combat illicit trafficking of nuclear materials and equipment across Russia's borders. The Second Line of Defense initiative complements other CTR initiatives and enhances Russia's capability to prevent the illegal transfer of nuclear materials, equipment, and technology. The immediate goal is to equip Russia's most vulnerable border sites with nuclear detection equipment. Subsequently, a sustainable counternuclear smuggling capability will be established. The program uses an equip-train-deter strategy by assisting in the installation of equipment at border sites and developing training programs for Russian customs officials.

Thus far five high-priority sites have been equipped with radiation monitors. Training programs have been instituted, and radiation-detecting equipment has been developed and tested for use at ports and sites of entry. Nevertheless, this is a monumental problem that will require years of cooperative effort before border controls are in place and become a viable line of defense against the illicit trafficking of fissile materials.

Disposition and Elimination of Fissile Materials

Deep reductions in the numbers of nuclear weapons have resulted in substantial quantities of surplus plutonium and HEU in the United States and Russia. As a result, 38 metric tons of weapon-grade plutonium and 174 metric tons of HEU were determined excess to U.S. defense needs. Furthermore, in 1995 President Bill Clinton ordered 200 tons of fissile materials—enough for thousands of nuclear warheads—to be permanently withdrawn from the U.S. nuclear stockpile, never again to be used to build nuclear warheads.

The United States is eliminating the proliferation threat from surplus HEU by "down-blending" the material to low-enriched uranium (LEU) for eventual sale and use as commercial reactor fuel.[18] Once down-blended, it can no longer be used to make a nuclear bomb. Material that cannot be economically converted will be disposed of as waste.[19]

The United States also declared an additional 50 metric tons of plutonium surplus to its defense needs, and the National Nuclear Safety Administration (NNSA) is pursuing a hybrid disposition strategy to eliminate the surplus.[20] Specifically, the plan is to irradiate it as mixed oxide (MOX) fuel in commercial reactors, then immobilize it in ceramic surrounded by high-level radioactive waste. Both approaches convert the surplus plutonium to

. From its headquarters in Moscow, the ISTC provides
om former Soviet countries with opportunities for redi-
to peaceful science. As defined in the international
ing the ISTC, this includes, but is not limited to, proj-
solving national and international technical problems,
sition to market-based economies, and supporting basic
h.
rogram has enjoyed some success, at least 3,000 scien-
e in WMD development have left Russia since 1992,
ing to work in Iran, Iraq, and North Korea. Still others
d in Russia are reportedly feeding information on WMD
clients via the Internet.[26] In addition, Russian technol-
ountries like Iran are accelerating the drain of WMD ex-
undercutting this nonproliferation effort.
s are integrated with other nonproliferation efforts, such as
s Initiative (NCI), which finances commercial projects that
ia to consolidate its nuclear weapon complex.[27] The NCI
een the United States and Russia, signed in 1998, seeks to
ns and equipment from the weapon complex, reduce its
rint, and create sustainable, alternative nonweapon work
ioning city economy. It also encourages investment from
corporations and the European Bank for Reconstruction and
which agreed in 2000 to make $30 million available for
loans and supports the MPC&A program by using Russian
d scientists to help secure Russia's fissile materials.
94 thousands of former Soviet scientists have received alter-
yment, and dozens of institutes have or are engaged in hun-
jects. U.S. industry partners have participated by contributing
ollars for commercial partnership projects, most of which have
undreds of long-term or permanent jobs and the establishment
d profitable commercial enterprises.

tiatives: Regional Security

the focus has been on cooperative measures, and will remain so
reseeable future, the former Soviet Union, the United States has
ged in small cooperative efforts to further discourage the demand
e proliferation danger. The regions of proliferation concern are the
East, South Asia, Northeast Asia, and Central Asia. The United
ntinues to engage in negotiations with other governments on re-
ecurity matters and collaboration on the application of technical so-
o smuggling and terrorism. Among other approaches, the regional

the so-called spent fuel standard so it can no longer be used in a weapon. The full extent to which either or both options are implemented will ultimately be determined by the results of technology demonstrations, additional environmental reviews, and detailed cost proposals.

Another option is using MOX fuel in Canadian deuterium uranium (CANDU) reactors in the event a multilateral agreement is negotiated among Russia, Canada, and the United States.[21] Furthermore, technical data on the performance of irradiating weapon-derived MOX fuel may also facilitate agreements to use the CANDU reactor option to help Russia dispose of its surplus plutonium.

Disposal options for surplus Russian fissile materials. In 1997 Russian President Boris Yeltsin made the first official declaration of excess Russian fissile materials, stating that up to 50 metric tons of weapon-grade plutonium and up to 500 metric tons of HEU were excess to Russian defense needs. The United States actively supports the effort to properly dispose of fissile materials in Russia. In 1998 the United States and Russia signed a scientific and technical cooperation agreement to conduct tests and demonstrations of plutonium disposition technologies. The United States, through the NNSA, will fund research and development of advanced reactors that might provide additional surplus plutonium disposition capacity in Russia.

Russia intends to dispose of its surplus plutonium in reactors by irradiating MOX fuel. In addition to the July 1998 joint U.S.-Russia cooperation agreement to advance technologies for plutonium management and disposition, in September 2000 the countries concluded a bilateral agreement on plutonium management and disposition. Under this agreement, the United States and Russia will proceed with roughly parallel programs to dispose of 68 metric tons of surplus weapon-grade plutonium.[22] The United States committed more than $200 million to help fund the Russian disposition program. That agreement sets 2007 as the target date to begin operating industrial-scale facilities, with a minimum disposition goal of 2 metric tons of plutonium per year.

Under these agreements, the United States has the flexibility to begin disposition unilaterally, as an example to Russia, or multilaterally or bilaterally with other nations. Proceeding in this way sends the message of U.S. commitment to nonproliferation and disarmament, encourages similar actions by Russia and the NIS, and will foster additional multilateral or bilateral disposition efforts and agreements.

HEU disposition initiatives. In 1993 the United States and Russia signed an HEU purchase agreement that covers the 500 metric tons that Russia declared will be converted over 20 years to LEU and sold to the United States Enrichment Corporation; Russia will receive approximately $12 billion in return. This quantity of LEU has enough energy to meet the electricity demands of the world for three years. More important, it represents the irreversible conversion of enough weapon-grade uranium equivalent to at least 20,000 nuclear weapons. This program is not without controversy, however. The potential for the United States to grow dependent on Russian-origin material for nuclear fuel has prompted worries by nuclear industry officials about the U.S. ability to cost-effectively produce fuel sufficient for commercial nuclear power plants.[23] One U.S. enrichment plant has already closed, leaving just one plant operating in the United States. Price considerations have also stalled at times full implementation.[24]

A key element of the program is the development of a transparency implementation system to meet the nuclear nonproliferation objectives of the HEU purchase agreement. Under that agreement, the United States will monitor the conversion of 110 metric tons of Russian weapon-grade HEU— the equivalent of roughly 4,400 nuclear weapons—to LEU for commercial sale. This includes the use of special monitoring teams visiting the four agreed Russian uranium processing facilities, where they will observe and monitor processing operations and review accountability documents. Portable nondestructive assay instruments were also developed to provide direct and independent confirmatory readings of HEU presence in closed containers, and a permanent down-blending monitoring system was installed at the blending facilities.

The trilateral initiative. In 1993 President Clinton offered to make excess fissile material available for IAEA inspection, thereby providing international transparency and removing weapon-origin fissile material from the defense programs of Russia and the United States in furtherance of the obligations of the two states under article 4 of the Nuclear Non-Proliferation Treaty. Since that time, the United States has unilaterally removed approximately 226 metric tons of HEU and plutonium from its nuclear stockpile. Of that amount, approximately 90 metric tons (73 tons HEU, 17 tons plutonium) has been made available for the application of IAEA safeguards, with the rest to be made available as soon as is practicable.

In April 1996 Russian President Yeltsin responded by pledging to make approximately 50 metric tons of weapon-origin plutonium available for IAEA verification at the Mayak storage facility. Much of the material declared by the United States and Russia remains in classified forms and therefore is not accessible for traditional IAEA inspections for fear that nuclear weapon design information would be inadvertently disclosed.

In September 1996 the United States, Russia, and the IAEA began to consider the practical implications of placing excess defense materials under IAEA verification at the earliest practical time. IAEA verification is intended to promote international confidence that fissile material made subject

to agency verificati[
programs.

This initiative a[
which are significant.[
that will enable the IA[
of declared materials w[
This verification must b[
tion to the inspector. The[
been to develop very hig[
ance that such materials a[

Nevertheless, substant[
these challenges and agreein[
the IAEA will have a critica[
IAEA safeguards is never ag[

Initiatives for Proliferation [
The Conundrum of Brain-D[

A critical step in reducing prolif[
prevent the brain-drain of scient[
izing in weapons of mass destru[
meaningful employment alternati[
weapons scientists work and live ra[
pursuing WMD know-how will ent[
projects. In 1996 the U.S. General[
many as 50,000 specialists pose a pr[

The United States recognized thi[
a number of initiatives to address it. I[
(IPP) was launched in 1994 with a go[
of Russia's nuclear weapons complex[
placed nuclear weapon workers. IPP a[
partnering with Russian and NIS institut[
civilian technologies in order to create [
ployment for former weapon scientists. 1[
corporations, principally through the U.S.[
promising technologies and provide seed n[
ment and to help bring these technologies to[

IPP is only one of several U.S. govern[
projects. IPP works in coordination with two[
the International Science and Technology Cen[
Science and Technology Center in Ukraine, as[
Research and Development Foundation. The IS[
organization established in 1992 between the Euro[

program takes what has been learned about preventing conflict through treaties, verification, and cooperative monitoring—as well as building peaceful cooperation through science—and makes this experience and technology available for other states to further their own security.

As part of this effort, in 1994 Sandia National Laboratories launched the Cooperative Monitoring Center to assist political and technical experts from around the world to acquire the technology-based tools they need to analyze, design, and implement nonproliferation, arms control, and other security measures. Their focus is on nonproliferation monitoring and verification technologies.[28]

The United States also undertook a four-year program beginning in 2001 to train and equip police and customs officials in 17 Eastern European countries to combat smuggling of WMD and related equipment. And with U.S. support, the IAEA has convened a number of conferences and studies to help countries develop laws, regulations, and procedures for enhancing nuclear material security and enforcing the application of IAEA safeguard standards.[29] Although these measures are small in comparison to the CTR program, they provide another line of defense to the continuing dangers of WMD proliferation.

Analysis

Despite the nearly $700 million annual U.S. budget for the CTR program, uncontrolled fissile material in the former Soviet Union remains one of the most urgent national security threats to the United States today. Russia's nuclear weapons are expected to continue to dwindle to 1,000 or fewer by 2020, yet this is a mixed blessing. Eliminating nuclear warheads aimed at the United States is gratifying, but Russia's bleak economic picture has subjected the nuclear storage system to new stresses. Warhead reductions have had the collateral effect of increasing near- to mid-term fissile material storage requirements, further increasing proliferation risks. The 2001 DOE Baker-Cutler Russia Task Force on Nonproliferation Programs stated that the "existing scope and management of the U.S. programs addressing this threat leaves an unacceptable risk of failure and the potential for catastrophic consequences." It recommended a $30 billion program to be carried over 8 to 10 years, with additional assistance from Europe and Japan. Russia would largely take over security efforts after that.[30]

Although the costs of these programs may seem high, they are insignificant when compared to the trillions the United States and Russia have spent building and maintaining their nuclear arsenals. Furthermore, as the above-mentioned DOE task force argued: "The national security benefits to U.S. citizens from securing and/or neutralizing the equivalent of more than 80,000 nuclear weapons and potential nuclear weapons would constitute the highest return on investment in any current U.S. national security and defense program."[31] Consequently, the task force recommended that the United States dedicate an additional $30 billion to these programs in coming years.

Critics, however, argue that the current program has become the "means by which Russia frees up resources to finance its military modernization programs."[32] Russia claims to lack the financial resources to invest in fissile material security and elimination yet continues to deploy its newest SS-27 ballistic missiles. Further, Congress has complained about the management of the program by DOE and higher-than-expected overhead costs, some of which are likely the result of corruption and mismanagement. Several of the initiatives discussed here have been criticized for excessive spending, inadequate program oversight, and failure to achieve their nonproliferation goals.[33]

Conclusion

Unquestionably these cooperative measures have made significant progress in reducing the proliferation threat, progress that certainly would not have occurred had the United States and other nations not made the commitment to provide assistance. These programs and initiatives have significantly contributed to the strengthening of physical controls, protection, and accountability; hastened the destruction of thousands of nuclear weapons and their delivery systems; accelerated the disposition of hundreds of tons of fissile materials; and provided opportunities for NIS nuclear weapon experts to retrain and refocus on more benign endeavors.

Yet much more remains to be done. More than 1,200 tons of HEU and at least 150 metric tons of plutonium exist in the Russian weapon complex. Buyers from Iraq, Iran, and other countries are actively seeking to buy fissile materials, technologies, and equipment. Controls at many facilities remain inadequate or nonexistent. The economic situations for the former nuclear cities and the scientists and technicians who reside in them remain bleak and will likely remain so for some time to come. The slow pace of Russian economic reforms, endemic corruption, and distrust on both sides contribute to the frustration and snail's-pace progress. The continuation of these cooperative efforts will require compromise and sacrifice. As long as Russia continues to accept this assistance, there is a window of opportunity to reduce and eventually eliminate the threat of former Soviet WMD.

The costs of ensuring adequate security and safe disposition of weapons and materials, though not insignificant, is dwarfed by the potential costs of the necessary defense responses and the real threats to U.S. security should the illicit diversion of fissile materials result in a nuclear nightmare. It would be a perilous move—potentially a strategic misstep of profound proportions—should the United States withdraw its support for these initiatives. The United States should take a flexible, multipronged approach, emphasizing cooperative approaches rather than handouts, and focus on specific deliverables to ensure that funds are spent for their intended purposes. Management errors should not be allowed to derail what is one of the most important programs to national security.

The potential consequences of not taking action to reduce these risks—measured in threats to our national security as well as the cost of defense responses to them—will be far higher than the cost of timely preventative action now. The costs of the necessary defense responses could easily dwarf the costs of protecting, securing, and disposing of these materials to prevent the threat from arising. Although the process will be frustrating and long-term—years of effort, perhaps two decades, will be needed—if these measures can keep fissile materials out of the hands of terrorists and rogue states, then it will be money, time, and effort well spent. We have a unique opportunity to help ensure that future generations will not be confronted with a comparable threat. It is an opportunity we cannot afford to miss.

Notes

1. Howard Baker and Lloyd Cutler, "A Report Card on the Department of Energy's Nonproliferation Programs with Russia," Secretary of Energy Advisory Board, U.S. Department of Energy, 10 January 2001, p. iii.

2. All former members of the Soviet Union became nonnuclear members of the Nuclear Non-Proliferation Treaty and signed and ratified the Chemical Weapons Convention and Biological Weapons Convention. The largest stockpile of chemical weapons in the world resides in the former Soviet Union and remains to be destroyed. Financial difficulties have delayed the destruction timetable for these weapons. The United States has helped fund some cleanup efforts, but there exists a large clandestine biological weapon capability of which the Russian Federation has yet to make a full accounting. Although the potential proliferation threat exists, U.S. and other international cooperative efforts have been meager compared to the nuclear initiatives. See Amy Smithson, *Toxic Archipelago: Preventing Proliferation from the Former Soviet Chemical and Biological Weapons Complexes* (Washington, DC: Henry L. Stimson Center, February 2000), p. 22.

3. Unless otherwise indicated, the use of the terms *fissile material* or *weapon-usable material* refers to plutonium and highly enriched uranium (HEU). HEU is uranium-235 enriched above 20 percent. Of course while weapon-usable in principle, it would take a much larger quantity of such material to produce a weapon than it would with 90 percent–enriched material. Unclassified sources suggest that 4 kilograms of plutonium or 20 kilograms of HEU are required for a nuclear weapon. David Albright, Frans Berkhout, and William Walker, *Plutonium and Highly Enriched Uranium 1996: World Inventories, Capabilities, and Policies* (New York: Oxford University Press, 1997), p. 8.

4. Although most lie within Russia, a number of small research institutes with tens of kilograms of fissile material continue to exist in Ukraine, Kazakhstan, Belarus, Latvia, Georgia, and Uzbekistan; they also pose high proliferation risks. Generally these countries have accepted U.S. and other donor countries' funding for improving security and accounting for these sites containing fissile materials. In 1994 Kazakhstan agreed to the shipment of 600 kilograms of HEU to safe storage at Oak Ridge, Tennessee, which eliminated the largest known stock of fissile materials remaining outside Russia.

5. Approximations of this quantity can be found in several unofficial sources, including Oleg Bukharin, "Security of Fissile Materials in Russia," *Annual Review of Energy Environment,* vol. 2 (1996); and Graham T. Allison et al., *Avoiding Nuclear Anarchy: Containing the Threat of Loose Russian Nuclear Weapons and Fissile Material,* CSIA Studies in International Security No. 12 (Cambridge: MIT Press 1996).

6. The START II agreement, although signed by Presidents Bush and Yeltsin in 1992, has never entered into force. Because of ratification conditions imposed by the Russian Duma with respect primarily to the United States adhering to the ABM Treaty, START II had no chance of ever being agreed to by the Senate and ratified by the Bush administration. Nevertheless, both sides have reduced their nuclear arsenals to the agreed START I levels (6,000 warheads) and agreed in the May 2002 Moscow Treaty to reduce the numbers further to a minimum range of 1,700–2,200 warheads by no later than 2012.

7. Notably, most of the stolen weapon-usable materials seized by authorities to date appear to have originated from facilities of this type.

8. Valentin Tikhonov, *Russia's Nuclear and Missile Complex: The Human Factor in Proliferation* (Washington, DC: Carnegie Endowment for International Peace, 2001).

9. "Leak Shows Nuclear Trafficking Doubled," *The Guardian* (London), 14 May 2001, p. 1. Rob Edwards, "Nuclear Boom: Attempts to Smuggle Radioactive Materials Have Doubled over the Past Five Years, Boosting Fears of Nuclear Terrorism," *New Scientist,* 9 May 2001, p. 1. Edwards cites Alex Schmid of the UN Terrorism Prevention Branch as suggesting that "there could be as many as 130 terrorist groups that pose a nuclear threat."

10. Edwards, "Attempts to Smuggle Radioactive Materials Have Doubled over the Past Five Years."

11. See Jon Brook Wolfsthal, Cristina Chuen, and Emily Ewell Daughtry, eds., *Status Report: Nuclear Weapons, Fissile Material, and Export Controls in the Former Soviet Union,* 6th ed. (Monterey, CA, and Washington, DC: Monterey Institute for International Studies and the Carnegie Endowment for International Peace, June 2001).

12. Public Law 102–228, 25 U.S.C. 2551.

13. For example, DoD negotiated and concluded, with eligible former Soviet states, agreements on strategic arms elimination, fissile material storage facility, nuclear weapons storage security, weapons transportation security, and nuclear core conversions, among other things.

14. This included, for example, exemption from all taxes, customs duties, and similar charges; immunity of personnel from foreign criminal jurisdiction; application of U.S. contracting rules; and the imposition of various other obligations, including the duty not to transfer any assistance without U.S. permission.

15. For example, in 1996 responsibility for the International Science and Technology Center, the Science and Technology Center of Ukraine, the Civilian Research

and Development Foundation, and export control activities were transferred to the State Department. Material protection, control, and accounting programs, the Nuclear Cities Initiatives, lab-to-lab initiatives, and most disposition programs were transferred to the Department of Energy. In 2000 Congress passed Public Law 106–65, creating the semiautonomous National Nuclear Security Administration to oversee nuclear nonproliferation and fissile material disposition issues.

16. DoD also has CTR programs to enhance the security of biological pathogen collection and for designing and assisting in site preparations for the construction of a chemical weapons destruction facility.

17. See the Defense Threat Reduction Agency (DTRA) website, www.dtra.mil/ctr/ctr_index.html. DTRA is charged with reducing the current proliferation threat to the United States and its allies and preventing future threats. DTRA is responsible for implementing on-site arms control inspection, escort, and monitoring activities, supporting arms control confidence-building activities, and developing treaty verification monitoring technologies.

18. A complicated five-step process of mixing highly enriched uranium with a much lower assay (diluted) uranium (typically naturally occurring uranium or depleted uranium) to produce LEU containing less that 20 percent uranium-235. LEU cannot be used for bombmaking.

19. Department of Energy, Press Release, "Clinton Administration Takes Strong Step to Reduce Global Nuclear Danger: Surplus Bomb-Grade Uranium Never Again to Be Used in Weapons," R-096–112, 31 July 1996.

20. The DOE considers another 14 metric tons of non–weapon grade plutonium as surplus.

21. DOE, Press Release, "[DOE] Announces Decision on the Storage and Disposition of Surplus Nuclear Weapons Materials," R-97–001, 14 January 1997.

22. The agreement requires that 68 metric tons of weapon-grade plutonium, 34 tons for each party, be disposed. This is enough plutonium for thousands of nuclear weapons. It will be disposed by irradiating it as fuel in reactors or by immobilizing it with high-level radioactive waste, rendering it suitable for geologic disposal. The agreement allows plutonium that may be designated as excess to defense needs in the future to come under the surplus program. $200 million has already been appropriated to help implement the Russian program. See White House, Press Release, "Vice President Al Gore Signs U.S.-Russia Plutonium Management and Disposition Agreement," 1 September 2000.

23. See John Heilprin, "Buying Russian Uranium May Hurt U.S. Producers," *Washington Post*, 30 December 2000, p. A11; Richard Falkenrath, "Uranium Blues: Economic Interest vs. National Security," *Milken Institute Review* 2, no. 4 (2000): 34–48.

24. See David Willman and Alan C. Miller, "U.S.-Russian Uranium Pact Stalls," *Los Angeles Times,* 16 January 2002; and Valeria Korchagina, "Russia, U.S. Extend Key Uranium Deal," *Moscow Times,* 27 February 2001, p. 5.

25. U.S. General Accounting Office, *Nuclear Nonproliferation: Limited Progress in Improving Nuclear Material Security in Russia and the Newly-Independent States* (Washington, DC: U.S. General Accounting Office, March 2000), p. 8.

26. Steve Goldstein, "Russia's Dejected Scientists See Bomb Skills as Ticket Out," *Philadelphia Inquirer,* 11 January 1999, www.phillynews.com/programs/aprint.

27. A detailed discussion of the Nuclear Cities Initiative can be accessed at the Energy website, www.nn.doe.gov/nci/ncihome.htm.

28. DOE has also funded work on regional security at other national laboratories, particularly the Lawrence Livermore National Laboratory.

29. See IAEA, "International Conference in Stockholm Address Protection of Nuclear Material and Radioactive Sources from Illicit Trafficking," www.iaea.org/worldatom/Press/P_release/ 2001/prn0109.shtml.

30. Baker and Cutler, "Report Card," p. 2.

31. Ibid., p. 3.

32. John Donnelly and George Lobsenz, "Rumsfeld Wants Review of Threat-Reduction Spending," *Defense Week,* 16 January 2001, p. 3.

33. See, for example, U.S. Government Accounting Office, "Concerns with DOE's Efforts to Reduce the Risks Posed by Russia's Unemployed Weapons Scientists," GAO/RECD-99–54, February 1999; also, Inspector General, Department of Defense, "Audit Report on the Comprehensive Threat Reduction Program" Report No. D-2001–074, 9 March 2001.

Suggested Readings

Albright, David, Frans Berkhout, and William Walker. *Plutonium and Highly Enriched Uranium, 1996: World Inventories, Capabilities, and Policies.* New York: Oxford University Press 1997.

Baker, Howard, and Lloyd Cutler. *A Report Card on the Department of Energy's Nonproliferation Programs with Russia.* Secretary of Energy Advisory Board. Washington, DC: U.S. Department of Energy, 10 January 2001.

Sokolski, Henry. *Best of Intentions: America's Campaign Against Strategic Weapons Proliferation.* Westport, CT: Praeger, 2001.

Tikhonov, Valentin. *Russia's Nuclear and Missile Complex: The Human Factor in Proliferation.* Washington, DC: Carnegie Endowment for International Peace, 2001.

Wolfsthal, Jon Brook, Cristina Chuen, and Emily Ewell Daughtry, eds. *Status Report: Nuclear Weapons, Fissile Material, and Export Controls in the Former Soviet Union.* 6th ed. Monterey, CA, and Washington, DC: Monterey Institute for International Studies and Carnegie Endowment for International Peace, June 2001.

PART 3

REGIONAL PERSPECTIVES

11

Europe

Jeffrey D. McCausland

There is no question that Europe was the central theater of the Cold War. From the end of World War II to the fall of the Berlin Wall, the continent witnessed the largest buildup of military forces in human history. As a result, arms control was a diplomatic tool for ensuring stability on the continent and preserving alliance solidarity.

Certain concepts were key to the North Atlantic Treaty Organization (NATO) strategic approach. Military sufficiency described the need to preserve sufficient forces and freedom of action to deter Warsaw Pact aggression and, should deterrence fail, defend NATO territory. Deterrence was important from the standpoint of not only the physical presence of conventional forces but also the linkage to NATO nuclear weapons. Any Soviet calculation about an attack on Western Europe had to consider the possibility of escalation and nuclear war. This was underscored by the forward presence of large numbers of U.S. forces in Central Europe. Furthermore, NATO policy retained the option to initiate the use of nuclear weapons due to its conventional inferiority vis-à-vis the Warsaw Pact.

Arms control supported conflict prevention and crisis management by providing transparency about the size and disposition of military forces, thereby reducing uncertainty and miscalculation. Periodic crises that could have resulted in war in Europe emphasized this need. In the waning days of the Soviet Union, this translated into assisting in the transition of the security environment and the development of a new relationship with the successor Russian Federation. Following the wars in the former Yugoslavia, arms control was also used in conflict resolution and the prevention of a reoccurrence of hostilities. This chapter will examine the principle conventional arms control agreements in Europe and their role during the 1999 Kosovo crisis.

Force Reduction Talks, Cooperative Security, and the Vienna Document

The Mutual and Balanced Force Reduction Talks (MBFR), which began in October 1973, were the first attempt to limit conventional forces in Europe. Initial Western proposals emphasized asymmetrical reductions to a level of parity in troop strength at 700,000 each for NATO and the Warsaw Pact.[1] The Soviets rejected this proposal and the concept of unequal reductions. This was a clear effort by Moscow to preserve the political status quo and continued control over Eastern Europe.

In response, the West added a nuclear package to its proposal in 1976. It consisted of a one-time reduction of U.S. theater nuclear systems in return for a reduction in Soviet manpower.[2] This responded to Soviet insistence that any proposal focusing solely on troops (the Warsaw Pact's advantage) was unfair without an associated reduction in Western nuclear systems (NATO's advantage). Although this demonstrated the linkage between conventional and nuclear forces, it was unsuccessful in breaking the impasse and was withdrawn in 1979.

Due to the continued unwillingness of the Soviet Union to accept significantly higher reductions in Warsaw Pact forces, the MBFR talks stalemated. Several important precedents were established, however, that were essential to future negotiations. The East eventually accepted the notion of a reduction in forces to a common ceiling and further agreed that Western data on NATO forces were valid.

The Conference on Security and Cooperation in Europe (CSCE, later renamed the Organization for Security and Cooperation in Europe, or OSCE) also convened in 1973. This negotiation was a Western concession to the Soviet Union in return for the latter's participation in MBFR, as it closely approximated an earlier Eastern request for a Europewide security conference. It also embodied the idea of détente that had been enunciated in NATO's Harmel report, which placed political efforts on a par with NATO military activities. The concluding document of the CSCE negotiations (the Helsinki Final Act) was signed by the 35 participants on 1 August 1975.[3] This launched the so-called CSCE process that called for balanced progress in three areas: security; science, economics, technology, and the environment; and human rights (or Baskets One, Two, and Three, respectively).

Basket One initially resulted in modest agreements on confidence- and security-building measures (CSBMs), referred to as the "Vienna Document." CSBMs were designed to reduce the "dangers of armed conflict and of misunderstanding or miscalculation of military activities which could give rise to apprehension."[4] CSBMs were a significant shift from technical arms control, changing the focus from reductions to transparency in military operations. The successful conclusion of this agreement was in many ways a compromise by the Soviet Union. The Soviet Union had long insisted that restrictions on military activities could not be agreed upon until reductions had first taken place, whereas the Western position had always been to seek CSBMs before reductions.

The first CSBM was a commitment to provide 21 days' advance notification to all signatories of any military exercise involving more than 25,000 troops. It also encouraged voluntary notification of smaller military training events, major military movements, and the invitation of observers to maneuvers. These provisions have evolved and the thresholds subsequently reduced; they now include the following (as described in Vienna Document 1999):

- Annual exchange of military information
- Consultation regarding unusual military activities
- Provisions for military contacts and cooperation
- Prior notification for exercises
- Observation of military activities
- Exchange of annual calendars for military exercises
- Compliance and verification measures
- Direct communications network between capitals
- Annual implementation assessment meetings
- Stabilizing measures during crisis situations
- Principles governing arms transfers

OSCE members also agreed to a military code of conduct in 1994. That code reaffirmed the principles in the Helsinki Final Act and established norms regarding the role of armed forces in democratic societies. The United States and its European allies formally cited Russia for violations of the code of conduct during Russian operations in Chechnya in the 1990s and requested observation of military activities there in accordance with the Vienna Document.

The Treaty on Conventional Armed Forces in Europe

The Treaty on Conventional Armed Forces in Europe (CFE) was signed on 19 November 1990 by the 22 members of NATO and the Warsaw Pact. It established limits on the aggregate total of conventional military hardware for the two blocs, required substantial reductions in each nation's conventional arsenal, and created an intrusive regime of inspections and verification.

The talks commenced in January 1988 and established the goals of strengthening stability and security in Europe through a conventional force balance while eliminating the capability for surprise attack. The final agreement required alliance, or "group," limitations on tanks, artillery, armored combat vehicles, combat aircraft, and attack helicopters—known collectively as treaty-limited equipment (TLE)—in an area stretching from the Atlantic Ocean to the Ural mountains. Each bloc's allocation is shown in Table 11.1.

Group limitations for NATO and the former Warsaw Pact were further circumscribed by a series of five geographic nested zones for land-based TLE. Limitations on helicopters and attack aircraft applied to the entire area of application due to their ability to rapidly reposition. This zonal approach was a derivative of the mandate's intent to reduce the possibility of surprise attack by precluding excessive force concentrations by either side. Subsequent national limits for each treaty signatory were determined in negotiations among the members of the two groups. The successor states of the Soviet Union within the area of application determined their respective limits from the total allocated to the Soviet Union in May 1992.

New negotiations began immediately after the CFE Treaty was signed. The so-called CFE-1A agreement (formally, the Concluding Act of the Negotiations on Personnel Strength of Conventional Armed Forces in Europe, signed on 6 July 1992) established limits on the personnel strength of military forces with the exception of sea-based naval units, internal security forces, and those assigned to United Nation duties. Unlike the CFE Treaty, the CFE-1A agreement is politically binding, not legally binding. It provided that the ceilings announced by each signatory would take effect 40 months after entry into force and contained provisions for information exchange, notification, and verification.

Although the CFE Treaty was signed in 1990, implementation was delayed until 1992 by the dissolution of the Warsaw Pact, the demise of the Soviet Union, and problems associated with Soviet TLE. Despite this delay, more than 58,000 pieces of TLE from both groups were destroyed and approximately 2,700 inspections conducted to ensure compliance by November 1995 (the end of the implementation period).[5] The Russian Federation had the greatest burden for destruction—roughly 20 percent of the total. By

Table 11.1 CFE Equipment Limits by Bloc

Treaty Limited Equipment (TLE)	Alliance Limit
Tanks	20,000
Artillery	20,000
Armored combat vehicles	30,000
Attack helicopters	2,000
Combat aircraft	6,800

the end of 2000 more than 70,000 pieces of TLE had been destroyed and 3,500 inspections conducted.[6] So-called cascading of equipment within each group was allowed, meaning that some countries could destroy old equipment and accept newer TLE from other alliance members as part of overall reductions. The export and sale of equipment designated for destruction to nonmembers was, however, prohibited.

Inspections may have contributed more to reducing tensions than actual reductions. The CFE Treaty proved valuable by assuaging concerns about German reunification and by providing transparency during the withdrawal of Soviet forces from Eastern Europe. Short-notice inspections were conducted of U.S. forces in Germany as they prepared for deployment to Bosnia in 1995, as well as during the 1999 Kosovo crisis. The treaty's greatest value may be the CFE system, which encourages confidence through transparency and provides a forum for the major European states to debate, agree, and maintain a set of rules about conventional military power on the continent.[7]

Full and final compliance with the CFE Treaty was endangered in late 1995 by Russian insistence that it could not comply with limits on its forces in the so-called flank zone, an area that includes both the military districts of Leningrad and the North Caucasus. A final compromise was achieved at the first review conference in May 1996 that permitted Russia higher force levels in the flank zone. The compromise established a May 1999 deadline for Moscow to meet the adjusted levels and reduced the overall size of the flank zone.[8] Yet the flank-zone problem continued and was exacerbated by Russian military operations in Chechnya (located within the flank region) as well as by Moscow's desire to maintain influence over the North Caucasus states.

Revising the CFE Treaty

The West indicated its willingness to consider adjustments to the CFE Treaty during the 1996 review conference. Actual discussions began in the winter of 1997 and progressed slowly throughout the next year. As spring 1999 arrived, it was clear that adaptation would be affected by ongoing developments in European security. In this regard the period 12 March–24 April 1999 was a watershed in NATO history due to four significant events. First, on 12 March three new nations (the Czech Republic, Hungary, and Poland) entered NATO. From the Russian perspective an adjusted CFE Treaty provided legal assurances about the size and deployment of NATO forces on the territory of these new members that was critical to Moscow's assessment of regional security.[9] Consequently, even though treaty modifications were warranted based on the dramatic changes that had occurred since 1990, the enlargement process gave the entire effort additional resonance. Second, NATO began bombing Serbia on 26 March. Third, on 30

March the states participating in the negotiations to adapt the CFE Treaty reached a major political agreement despite the ongoing hostilities.[10] This was particularly noteworthy, for Moscow had severed and/or suspended other political ties with NATO (e.g., the NATO-Russia Council). Furthermore, these ongoing negotiations focused on the conventional force balance in Central Europe during the first actual conflict involving all NATO members and the largest air campaign in Europe since World War II. Finally, NATO issued its new Strategic Concept during the Washington summit that was held during 23–24 April.

On 19 November 1999 (the ninth anniversary of the CFE Treaty) 30 leaders signed the adapted treaty.[11] It confirmed a new structure based on a system of national and territorial ceilings to replace the zonal approach. This reflected the greater multilateral character of the emerging security environment. The adapted treaty further noted that the presence of foreign forces on any state's territory was allowed only if consistent with the principle of host-nation consent. This was critical to newly independent democracies throughout Eastern Europe and the former Soviet Union.

NATO also declared unilateral limitations on force deployments early on in the enlargement process. NATO announced that it saw no need to permanently station significant forces on the territories of new members. Although this acknowledged the security situation and attempted to ease Russian concerns, the three new NATO members were concerned as well that the NATO goal of military sufficiency could be undermined. Consequently, NATO negotiated operational flexibilities such as the right to deploy equipment temporarily on the territory of an ally during a crisis.

The accord also made changes to the flank regime in order to reconcile this portion of the original treaty to a revised structure. It noted that the existing flank regime remained legally binding on all parties but allowed Russia modest force increases in that zone. Moscow also began bilateral discussions on the reduction of its forces from Georgia and withdrawal from Moldova consistent with the principle of host-nation consent. Finally, the adapted agreement concluded key verification enhancements and contained important national statements. For example, Russia pledged to restrain its force levels adjacent to the Baltic states as well as Poland. Overall, the United States accepted a reduction of more than 45 percent in the amount of ground TLE it was authorized to have in the region. Finally, each state accepted a moderate increase in its annual inspection requirements and commitments to pursue continued reductions.

The final negotiations and eventual ratification were complicated by Russia's failure to meet the revised flank totals agreed at the review conference by the June 1999 deadline.[12] Although Moscow remained within its overall national limits for all categories of TLE, it significantly exceeded its allocation in the North Caucasus area. This was exacerbated as hostilities resumed in Chechnya in October 1999. Moscow did formally announce that its deployment to the Chechnya region to meet the emerging crisis would exceed treaty limits, thereby demonstrating at least verbal commitment to the agreement. Still, Russian failure to comply with treaty provisions, coupled with its continued presence in Georgia and Moldova, made final ratification of the adapted treaty problematic. U.S. President Bill Clinton announced at the conclusion of the summit that he would not submit the agreement for ratification by the Senate until Russia had fully complied.[13] That action was supported by all NATO members.

Russia's inability or unwillingness to resolve these issues continues. Some observers believed that Russian military leaders, due to the uncertain situation in Chechnya, resisted complying with force limitations that might have to be violated subsequently if hostilities escalated. Clearly, Russia's continued presence in Georgia beyond its self-imposed 1 August 2001 deadline reflected a desire to maintain influence over the Georgian government.

Arms Control in the Balkans: The Dayton Accords

The Dayton Accords, signed in November 1995, ended the conflict in Bosnia. Annex 1A of the accords included ambitious arms control and confidence-building proposals for the signatories to be negotiated under the auspices of the OSCE. Under article 2 state parties agreed to immediately commence negotiations on CSBMs. They also agreed (under article 4) to begin negotiations to establish reduced levels of armament and military manpower. Article 4 also established a deadline of 11 June 1996 to achieve an agreement. Finally, the agreement (article 5) called for subsequent negotiations with the goal of establishing a regional balance in and around the former Yugoslavia.

Surprisingly, the parties achieved agreement on a package of CSBMs by 26 January 1996. The accord used existing CSBMs contained in the Vienna Document as a model, and the measures became effective upon signature.[14] All of the states of the former Yugoslavia were also subject to the CSBMs listed in the Vienna Documents as well as the military code of conduct upon achieving membership in the OSCE. Eventually this applied to all parties with the exception of the Federal Republic of Yugoslavia (Serbia and Montenegro). Belgrade's OSCE membership had been suspended in July 1992 as the war in the region intensified, and it was not restored until the demise of the Slobodan Milosevic government in 2000.

Although success in achieving the agreement on CSBMs was significant, final settlement of the article 4 reduction accord proceeded slowly. Dayton established equipment limits based on population that would automatically apply if no agreement was reached by the deadline. Consequently, the arms control process could not occur in isolation. Success for these negotiations was dependent upon the outcome in other areas of the accord, as well as the emerging political climate among the former warring parties. Failure of the Implementation Force, for example, to implement the physical movement of forces required, or a breach in the agreement to conduct elections, would have made the negotiations moot.

During discussions a serious disagreement existed among the Contact Group (which included the United States, Russia, France, Great Britain, and Germany) over the U.S. plan to assist in the training and reequipping of Croatian and Muslim forces for a Bosnian Federation Army.[15] European participants argued that this effort could potentially undermine the negotiations and were akin to pouring gasoline on smoking embers. This divergence between the United States and its allies demonstrated not only a differing approach to cooperative security in this case but also the beginning of a more united European security perspective. This development has continued subsequently with the advent of the European Security and Defense Identity initiative.

An agreement was achieved in the final moments prior to the deadline in June 1996. The parties eventually accepted the default ratios described in Dayton article 4. They also made politically binding pledges to reduce military manpower, not unlike CFE-1A.[16] The reductions did, however, reflect economic necessity rather than strict military analysis. Furthermore, although it had great political significance, the verification and definition of actual military manpower levels (particularly in states with large paramilitary forces) are virtually impossible.

Implementation proceeded slowly, with widespread complaints by all about cheating and the costs associated with destruction. The efforts underscored some of the essential coordination difficulties based on the structure of the Dayton Accords that required cooperation between the OSCE, the European Union, and the United Nations.

Another review conference was held in June 1998. At that meeting the state parties declared the agreements successfully implemented and began discussions for an article 5 mandate. Article 5 prescribed that the OSCE should assist the parties to achieve the goal of "establishing a regional balance in and around the former Yugoslavia" and included states (i.e., Hungary and Romania) that had not been directly involved in the wars in Yugoslavia.[17] No agreement, however, was achieved due to the onset of hostilities in Kosovo and the desire by some Balkan states to eventually accede to CFE.

Arms Control During War and Conflict Resolution

As the Kosovo war unfolded in the spring of 1999, conventional arms control demonstrated its inherent value as well as potential problems and pitfalls. In

April 1999 Belarus made formal inquiries of the United States, Britain, France, and others about military operations in and around the former Yugoslavia consistent with chapter 2 of the Vienna Document. Those countries, as well as the host states of Albania and Macedonia, also provided required reports when NATO forces operating on their territory exceeded certain prescribed levels. In early May Russia formally requested to send observers to Macedonia (and subsequently Albania) to view the activities of NATO forces in those two countries under chapter 8 of the Vienna Document.[18]

NATO (largely at U.S. insistence) severely restricted the area observers could enter in Macedonia. Moscow formally démarched the NATO countries for this as a violation of the Vienna Document and argued that access had been so limited as to imply that the observation had in fact not occurred. The Macedonian observation also caused serious disagreements within NATO, as many European allies indicated their willingness to allow thorough observations.[19] During a subsequent visit by Russian military observers in Albania, it was clear that allied forces were directed to follow the instructions provided by their national capitals and comply with the provisions of the CSBMs as opposed to orders coming from NATO headquarters.

Russia also requested so-called challenge inspections of NATO airbases in Italy and Hungary consistent with the provisions of the CFE Treaty. This included the NATO base at Aviano, Italy, one of the primary facilities for mounting the air campaign against Belgrade. Although this was difficult given the circumstances of an ongoing air offensive, NATO accepted the Russian requests as legally binding under the treaty, and military officials complied appropriately.

Clearly the role that conventional arms control played in the Kosovo crisis was mixed. In the case of the Vienna Document observations, arms control did not fully achieve its purpose of eliminating tensions with countries that were not immediately involved in a crisis. The problems associated with Vienna Document observations in Macedonia and Albania also revealed serious disagreement between the United States and its allies over the role of arms control as part of cooperative security. Furthermore, the agreements had no direct bearing on preventing the conflict between NATO and the former Yugoslavia, as Belgrade was neither a signatory to CFE nor an active OSCE member and therefore not susceptible to the Vienna Document. Still, the transparency provided to NATO operations by the inspections in Italy and Hungary underscored the value of conventional arms control as a means of reassuring neighboring states during a crisis.

Conclusion

NATO members agreed in the 1999 Strategic Concept that arms control continues to have "a major role in the achievement of the Alliance's security and objectives in future."[20] In Europe these efforts have now shifted from challenging the status quo to locking it into place. Corresponding deterrence strategies are less focused on deterring a specific adversary and more concerned with deterring a condition. They also seek to facilitate conflict resolution and the continued development of a European security architecture. This evolution will undoubtedly include further refinement of the European Security and Defense Identity and its relationship to NATO in the future. Obviously, existing treaties and the future role of arms control as a tool of NATO and national strategy must be reexamined in light of the tragic events of 11 September 2001 and the war on terrorism.

NATO will, however, continue to confront issues of military sufficiency as its purpose evolves, it accepts new members, and its relationships develop. As formal military threats to Europe decline, some experts may assume that U.S. forces in Europe are less intended for NATO defense and more focused on power projection. As a result, Europeans may become less concerned about ebbing Russian military strength and more focused on limiting those U.S. operational flexibilities that they construe to be provocative. NATO must also consider how arms control affects the expanded military requirements brought about by enlargement, particularly if states such as those in the Baltic region are admitted to NATO and join the CFE regime.[21] Consequently, greater care must be taken to ensure that arms control policy reflects a common view of cooperative security and does not portend divisions in the transatlantic relationship.

Efforts to preserve and adapt conventional arrangements will continue to affect the nuclear relationship and the evolving role of Russia in Europe. The Russian Federation will likely continue to reduce its conventional forces consistent with available resources. Some Russian leaders have argued that this growing conventional military vulnerability demands increased reliance on nuclear weapons.[22] The entry of new members into NATO, coupled with the commencement of the Kosovo conflict two weeks later, underscored this perceived Russian weakness. Reports that Russia had moved tactical nuclear weapons to Kaliningrad (in violation of a 1991 commitment not to deploy such weapons to the Baltic region), if true, could be in response to these events and reflect this change in policy.[23] The admission of additional new members to NATO following the 2002 NATO summit could cause additional friction in the U.S.-Russia relationship. Conventional arms control could serve to reduce concerns, forestall a corresponding greater reliance on nuclear weapons by Moscow, and encourage progress in other areas.

The Balkan wars of the 1990s are sad reminders that Europe is not immune to conventional conflict despite some 50 years of peace following World War II. Arms control can continue to assist in the resolution of conflicts, forestall their reoccurrence, and contribute to crisis management.

Policymakers have attempted (with mixed results) to use arms control as part of overall political settlements. This occurred in the case of the Irish Republican Army in Northern Ireland as well as between the Kosovo Liberation Army and NATO, whereby the rebel groups agreed to turn in their weapons at the end of the conflict.

Most recently NATO undertook a mission in Macedonia solely focused on arms control. Operation ESSENTIAL HARVEST was designed to collect weapons from ethnic Albanian militants in Macedonia. This was part of a larger political settlement whereby the Macedonian government agreed to grant ethnic Albanians greater constitutional rights. The operation was completed within the prescribed 30-day period, and the 3,800 weapons collected exceeded mission goals.[24]

Arms control could also serve as a brake on future wars and help to resolve existing disputes, such as the ongoing struggle between Armenia and Azerbaijan over Nagorno-Karabakh. Due to the continued regionalization of conflict, Western policymakers should also examine how the lessons learned from efforts in Europe could be applied appropriately in other regions (such as the Middle East, Korea, and South Asia) and encourage their use.[25]

The twentieth century began with a war in the Balkans and ended in the same manner. Arms control is not a panacea for European security, but the record of destruction during the twentieth century demands that every attempt be made to avoid such folly in the future. Many noted historians have argued that the immediate cause of World War I in 1914 was the decision by European leaders to begin mobilizing their armies. This caused a chain reaction as potential adversaries reacted in order to avoid being vulnerable to attack. It is impossible to calculate whether arms control arrangements such as those outlined in this chapter might have provided sufficient restraint during those tense moments and precluded the resulting conflict. Still, it is clear that the CFE Treaty, the Vienna Documents, and arms control arrangements associated with the Dayton Accords offer transparency mechanisms, force limits, and reassurances that might serve to reduce tensions between potential protagonists during a crisis and assist in conflict resolution. Arms control remains the best chance for the West to give meaning to President Clinton's statement following CFE adaptation: "Together, we are building a Europe in which armies prepare to stand beside their neighbors, not against them, and security depends on cooperation, not competition."[26]

Notes

1. James Golden and Asa Clark, eds., *Conventional Deterrence* (Lexington, MA: D. C. Heath, 1984), pp. 30–36.

2. John G. Keliher, *The Negotiations on Mutual and Balanced Force Reductions* (New York: Pergamon, 1980), p. 146.

3. Richard Schifter, "The Conference on Security and Cooperation in Europe: Ancient History or New Opportunities?" *Washington Quarterly* (Autumn 1993): 123.

4. U.S. Arms Control and Disarmament Agency, *Arms Control and Disarmament Agreements* (Washington, DC: U.S. Government Printing Office, 1990), pp. 319–320.

5. Organization for Security and Cooperation in Europe, "Final Document of the First Conference to Review Operations of the CFE Treaty" (Vienna: OSCE, 1996), p. 2.

6. U.S. Department of Defense, *Strengthening Transatlantic Security: A U.S. Strategy for the 21st Century* (Washington, DC: U.S. Government Printing Office, 2000), p. 41.

7. Sherman Garnett, "The CFE Flank Agreement" (Washington, DC: Carnegie Endowment for International Peace, 1997), p. 1.

8. Lynn Davis, Undersecretary of State for Arms Control and International Security Policy, testimony before the Senate Foreign Relations Committee Subcommittee on European Affairs, 29 April 1997.

9. Michael Mandelbaum, *The Dawn of Peace in Europe* (New York: Twentieth Century Fund, 1996), pp. 61–63. See also Frederick Hammersen, "The Disquieting Voice of Russian Resentment," *Parameters* (Summer 1998): 39–55.

10. U.S. Department of State, "Adaptation of the Treaty on Conventional Armed Forces in Europe (CFE) and the Decision of the Joint Consultative Group on Treaty Adaptation" (Washington: U.S. Government Printing Office, 6 April 1999). See also Wayne Boese, "CFE Parties Outline Adapted Treaty; Limits to Allow NATO Growth," *Arms Control Today* (March 1999): 28.

11. The White House, Office of the White House Press Secretary, "Adaptation of the Treaty on Conventional Armed Forces in Europe (CFE)," Istanbul, Turkey, 19 November 1999.

12. Wayne Boese, "Russian Compliance with CFE Flank Limit in Doubt," *Arms Control Today* (July 1999): 46.

13. The White House, Office of the White House Press Secretary, "Statement by the President," Washington, DC, 19 November 1999.

14. Organization for Security and Cooperation in Europe, Press Release, "Parties Sign Agreement on Confidence and Security Building Measures for Bosnia and Herzegovina," Vienna, Austria, 26 January 1996.

15. Bryan Bender, "Alliance's Bosnian Train and Equip Project Will Resume," *Jane's Defence Weekly,* 17 June 1998, p. 22.

16. Michael O'Hanlon, "Arms Control and Military Stability in the Balkans," *Arms Control Today* (August 1996): 5.

17. OSCE, "Regional Stability—Article V of Annex 1B of the General Framework for Peace in Bosnia and Herzegovina," Vienna, Austria, 13 November 1998.

18. Lynn Hansen, "Conventional Arms Control—Has It a Future?" Paper delivered at the Defense Threat Reduction Agency's Eighth Annual International Conference on Controlling Arms, Norfolk, VA, 2 June 1999, p. 7.

19. Ibid. See also Christopher Donnelly, "Russia After Primakov." Paper delivered at the Finnish National Defense College, 10 June 1999, p. 4.

20. North Atlantic Treaty Organization, *The Alliance's Strategic Concept*, Press Communiqué, NAC S(99)65, 1999, p. 10.

21. Klaus Bolving, *Baltic CFE Membership* (Copenhagen, Denmark: Danish Institute of International Affairs, 2001), p. 12.

22. Alexander A. Pikayev, "After Yugoslavia: Shifting Russian Priorities on Arms Control and Non-Proliferation," Presentation at the North Atlantic Council, 8 June 1999, p. 12. See also Richard F. Staar, *The New Military in Russia* (Annapolis, MD: Naval Institute Press, 1996), pp. 29–37, 192.

23. Philipp C. Bleek, "Moscow Reportedly Moves Tactical Nuclear Arms to Baltics," *Arms Control Today* (January 2001): 33.

24. Carlotta Gall, "NATO Chief Urges Macedonia to Carry Out Terms of Peace Pact," *New York Times,* 26 September 2001.

25. James Brown, ed. *New Horizons and Challenges in Arms Control and Verification* (Amsterdam: VU University Press, 1994) pp. 53–56.

26. Office of the White House Press Secretary, "Presidential Statement on the Adaptation of the Treaty on Conventional Armed Forces in Europe (CFE)," Istanbul, Turkey, 19 November 1999.

Suggested Readings

Daalder, Ivo. *Cooperative Arms Control: A New Agenda for the Post–Cold War Era.* College Park, MD: Center for International Security Studies, 1992.

Dean, Jonathan. *Ending Europe's Wars.* New York: Twentieth Century Fund, 1994.

Falkenrath, Richard. *Shaping Europe's Military Order.* Cambridge: MIT Press, 1994.

Freedman, Lawrence, Catherine Kelleher, and Jane Sharp, eds. *The Treaty on Conventional Armed Forces in Europe: The Politics of Post-War Arms Control.* Baden-Baden, Germany: Nomos Verlagsgesellschaft, 1996.

Keliher, John G. *The Negotiations on Mutual and Balanced Force Reductions.* New York: Pergamon, 1980.

Mandelbaum, Michael. *The Dawn of Peace in Europe.* New York: Twentieth Century Fund, 1996.

12

The Middle East

Glen M. Segell

The overall reading of arms control in the Middle East is pessimistic.[1] The antagonistic mannerisms of the populace and the animosity among states do not tend toward a reduction in current tensions or an amelioration of conflicts, whether they be historic or contemporary over resources such as oil and water.[2] The early twenty-first century is a continuation of the 1990s that were a legacy of unresolved Cold War arms control issues. Global arms control initiatives have not prevented an increase in the flow of arms or prevented the escalation in the proliferation of weapons of mass destruction (WMD). There continues to be an unabated acquisition of large arsenals of all types of weapons. Equality in capability has not led to mutual deterrence, and arms control initiatives within the region have not attained a level of cooperative security that would reduce the frequency and intensity of conflicts.[3]

The Middle East shows that the causes and necessity for arms control do not differ radically from elsewhere in the world. Global arms control processes do not, however, always have practical applicability in regional frameworks such as the Middle East. Arms control processes originating from and between the United States, Russia, and European Union (EU) states, as applied in and between Middle East countries, have in the past led to dramatic failures in the goals of reducing the intensity and frequency of conflicts in the Middle East. In the main this has been due to linguistic and cultural differences. These conflicts are increasingly associated with an increase in anti-Western nongovernmental Islamic civil society, disputes over natural resources wealth, and inherent leadership instability. Arms control efforts originating within the region have not been overtly successful due to idiosyncratic dictatorial leadership, religious and ethnic differences, and ongoing resource and border disputes.

Cooperative security appears to be the singular first step toward achieving any success in arms control aimed at the intensity of the conflicts.

Cooperative security stresses the largely informal cooperation and dialogue between states in a region in the development and implementation of a set of agreed regional principals of conduct or norms. Within such cooperative security arrangements there is a need for political solutions to the frequency of the conflicts. Confidence-building, openness, and transparency measures to reduce the likelihood of surprise attack and lessen the demand for all types of weapons are essential for establishing such dialogue and norms in implementing a program of arms control. Two approaches are needed: by states within the region, and by the global arms control regime.

Approaches to Arms Control in the Middle East

The Middle East stands alone among regions of the world in that it has not succeeded as a bloc in signing a regional cooperative security agreement on arms control.[4] The progression of arms control initiatives has historically been hampered there, marked by multiple, overlapping conflicts at the national, regional, and subregional levels. Many of these conflicts have multiple causes and effects, from the internal security of states to their relations with each other and to states outside the region.

In considering these conflicts and associated arms control efforts, the Middle East can be divided into three subregions: the central subregion, with a focus on the Israeli-Palestinian conflict; Maghreb/North Africa, with a focus on militarily and economically powerful—but politically unstable—dictator-led small states; and the Persian Gulf, with a focus on bellicose Iran and Iraq and the Gulf Cooperation Council (GCC), which seeks cooperative security.[5]

The Central Subregion

The central subregion of the Middle East is the most volatile for cooperative security arrangements and the most problematic for arms control efforts. This subregion stretches north from the Suez Canal to the Black Sea and encompasses the states of Egypt, Israel, Jordan, Lebanon, and Syria, with Turkey as the NATO neighbor.[6] The subregion has experienced a high frequency of conflicts of increasing intensity. Arms control efforts relating to the acquisition of large arsenals of weapons and the proliferation of WMD have not been successful.[7] The only regional party to the Biological and Toxin Weapons Convention (commonly cited as the Biological Weapons Convention, or BWC), for example, is Lebanon. The Chemical Weapons Convention (CWC) has been even less successful, with no signatory states in the subregion.[8] Israel has been the only real opponent to the Nuclear Non-Proliferation Treaty (NPT), yet it signed the Comprehensive Nuclear Test

Ban Treaty (CTBT), whose other signatories were Egypt and Jordan.[9] That latter treaty, however, has fallen by the wayside since the United States voted not to ratify it.[10] Similarly, the Environmental Modification Convention has been supported only by Egypt and Lebanon. The Limited Test Ban Treaty may prove to be a positive step because it has been signed and ratified by Egypt, Israel, Jordan, Lebanon, and Syria.[11]

The numerous failures of arms control efforts are indicative of the necessity for cooperative security objectives. Cooperative security endeavors highlight that arms control efforts can succeed only if there exists the political will of all parties to resolve their differences and establish a dialogue with a view toward arms control. Exacerbating such endeavors is the difference in arms control approaches between Israel and its neighbors. The Israeli approach is based on the view that global treaties are not readily applicable to the Middle East environment and that arms control is closely linked to the development of regional security structures.[12] This position explains Israel's refusal to sign the NPT.[13]

This approach to arms control is also reflected in the Israeli position on the creation of a Middle East nuclear weapon–free zone, which it has supported in the United Nations (UN) for more than 20 years.[14] The Israeli policy includes the development of regionally based verification systems and mutual inspection in order to ensure that the verification failures that were characteristic of the International Atomic Energy Agency (IAEA) inspections in Iraq during the 1970s are not repeated.[15] Israel has also placed primary emphasis on the multilateral working group on arms control and regional security (ACRS), which began to function in late 1991 following the Middle East peace conference in Madrid.[16] Fundamental to this arms control approach is to instill among states the recognition that security is shared by all people of the region, rather than being an object of state competition.[17] The role of cooperative security within such an approach is to turn the focus on the reduction of tensions.[18]

This arms control approach has not been successful because it is dichotomous with the mutual lack of trust between Israel and its neighbors. For public relations purposes Israel needs to appear to support arms control, but it also aims to deter its neighbors through the calculated ambiguity of its nuclear status. The various international regimes aimed at countering the proliferation of WMD have not succeeded in restraining the Islamic world in its quest to seek methods, including chemical and biological weapons, to counter the perception of Israel's nuclear capability and formidable conventional arsenal.[19] Egypt has also been acquiring satellite reconnaissance capability that is already available to Israel, while Israel has a limited theater missile defense system through the ARROW program. Arms control could flourish within the central subregion if Israel's Arab neighbors recognized that Israel shows no aggressive intent in its foreign policy and does not have the capacity to occupy neighboring states. Similarly, Israel could enhance this process by entering a cooperative security dialogue to establish a set of norms to alter its procurement policy, research-and-development facility buildup, and large-scale worldwide weapon exports.[20]

The arms buildup is also dichotomous with the second approach to arms control in the subregion. This second approach has been adopted by the Arab states during international arms control negotiations. It is based upon national arms control policies that emphasize the primacy of global instruments and institutions, such as the NPT and IAEA.[21] This difference in approach was a central factor in the deadlock that took place in the context of the ACRS talks in 1994.[22] Despite the existence of a long-standing peace agreement between Egypt and Israel, there was clearly a dispute between the two countries on the implementation of arms control. Egypt demanded that Israel sign and ratify the NPT and has made adherence to the CWC dependent on this change in Israeli policy. In its policies regarding the development of a Middle East nuclear weapon–free zone, Egypt has called for inspection and verification in the context of the NPT and under the auspices of the IAEA.[23]

A recent positive proposal as a step forward has been the Middle East arms control technology demonstration project aimed at joint and cooperative arms control technology evaluations without regard to the ongoing domestic violence in Israel. The initial focus is on Egypt, Jordan, and Israel, because the existing peace treaties among these countries may ultimately allow cooperative technology projects internationally. The first step would be an arms control technology outpost in Egypt; funding and approval are currently being sought.[24]

The Maghreb/North Africa Subregion

These two disparate approaches to arms control initiatives and the simultaneous weapon procurement programs indicate the basic dilemma: that states in the central subregion suffer from a zero-sum mentality regarding arms control. That is reflected in the Maghreb/North Africa subregion, which stretches westward and southward of the central region and includes Algeria, Chad, Djibouti, Libya, Morocco, Tunisia, and Sudan. Arms control has not flourished in these dictatorial states, in which the political systems mix African with Mediterranean cultures, and Christianity with Islam.[25] There has been no constructive success in arms control agreements between these neighboring states despite a modicum of acceptance of the international arms control regime. The only party to the BWC has been Libya, although Morocco is a signatory. The CWC has been signed by Morocco and Tunisia. Similarly, the CTBT has seen sparse support, with Algeria, Morocco, and Sudan being the only signators from this subregion. The only support for the Environmental Modification Convention has come from Algeria and Tunisia. Algeria has signed but not ratified the Limited Test Ban Treaty, though Libya and Tunisia have signed and ratified the treaty.

Despite these agreements on paper, Libya remains an exceptional cause for concern in all aspects of the proliferation of WMD, including long-range extraregional deployment with missiles. Sudan has clearly demonstrated capability and intent in the development of chemical warfare capabilities.[26]

The Persian Gulf Subregion

This zero-sum mentality of arms control implementation is juxtaposed with the acceptance by smaller states of limited cooperative security in the Persian Gulf subregion. This subregion sits closer to Asia, stretching from the Red Sea to the Indian Ocean, crossing the Arabian Peninsula to India and north to the Caspian Sea. It includes the states of Bahrain, Kuwait, Oman, Quatar, Saudi Arabia, the United Arab Emirates, Iran, Iraq, and Yemen. Iran and Iraq are part of an "axis of evil," arming to threaten the peace of the world by aggressively pursuing the acquisition of WMD and through the support of agents of terror.[27]

Arms control in this subregion has depended upon the longevity of state leadership and political systems. The changes in leadership and political systems in both Iran and Iraq, plus the establishment of the GCC, challenge the validity and longevity of international arms control treaties signed or ratified by predecessor governments.[28] Iran, Iraq, Kuwait, Oman, Qatar, and Yemen are parties to the BWC; yet Iran, Iraq, and Yemen have contemplated or actually violated the convention.[29] The CWC has been more successful, with Oman, Qatar, Saudi Arabia, the United Arab Emirates, and Yemen signing it. Similarly, the CTBT has seen wide support; signatories include Bahrain, Brunei, Iran, Kuwait, Qatar, the United Arab Emirates, and Yemen. The Environmental Modification Convention has been signed by Brunei, Iran, Iraq, Kuwait, and Yemen. The Limited Test Ban Treaty, even though applauded, has not provoked intense interest. Yemen has signed but not ratified it, and Iran, Iraq, Kuwait, and Tunisia have signed and ratified.

The member states of the Gulf Cooperation Council have sought cooperation rather than conflict. Their relatively small territory, populations, and oil revenues do not lead to conflict. This cooperation has been spurred by the collective need to protect against Iran and Iraq.[30] Despite such cooperation among GCC states, arms control has not flourished in the subregion due to the tensions between the GCC and the bellicose Iran and Iraq. This situation invites a quasi–Cold War, controlling the use of weapons to the GCC through constant supply, training, and provision of spare parts by the United States and European Union. Arms control efforts are further thwarted by the tensions between Iran and Iraq, which highlight the rift in the Islamic world between the Shia and Sunni sects. This has brought Pakistan into the Middle East arms control process via the Pakistan nuclear tests of 1998 (India officially joined the nuclear club that same year), marking the creation of the first so-called Islamic bomb.[31] The existence of such a weapon generates a psychological strength for the Muslim Middle East and highlights how risks have increased in intensity.[32]

The Indian and Pakistani nuclear tests were seen by some as evidence of the weakness of the global arms control system, whereas others, including the U.S. government, cited these developments as evidence of the need to increase the salience of global arms control agreements and institutions.[33] This perception contributed to increased U.S. emphasis on negotiating the Fissile Material Cut-Off Treaty and was a factor in the weight given to the preparation conferences leading up to the 2000 NPT review conference. The arms control efforts of this subregion are thus closely interconnected with neighboring regions.[34]

*   *   *

The approach to arms control within the three subregions of the Middle East—the central subregion, Maghreb/North Africa, and the Persian Gulf—has not provided any movement toward reducing the frequency and intensity of conflicts in the region. Negotiations are dependent upon the current leadership and political systems of individual states. A change in leadership either way could change the status quo. This could be for the better—as in the case of Libya—or for the worse, should Islamic fundamentalism give rise to internal instability in Egypt. Despite this, there is a constant escalation in the procurement of weapons (both in quantity and quality), a constant cause of concern for arms control efforts. The only positive event has been the reevaluation of Israel's nuclear capability due to the natural processes of uranium decay. Some analysts now claim Israel's arsenal of nuclear warheads is 20, not 200 as once estimated.[35]

The Middle East and Global Arms Control Efforts

The ultimate purposes of the various international arms control regimes in the Middle East are to prevent the use of any form of WMD in the region, to restrict any regional conflict from escalating outside the region (such as the launching of ballistic missiles against European and North American targets), and to bring about an amelioration in local conflicts.[36] Cooperative security fits hand-in-glove with arms control because a state's intention to join or to refrain from joining a treaty is dependent on whether relative or absolute gains are the objective. This issue is context-relative, meaning that various factors may be involved depending on the issue under consideration as well as the particular time in question. Defection from a treaty, or failure by a state to join a treaty, can be motivated by that state's desire to obtain potential relative gains.

The international arms control regimes dominated by the United States have two options to instill arms control through cooperative security in the Middle East.[37] The first option is via formal diplomacy, that is, through adherence to the conventions and treaties of the international arms control regimes. As already noted, very few states in the Middle East are signatories to these conventions and treaties, and even fewer have ratified and adhere to them.[38] The case of the UN Special Commission on Iraq (UNSCOM) during the 1990s further highlights the difficulties in compliance and verification by international arms control regimes.

The second option resembles the Cold War policy of linking the defense capability of states in the region to the extraregional provision of weapons, spare parts, components, and training. In this extraregional provision of weapons, the international arms control regime is also hampered by its efforts to curtail and to counter the proliferation of such weapons. The supply of weapons is a traditionally powerful but limited mechanism for the supplier country to control the military activities of countries in the region. Even now, bilateral and multilateral peace processes aimed at regional cooperative security with superpower security assurances have not provided arms control successes. In the instances where weapon provision is linked to global arms control efforts in the Middle East, weapon procurement by states provides three potential tiers of cooperative security to enhance arms control: conventional, WMD nonproliferation, and WMD counterproliferation.[39]

Conventional

The lowest and broadest tier of global arms control initiatives in the Middle East is aimed at cooperative security to curtail the frequency of conflicts. The frequency of the conflicts is typified by the use of conventional weapons. The causes of the conflicts are domestic, regional, and global. Global arms control efforts for such conflicts have two focuses. The first is international efforts aimed at controlling the proliferation of global sales in conventional weapons. This is arms control by controlling of the flow of arms. In this, the Middle East is not unique from other regions.[40]

Efforts such as the 1997 Mine Ban Treaty (also known as the Ottawa Treaty) and the UN Register of Conventional Arms have not been successful.[41] It is only necessary to look at the changes in leadership and political systems to understand the reasons. In the 1990s, when the Mine Ban Treaty was negotiated, states in the Middle East had long since attained statehood and had no wish to sign such treaties simply to be part of the international club; neither did their dictatorial leaders wish to appease the United States. Thus the Mine Ban Treaty attracted only six Middle East signatories: Algeria, Brunei, Qatar, Sudan, Tunisia, and Yemen. A similar fate has befallen global supplier agreements such as the Missile Technology Control Regime. These arms control efforts have been further hampered by the glut of conventional weapons on the world market, primarily coming from the former Warsaw Pact arsenals. It is unlikely anytime soon that there will be a reduction in the size of the armed forces and the conventional weapon arsenals of states in the Middle East; it may take decades.

WMD Nonproliferation

The second and third tier of arms control efforts (WMD nonproliferation and counterproliferation) aim to curtail the intensity of conflicts. Following each conflict, the parties rebuilt their military capacity with more sophisticated weapons. Some states, such as Egypt, Iran, Iraq, and Israel, have developed indigenous research, development, and production capabilities to reduce their dependence on extraregional supplies of weapons.

The second tier of arms control efforts—WMD nonproliferation—is unique to the Middle East. It is aimed at bilateral and multilateral negotiations among states with the goal of establishing cooperative security requirements to prevent the acquisition of WMD and to reduce the risk of conflict. Bilateral efforts focus on specific issues of defense and security with the goal of a peace treaty, usually sponsored by the United States. Norway has also been a major peacebroker. Such efforts are closely equated to the Cold War arms control efforts of open diplomacy and treaties. The Camp David Accords of 1977 and the Oslo Accords of 1993 are the best examples, for they have established a modicum of cooperative security in the Middle East. Multilateral efforts focus on the broader security agenda of risks that could lead to confrontations, such as quarrels over water resources. Such multilateral efforts are closely equated with tacit diplomacy and the model of quasifederal state-building based upon the European Union model of cooperation.

Attempts to impose the demands of a U.S. foreign policy agenda (e.g., as written in the NPT and CWC international arms control regimes) do not allow for regional distinctions among stable and unstable subregions, or among status-quo and revisionist states as in the Middle East. The needs and desires of individual countries and ethnic groups are not addressed, leaving such arms control processes meaningless to some states within the region and subsequently not adhered to by them. Such regimes generate uniformity or universality and often become a media tool for states such as

Iraq, Iran, Libya, and Syria to demand access to the technology and weapons that should be regulated. The continuing argument regarding universality versus Israeli exceptionality in the NPT regime is a major source of friction and tension, rather than a source of cooperation or a basis for the development of regional security.

WMD Counterproliferation

The third tier of arms control efforts involves counterproliferation efforts aimed at states that already have WMD capability. The ultimate, and somewhat utopian, goal is to create a WMD-free zone. Such efforts have not been particularly successful. The ability of global arms control regimes to monitor states in the region ultimately depends on those states' willingness to permit monitoring and/or inspectors. Even if Middle East states had signed and ratified these global systems, their value could be measured only in relation to viable means for verification and monitoring. Certain realities cannot be ignored. The UNSCOM experience in Iraq clearly demonstrated that even with the most intrusive inspection and verification systems in the history of arms control, closed totalitarian states are capable of concealing weapons and facilities for many years.[42] The lesson of the failure of UNSCOM nevertheless provides valuable experience for future arms control negotiations on verification and compliance. In technical terms UNSCOM was a success, despite the failure of Iraq to comply with Security Council Resolution 687 (1991). This led to the establishment of UNMOVIC following the Amorin Report and the adoption of Security Council Resolution 1284 (1999), which still provides valuable experience for future arms control monitoring, verification, and control.[43] If normal diplomatic arms control measures fail at WMD counterproliferation, then the use of military means by threatened states and superpowers cannot be ruled out to guarantee global security and enhance regional cooperative security, as in the case of the United States against Iraq.

The success of all three tiers of global arms control efforts ultimately depends on establishing a set of norms and a dialogue among states in the region. Such norms and dialogue are components of cooperative security. In these efforts, nonstate actors cannot be expected to be mere parties to treaties but must adhere to their spirit of compliance.

Conclusion

There are few signs of success and many indications of failure in arms control efforts in the Middle East. There is little chance for successful arms control as long as there is a continuation of the factors that promote proliferation, especially the political-religious cultures in Libya, Iran, and Iraq; the ongoing Israel-Palestinian dispute; and domestic instability in most countries of the Middle East. This is clearly seen in the steady procurement of large arsenals of conventional and nonconventional weapons and a proliferation of WMD that is leading the region toward a security abyss. In the short term, the prospects for arms control in the Middle East are dimmer today compared to the early 1990s. The key to stability and arms control success is most likely to stem from cooperative security within the region, including constructive dialogue and the establishment of an agreed set of norms and conduct to reduce threats. Such regional cooperative security will require a global foundation of arms export controls and nonproliferation regimes.

Notes

1. The U.S. State Department does not have a Middle East section. It has a Near East section, which handles the following countries: Algeria, Bahrain, Egypt, Iran, Iraq, Israel, Jordan, Kuwait, Lebanon, Libya, Morocco, Oman, Qatar, Saudi Arabia, Syria, Tunisia, and Yemen. This chapter also considers Sudan, Chad, and Djibouti, which fall under the State Department's Africa section.

2. G. Ben-Dor, "Regional Culture and the NACD in the Middle East," *Contemporary Security Policy* 19, no. 1 (1998): 189–218.

3. The intensity of conflicts is best understood as the range from low-intensity conventional weapons toward weapons of mass destruction such as nuclear, biological, and chemical weapons and the means to deliver them over a distance, such as ballistic missiles. The frequency of conflicts is best understood in the number of years between a risk turning into a threat, then into a conflict, and finally into a war, usually fought with conventional weapons.

4. Other regional agreements included the Africa Nuclear Weapon Free Zone Treaty, the Antarctic Treaty, the Latin America Nuclear Weapon Free Zone Treaty, the South Pacific Nuclear Free Zone Treaty, the Southeast Asia Nuclear Weapon Free Zone, and the Conventional Armed Forces in Europe Treaty.

5. See Shahram Chubin, *Iran's National Security Policy: Capabilities, Intentions, and Impact* (Washington, DC: Carnegie Endowment for International Peace, 1994), and "Saddam Is the Problem," *Jerusalem Post*, 28 August 1998.

6. Dany Shoham, "Chemical and Biological Weapons in Egypt," *Non-Proliferation Review* (Spring/Summer 1998); and Steve Rodan, "Israel Is in Dilemma over Ratifying CWC," *Jerusalem Post*, 23 July 1997.

7. B. Frankel et al., "Middle East Arms Control and Regional Security Dilemmas," Carnegie International Non-Proliferation Conference: Repairing the Regime Preventing the Spread of Weapons of Mass Destruction (Washington, DC: Carnegie Endowment for International Peace, January 1999).

8. Amy E. Smithson, "Playing Politics with the Chemical Weapons Convention," *Current History* (April 1997): 162–166.

9. Gerald M. Steinberg, "The 1995 NPT Extension and Review Conference and the Arab-Israeli Peace Process," *Non-Proliferation Review* (Fall 1996), pp. 17–29; J. Bandyopadhyaya and A. Mukherjee, "International Regimes and World Peace: A Case Study of NPT and CTBT," *International Studies* (October–December 2000):

303–333; and K. Dekiba, "Comprehensive Test Ban Treaty (CTBT): Is It Comprehensive?" *Pakistan Horizon* (January 2000): 7–15.

10. Eric Schmitt, "Senate Kills Test Ban Treaty in Crushing Loss for Clinton," *New York Times*, 14 October 1999.

11. "A Middle Eastern Conference on Mines in Jordan," *Arabic News.com*, www.arabicnews.com/ansub/Daily/Day/980711/1998071127.html.

12. M. A. Heller, "Weapons of Mass Destruction and Euro-Mediterranean Policies of Arms Control: An Israeli Perspective," *Mediterranean Politics* (Spring 2000): 158–166; also, Rebecca Johnson, "The Conference on Disarmament," *Disarmament Diplomacy* (July–August 1997), www.acronym.org.uk/dd/dd171/17genev.htm.

13. D. A. Ozga, "Back to Basics on the NPT Review Process," *Security Dialogue* (March 2000): 41–54.

14. Shalhevet Freier, "A Nuclear-Weapon-Free Zone in the Middle East and Effective Verification," *Disarmament: A Periodic Review by the United Nations* 16, no. 3 (1993): 66–91.

15. O. J. Heinonen, "The IAEA Safeguards System: A Critical Analysis." Paper presented at the Hellenic Foundation for European and Foreign Policy, Athens, Greece, September 1994.

16. The Arms Control and Regional Security (ACRS) working group is one of the five working groups set up in the multilateral track of the peace process. ACRS members are as follows: Regional Parties—Jordan, Israel, Palestinians, Saudi Arabia, Oman, Bahrain, Qatar, Kuwait, United Arab Emirates, Yemen, Egypt, Tunis, Algeria, Morocco, and Mauritania; Co-Gavel Holders—United States and Russian Federation; Extra-Regional Parties (Active)—Australia, Austria, Belgium, Canada, China, Denmark, Finland, France, Germany, Greece, Iceland, India, Ireland, Italy, Japan, the Netherlands, Norway, Portugal, Spain, Sweden, Switzerland, Turkey, Ukraine, United Kingdom, European Union, OSCE, United Nations, and the IAEA.

17. P. Jones, "Arms Control in the Middle East: Some Reflections on ACRS," *Security Dialogue* 28, no. 1 (1997): 57–70.

18. U.S. Department of State, Bureau of Political-Military Affairs, "Confidence and Security Building Measures: Middle East Peace Process Arms Control and Regional Security (ACRS) Working Group Fact Sheet," Washington, DC, June 26, 2000.

19. H. Mashhadi, "Biological Warfare and Disarmament Problems, Perspectives, and Possible Solutions: Complementary Measures Inside and Outside the Framework of the BWC," *Politics and the Life Sciences* (March 1999): 98–102; also, J. P. Zanders and E. M. French, "Article XI of the Chemical Weapons Convention: Between Irrelevance and Indispensability," *Contemporary Security Policy* (April 1999): 56–85.

20. Y. Shichor, "Israel's Military Transfers to China and Taiwan," *Survival* (Spring 1998): 68–91.

21. Mostafa Elwi Saif, "Nuclear Weapons and Arms Control in the Middle East: An Egyptian View," www.uspid.dsi.unimi.it/proceed/cast97/elwisaif.html.

22. Joel Peters, *Pathways to Peace: The Multilateral Arab-Israeli Talks* (London: Royal Institute of International Affairs, 1996); and Bruce W. Jentleson, *The Middle East Arms Control and Regional Security (ACRS) Talks: Progress, Problems, Prospects*, Policy Paper No. 26 (San Diego: Institute on Global Conflict and Cooperation, University of California, 1996).

23. H. Schenker, "Apocalypse Tomorrow? Nearing the Nuclear Edge: The Case for Non-Conventional Weapons Arms Control and a Nuclear Weapons Free Zone in the Region," *Palestine-Israel Journal of Politics, Economics and Culture* 6, no. 3 (1999): 91–96.

24. Middle East Arms Control Technology Demonstration Project, Final Report, Middle East Regional Program, Cooperative Monitoring Center, Sandia National Laboratories, Albuquerque, New Mexico, November 2001, www.cmc.sandia.gov/ Links/regions/MidEast/MEarmscontroltech/MEarmscontroltech.htm.

25. A. Biad, "Conflict Prevention in the Euro-Med Partnership: Challenges and Prospects," *International Spectator* (April–June 1999): 109–122.

26. Steven Lee Myers and Tim Weiner, "Possible Benign Use Is Seen for Chemical Factory in Sudan," *New York Times*, 27 August 1998.

27. The President's State of the Union Address, United States Capitol (Washington, DC: Office of the White House Press Secretary, 29 January 2002).

28. Anthony H. Cordesman, *Iran's Military Forces in Transition* (Westport, CT: Praeger, 1999); also, Barbara Crossette, "Iraq Still Trying to Conceal Arms Programs, Report Says," *New York Times*, 27 January 1999, and "Former UN Weapons Inspector: Iraqi Arsenal Undiminished," Associated Press, 28 September 1999.

29. Seth W. Carus, "Iran's Weapons of Mass Destruction: Implications and Responses," *Middle East Review of International Affairs* 2, no. 1 (March 1998): 1–14; Martha Raddatz, "Ominous Rebuilding: Iraq Apparently Again Trying to Make Chemical, Biological Weapons," *ABCNEWS*, 12 July 1999, www.abcnews.go.com.

30. Peter Jones, "Iran's Threat Perceptions and Arms Control Policies," *Non-Proliferation Review* (Fall 1998): 39–55.

31. S. Yasmeen, "Pakistan's Nuclear Tests: Domestic Debate and International Determinants," *Australian Journal of International Affairs* (April 1999): 43–56; and Herbert Krosney and Steven Weismann, *The Islamic Bomb* (New York: Times Books, 1981).

32. Pervez Hoodbbhoy, "Myth-Building: The Islamic Bomb," *Bulletin of the Atomic Scientists* (June 1993): 42.

33. Pakistan Minister of Information Mushahid Hussain, interview with *Der Spiegel*, 8 June 1998.

34. To this end it should be noted that Israel, Egypt, Jordan, Tunisia, Algeria, and Morocco (all Mediterranean states) have observer status at the Organization for Security and Cooperation in Europe (OSCE), enabling them to participate in some of the organization's activities and to hold dialogues on issues of common interest, including security, with OSCE members.

35. Discussion with Brigadier-General Yom-Tov Samia, Commanding Officer, Southern District, Israeli Defense Forces, Southern Command Headquarters, Beersheba, July 1999.

36. Commission to Assess the Ballistic Missile Threat to the United States, *Executive Summary of the Report of the Commission to Assess the Ballistic Missile Threat to the United States* (Washington, DC: U.S. Government Printing Office, 15 July 1998).

37. For Russia's role, see Y. Klein, "Russia and a Conventional Arms Non-Proliferation Regime in the Middle East," *Contemporary Security Policy* 16, no. 1 (1995): 1352–1360; and for the European perspective, see P. Boniface, "Arms Control in the Mediterranean Area: A European Perspective," *Mediterranean Politics* (Spring 2000): 167–188.

38. U.S. Arms Control and Disarmament Agency, "Adherence to and Compliance with Arms Control Agreements," *1997 Annual Report to Congress by the U.S. Arms Control and Disarmament Agency* (Washington, DC: ACDA, 1998), www.state.gov/www/global/arms/reports/annual/comp97.html.

39. States in the Middle East procure weapons for four reasons: domestic security, prestige, external security against neighbors, and indirect external security through brokerage and sales.

40. M. Brzoska, "Prospects for a Common Arms Transfer Policy from the European Union to the Middle East," *Contemporary Security Policy* 16, no. 1 (1995): 4–18.

41. Statement by Dr. M. H. Adeli, Iranian ambassador to Canada, at the signing conference for the Convention on the Prohibition of the Use, Production, Transfer, and Stockpiling of Anti-personnel Mines and Their Destruction, Ottawa, 2–4 December 1997, in *Disarmament Diplomacy* (December 1997): 29; and Statement by David Sultan, the Israeli ambassador, in ibid., pp. 33–34.

42. S. Black, "UNSCOM and the Iraqi Biological Weapons Program: Implications for Arms Control," *Politics and the Life Sciences* (March 1999): 62–69; also, A. Saikal, "Iraq, UNSCOM, and the U.S.: A UN Debacle?" *Australian Journal of International Affairs* (November 1999): 283–294.

43. Patricia Lewis, "From UNSCOM to UNMOVIC: The United Nations and Iraq," www.unog.ch/unidir/1-02-elewis.pdf.

Suggested Readings

Center for Middle Eastern Studies, www.menic.utexas.edu/menic.html.

Center for Nonproliferation Studies, www.cns.miis.edu/research/mideast.htm.

Center for Strategic and International Studies, www.csis.org/mideast/index.html.

Frankel, B., A. Levite, K. Hamza, and B. Jentleson. "Middle East Arms Control and Regional Security Dilemmas." In Joseph Cirincione, ed. *Carnegie International Non-Proliferation Conference: Repairing the Regime Preventing the Spread of Weapons of Mass Destruction*. Washington, DC: Routledge, 2000, pp. 195–204.

Feldman, Shai, and Ariel Levite, eds. *Arms Control and the New Middle East Security Environment*. Boulder: Westview, 1994.

Jaffee Center for Strategic Studies, www.tau.ac.il/jcss.

Middle East Newsline (daily news and in-depth articles), www.mnewsline.com.

Rauf, Tariq, ed. *Regional Approaches to Curbing Nuclear Proliferation in the Middle East and South Asia*. Ottawa, Canada: Canadian Centre for Global Security, 1992.

13

Africa

Christopher Carr

It is plausible that there has developed in Africa what may be the archetype for arms proliferation in the first decades of the twenty-first century. Compared to the acquisition of weapons of mass destruction (WMD) by major regional actors, this form of proliferation does not pose a clear and obvious threat to the United States or even to Europe. But in its own way such activity endangers the national and security interests of the postindustrial powers. Because such interests provide those powers influence and primacy, anything that challenges them in a wider sense threatens those states. Therefore, even though the arms that have proliferated and destabilized Africa are at the farthest end of the spectrum from strategic missiles and chemical or biological warheads, they are a corrosive and insidious contributor to the collapse of order and state primacy on the continent. "Small arms" they may be, but the problems they pose are neither small nor marginal to the concept of stability that lies at the heart of all arms control issues.

The proliferation of small arms, or light weapons, in Africa cannot be laid at the doorstep of any one agent or traceable to any particular social and political problem. Many of the arms that threaten human security on the continent were given by former colonial powers to form the hardware base for the armies of newly independent states. Others, particularly in the African Horn and in southern Africa, were the small change of Cold War superpower rivalry, in which the United States and the Soviet Union fought sideshow proxy wars with minimal commitment on their own behalf but with maximum effects upon such countries as Angola, Mozambique, and Somalia. Additional arms flowed into the continent as instruments to either sustain or challenge the last vestiges of colonial or white supremacy in such places as Rhodesia and South Africa. And still other weapons were trafficked into the continent to support those hybrid interstate/intrastate conflicts exemplified by the Great Lakes and the Liberia–Sierra Leone–Guinea wars. The cumulative impact of this influx has been to create large geo-political subdivisions in Africa that are some of the most highly weaponized areas in the world.

Arms control in Africa is centered upon two distinctively different sets of problems. The first relates to new arms flowing into the continent from external sources. The bulk of these arms go to forces engaged in extant conflicts. Many of them are provided by nonstate actors trafficking in arms, often in contravention of embargoes and restrictions. The second movement of arms relates to weapons that already exist on the continent and that leech from one area of conflict into a neighboring region, often infecting the latter with instability and insecurity. Both types of activities pose different types of challenges to the arms control community; neither is solvable by traditional regimes and strictures. Indeed, such is the depth and complexity associated with arms trafficking into and within Africa that it would appear that arms proliferation on that continent, like the poor, will always be with us. However, although there is little evidence of major collective agreements forming on a transcontinental or even regional basis, there has emerged a patchwork quilt of responses that in its own way may form the prototype of a new form of arms control regime. Before looking at that possibility, however, I will review the status of traditional arms control measures on the continent.

Weapons of Mass Destruction and Arms Control in Africa

On the continent of Africa only one state has engaged in formal programs to develop WMD. South Africa's nuclear weapon program, begun in 1974 under the white minority apartheid regime, bore fruit in the 1980s in the form of a half-dozen low-yield nuclear devices. A similar (although less well managed) clandestine program involving chemical and biological weapon (CBW) research had also been undertaken in South Africa during the 1980s. However, with the accession to power of the reformist government of F. W. de Klerk in 1989, the regime in Pretoria decided to terminate its nuclear weapon program and to sign the Nuclear Non-Proliferation Treaty. South Africa's CBW program, code-named PROJECT COAST, was also terminated by de Klerk after a government report indicated that there had been major irregularities in oversight and accounting.[1]

South Africa's decision to destroy its nuclear stockpile was made unilaterally, but the destruction of the devices and of the program's databank was audited and ratified by the International Atomic Energy Agency (IAEA). In late 1994 the IAEA declared that the South African nuclear weapon facilities had been dismantled beyond reconstitution.

South Africa conducted its CBW program even though it had become a party to the Biological Weapons Convention in 1975. The bioweapon element of the program had included work on cholera, anthrax, and botulism. Subsequent investigations indicated that both chemical and biological agents had been used by the apartheid regime in its confrontations with other African states. When the CBW program came to light during the presidency of Nelson Mandela, the South African majority government renewed its pledge to eschew CBW. As a concrete indicator of its commitment, it signed the Chemical Weapons Convention in 1995.

In the spirit of this renunciation of WMD in its own country, South Africa in 1996 sponsored a multilateral agreement to make Africa a nuclear weapon–free zone. The Treaty of Pelindaba included a pledge by 49 of the 53 members of the Organization of African Unity to permanently eschew any attempts to achieve nuclear weapon status, to maintain control over civilian nuclear programs, and to outlaw the dumping of nuclear waste on the continent.

There is, perhaps, a certain irony in the relative ease with which the entire continent of Africa was willing to subscribe to the concept of a nuclear weapon–free zone. In reality, however, the construction of WMD was beyond the capabilities of virtually all African states, so the Treaty of Pelindaba was a symbolic gesture of easy self-denial. The real arms proliferation issue bedeviling Africa is the mass of light weapons that flows into and among the states of that continent. Controlling them is another matter.

Arms Trafficking into Africa

Firearms were first introduced into Africa in the early seventeenth century. Although local chiefs and monarchs were initially encouraged to acquire muskets and artillery from the Europeans, it was the policy of most later colonial administrations to maintain a near-monopoly over arms on the continent. Upon independence, this monopoly of arms was vested in the governments of the new African states, many of which abused this power and were then challenged by guerrilla groups that were armed by external actors (the Soviet Union, the United States, France, and Libya, among others). Similarly, some colonial and white minority regimes did not succumb to the winds of change in Africa without a fight, and the forces that would eventually prevail against those regimes absorbed arms sent from Washington, Moscow, Beijing, and North Korea.

In the Portuguese colonies of Angola and Mozambique, resistance movements, primarily armed by the Soviet Union and its allies, achieved a level of systemic violence that, by the time freedom had been achieved, immediately transformed into civil war. In Rhodesia and South Africa, sanctions-busters provided a system of supply and transportation to the white minority regimes. By the 1990s this had become one of the most sophisticated illicit arms trafficking networks ever devised. Similarly, the armed resistance movements in those countries were beneficiaries of external support and arms largesse, again principally from the Soviet Union and its allies. Many of the actors and most of the techniques perfected by arms traffickers during these times provided the foundation for illegal and illicit transfers into Rwanda, the Congo, Liberia, Sierra Leone, and Sudan during the 1990s and into the twenty-first century.

There are very few full-time arms traffickers engaged in selling and transporting arms into Africa. Even the increased tempo of conflict in the 1990s was not enough to sustain dedicated arms networks. Such activity was usually undertaken in concert with activities such as drug trafficking, natural resource exploitation (particularly diamonds), and, for the multiplicity of airlines involved, the transport of black-market goods. Arms trading in Africa has also been affected by this cross-pollination of criminal communities, with arms being increasingly countertraded for minerals, timber, and even animal products. The involvement of many small Canadian and European diamond-mining companies in the traffic in arms was obvious enough to warrant an investigation into the phenomenon by the United Nations, even creating a cause célèbre surrounding so-called conflict diamonds.[2]

Arms trafficking into Africa takes the standard form of illicit supply. Middlemen, or arms brokers, are contacted by buyers, who may or may not represent a legal government. The brokers themselves put together a package of sellers, financiers, document providers, and transportation managers. There is enough specificity in the nature of arms trafficking that brokers are an integral element in the process (the documents alone, including end-use certificates [EUCs], require specialist knowledge). As a result, the brokers themselves have become the subject of certain control measures. Nevertheless, prosecuting arms brokers has not been a priority for most states, and brokering remains the most lucrative aspect of arms trafficking.[3]

The trade in illegal EUCs and other documents is also rife in Africa. Two specific types of EUCs have been used to facilitate illicit or illegal arms trafficking in Africa. The first type is fake EUCs, which are counterfeit documents concocted by traffickers. Often crudely made, they are used in extremis or to save money.[4] The second type is false documents, most often acquired with the connivance of corrupt officials and for considerable sums (the cost is on a sliding scale according to the size of the deal, but EUCs priced between $20,000 and $50,000 are not unusual).[5] The United Nations has identified false EUCs emanating from the Democratic Republic of Congo, Zaire, Togo, Nigeria, and other states in Africa, most often in relationship to arms being trafficked into the continuing conflict in Angola and into the Great Lakes region. Proposals to regularize and regulate the issuance of EUCs have not proven fruitful.

Most arms that have been trafficked into Africa since the end of the Cold War have originated in Western and Eastern Europe, Russia, and East Asia. In order to reach Africa they have been transported by ship or, increasingly, by air. The coastal fleets of Denmark and the Black Sea states have been the major maritime shippers of illicit arms into Africa, and they are now supplemented by fleets of aircraft ferrying arms from Bulgaria, Ukraine, and other malleable arms-manufacturing states.[6] Sometimes single-aircraft cargo airlines—more often major charter services—these companies mix support for nongovernmental organization (NGO) operations and other legitimate contracts with arms trafficking. Many of the aircraft are underserviced and often bear false certificates of airworthiness and dubious licenses.

An ancillary element of the uncontrolled flow of arms into Africa by air is the lack of radar coverage on the continent, a shortfall that facilitates such movements. Even the more sophisticated states, such as Kenya, do not have full radar coverage of their airspace. This allows unauthorized aircraft to fly through their airspace and even to land, refuel, and take off without oversight or interception.[7] Assuming that ground-based radar systems would be maintained and kept operational, increased radar coverage would appear to be one way in which the free flow of arms across the continent might be inhibited. As a stop-gap measure, use of airborne radar, most particularly the U.S./NATO AWACS system, might serve to increase monitoring of the most intensively trafficked areas and therefore increase the likelihood of intercepting illegal flights.[8]

Arms trafficking into Africa is a mature process. Since at least the early 1970s arms brokers, sellers, document providers, and transportation specialists have provided arms to Biafran forces, Rhodesian white supremacists, Angolan rebels, and Sudanese irredentists. This has often taken place in open contravention of United Nations or national sanctions and with the connivance of corrupt state officials. Throughout this period a number of scandals have been made public within the originating countries (French arms sales to Angola, British sales to Sierra Leone, and South African sales to Yemen were all the subject of major inquiries), and there has been a general condemnation of illicit and illegal arms trafficking into sub-Saharan Africa. Nevertheless, with the possible exception of a concerted effort to delink the diamond trade from arms trafficking, little has been attempted or achieved in respect to halting this trafficking. Ironically, it would take very little to deter those who participate in such activities as an ancillary aspect of their business. There are profits to be made in other areas of exploitation within the African economies. But a combination of venal public officials, a well-established network of supply, and the constant need for arms and ammunition engendered by civil war have turned arms trafficking into Africa from a risky business into a profitable and normative commercial activity.

Arms Trafficking Within Africa

Arms flowing into Africa from outside the continent may be difficult to inhibit, but arms flowing from area to area within the continent pose an altogether different set of control problems. The tens of millions of small arms that already exist beyond the authority of national governments in Africa pose more than a short-term threat to the established order in Africa; because of the longevity of arms (certain weapons still in use in Somalia are World War II–vintage) they will continue to destabilize regimes and regions in the foreseeable future.[9] The estimated 2 million arms that remained in Mozambique at the end of that country's civil war in the mid-1990s not only served to inject uncertainty into human security in that country but also spread insidiously into South Africa, Zimbabwe, and Malawi.[10] Similarly, arms looted from the arsenals of Uganda at the end of dictator Idi Amin's regime in the 1970s began a localized arms race among the pastoral tribes of East Africa. This resulted in the deaths of thousands of clan members of traditional societies; it also threatened a way of life that had existed for millennia.[11]

In certain parts of Africa the threat posed by existing stocks of weapons is the dominant security concern. In Kenya, arms from the conflicts in southern Sudan and Somalia created a virtual no-go area in the northern and eastern parts of that country. Weapons also infiltrated the Nairobi metropolitan area, helping to create a climate of violence in that city that had wider political ramifications.[12] In South Africa weapons that remained from the struggle against the apartheid regime were prolific enough to turn cities such as Johannesburg into the most violent urban areas in the world. Arms from the conflict in Liberia leeched into Sierra Leone and helped feed that country's civil war; those arms then spread across the border into Guinea, bringing the three countries into a tripartite conflict. And the arms that the Rwandan *interahamwe* forces took with them into the Democratic Republic of the Congo after the 1994 Rwandan genocide helped fuel the instability that gave rise to the Great Lakes conflict. Clearly, then, large quantities of uncontrolled arms are a major contributor to the chronic instability that has retarded the social, political, and economic evolution of Africa in the postcolonial period. This problem must be addressed before progress can be made in national security and human security.

Controlling arms that already exist on the continent is less a matter of traditional international agreement than it is of multiple activities by interstate, state, and substate actors that chip away at the tens of millions of arms that remain in the hands of groups and individuals in Africa. Although traditional types of arms control agreements do exist in Africa, for the most part such action as has been taken to manage and control arms has been less conventional. Grassroots bodies, in concert with international NGOs and often with the help of monies from foreign governments or international governmental organizations (IGOs), have emerged with plans and activities that are small in scale but related to local conditions and that (if sufficiently funded) have the type of long-term, persistent application that is the key to reclaiming arms in Africa. Similarly, governments with shared borders and security concerns have established mechanisms of coordination and activity that may only have a limited direct impact on the flow of arms within the continent but that serve as confidence-building measures in respect of future major regional efforts to control arms.

Mozambique and the TAE Project

Mozambique is one of the prime exemplars of the insecurity created by arms saturation within a country. Local insurgents fought for decades against the Portuguese colonial regime. After independence in 1975 a brutal civil war claimed between 350,000 and 600,000 lives over the subsequent 17 years. During the civil war arms were dispensed to the populace on an unregulated basis, with assault rifles being handed out during political rallies without any record as to numbers or the identities of recipients. When the civil war abated in 1992 the issue of decommissioning the arms in the hands of the opposing forces, FRELIMO and RENAMO, was deferred, leaving large stockpiles under the control of local commanders and even larger quantities in the hands of individual former fighters. Such was the proliferation of weapons in Mozambique in the 1990s that AK-type assault rifles were being exchanged for a chicken or sold for less than US$20.[13] Armed crime elements paralyzed communications and trade within the country, and local paramilitary groups threatened the primacy of the government.

During this same period Mozambique had achieved world attention as one of the most heavily mined areas in the world. The antilandmine movement that began in the early 1990s was initially founded by existing or issue-specific NGOs whose activist strategy forced the international community to take a position on the matter. Mozambique (along with Cambodia) was used as a worst-case example by the movement and therefore attracted global interest in regard to its parlous security situation. The country therefore became an example of a new form of arms control initiative: one that did not emerge from the deliberations of state actors but rather from the frustrations of local people as articulated through the international NGO network. Although only partially successful (landmine clearance at a concerted level did not begin in Mozambique until 2000), this bottom-up type of movement provided the template for the light weapons antiproliferation activity that emerged internationally in the late 1990s and that to a limited extent began to emerge in Mozambique by the end of that decade.

Judged by the initial results, the attempt by NGOs to disarm the population of Mozambique could not be considered a success. One of the most dedicated of such efforts, coordinated by the religious-based organization Transformacao de Armas em Enxadas [Transforming Arms into Plowshares] (TAE), was able to retrieve some 2,500 firearms from the population between 1995 and 2000.[14] Given the estimated 2 million arms in civilian hands in Mozambique, this would appear to reflect a failed effort. But the core of the effort, in which goods such as sewing machines and bicycles were exchanged for arms, could yet serve as a future model. Indeed, lack of such exchange goods during the formative years of the program probably served to sabotage the TAE efforts to establish the program on a comprehensive nationwide basis. This swords-into-plowshares concept was initially well received at the popular and governmental levels and resulted in such unforeseen results as voluntary arms decommissioning by mothers who were tired of their children being injured and killed by uncontrolled weapons.

An important aspect of the TAE program was the almost instantaneous destruction of arms that were retrieved. Experience in Mozambique (and elsewhere in Africa) had led TAE and other light weapon controllers to the conclusion that if arms were stockpiled intact they would often find their way back into the community. Destruction of arms in place not only prevented such an eventuality but also gave confidence to those who had surrendered their arms that they were not participating in a sham exercise. The provision of inexpensive, field-operable methods of destruction are an intrinsic element of such programs and would enhance the success of activities of groups such as TAE.[15]

The RACHEL Operations

Mozambique was also the setting for another unconventional form of arms control activity, centered on crossborder military cooperation. Since 1996 the governments of South Africa and Mozambique have jointly participated in an arms management program code-named RACHEL. This activity, in which units of a special task force from South Africa operate with Mozambican counterparts to identify, locate, and destroy arms caches within Mozambique, has proven to be a model of cooperation based upon shared security concerns. In the mid-1990s South African police authorities became aware that large quantities of light weapons were moving across the border from Mozambique and were contributing to the lethality of urban crime in South African cities. Mozambican authorities were approached regarding a joint interdiction program, and the RACHEL series of operations was inaugurated in 1996.[16]

RACHEL was a two-part activity. The first part—the identification of caches of arms within Mozambique—was carried out over a number of months in a given year and was dependent upon a network of informants pinpointing the arms for Mozambican and South African authorities. Later in the RACHEL series these informants were given global-positioning-system receivers to more accurately locate the arms. In the second phase of the operation, South African police authorities flew or drove over the border into Mozambique, linked up with Mozambican military elements, and began a search-and-destroy mission against the identified arms caches. RACHEL 1 resulted in the destruction of more than 1,000 weapons over a two-week period, with the total number of weapons destroyed during the first four RACHEL operations totaling more than 12,000.

RACHEL was initially funded by the South African government, but as the zone of operations moved farther north and away from the South African border, it became increasingly difficult to rationalize the expenditures to South African taxpayers. The RACHEL operations in 1999 and 2000 were thus subsidized by the Belgian government, and the operation in 2001 was underwritten by the United Nations.[17] The program itself has been hampered by communications and mobility problems, with operations being undertaken in an area where no formal road system exists and where security can be compromised by helicopter operations. In 2001, for example, arms were removed from five identified caches before they could be destroyed. Nevertheless, the program was deemed a qualified success by the two participating countries, and it remains a unique crossborder arms control initiative.

The Mozambique arms control activities were a combination of state, IGO, and NGO responses to the complex problem of deactivating arms in a highly weaponized community. Absent the prospect of a comprehensive continentwide agreement on controlling arms within Africa, these types of measures may well be the future of arms control in the region. However, there have been a number of attempts to achieve more formal, traditional types of interstate agreements in sub-Saharan Africa. One of the most comprehensive, the Mali initiative, indicates the possibility of forging African arms control alliances.

The Mali Initiative

On 31 October 1998 the 16 members of the Economic Community of West African States (ECOWAS) declared a "moratorium on the importation, exportation and manufacture of light weapons."[18] The moratorium, designed to last three years, followed a proposal by the state of Mali that West Africa should seriously tackle the problem of some 5 million uncontrolled light weapons that threatened regional security. Mali itself had been confronted by an armed rebellion in the early 1990s and had made a specific effort to deweaponize its own country after the cessation of hostilities in 1995. Encouraged by the response of the international community to its domestic arms management program, Mali had been able to persuade fellow ECOWAS members to subscribe to the spirit of arms control through a moratorium. Unfortunately, at least three of the signatories (Liberia, Burkina Faso, and Togo) were later to be implicated by the United Nations and the NGO community of participation in arms trafficking into either Sierra Leone or Angola or both. Nevertheless, the Mali initiative was used as a model for the Nairobi Declaration on Small Arms and Light Weapons, which was supported by the foreign ministers of all of the states of East Africa in March 2000.[19]

Conclusion

The arms that saturate the continent of Africa are symbols of its violent past as well as harbingers of its insecure future. The finely crafted arms control agreements that are the objective of established states, governed as they are by the rules of law and statecraft, are unlikely to emerge in Africa. The threat posed by automatic weapons to the Kuria tribe on the Kenya-Tanzania border will not be mitigated by pronouncements made in capitals thousands of miles away. Similarly, it is fanciful to think that those who are beyond any law in Somalia, Angola, and Sierra Leone will willingly or unwittingly surrender the instruments upon which they depend for their livelihood, status, and survival. Unfortunately, while they continue to cling to their symbols of lethal insurance they are exacerbating the very human insecurity that forestalls the possibility of social, economic, and political progress.

Arms control in Africa will be achievable when societies become so tired of constant, debilitating conflict that they viscerally reject the rule of the gun. In Lebanon, this took nearly 20 years to be achieved; in Northern Ireland, it took more than 30. In the meantime, all that the international community can do is support NGO, IGO, and state actors that are willing to sop up the arms, in the tens and in the thousands, that already exist on the continent and to inhibit the commerce of the arms traffickers that would replace destroyed weapons with new ones.

Notes

1. See Truth and Reconciliation Commission, Final Report, *South Africa's Chemical and Biological Warfare Programme: Special Investigation into Project Coast,* vol. 2, chap. 6 (Pretoria, South Africa: Truth and Reconciliation Commission, October 1998).

2. One of the best examples of the comingling of mining interests and arms trafficking occurred in Sierra Leone. In 1998 Rakesh Saxena, an Indian national who was a fugitive from Thai authorities and residing in Canada, contacted a British private military company, Sandline International, to broker an arms deal to help support the cause of the then-exiled Sierra Leonean leader Tejan Kabbah. Sandline itself had connections with two other Canadian mining companies that had been

active in Sierra Leone. In its own review of the impact of conflict diamonds on Sierra Leone's civil war, the United Nations accused the Liberian regime of Charles Taylor, in league with international diamond brokers, of maintaining a trade in diamonds that involved a countertrade program that provided the rebels of the Revolutionary United Front in Sierra Leone with the arms that it needed to continue to fight against the government in Freetown. See *Report of the Sierra Leone Arms Investigation: Sir Thomas Legg and Sir Robin Ibbs* (The Legg Report) (London: Her Majesty's Stationery Office, July 1998). Also see United Nations, *Report of the Panel of Experts Appointed Pursuant to UN Security Council Resolution 1306 (2000), Paragraph 19, In Relation to Sierra Leone* (New York: United Nations, December 2000).

3. In the first five years of the antibrokering amendment to the U.S. Arms Export Control Act, not a single individual was prosecuted. Loretta Bondi and Elise Keppler, *Casting the Net? The Implications of the U.S. Law on Arms Brokering* (New York: Fund for Peace, 2000), p. 21.

4. Commission of Inquiry, *First Report of the Commission of Inquiry into Alleged Arms Transactions Between Armscor and One Eli Wazan and Other Related Matters: Cameron Commission* (Cape Town, South Africa: Government Printing Office, 21 June 1995). In a case investigated by the South African Cameron Commission, for example, there were several misspellings in the EUC, and the "purchasing" agency no longer existed.

5. In 1992 Croatian officials allegedly paid $35,000 for an EUC purported to be an official document from a Nigerian military official. The EUC used in the Wazan case, above, cost $50,000. *The Independent* (London), 10 October 1992.

6. Danish ships are used in arms trafficking because they are relatively low tonnage and inconspicuous, and most have on-board cranes that allow them to offload in small ports. They were used in the Iran-contra enterprise and in the Wazan affair and have been implicated in arms trafficking into Angola and apartheid-era South Africa. Uli Schmetzer, "Arms Float to Iran via the Danes," *Chicago Tribune,* 30 November 1986; Stefaans Brummer, "South Africa's Arms Dealing Underworld," *Mail and Guardian,* Johannesburg, 2 June 1995.

7. Robert Holloway, "Air Transport a Little Known Key to Arms Smuggling," Agence France Presse, 27 March 2001.

8. In 1999 the chair of the UN Sanctions Committee on Angola, Ambassador Robert Fowler, raised the possibility of AWACs aircraft being used to interdict sanctions busters flying into Angola. *Angola Peace Monitor,* published by Action for Southern Africa, 28 July 1999, www.anc.org.za/angola/apm0511.html.

9. Some of the arms recovered during the RACHEL operations had been stored in holes in the ground for more than a decade and were rusty yet serviceable when retrieved.

10. "Mozambique–South Africa: Arms Trafficking Worries Governments," Inter Press Service, 27 October 1993.

11. Michael Quam, "Creating Peace in an Armed Society: Karamoja, Uganda, 1996," *African Studies Quarterly* 1, no. 1 (1997): www.web.africa.ufl.edu/asq/v1/v1.htm.

12. "Gunrunning Is Out of Control, Admits State," *The Nation* (Nairobi), 14 February 2001.

13. Alex Vines, *The Struggle Continues: Light Weapons Destruction in Mozambique* (London: British American Security Information Council, April 1998).

14. Christian Council of Mozambique, *Tools for Arms Project/Weapons for Ploughshares: Total of Weapons Collected up Until April 2000* (Maputo, Mozambique: CCM, 2000).

15. This author witnessed TAE destroying arms in 1999. The process, using saws and cutting instruments, was laborious but effective. The machinery was heavy enough that it needed a truck to transport it. Lighter, more transportable equipment was clearly more desirable.

16. Martinho Chachiua, *Arms Management Programme: Operations Rachel, 1996–1999,* Monograph Series No. 38 (Pretoria, South Africa: Institute for Security Studies, June 1999).

17. "International Interest in Operation Rachel Expanding," South African Press Association, 20 May 2001.

18. ECOWAS, *ECOWAS Moratorium on the Importation, Exportation, and Manufacture of Light Weapons* (Abuja, Nigeria: Government Document, 31 October 1998).

19. *The Nairobi Declaration on the Problem of the Proliferation of Illicit Small Arms and Light Weapons in the Great Lakes Region and the Horn of Africa* (Nairobi, Kenya: Government Document, 15 March 2000).

Suggested Readings

Austin, Kathi. *Stoking the Fires: Military Assistance and Arms Trafficking in Burundi.* New York: Human Rights Watch Arms Project, 1997.

Burgess, S., and H. Purkitt. *The Rollback of South Africa's Biological Warfare Program.* INSS Occasional Paper No. 37. Colorado Springs, CO: USAF Institute for National Security Studies, 2001.

Forberg, E., and U. Terlinden. *Small Arms in Somaliland: Their Role and Diffusion.* Berlin: Information Center for Transatlantic Security, 1999.

United Nations. *Report of the Panel of Experts Appointed Pursuant to UN Security Council Resolution 1306 (2000); Paragraph 19 in Relation to Sierra Leone (Conflict Diamonds).* New York: United Nations, December 2000.

14

South Asia

Peter R. Lavoy

The strategic competition between India and Pakistan is undergoing a modest revolution. The nuclear explosive tests the two rivals conducted in May 1998, and the subsequent steps each has taken to expand and improve the operational readiness of its nuclear forces, have convinced most observers that the elimination of nuclear weapons in South Asia is a futile goal. The key issues today are how to safeguard and secure each side's nuclear arsenal and how to stabilize their strategic competition. Even the U.S. government has abandoned its decades-old nonproliferation policy for India and Pakistan and is now reconciled to encourage them to exploit the deterrence value of nuclear weapons, albeit with caution and restraint.[1]

A parallel strategic shift between opposing powers occurred in the mid-1950s when it became clear that the United States and the Soviet Union would not abandon their nuclear stockpiles but instead would seek security and advantage through deterrence strategies.[2] Fearing that the search for more and more devastating deterrence arsenals would cause the superpower political crisis to escalate to military confrontation, policy analysts proposed arms control as a way for Washington and Moscow to consider the impact their military postures had upon one another and to promote strategic stability.[3] This logic now grips South Asia. Outside observers believe that arms control is required for India and Pakistan to avoid a fifth war. But there is no consensus on what kind of arms control India and Pakistan need or whether meaningful arms control is even attainable in the subcontinent.

This chapter is organized into two main sections. In the first, I review the conditions that made arms control so difficult for India and Pakistan to achieve during the 1980s and 1990s—a period when each state secretly was building nuclear weapons and the United States was trying to stop them. In the second section, I describe the post-1998 security predicament of South Asia, where India and Pakistan are expanding their declared nuclear weapons arsenals yet continue to prepare for conventional war. Here I identify several conditions that could improve the stability of deterrence between India and Pakistan and examine how arms control might help them. Real security in South Asia rests on the ability of India and Pakistan to overcome political, psychological, and bureaucratic hurdles to establishing mutual deterrence. Arms control, if designed and implemented carefully, can help to stabilize this relationship.

Impediments to Arms Control in South Asia

India and Pakistan have been slow to develop a stable strategic order in South Asia. Each side engages in coercive strategic behavior—expensive arms buildups, provocative troop movements and military exercises near tense borders, support for insurgent groups in the other country, and cross-border firing along the line of control in Kashmir.[4] Yet both sides recognize that they cannot afford to escalate to full-scale combat, much less nuclear war. In response to numerous military crises, Indian and Pakistani leaders have learned to conduct military operations more cautiously and even concluded several confidence-building measures (CBMs) on issues of marginal military importance, but they do not yet accept arms control as a way to enhance security.

Effective arms control requires India, Pakistan, and the United States—the only outside power able to facilitate regional negotiations and agreements—to develop the institutions and attitudes required for strategic stability. During the 1980s and 1990s four obstacles impeded the creation of arms control in South Asia: (1) a diplomatic preoccupation with nuclear disarmament to the detriment of nuclear restraint; (2) a reluctance to acknowledge the military orientation of Indian and Pakistani nuclear programs to permit a realistic debate about appropriate nuclear forces and strategies; (3) both states' refusal to pursue arms control as an instrument of national security; and (4) the persistence of resentment and defiance among the three powers.

The Inertia of Disarmament Diplomacy

A major barrier to achieving arms control in South Asia during the past two decades was the emphasis on disarmament and denuclearization by India, Pakistan, and the United States. Persistent pleas for the elimination of nuclear arms at the global level by New Delhi, and regionally by Islamabad and Washington, precluded the introduction of pragmatic arms control proposals.

India and global disarmament. India was a longtime opponent of nuclear deterrence and arms control. Even before becoming independent, India's first leader, Jawaharlal Nehru, campaigned to ban nuclear weapons. Like Mahatma Gandhi, the leader of India's nonviolent independence struggle, Nehru argued that the prospect of nuclear violence could not be countered by threats of nuclear retaliation, for that would spell suicide for humanity. Prior to the current leader, Atal Behari Vajpayee, every Indian prime minister viewed deterrence as an immoral and irrational basis for national security. They also distinguished arms control from disarmament, rejecting the former as an inappropriate response to the nuclear danger. Viewing horizontal proliferation (i.e., an increase in the number of nuclear-armed states) and vertical proliferation (growth of existing nuclear arsenals) as twin evils, India was more outspoken about the latter and called for both problems to be solved simultaneously. This perspective led Prime Minister Rajiv Gandhi to issue (with Soviet Premier Mikhail Gorbachev) the 1986 Delhi Declaration on Principles for a Nuclear-Weapon Free and Non-Violent World, calling for "the balance of terror [to] give way to comprehensive international security" through nuclear disarmament, a just political settlement of conflicts, peaceful negotiation and coexistence, and cooperation in political, economic, and humanitarian spheres.[5] Two years later Gandhi issued an action plan on nuclear disarmament.[6] This approach formed the basis of Indian policy until Vajpayee and the Bharatiya Janata Party came to power in 1998.

Pakistan and regional disarmament. Pakistan did not participate actively in the global nuclear debate during the 1950s, but in the 1960s it labored to draw international attention to the military potential of India's civil nuclear program and to raise the political cost to India of developing nuclear arms. In 1962 Pakistani President Ayub Khan urged the world community to devise "a treaty to outlaw the further spread of nuclear weapons."[7] During subsequent negotiations over the Nuclear Non-Proliferation Treaty (NPT), Pakistani diplomat Agha Shahi argued that although vertical proliferation needed to be controlled, the world's "top priority" was to curb horizontal proliferation and that "to tie the question of non-proliferation of nuclear weapons to other measures restricting the nuclear arms race could only result in an impasse."[8] In the end Pakistan refused to sign the NPT because it was not binding on India, which did not sign, and because it contained no guarantee for Pakistan's security.

Shortly after the NPT entered into force—and only a month after India defeated Pakistan in the 1971 Bangladesh War—Islamabad launched a two-track policy to match and contain India's growing nuclear capability. In January 1972 Prime Minister Zulfikar Ali Bhutto secretly directed Pakistani scientists to begin a nuclear weapon development program. Several months later Bhutto initiated the second track: a reinvigorated diplomatic effort to prevent India from obtaining nuclear weapons. This culminated in Pakistan's submission of the South Asia Nuclear Weapon Free Zone plan to the United Nations (UN) in November 1974, six months after India's first nuclear test. Bhutto's successors continued this strategy. General Zia ul-Haq repeatedly offered India six nonproliferation measures during his 11-year rule: mutual renunciation of nuclear arms, inspection of each side's nuclear facilities, acceptance of full-scope nuclear safeguards, accession to the NPT, a bilateral nuclear test ban, and a UN conference on nuclear nonproliferation in South Asia.[9] In 1991 Prime Minister Nawaz Sharif also invited the United States, Russia, and China to discuss nuclear nonproliferation with India and Pakistan. India rejected each of these regional disarmament ideas.

The United States and nuclear nonproliferation. A consistent goal of U.S. nonproliferation policy was to prevent India and Pakistan from obtaining nuclear weapons. U.S. efforts to curb nuclear proliferation rest on the premise that new nuclear forces are inherently dangerous and inimical to U.S. interests. And though nonproliferation has been a steady goal, Washington has changed its strategy for controlling the bomb's spread globally and in South Asia.[10] Breaking with early U.S. efforts to pressure India and Pakistan to abandon their nuclear efforts and join the NPT, the Bill Clinton administration urged them first to cap, then over time reduce, and finally eliminate their nuclear programs. Toward that end, Washington emphasized nonproliferation in bilateral discussions with New Delhi and Islamabad; it urged them to stop producing fissile material for weapons; it withheld military technology from India and economic and military aid from Pakistan (under the Pressler amendment to the Foreign Assistance Act); it supported direct India-Pakistan talks on regional security and nonproliferation; it pressed China to stop nuclear and missile assistance to Pakistan; and it engaged other states to apply similar nonproliferation pressures on India and Pakistan.

Because Washington had little to show for its efforts, many officials within the Clinton administration came to regard nuclear disarmament as unobtainable in South Asia. U.S. Secretary of Defense William Perry evinced this view in January 1995: "I recognized that the nuclear ambitions of India and Pakistan flow from a dynamic that we are unlikely to be able to influence in the near term. We might be able to [gain] influence over the long haul, but only if in the meantime we can prevent the tension from flaring into another conflict."[11] Since the Indian and Pakistani nuclear tests of 1998, George W. Bush's election as U.S. president in 2000, and the 11 September 2001 terrorist attacks against the United States, counterterrorism, foreign trade and investment, and avoiding a fifth India-Pakistan war apparently have replaced nuclear nonproliferation at the top of the U.S. foreign policy agenda for South Asia.

The Pathologies of Nuclear Opacity

The refusal of India and Pakistan to openly declare their nuclear weapon capabilities and intentions posed two problems for regional security since the early 1980s. First, some experts judged the strategic competition between the rivals to be less stable politically and militarily because their nuclear forces were covert, or "opaque," rather than openly declared, like those of the United States and Russia.[12] Indian General K. Sundarji claimed that nuclear opacity resulted in two strategic complications. The first was "due to the possibility of a war between India and Pakistan being triggered through miscalculation of each others' nuclear status, as well as ignorance of the nuclear doctrines that the two countries are likely to go by, which would culminate in a tragic nuclear exchange"; the second was "due to the difficulties of ensuring the safety of nuclear warheads and the prevention of unauthorized use when in a clandestine state."[13] Overt nuclear forces and clearly communicated nuclear doctrines were considered to be much more stable.

A second problem was that nuclear opacity impeded Pakistani and Indian efforts to openly propose, negotiate, and accept nuclear arms control agreements, even though that condition might have enabled policymakers to formulate measures in private that would be politically unpopular if publicized. Nuclear weapons have a meaning in South Asia well beyond their value as military instruments. For most of the region's population these weapons symbolize national sovereignty and security. If either state's leadership were to embrace arms control, it would be difficult to cultivate popular support for measures that are understood by few citizens owing to years of government secrecy. Moreover, neither state had a bureaucracy—civilian or military—to formulate and popularize arms control proposals.[14] Opaque nuclear proliferation may have constrained a regional arms race and provided policymakers flexibility in negotiations, but it also inhibited Indian and Pakistani leaders from cultivating domestic (and even bureaucratic) constituencies for arms control.

The Reluctance to Pursue Arms Control

New Delhi and Islamabad have devoted some energy to bilateral arms control, but neither side has accepted limits on military activities that it realistically might wish to pursue at some point in the future. Past and existing India-Pakistan treaties and CBMs have helped to reduce tensions and resolve troublesome disputes, but they have not significantly altered the sources of insecurity for either country.

Islamabad and New Delhi concluded their most meaningful CBMs after their first three wars (1947–1948, 1965, and 1971). The high costs of those conflicts led them to negotiate measures for troop disengagements and to make minor territorial adjustments along disputed borders; but because the settlements did not solve basic problems—especially those underlying the Kashmir dispute—neither party considered them conclusive. "At best," Douglas Makeig observed, "the Karachi Agreement (1949), the Tashkent Agreement (1966), and the Simla Accord (1972) should be considered formalized, armed truces under which both sides expressed a preference for negotiations over war."[15]

Today India and Pakistan observe several conventional CBMs. Driven to avoid a repeat of the second India-Pakistan war, the two sides agreed in 1966 to provide prior notification of border exercises. In 1982 they established the Indo-Pakistan Joint Commission. Aiming to create a forum for bilateral cooperation in communications, consular affairs, cultural exchanges, trade, smuggling, and, more recently, drug-trafficking, the commission convened several sessions at the foreign minister level and more sessions at lower levels. As separatist violence broke out in Indian-held Kashmir in 1990, Indian and Pakistani troops fought armed skirmishes along the Kashmir Line of Control. The heightened risk of war again signaled the need for confidence-building. The foreign secretaries of Pakistan and India met in New Delhi in April 1991 and signed two CBMs: one pledging nonviolation by military aircraft of each other's airspace, the other requiring each side to provide advance notification of military exercises and troop movements along common borders. India and Pakistan subsequently established a hot line between their military commanders.

Despite these steps, few regional CBMs actually operate as intended. Both sides violate no-fly zones for combat aircraft and helicopters in order to map terrain across the border. The agreement on prior notification of military exercises reportedly is often violated. Abuses of the military hot line also occur. After opening fire and inflicting casualties on enemy troops in Kashmir and on the Siachin Glacier, for example, the attacking party can call the enemy on the hot line to prevent hostilities from widening. Military and civilian officials evidently still remain skeptical that arms control can fundamentally enhance national security.

Resentment and Defiance

Another barrier to arms control in the 1980s and 1990s was the resentment and defiance that damaged relations among India, Pakistan, and the United States. The lack of trust and understanding between India and Pakistan is well known: neither side is willing to initiate a relationship of reciprocated good gestures. The animosity created by differences over the nuclear issue between Washington and India and Pakistan also was destructive. U.S. non-proliferation pressure precluded open discussions between India and Pakistan on regional security. Pakistan resented the imposition of the Pressler amendment, which it saw as discriminatory, and India objected as strongly to U.S. pressure for it to join the NPT and curb its space and missile activities. As a result, more Indian and Pakistani diplomatic energy went to diverting U.S. pressure than to devising arms control to promote regional security.

South Asia's Strategic Predicament

In the aftermath of the 1998 nuclear tests, there is greater openness about nuclear weapons and military doctrines in South Asia—but still no strategic stability and arms control. The two rivals made real progress toward those objectives in February 1999 when Indian Prime Minister Vajpayee held landmark meetings with Pakistani Prime Minister Nawaz Sharif in Lahore, Pakistan. But hopes were dashed just weeks later when Pakistani forces and pro-Pakistan insurgents launched a military campaign to take key territory in the Kargil sector on the Indian side of the Kashmir Line of Control. The Kargil conflict—the fourth India-Pakistan war—resulted in approximately 1,000 casualties on each side and reversed the confidence-building momentum created at Lahore. Thus observers have come to question whether progress toward deterrence stability and arms control can be restored in the wake of the U.S. campaign against the al-Qaida terrorist network and the Taliban regime in Afghanistan. The U.S. war on terrorism created even more resentment between India and Pakistan but might alter the strategic and political landscape such that cooperation is again desirable.

The Lahore summit was a watershed event in the strained history of India-Pakistan relations. The main outcomes were a declaration signed by the two prime ministers to intensify efforts to resolve all divisive issues. This included agreement on the political status of Kashmir, as well as a memorandum of understanding committing each country to:

- Engage in bilateral consultations on security concepts and nuclear doctrines, with a view toward developing nuclear and conventional CBMs;
- Provide each party with advance notification of ballistic missile flight tests;
- Undertake national measures to reduce the risks of accidental and unauthorized use of nuclear weapons; notify the other party immediately in the event of any accidental, unauthorized, or unexplained

incident; and identify or establish an appropriate communications mechanism for this purpose;

- Continue to abide by their respective unilateral moratoriums on conducting further nuclear test explosions;
- Conclude an agreement on prevention of incidents at sea in order to ensure safety of navigation by naval vessels and aircraft belonging to the two parties;
- Periodically review the implementation of existing CBMs and, where necessary, set up appropriate consultative mechanisms to monitor and ensure effective implementation of those CBMs;
- Review the existing communications links (e.g., between the respective directors-general of military operations) with a view toward upgrading and improving those links and to provide for fail-safe and secure communications; and
- Engage in bilateral consultations on security, disarmament, and nonproliferation issues within the context of negotiations on those issues in multilateral forums.[16]

If these measures had been implemented, India and Pakistan would be well on their way toward establishing an arms control regime that could rival, even surpass, that of the superpowers during the Cold War. But almost before the ink dried on this document India and Pakistan were at war again—this time in the snow-covered mountains near Kashmir.

Pakistan's bid to occupy Indian-controlled territory in Kargil was viewed by the Indian government as "a cynical breach of the trust on which the Lahore process was posited."[17] Particularly galling to the Indian leadership was the fact that "the Kargil aggression was underway even as the Pakistani Prime Minister was meeting the Indian Prime Minister at Lahore."[18] Although Kargil heightened tensions, the conflict itself remained limited because both sides wished to avoid escalation to a general war—one that could lead to the use of nuclear weapons. Therefore, even as Kargil underscored the risks involved in conflict, it also demonstrated that India and Pakistan appreciate the importance of caution and restraint in their strategic competition. This, of course, is an essential condition for arms control and deterrence stability.

India-Pakistan relations plummeted further in the aftermath of the 11 September 2001 terrorist attacks against New York and Washington and the U.S.-led war against the Taliban and Al-Qaida in neighboring Afghanistan.[19] India was particularly concerned that Taliban and Al-Qaida extremists would flee Afghanistan and take up arms against India in Kashmir and elsewhere. Such fears were apparently realized when the Indian parliament was attacked on 13 December 2001 by terrorists who India claimed belonged to two Pakistan-based militant groups: Lashkar-e-Taiba and Jaish-e-Mohammed.[20]

Pakistan's government denied that any groups based in Pakistan carried out the attacks. Despite this denial, Indian Prime Minister Atal Behari Vajpayee ordered the mobilization of the military and demanded that Pakistan eliminate militant groups operating against India from Pakistani territory and in Kashmir. He further announced that India would respond to this act of terrorism and that the use of military force will be one possible option.[21] Pakistan in turn mobilized its army. In mid-2002 the two armies were facing each other across the Line of Control in Kashmir and along the 2,200-mile international border.

This was the first time since 1971 that both countries were actually poised for full-scale war with one another. Earlier mobilizations of the two armies—in 1987 and 1990—were different in scale, because the strike elements of each force were not fully activated, and no landmines were deployed. Reports suggest that in the current situation both countries have also activated their strategic nuclear assets.[22]

Prime Minister Vajpayee and President Musharraf attended a meeting among heads of state of the South Asian Association for Regional Cooperation (SAARC), held in Kathmandu, Nepal, on 4–6 January 2002. Foreign ministers of the two countries also met on the side during the summit. Although these meetings did not result in a substantive dialogue between the two governments, statements made to the media by both leaders indicated a mutual desire for reconciliation and a defusing of the crisis.

While Indian officials acknowledged that steps taken by Pakistan's government were a positive sign, most remained skeptical about Pakistan's commitment to curb anti-India activities. Pakistani leaders continued to maintain that terrorism in other parts of the world could not be equated with the violence in Kashmir, which they characterized as part of an ongoing struggle for freedom by the Kashmiri people against the Indian government. The Indian position, by contrast, is that the insurgency in Kashmir and other parts of India is a direct result of crossborder terrorism perpetrated by Pakistan. Indian officials insist that it is up to Pakistan to halt all manifestations of terrorism as a precondition to peace between the two countries, failing which the current military impasse will continue and may lead to war.

The strategic predicament India and Pakistan face today can be summed up in three points: (1) The rivals continue to have serious conflicts of interest, especially over Kashmir, and a deep mistrust of one another; (2) each side is prepared to use military force, including nuclear weapons, to protect its security interests; but (3) neither wants war because of political considerations, because of the risk of escalation, and because neither side has enough of an edge in conventional military forces to win anything of political significance.[23] Because South Asia is prone to all kinds of crises, the risk of conflict will be an indelible feature of India-Pakistan relations, even in a condition of mutual nuclear deterrence.

In such an environment, the incentives for India and Pakistan to maintain their conventional and nuclear military readiness are obvious. Not only is this the overriding strategic imperative for Islamabad and New Delhi; the United States and other outside powers now accept this requirement as well. What is less well understood by Indian and Pakistani political and military leaders is the strategic necessity of restraint and reciprocity. As Bernard Brodie counseled in 1959,

> Deterrence . . . depends on a subjective feeling which we are trying to create in the opponent's mind, a feeling compounded of respect and fear, and we have to ask ourselves whether it is not possible to overshoot the mark. It is possible to make him fear us too much, especially if what we make him fear is our over-readiness to react, whether or not he translates it into clear evidence of our aggressive intent. The effective operation of deterrence over the long term requires that the other party be willing to live with our possession of the capability upon which it rests.[24]

In other words, fielding nuclear weapons, ballistic missiles, and conventional forces ultimately might be the easiest prerequisite for deterrence; far more challenging—but no less critical—are steps designed to make each competitor feel confident that the other accepts its right to exist. Here is where arms control can help.

Conclusion

The advent of nuclear weapon capabilities in South Asia poses new risks for India and Pakistan. The United States and the Soviet Union were able to manage similar risks during the Cold War, but never was it an easy task. After several dangerous episodes, the Cuban missile crisis in particular, Washington and Moscow eventually learned to bring their foreign policy practices, defense programs, and military behavior in line with the requirement of avoiding nuclear war. India and Pakistan are now on the verge of undergoing a similar learning process. The outcome remains to be seen, but the risk of nuclear war in South Asia might be controlled with the effective application of arms control measures by India, Pakistan, and the United States as they attempt to stabilize mutual deterrence on the subcontinent.

Notes

The views expressed in this chapter are the author's alone and do not represent the positions of the Naval Postgraduate School or the U.S. Department of Defense.

1. This policy shift was signaled by Deputy Secretary of State Strobe Talbott in a February 1999 interview with *India Today*: "Your prime minister on several occasions used the phrase 'credible minimum deterrence.' Now the two adjectives,

credible and minimum, need to be reconciled. It needs to be credible in order to deter. But it needs to be minimum in order not to provoke a devastatingly and expensive arms race." *India Today*, 15 February 1999. President Bush hastened this policy reversal: on 22 September 2001 he lifted the sanctions placed on India and in May 1998 those on Pakistan. For background, see K. Santhanam et al., "A Study of the Waiver of U.S. Sanctions," Institute for Defense Studies and Analyses, www. idsa-india.org/u%20s%20lift.htm.

2. See Forrest Waller, Chapter 6 in this volume.

3. Bernard Brodie led the campaign "to limit or control the unsettling effects of our deterrent posture." Bernard Brodie, *Strategy in the Missile Age* (Princeton, NJ: Princeton University Press, 1965 [1959]), p. 397.

4. For background, see Peter R. Lavoy, "The Costs of Nuclear Weapons in South Asia," in D. R. SarDesai and Raju G. C. Thomas, eds., *Nuclear India in the Twenty-First Century* (New York: Palgrave, 2002).

5. Text contained in *Disarmament: India's Initiatives* (New Delhi: Indian Ministry of External Affairs, 1988), pp. 81–86.

6. Presenting India's action plan to the United Nations, Gandhi condemned nuclear deterrence as a justification for arms, threats, and violence; a source of international hostility; the cause of economic calamity; a spur to nuclear proliferation; and the root of the inevitable risk of global annihilation. "A World Free of Nuclear Weapons," in *India and Disarmament* (New Delhi: Ministry of External Affairs, 1988), pp. 280–294.

7. President Ayub Khan's statement to the UN General Assembly is quoted in Hameed A.K. Rai, *Pakistan in the United Nations* (Lahore, Pakistan: Aziz, 1979), p. 241.

8. Quoted in *Documents on Disarmament, 1967* (Washington, DC: U.S. Government Printing Office, 1968), p. 671; and *Documents on Disarmament, 1968* (Washington, DC: U.S. Government Printing Office, 1968), p. 318.

9. Ali Sarwar Naqvi, "Pakistan: Seeking Regional Peace and Progress in Non-Nuclear South Asia," *Arms Control Today* (June 1993): 11.

10. See Peter R. Lavoy, "Learning and the Evolution of Cooperation in U.S. and Soviet Nonproliferation Activities," in George W. Breslauer and Philip E. Tetlock, eds., *Learning in U.S. and Soviet Foreign Policy* (Boulder: Westview, 1991), pp. 735–783.

11. Quoted in *Defense News,* 6–12 February 1995, p. 16.

12. For example, Shai Feldman has argued that covert nuclear weapon programs entail closed decisionmaking without wider scrutiny, dominance of the military in the formulation of doctrine, biases toward offense and preemption, and strained crisis management and nuclear signaling. Shai Feldman, *Israeli Nuclear Deterrence* (New York: Columbia University Press, 1982). See also Avner Cohen and Benjamin Frankel, "Opaque Nuclear Proliferation," in Benjamin Frankel, ed., *Opaque Nuclear Proliferation: Methodological and Political Implications* (London: Frank Cass, 1991), pp. 14–44.

13. K. Sundarji, "Former Military Chief Discusses Nuclear Options," *India Express* (Mumbai), 20 December 1992.

14. See Stephen P. Cohen, *India: Emerging Power* (Washington, DC: Brookings Institution, 2001), pp. 73–74.

15. Douglas C. Makeig, "War, No-War, and the India-Pakistan Negotiating Process," *Pacific Affairs* (Summer 1987): 272.

16. The memorandum of understanding and other documents from the February 1999 Lahore summit can be found on the Henry L. Stimson Center website, www.stimson.org/southasia/?sn=sa20020109215.

17. This sentiment is uttered by Indian political and military leaders and appears in India's official review of the war, Government of India, *From Surprise to Reckoning: The Kargil Review Committee Report* (New Delhi: Sage, 2000), p. 69.

18. Ibid.

19. This section is drawn from Peter R. Lavoy and Surinder Rana, "Standoff Between India and Pakistan," *Strategic Insight: South Asia* (Monterey, CA: Center for Contemporary Conflict, Naval Postgraduate School, February-March 2002), www.ccc.nps.navy.mil/rsepResources/si/mar02/southAsia.asp.

20. Prashant Pandey, "Jaish, Lashkar Carried out Attack with ISI Guidance: Police," *Hindu* (Madras, India), 16 December 2001.

21. "All Options are Open PM," *Hindu*, 19 December 2001.

22. "India's Missile System 'In Position': Fernandes," *Hindu,* 26 December 2001.

23. For background, see Ashley Tellis, *Stability in South Asia* (Santa Monica, CA: RAND, 1997); and Neil Joeck, *Maintaining Nuclear Stability in South Asia,* Adelphi Paper No. 312 (London: International Institute for Strategic Studies, 1997).

24. Brodie, *Strategy in the Missile Age,* p. 397.

Suggested Readings

Cohen, Stephen P. *India: Emerging Power.* Washington, DC: Brookings Institution, 2001.

Kux, Dennis. *The United States and Pakistan, 1947–2000: Disenchanted Allies.* Baltimore: Johns Hopkins University Press, 2001.

Perkovich, George. *India's Nuclear Bomb: The Impact on Global Proliferation.* Berkeley: University of California Press, 1999.

Tellis, Ashley J. *India's Emerging Nuclear Posture: Between Recessed Deterrent and Ready Arsenal.* Santa Monica, CA: RAND, 2001.

15

East Asia

Brad Roberts

What role has arms control played in East Asia? What role should it play in shaping the future East Asian security environment? Such questions have not received sustained attention from analysts interested in arms control, as attention focused instead on arms control in the East-West context.[1] But with the evolving security situation in East Asia after the Cold War, it is necessary to revisit basic questions such as these. East Asia is a dynamic region, and concern about the possible further proliferation of nuclear, biological, and chemical (NBC) weapons and missile delivery systems is rising. Moreover, there is a distinct history of arms control in the region, one that includes both successes and failures. Understanding the past and present role of arms control can tell us something of its future there.

I begin with a review of the history of arms control in East Asia, giving special attention to the evolving role of arms control since the end of the Cold War. This is a surprisingly extensive history, rich in implications for the future. I then consider the near-term future with a discussion of alternative possible arms control outcomes. I conclude with a review of implications for the general strategy of arms control as well as the strategy of security in East Asia. I broadly define the region of East Asia to include not just the states of Northeast and Southeast Asia but also the contiguous oceanic and geographic regions to the extent they bear on arms control choices in one or both of the primary subregions. I also consider, as appropriate, the role of the United States and the Russian Federation as arms control actors in East Asia.

Pre–Cold War Arms Control

A natural starting point for a review of the modern history of arms control in East Asia is the same as for many other regions: the Hague conferences, held near the turn of the twentieth century, a time of rising concern about the impact of the Industrial Revolution and the highly competitive balance-of-power system on the prospects for war and its conduct. But in East Asia, as elsewhere, there are some practices analogous to modern arms control that predate that era. Japan's centuries-long effort to preserve the samurai sword culture from the changes wrought by the gun, for example, is roughly analogous to the effort of the Catholic Church to outlaw the use of the crossbow among civilized armies.[2] Also prior to the modern era a body of analysis and opinion developed in some East Asian societies, as elsewhere, about "just war" rules for the conduct of war conducive to a "just peace."

The second Hague conference, in 1907, in some ways signaled Japan's arrival as a major global power, coming as it did toward the end of the four-decade-long Meiji restoration and the radical transformation of Japan from an isolated, preindustrial society into a modern, imperial state. At the first conference, in 1899, Japan played almost no role at all. But the 1904–1905 Russo-Japanese war raised important questions about the rights of neutrals in war, and the 1907 convention focused in significant measure on codifying such rights in international law.[3]

This era also included limited efforts to control the international arms trade in the form of two embargoes on the sale of arms to factions in China. The first such embargo, in 1900, was largely informal, reflecting the decision of a number of arms manufacturers not to sell arms to factions during the Boxer Rebellion. The second was a more formal embargo, in 1919, when eight major countries tried to calm the power struggle then raging among Chinese warlords.[4]

World War I and its aftermath had a number of implications for arms control in East Asia. The decision of the U.S. Senate not to join the League of Nations or to ratify the Versailles Treaty had far-reaching implications. By withholding its consent to those measures, Washington was also withholding recognition of certain rights and mandates bestowed on Japan by the League. Such decisions had a major impact on Japan, on U.S.-Japanese relations, and on the drift toward war in the Pacific.

But there were also more arms control–specific implications of World War I. Public revulsion to the war's carnage led to a strong political commitment in some countries to control the arms trade and to seek disarmament. This impulse was felt especially strongly in Australia, which focused diplomatic energies on pursuit of these agendas—an impulse that remains strong today. Canberra played an important role in negotiating the Geneva Protocol in 1925 that banned the use of chemical and biological weapons (CBW).[5] Of course, this impulse has been criticized by some analysts and policymakers as precisely the wrong lesson of World War I, on the argument that arms races are merely the symptoms of the absence of peace, not the cause of war; controlling weapons without dealing with the actual political causes of war, they say, only aggravates international security.[6]

Another important result of the World War I experience was the naval arms control process. This process was set in motion in 1921 and 1922 at the Washington Conference on Naval Disarmament and Far Eastern Affairs—an Asian dimension that is often overlooked by arms control historians. It also grew out of the perception that arms races had made more war likely. The process produced three treaties, only one of which related to the disposition of military forces.[7] The Five-Power Treaty on Naval Armament Limitation was signed in February 1922 and established a ratio of 5:5:3 for capital ships (battleships and cruisers) of the navies of the United States, Britain, and Japan. Japan won a concession from the United States and Britain to maintain the status quo regarding its fortifications in the Pacific. The treaty also limited the tonnage for the newest naval weapon—the aircraft carrier. A supplemental measure was agreed on in 1930 in part to meet Japanese demands for a more favorable balance, with adoption of a 10:7 ratio between the United States and Japan for auxiliary ships and parity in submarines. This agreement was to expire in 1936.[8]

These naval measures are typically recalled among contemporary arms control scholars as demonstrating the destabilizing consequences of ill-considered measures. Ostensibly they signal the advantages that authoritarian states have in arms control, as they cheat on such measures to gain military advantages, and the weaknesses of democracies, which seem to overcomply and fail to deal with evidence of noncompliance by another party.[9] This history lends itself also to an alternative explanation. Treaty negotiators hoped to ensure that if war came it would not be as a result of a naval arms race. They also sought to ensure that if war came no one could gain a decisive advantage through exploitation of naval means. Moreover, they were seeking to create mechanisms that made developments in the military competition largely predictable and that provided warning of militarily significant shifts in the balance of power.[10] In these respects, the treaties were somewhat more successful.

When war erupted in Asia in the 1930s, the naval treaties were, of course, swept aside. Not so the Geneva Protocol. Both Japan and the United States were signatories of the protocol, though neither deposited instruments of ratification to become state parties until the 1970s. Japan employed both chemical and biological weapons in its war against China. But it refrained from doing so in its war against the United States in the Pacific, just as the United States refrained from using such weapons against Japan. This pattern of restraint mirrors the situation in Europe, where all states readied for chemical and biological warfare but none waged it. This experience is recalled by some as proof of the axiom that the threat of retaliation in kind deters the use of such weapons, whereas others recall it as proof of the existence of a strong anti-CBW norm that leaders violate only at the risk of losing public support.[11] World War II ended with a strong antiwar constitution for Japan, a constitution that differs from Germany's in that it does not include the explicit prohibition against the development and possession of NBC weapons.

Cold War Arms Control

Whatever the real and perceived failures of arms control in East Asia during the interwar period, this history did not prevent leaders in the subsequent era from pursuing further measures. In this section I survey arms control milestones by decade.

In the 1950s there were two important arms control benchmarks. The first was the continuing dispute about the Geneva Protocol. The recently established People's Republic of China joined the protocol in 1952, in part to gain political visibility for its claim that the United States was employing biological weapons in the Korean War and against Chinese territory. A debate on these claims has percolated ever since, with some Western scholars arguing that the evidence is highly suggestive of such U.S. use.[12] Others argue that the evidence points to a public disinformation campaign by the KGB (the Soviet intelligence agency).[13]

The other benchmark was the conclusion of the Antarctic Treaty in 1959. That treaty was in part a demilitarization measure, but a central purpose was to settle multiple competing claims to the region. From an East Asian perspective, it is noteworthy in that both Australia and New Zealand were among the original claimants. The treaty itself has provisions for verification and resolution of compliance questions.[14]

In Asia, as elsewhere, the 1960s were dominated by the nuclear issue. President John F. Kennedy's aggressive pursuit of a test ban had significant implications in the region, as the resultant Limited Test Ban Treaty (LTBT) of 1963 brought to an end U.S. atmospheric tests in the Pacific. Moscow's acceptance of the LTBT was also seen in Beijing as Moscow's final sellout of China's as yet unfulfilled nuclear ambitions, as the Soviet Union abandoned its cooperative development programs with China in the name of nuclear cooperation with the United States.[15] China exploded a nuclear device in 1964 and championed the principle of no-first-use for all of the nuclear weapon states.

Conclusion of the Nuclear Non-Proliferation Treaty (NPT) in 1968 had wide-ranging implications for Asia. It effectively closed the door on nuclear weapon programs or ambitions in a number of countries.[16] In preceding years, Australia had actively pursued purchase of nuclear weapons and delivery platforms.[17] Indonesia, concerned with Australian ambitions, apparently sought a deal with Beijing whereby China would explode a nuclear device in the territory of Indonesia that Jakarta could call its own.[18]

South Korea also had nuclear weapon ambitions in this period.[19] But perhaps the most important nuclear door closed was on Japan. Japan did not complete its ratification of the NPT until 1976, and this only after extended debate about its potential future nuclear requirements and its interests in a treaty of unlimited duration and the safeguards on its commercial power industry.[20]

The 1970s saw an expansion of the global treaty regime in ways that brought Asian states into a number of new mechanisms, including the Seabed Treaty of 1971,[21] the Biological and Toxin Weapons Convention of 1972 (commonly cited as the Biological Weapons Convention, or BWC),[22] and the Environmental Modification Convention, which bans the manipulation of the environment for military purposes.[23]

The accession of the People's Republic of China to China's seat in the United Nations and at the Security Council in 1971 also had certain arms control implications. This brought with it a Chinese decision to join additional multilateral arms control measures beyond the Geneva Protocol, including the BWC and the Latin America Nuclear Weapon Free Zone, which China was expected to sign as one of the recognized nuclear weapon states under the NPT.

The 1980s saw an expansion of China's participation in arms control regimes. It joined the Antarctic Treaty, joined the International Atomic Energy Agency (IAEA), and renounced atmospheric testing of nuclear weapons (though it did not join the LTBT).[24] This period also witnessed rising concern about potential Taiwanese nuclear weapon ambitions and efforts by the United States to prevent Taipei from implementing a development program—efforts largely made possible by the existence of the NPT and IAEA mechanisms.[25]

The year 1985 also saw conclusion of the Treaty of Rarotonga and, with it, creation of a South Pacific Nuclear Weapon Free Zone. China and the Soviet Union adhered to the relevant protocols, whereas the United States, Britain, and France did not until the 1990s.[26]

During this period the unfolding détente and rapid arms control progress between Washington and Moscow had some important implications for Asia. Conclusion of the Intermediate-Range Nuclear Forces (INF) Treaty came about only after significant discussion of possible repercussions in Asia. An initial framework that would have allowed Soviet retention of some intermediate-range forces caused considerable concern in both Japan and China about the possible redeployment of SS-20 nuclear-tipped missiles from Europe to Asia. Their concern helped fuel the decision to seek the so-called double-zero option that was the basis of the final INF agreement.[27] Similar concerns were voiced in Asia about the possible impact of the Conventional Armed Forces in Europe Treaty.

Post–Cold War Arms Control

The end of bipolar confrontation between Moscow and Washington, the collapse of the Soviet Union, and the near-brush with NBC weapons in the 1991 Gulf War brought an acceleration of international cooperation on arms control and nonproliferation that has also affected Asian countries.

Bilateral U.S.-Soviet agreements have had an important impact on Asia. The treaty process pursuant to the Strategic Arms Reduction Talks (START) has brought with it a significant drawdown of strategic nuclear forces deployed by both in Asia. The presidential nuclear initiatives (PNIs) pursued by Presidents George Bush and Mikhail Gorbachev led to the withdrawal of U.S. tactical nuclear weapons from Korea as well as the removal of such weapons from U.S. naval vessels; Russia's compliance remains uncertain.[28] Activities under the Cooperative Threat Reduction (CTR) program have also helped to ease concerns in Asia about so-called loose nukes from Russia finding their way into Asian hands. Some rising Asian concerns about environmentally destructive and abandoned former Soviet military systems in Pacific regions are also evident. Japan has sought to cooperate with the Russian Federation to promote dismantlement of Russian nuclear submarines in the region.

The multilateral treaty regime has been expanded through conclusion of the Chemical Weapons Convention (CWC). It has provided a new tool for states in the region to address long-standing concerns about chemical weapons and, especially, for final Sino-Japanese resolution of issues related to old and abandoned Japanese stocks in China (and their associated history). It has also brought revelations about chemical warfare preparations by South Korea.[29]

The 1990s opened with China's decisions to sign the NPT and then to sign the Comprehensive Test Ban Treaty (CTBT), decisions that seemed to signal a surprise willingness not to complete modernization of its nuclear forces. China also took numerous steps during the 1990s to bring its arms and technology transfer policies into closer compliance with the preferences of the United States and international norms, although by the end of the decade there were still concerns about whether it was fully honoring its commitments in this regard and should not do more.[30]

This period also included the rising drama associated with North Korea's nuclear weapon program, its noncompliance with NPT, a near-war of nuclear preemption by the United States, and subsequent conclusion of the U.S.–North Korea Agreed Framework—and very unsatisfying implementation.[31] In part because of the North Korean experience, but also because of revelations about Iraq's nuclear program, members of the IAEA moved forward with negotiation of an enhanced safeguards program, with significant interest expressed by some Asian nations. The effects on Asia of nuclear tests by India and Pakistan in 1998 are a matter of continuing debate. At the very least, they were interpreted in East Asia, and especially Japan, as signaling a possible further erosion of the nuclear nonproliferation regime—not least because of the vivid demonstration of the inability of the major powers acting in their roles as permanent members of the UN Security Council to reverse or even meaningfully punish the two proliferators. East Asian states did not overlook Beijing's complicity in assisting Pakistan to acquire a nuclear capability and saw its post-test diplomacy as little more than an effort to save face for a dramatic policy mistake.

In Southeast Asia in particular during this period there was also a very active pursuit of confidence- and security-building measures (CSBMs), to include the fullest possible participation in and implementation of existing arms control agreements.[32] States in the region pushed for full participation in the UN Register of Conventional Arms, largely because of fears that their robust economies might generate conventional arms races, fears that attenuated with the financial crisis late in the decade. These states also brought into being a new Southeast Asia Nuclear Weapon Free Zone.[33]

Arms Control 2002

More than a decade after the end of the Cold War, arms control mechanisms play an important role in East Asia, though less prominent than in the transatlantic community and, until recently, in U.S.-Russia relations. But it should not be dismissed lightly. It is useful to think of three levels of arms control activity in the region: (1) the bilateral U.S.-Russia overlay; (2) the global treaty regime as evident in the region; and (3) local mechanisms, both regional and subregional. In each case, it is important to recognize that the world is at a major fork in the road and that strategically significant questions have come to the fore about next steps.

At the bilateral level, the regional implications of START, INF, CTR, and the PNIs have already been identified. The fork in the road is defined by the choices yet to be made in Washington and Moscow about whether and how to move away from the offense-defense framework embodied in the START and Anti-Ballistic Missile Treaties. Possible cessation of formal U.S.-Russia arms control has generated anxiety among many Asian nations. Continuation of restraint and cooperation by Washington and Moscow, whether in a formal or informal mode, would go a long way to attenuate such concerns.

At the global level implementation of measures such as the NPT, BWC, CWC, and UN Register of Conventional Arms has significant implications for the region. Successful resolution of compliance challenges posed by North Korea and Iraq would bolster confidence in arms control more generally, not least by signaling the ability of the major powers to co-operate toward and meaningfully accomplish such ends. Failure to achieve such resolution is likely to have long-term erosive effects on the willing-ness of states in the region to participate in arms control agreements. The global multilateral mechanisms stand at something of a crossroads. After more than a decade of effort started by the Gulf War, there is not a lot of progress to show for efforts to strengthen the anti-NBC global treaty regime. Whether the treaty regime will continue to hold together is an open question. If it begins to unravel, repercussions will certainly be felt in East Asia. Reopening the nuclear doors closed in the 1960s would have far-reaching implications.

At the regional level, numerous mechanisms have been brought into being, and more are under discussion. Nuclear weapon–free zones have been codified in the South Pacific and in Southeast Asia. Similar mecha-nisms are under discussion in Northeast Asia[34] and Central Asia.[35] And CSBMs have been pursued in various guises and with increasing interest since the end of the Cold War. But in some sense these regional mecha-nisms reflect a willingness to do the easy things; now leaders in the region must consider whether there is virtue in doing some of the more difficult things. Measures that would increase the transparency of military prepara-tions in the region are widely rejected as inconsistent with the interests of societies unaccustomed to military transparency, just as formal restraint measures are typically rejected as European inventions ill-suited to Asian societies that prefer a less formal style of interstate relations.

The Future of Arms Control in East Asia

This brief historical review would seem to point to a continuing role for arms control in East Asia. After all, the existence of such a long and multi-faceted history suggests an openness to arms control tools on the part of de-cisionmakers in the region. A certain momentum attaches to the implemen-tation of existing measures, not least through the creation of bureaucratic and political constituencies associated with such implementation. Yet the forks in the road are real indeed, and so I proceed with an exploration of two alternative futures. The first is defined by the unraveling of arms control in East Asia; the second is defined by continued progress in implementing ex-isting measures, leading to an expansion of arms control approaches.

Unraveling of Arms Control

What would the unraveling of arms control in East Asia look like? It could begin with failure of the Agreed Framework or follow-on measures with

North Korea and that country's overt declaration of a nuclear capability. It could begin with more NBC capabilities from the former Soviet Union somehow leaking into the region, perhaps appearing during a moment of crisis as a newly declared capability. It could begin with Chinese resumption of illicit transfers of NBC and/or missile technologies to other states. And it could begin at the 2005 NPT review conference. If by then the CTBT has not entered into force (or if the test moratorium has ended), there seems some significant possibility that some East Asian states will move away from the NPT as a way to protest the failure of the nuclear weapon states to deliver on the promises made at the 1995 review and extension conference. An unraveling of the arms control regime in East Asia would likely precipitate some states to reconsider nuclear options, including most prominently U.S. friends and allies there. A determination by Japan, Taiwan, or a reunified Korea that possession of a national nuclear deterrent is essential their national security would be a sharp blow to the nonproliferation regime—and to U.S. credibility as a security guarantor.

Expanded Arms Control Efforts

What might an expansion of arms control look like? It could begin—indeed, it seems that it must begin—with successful implementation of the global treaty regime in the form of successful resolution of the compliance challenges posed by North Korea and Iraq. Entry into force of the CTBT, an unlikely prospect at this writing, could have a positive reinforcing effect on the global treaty regime, not least by signaling continued Chinese nuclear restraint. Expansion of arms control could proceed with full implementation of the enhanced IAEA safeguards program, negotiation and entry into force of the Fissile Material Cut-Off Treaty, and adaptation of the Open Skies program to Asian purposes. There is continued discussion in Asia of long-standing Chinese interest in a declaration of no-first-use by the nuclear weapon states.[36] China also has an agenda to expand the restraints codified in the Outer Space Treaty of 1967.[37] Expansion could entail new regional mechanisms, including nuclear weapon–free zones in Northeast and Central Asia, as well as what some have promoted as PACATOM (a possible Asian analogue to EURATOM, the European Atomic Energy Agency) to enhance control of the regional nuclear fuel cycle and associated materials.[38] The Korean situation seems likely to generate new arms control questions, whether along the track toward reunification if that becomes possible (which will raise questions about the nuclear status of the successor state), or along the track of continued stalemate (with questions about the Agreed Framework and possible successor measures). The Taiwan situation also seems likely to generate some new arms control questions, including a possible freeze on deployments on the mainland of new short- and medium-range ballistic missiles, or new measures of cross-strait transparency, or even a new formal understanding between the United States and the People's Republic of China of the nature of arms sales that Washington will conduct with Taipei.[39]

A central question about the future of arms control in East Asia relates to the U.S.-China nuclear relationship. Until now China has been a bystander in the nuclear arms control process, except as a participant in the NPT and CTBT—neither of which requires a cessation of Chinese nuclear modernization or a reduction of its forces. This past practice is understandable enough, in the sense that the Chinese nuclear arsenal is a small fraction of the arsenal of the superpowers—numbering somewhere between 300 and 700 warheads, only 20 or so of which are understood to be deliverable at intercontinental ranges (remembering, of course, that all of China's Asian neighbors are at less than intercontinental range).[40] But as U.S. and Russian arsenals continue to shrink, there is a logical question as to when China should join the reductions process. And as the United States moves to deploy ballistic missile defenses, there are also logical questions as to whether or how China might increase its arsenal to overwhelm those defenses. Some form of negotiated restraint on China's part could be helpful in firming up Russian and U.S. willingness to make very deep cuts in their nuclear arsenals. Clearly the potential for formal arms control with the Chinese in the strategic realm will be driven largely by whether or not there is formal arms control in the U.S.-Russia realm.

A Third Alternative

These two arms control alternatives are set out rather starkly. History suggests a third possibility: simply muddling through, pushing forward on arms control where possible while coping with its failures and imperfections where necessary. Muddling through is always an option in international politics. But there is good reason for skepticism that arms control will simply muddle along. The forks in the road are real. The challenges posed by North Korea are increasingly prominent. More than a decade of effort to strengthen the multilateral global regime has not gotten very far. Unraveling is a real possibility, one that could lead to a rapid proliferation of weapons of mass destruction in the region given the high degree of latent capability that is evident there.

What factors will determine the course ahead? Certainly in each of the numerous countries in East Asia different factors and interests will shape the willingness to pursue arms control more aggressively in the period ahead—or to abandon arms control and pursue weapon programs. What factors can have crosscutting effects that will influence thinking in multiple countries? The list of possible factors is long and must include a visible collapse or outright failure of arms control elsewhere in the world, the use of banned weapons to positive effect in some future war, or an accident like Chernobyl that dramatically changes public perceptions. Perhaps the key question is political: Will the United States and China be able to find sufficient common ground to pursue an arms control agenda cooperatively and more aggressively than is currently the case? The relationship between the two countries is, after all, the major uncertainty in the East Asian security environment. Arms control cooperation between them could pay significant dividends at the regional and global levels. But confrontation between them could lead China to choose to play the role of spoiler to the U.S. ambition of promoting stability through arms control and nonproliferation.[41] More than a decade after the Cold War ended the evidence remains ambiguous.

Conclusion

In East Asia, as elsewhere, arms control has played a significant but by no means singular role. Arms control has not been the primary tool for building security in the region. A stable balance of power, formal alliance relationships, and political and economic modernization have all played essential roles in constructing the existing security order. But arms control has been far from irrelevant, as policymakers have demonstrated over many decades a willingness to consider specific mechanisms and to participate in their implementation. As the experience in other regions well suggests, arms control is no panacea. But states seem to value specific forms of military restraint and to exercise restraint of their own in exchange.

These conclusions are relevant to the ongoing U.S. policy debate about the role of arms control within U.S. strategy. Is arms control merely a vestige of the Cold War, to be set aside for the exigencies of a new era? The experience in East Asia suggests that the answer is no. Arms control in East Asia predates the Cold War, and the end of the Cold War has brought an expansion of arms control in that region. This history is suggestive of two further insights into the current debate. First, multilateral approaches to security can be helpful but cannot be pursued as a substitute for bilateral and other measures; the policymaker typically wants as broad a set of tools as possible, and multilateral mechanisms belong in the toolkit despite their imperfections. Second, arms control does not work without leadership. If the United States wishes to shape the region in ways that suit its interests, it should welcome that leadership role. Others, especially China, are ready to exert leadership if the United States chooses not to. It seems unreasonable to expect that China would always pursue arms control in ways that suit U.S. interests.

These conclusions are also relevant to the scholarly debate about the classic functions of arms control as described by Thomas Schelling and

Morton Halperin. In East Asia today arms control is a tool for setting expectations about the durability of the balance of power and the types of strategic relations that will prevail between Washington and Beijing. It is a source of reassurance that states with increasingly robust weapon capabilities will not suddenly create new weapons and new strategic realities, thus dampening the need to hedge against such possibilities. Arms control helps to inhibit the spillover effects of developments from one subregion to another. Export licensing procedures required of state parties to the nuclear, biological, and chemical control regimes also promote the exploitation of dual-use technologies and materials for commercial and other public purposes, technologies that might otherwise be constrained for fear of their potential misapplication to military purposes. Arms control helps to consolidate and accelerate the transparency of heretofore closed societies. It also helps to address basic questions of power in the region by tying U.S. power to common purposes and engaging China in existing institutions and processes. In these ways the functions of arms control would appear in East Asia to extend well beyond the classic ones. As the region moves from a competitive balance-of-power system to more cooperative approaches to common security challenges, arms control measures will offer valuable benefits.

Notes

The author is grateful for research and other assistance provided by Michael Fleischer. The author is also grateful for comments on earlier drafts of this chapter provided by Jeffrey Larsen and Michael Wheeler. The author alone is responsible for the final arguments presented here, and the views expressed here should not be attributed to the Institute for Defense Analyses or any of its sponsors.

1. One indicator of this predisposition is the fact that the 1996 edition of this book did not include a chapter on East Asia.

2. Richard P. Cronin, "Japan," in Richard Dean Burns, ed., *Encyclopedia of Arms Control and Disarmament* (New York: Charles Scribner's Sons, 1993), pp. 129–130.

3. Ibid., p. 135.

4. Walter C. Clemens, Jr., "China," in Burns, *Encyclopedia of Arms Control and Disarmament,* p. 62.

5. The protocol itself was the one significant agreed measure in a conference that otherwise failed to deliver any significant agreement on its primary agenda, which was the control of the arms trade. See Josef Goldblat, *Arms Control Agreements: A Handbook* (Stockholm: Praeger, 1982), pp. 5–6, and U.S. Arms Control and Disarmament Agency, *Arms Control and Disarmament Agreements: Texts and Histories of the Negotiations* (Washington, DC: U.S. Arms Control and Disarmament Agency, 1996), pp. 10–19.

6. Patrick Glynn, *Closing Pandora's Box: Arms Races, Arms Control, and the History of the Cold War* (New York: Basic, 1992); see also Glynn, "The Sarajevo Fallacy: The Historical and Intellectual Origins of Arms Control Theology," *National Interest* (Fall 1987): 3–32.

7. Of the other two treaties, one committed signatories to promote the integrity of China, and the other entailed abrogation of the Anglo-Japanese alliance as well as a commitment to consult jointly over threats emerging in the Pacific. See Cronin, "Japan," p. 137.

8. Janet M. Manson, "Regulating Submarine Warfare, 1919–1945," in Burns, *Encyclopedia of Arms Control and Disarmament,* pp. 737–747.

9. Stephen E. Pelz, *Race to Pearl Harbor: The Failure of the Second London Naval Conference and the Onset of World War II* (Cambridge: Harvard University Press, 1974).

10. Caroline F. Ziemke, "Peace Without Strings? Interwar Naval Arms Control Revisited," *Washington Quarterly* (Autumn 1992): 87–109.

11. John Moon, "Chemical Weapons and Deterrence: The World War II Experience," *International Security* (Spring 1984): 3–35.

12. Stephen Endicott and Edward Hagerman, *The United States and Biological Warfare* (Bloomington: Indiana University Press, 1998).

13. Milton Leitenberg, *New Russian Evidence on the Korean War Biological Warfare Allegations: Background and Analysis* (Washington, DC: Woodrow Wilson Center for International Scholars, 1999).

14. Christopher C. Joyner, "The Antarctic State Treaty, 1959 to the Present," in Burns, *Encyclopedia of Arms Control and Disarmament,* pp. 817–825.

15. Benjamin S. Loeb, "Test Ban Proposals and Agreements," in Burns, *Encyclopedia of Arms Control and Disarmament,* pp. 827–846.

16. For a more comprehensive discussion of nuclear weapons histories and ambitions in Asia, see Brad Roberts and Shen Dingli, "Future of Nuclear Weapons in Asia," in Burkard Schmitt, ed., *Future of Nuclear Deterrence* (Paris: Western European Union, 2001). See also conference summary, "Nuclear Weapons Challenges in Asia," Asia-Pacific Center for Security Studies, 22 April 2000, Honolulu, HI, www.apcsss.org.

17. Jim Walsh, "Surprise Down Under: The Secret History of Australia's Nuclear Ambitions," *Nonproliferation Review* (Fall 1997): 1–20.

18. Robert M. Cornejo, "When Sukarno Sought the Bomb: Indonesian Nuclear Aspirations in the Mid-1960s," *Nonproliferation Review* (Summer 2000): 31–43.

19. See "Seoul Planned Nuclear Weapons Until 1991," *Jane's Defence Weekly,* April 2, 1994, p. 1; Selig Harrison's discussion of South Korea in "Japan and Nuclear Weapons," in Selig Harrison, ed., *Japan's Nuclear Future: The Plutonium Debate and East Asian Security* (Washington, DC: Carnegie Endowment for International Peace, 1996), pp. 3–5; and Andrew J. Mack, *Proliferation in Northeast Asia,* Occasional Paper No. 28 (Washington, DC: Henry L. Stimson Center, July 1996), pp. 19–23.

20. See Harrison, *Japan's Nuclear Future.*

21. Bennett Ramberg, "The Seabed Treaty," in Burns, *Encyclopedia of Arms Control and Disarmament,* pp. 887–894.

22. Charles C. Floweree, "Chemical and Biological Weapons and Arms Control," in Burns, *Encyclopedia of Arms Control and Disarmament,* pp. 999–1020.

23. Arthur H. Westing, "The Environmental Modification Convention," in Burns, *Encyclopedia of Arms Control and Disarmament,* pp. 947–954.

24. Iain Johnston and Paul Evans, "China's Engagement with Multilateral Security Institutions," in Iain Johnston and Robert S. Ross, *Emerging China* (New York: Routledge, 1999); see also Clemens, "China," p. 67.

25. David Albright and Corey Gay, "Taiwan: Nuclear Nightmare Avoided," *Bulletin of the Atomic Scientists* (January/February 1998): 54–60; and Mack, *Proliferation in Northeast Asia,* pp. 7–11.

26. John Redick, "Nuclear Weapon Free Zones," in *Encyclopedia of Arms Control and Disarmament*, Burns, pp. 1083–1085.

27. Janne E. Nolan, "The INF Treaty: Eliminating Intermediate-Range Nuclear Missiles," in Burns, *Encyclopedia of Arms Control and Disarmament*, p. 958.

28. Patrick Garrity, "Nuclear Weapons and Asian-Pacific Security," *National Security Studies Quarterly* (Winter 1998): 60.

29. Jonathan B. Tucker, "The Chemical Weapons Convention: Has It Enhanced U.S. Security?" *Arms Control Today* 31, no. 3 (April 2001): 8.

30. Shirley A. Kan, *China's Compliance with International Arms Control Agreements*, Report for Congress (Washington, DC: Congressional Research Service, updated periodically).

31. Ralph A. Cossa, *Monitoring the Agreed Framework: A Third Anniversary "Report Card"* (Honolulu, HI: Pacific Forum CSIS, October 1997); *Nuclear Nonproliferation: Implementation of the U.S./North Korean Agreed Framework on Nuclear Issues*, GAO/RCED/NSIAD-97-165, Report to the Chairman, Committee on Energy and Natural Resources, U.S. Senate (Washington, DC: U.S. General Accounting Office, June 1997); and David Albright et al., *Solving the North Korean Nuclear Puzzle* (Washington, DC: Institute for Science and International Security, 2000).

32. The ASEAN Regional Forum, which was created in 1994 to facilitate a security dialogue among states in the region, embraced CSBMs and nonproliferation as essential tools for further development of cooperative approaches to regional security challenges. See Ralph Cossa, ed., *Confidence and Security Building in the Asia-Pacific* (Washington, DC: CSIS for the U.S. Committee of the Council for Security Cooperation in the Asia Pacific, 1995).

33. The Treaty on the Southeast Asia Nuclear Weapon Free Zone, or Bangkok Treaty, was signed in 1995 and entered into law in 1997. Zachary Davis, "The Spread of Nuclear-Weapon-Free Zones: Building a New Nuclear Bargain," *Arms Control Today* (February 1996): 15–19.

34. John Endicott, "A Limited Nuclear-Weapons-Free Zone in Northeast Asia: A Track-II Initiative," *Disarmament Diplomacy* (March 1999): 19–22. See also Hiromichi Umebayashi, "Northeast Asia Nuclear Weapon-Free Zone: A Perspective from Japan," delivered to INES2000 International Conference, Stockholm, June 14–19, 2000, www.tni.org/nwsfz.

35. Oumerserik Kasanov, "On the Creation of a Nuclear-Weapon-Free Zone in Central Asia," *Nonproliferation Review* (Fall 1998): 144–147.

36. Some would like to see this adapted as a no-first-use of weapons of mass destruction in order to preserve an option to retaliate for massively destructive chemical and biological attacks with nuclear means. Michael J. Green and Kutsuhisa Furukawa, "New Ambitions, Old Obstacles: Japan and Its Search for an Arms Control Strategy," *Arms Control Today* (July/August 2000), pp. 17–24.

37. This agreement bans the placement of weapons of mass destruction in outer space, as well as the militarization of celestial bodies. See Raymond L. Gartoff, "The Outer Space Treaty," in Burns, *Encyclopedia of Arms Control and Disarmament*, pp. 877–886. China hopes to expand the writ of the treaty to prevent further U.S. exploitation of space for military purposes.

38. Robert A. Manning, "PACATOM: Nuclear Cooperation in Asia," *Washington Quarterly* (Spring 1997): 221–222.

39. Monte R. Bullard, "Undiscussed Linkages: Implications of Taiwan Straits Security Activity on Global Arms Control and Nonproliferation," Report of the Center for Nonproliferation Studies, October 2000, www.cns.miis.edu/pubs/reports.

40. Robert Manning, Ronald Montaperto, and Brad Roberts, *China, Nuclear Weapons, and Arms Control* (New York: Council on Foreign Relations, 2000).

41. The possibilities for U.S.-China cooperation in the arms control realm are discussed in Roberts and Shen, "The Asian Nuclear Dynamic," in Schmitt, *Future of Nuclear Deterrence*.

Suggested Readings

Larsen, Jeffrey A., and Thomas Miller, eds. *Arms Control in the Asia-Pacific Region*. Colorado Springs, CO: USAF Institute for National Security Studies, 1999.

Manning, Robert, Ronald Montaperto, and Brad Roberts. *China, Nuclear Weapons, and Arms Control*. New York: Council on Foreign Relations, 2000.

Thakur, Ramesh, ed. *Keeping Proliferation At Bay*. Jakarta, Indonesia: Centre for Strategic and International Studies, 1998.

PART 4

FUTURE CHALLENGES FOR ARMS CONTROL

16

The Future of the Offense-Defense Relationship

Kerry M. Kartchner

Beginning in the early 1960s an unbalanced offense-defense relationship—in which strategic offensive weapons were dominant and strategic defenses were denigrated—was the basis of the U.S. strategic relationship with the Soviet Union (now the Russian Federation). It was also the essence of U.S. deterrence and targeting doctrine, as well as a key precondition for progress in strategic arms control. This offense dominant relationship was based on the assumptions that for deterrence purposes a good offense was the best defense and that deploying defenses would provoke an arms race and create incentives for striking first in a crisis. Not only were missile defenses believed to be destablizing; they were considered technologically infeasible and cost-prohibitive.[1] Consequently, in the arms control arena strict limits on missile defenses (but not on other forms of defense) have been an explicit precondition for offensive arms limitation and reduction.

The United States and the Soviet Union signed the Anti-Ballistic Missile (ABM) Treaty in 1972, enshrining these assumptions. The ABM Treaty prohibited either side from building a missile defense of its national territory and, as amended in 1974, allowed only a modest defense of either one intercontinental ballistic missile (ICBM) base, or the nation's capital. The United States completed its one ABM site at the Grand Forks ICBM base in North Dakota in 1972 but elected to shut it down only months after it began operation in 1976, concluding that it made little contribution to U.S. security and that it was inconsistent with the offense-defense relationship codified in the ABM Treaty. The Soviet Union chose to retain its ABM system around Moscow and has since upgraded it three times with new interceptor missiles and new radars. It is still in operation today, the only strategic missile defense system in the world.

From the time the ABM Treaty was signed until recently, Russia had predicated its willingness to enter into strategic arms reduction agreements on U.S. adherence to the ABM Treaty and threatened to abandon these offensive arms agreements if the United States were to ever withdraw from the treaty. This linkage was codified in language contained in documents associated with virtually every Cold War–era nuclear arms agreement signed since then, including the first treaty pursuant to the Strategic Arms Reduction Talks (START I, signed in June 1991), which provided for deep reductions in strategic offensive arms.

The United States agreed to give up its right to a national defense against ballistic missile attack in the ABM Treaty in return for Soviet agreement to limit strategic offensive arms in the first Strategic Arms Limitation Talks (SALT). The United States agreed to this compromise in 1972 for several reasons. The nature and character of the major threats faced by the United States and its allies at the time were best deterred, it was believed, by deploying the capability to conduct a massive offensive retaliation. Defensive weapons such as ABM systems had virtually no role in this deterrence strategy. The state of existing ABM and strategic offensive technology and the relative costs of this technology favored offensive weapons. A nationwide ABM defense was considered technologically impractical and fiscally prohibitive. Moreover, many believed that were the United States to deploy robust missile defenses, it would oblige the Soviet Union to field additional strategic offensive weapons to compensate for these defenses, thus feeding a cost-exorbitant and strategically destabilizing action-reaction arms race. Finally, there was a widespread view that the deployment of robust missile defenses would increase pressures for the other side to launch a preemptive first strike in the midst of a crisis, for fear that such defenses would confer an advantage to whoever struck first. They were thus considered to be crisis-destabilizing.

Today, however, each of these assumptions is subject to reconsideration, including the principle that strict limits on ABM systems, as embodied in the ABM Treaty, are necessary to preserve the gains of the START process and to sustain efforts to further reduce strategic offensive arms. Traditional assumptions concerning the offense-defense relationship are increasingly losing salience in favor of the emergence of a new or transformed offense-defense relationship. As the Cold War threat of a massive nuclear strike has receded, new threats have emerged related to the proliferation of weapons of mass destruction and ballistic missiles. These new threats require rethinking the traditional exclusive reliance on offense-dominant deterrence. A good offense may no longer be the best, or even a sufficient, defense. At the same time, the United States and Russia no longer consider one another enemies.

The idea of a preemptive first strike by Russia against the United States at any time in the foreseeable future is virtually inconceivable, as is the possibility of an economically emaciated Russia renewing an arms race with the United States. Remarkable advances in electro-optical, computing, communications, materials science, and rocket propulsion technology make missile defenses increasingly feasible and affordable. For these reasons, preserving the traditional offense-defense relationship may no longer be a necessary condition for further progress in strategic offensive arms reductions. U.S. willingness to engage in further negotiations on strategic offensive arms reductions may in fact be conditioned on relief from ABM Treaty restrictions on the number and basing of missile defenses, thus turning the traditional offense-defense relationship on its head.

In this chapter I critically examine the assumptions of the traditional offense-defense relationship noted above. I conclude by proposing four alternative future models of the strategic offense-defense arms control relationship.

Emerging Threats and the Inadequacy of Offense-Dominant Deterrence

Classic deterrence theory as applied to strategic nuclear weapons was developed in the late 1950s. It asserted that there were basically three ways to deter or to influence someone not to do something they might otherwise do: by threatening to punish the deterree; by threatening to deny or prevent the deterree from achieving his objective through limiting the damage he could inflict (that is, defending the assets he wanted to attack or defeating him militarily on the field of battle); and by offering him a reward for refraining from engaging in the undesired activity. The United States used some elements of all three to deter nuclear war, applied in different ways at different times, throughout the Cold War era. But beginning in the late 1960s deterrence of nuclear attack came to rest almost exclusively on the first method pursuant to the principle of assured destruction. Deterrence was achieved by assuring the destruction of whatever the deterree most valued, most often assumed to be his population and his industrial base.

Now, however, the emergence of a new, more complicated, and less predictable threat environment—with the proliferation of weapons of mass destruction and ballistic missiles to many states in some of the most politically unstable regions of the world—has brought into question the exclusive reliance on offensive retaliation for deterrence purposes. Just as a good stockbroker will diversify holdings in the face of increasing unpredictability and volatility in the market, the United States has concluded that it needs to diversify its approach to deterrence. This means incorporating, or rehabilitating, elements of the other approaches to deterrence—damage limitation in particular.

Deterrence as a general objective must and will remain a critical component of the U.S. national security posture. However, many of the conditions and assumptions that long guided Western thought about deterrence and its supporting strategic force posture have changed fundamentally. President George W. Bush referred to this need to diversify deterrence in his 1 May 2001 speech at National Defense University: "We need new concepts of deterrence that rely on both offensive and defensive forces. Deterrence can no longer be based solely on the threat of nuclear retaliation."[2] Reservations about whether the traditional reliance on purely offensive retaliatory threats would be sufficient in all cases to dissuade leaders of rogue states from attacking the United States or its forces and allies overseas are based on the following considerations.

First, leaders of rogue states may feel less constrained in their use of force, and may be more prone to take risks, than were U.S. adversaries during the Cold War. Although we came to assume that Soviet leaders were fundamentally risk-averse, rogue-state leaders have shown a willingness to take substantial risks, even if such gambles involved a major sacrifice of the lives of their people and the treasure of their nations.

Second, the foundation of past deterrent success—a mutually understood diplomatic vocabulary and established communications channels—may not exist or may be difficult to establish with rogue states. The miscalculations, misinterpretations, and misunderstandings that might result could have potentially catastrophic implications for deterrence during acute regional crises.

Third, the United States and its allies may not understand the fundamental political and military values within potential aggressor governments well enough to effectively implement deterrence by offensive threats alone. How one defines the term *rational* varies from one culture to another. Misperceptions of what another international actor may consider rational could lead to serious miscalculations, or to expressing threats that are not believed or are misunderstood, or even to conveying peaceful overtures that are misinterpreted or ignored.

Fourth, there may be significant asymmetries in the stakes involved in a regional crisis that could work to undermine deterrence. For example, some potential adversaries may believe that whereas their own survival is at stake in a regional conflict the survival of the United States is not. As a consequence, these adversaries may calculate that the United States, with less to lose, may decline to intervene or may back down if the stakes are raised.

Fifth, leaders of rogue states may believe that they have more to lose from *not acting* than from taking a particular course of action. Failure to act may cause a leader to lose face within his ruling party or power base.

Sixth, potential adversaries may hope that the acquisition of nuclear, biological, or chemical (NBC) weapons and delivery systems such as long-range ballistic missiles would deter the United States from intervening in, or leading coalitions against, their efforts at regional aggression; or perhaps these states may believe that such capabilities would give them the ability to threaten allied countries in order to dissuade them from joining such coalitions.

Finally, according to U.S. intelligence assessments the leaders of such states see NBC weapons and ballistic missile capabilities as tools of coercion, terror, blackmail, and aggression. NBC weapons, as well as ballistic missiles, may also be regarded as symbols of power and prestige by rogue states. Under such conditions there may be less restraint against employing such weapons. Moreover, using nuclear weapons may not carry the same stigma as it does among established nuclear powers.

Several other concerns regarding the adequacy and inadequacy of traditional offense-dominant deterrence warrant mention. One is the possibility that the United States and its allies could themselves be the subject of deterrence or subject to coercion by rogue states, thus limiting U.S. freedom of action to protect its allies and interests abroad. As one observer has speculated, "Increasingly the concept of deterrence will be used against us."[3]

Some U.S. and European commentators claim that overwhelming U.S. conventional military superiority alone constitutes an adequate deterrent against any attack by a rogue state. They scoff at the notion that the United States could be deterred or dissuaded from intervening on behalf of its own interests by much smaller states. But there are documented historical instances in which military superiority was no guarantee against being attacked by relatively weaker states. In a study of deterrence failures throughout history, RAND analyst Barry Wolf identified three types of circumstances under which weaker states actually attacked stronger states: (1) The weaker state was highly motivated by a strong commitment to particular values, by the agenda of a psychopathological leader, or by a cost-benefit calculus that differed from the international norm or expectation and was thus irrational by definition; (2) the weaker state misperceived some aspect of the situation (e.g., the weaker state perceived a vulnerability that did not exist, expected no retaliation from the strong state, or believed that allies would come to its aid); and (3) the stronger state was vulnerable in some respect relative to the weaker state, and the weaker state exploited this asymmetry.[4]

One or more of these conditions could manifest themselves in future conflicts, resulting in deterrence failure. Finally, some threats may be undeterrable by their very nature. These include the accidental or unauthorized launch of a long-range ballistic missile, an eventuality that many believe is increasingly likely. The threat of offensive retaliation would have little bearing on preventing such incidents, thus falling outside the range of threats addressed by deterrence alone.

Offensive nuclear forces are and will remain a key component of U.S. deterrence. U.S. officials have stated that no group or nation should doubt that the United States will continue to depend on the certainty of a devastating response to any attack on the United States or its allies. However, ballistic missile defenses may be able to enhance traditional deterrence by denying rogue states the ability to reliably and predictably inflict mass destruction on other nations. By complicating the rogue leader's calculation of success, these defenses add to a potential aggressor's uncertainty and weaken his confidence. Effective missile defenses may also serve to undercut the value that a potential aggressor places on ballistic missiles as a means of delivery, thereby advancing U.S. nonproliferation goals. With these considerations in mind, the new strategic framework envisions that appropriately sized and effective missile defenses can be a force for stability and security.

Missile Defense Technology and Affordability

Fundamental changes are occurring in the offense-defense relationship for reasons other than a changed threat environment and new requirements for a diversified approach to deterrence. Advances in technology and new perceptions of affordability are providing grounds for rethinking the technical and fiscal aspects of the traditional offense-defense relationship. While considerable skepticism still exists regarding the technical feasibility of missile defense, many believe that progress across a broad range of technical disciplines has made effective missile defenses increasingly feasible and affordable.[5] According to congressional testimony and other reports, these advances have taken place in the following technologies with particular application to missile defense:[6]

- Computing technology and telecommunications, specifically exponential increases in computing power coupled with dramatic decreases in the size of computers and memory storage devices;
- Thrust and rocketry, including the development of very small liquid propulsion rocket systems (necessary for advanced interceptor maneuvering);
- Materials science (e.g., ceramic radomes for less weight, greater strength, and enhanced electromagnetic transparency);
- Miniaturization and solid-state electronics (gyros) and spacecraft optical systems;
- Visible, infrared, and ultraviolet sensors for spacecraft and interceptors;
- Weaponization of laser systems for both airborne and space-based platforms;
- Characterization and processing of ballistic missile/reentry vehicle phenomenology (necessary to locate, identify, and track targets in

space, as well as to discriminate between reentry vehicles and decoys); and
- Advances in new radar systems, specifically improvements both in the transmit-receive function and in terms of data processing.

Some believe that these developments promise to alter the very basis of the offense-defense relationship. For example, according to William R. Graham, former White House science adviser and member of several presidentially chartered commissions to assess technology, in a statement provided to the House Armed Services Committee, "As missile defense technologies have improved the advantage has shifted from the offense to the defense."[7] Nevertheless, most would agree that more realistic testing remains to be done to convince most skeptics that issues of basic physics associated with intercepting ballistic missiles have been resolved and that only engineering problems remain to be worked out.

Cost-effectiveness is another of the criteria that led to the disparagement of damage-limitation capabilities and ABM systems during the Cold War, as well as the promotion of offense-dominant deterrence. It has been assumed since the mid-1960s that offensive forces (bombers, ICBMs, submarines, and submarine-launched ballistic missiles [SLBMs]) were cheaper to build than defensive weapons like ABM systems and thus a more cost-effective investment for the defense budget. However, the current debate has not been cast so much in terms of the cost-effectiveness of ballistic missile defenses versus proportional quantities of offensive forces but rather in terms of how much missile defense can be afforded. U.S. officials have addressed cost issues by making several points, all of which address affordability rather than relative cost-effectiveness. Projected costs for missile defense are proportional to other major defense acquisition programs. The amount of resources devoted to ballistic missile defense will represent 2–3 percent of the total U.S. defense budget. Furthermore, funding for ballistic missile defense will still amount to only about one-half that devoted to countering terrorism and defending against other proliferation threats. Although some might argue that resources devoted to missile defense unjustifiably detract from and compete with resources that should be directed to other allegedly higher priorities, there seems to be a broad political consensus that the above figures represent a reasonable allocation of defense budget dollars to strategic defenses.

The Unlikely Prospect of a Renewed Arms Race with Russia

Fear of reigniting an arms race is frequently cited as a principal reason for preserving the existing offense-defense relationship. The 1960s theory of an action-reaction arms race, precipitated by one side deploying ABM systems and the other responding by deploying more offensive weapons, was the original rationale for U.S. interest in the ABM Treaty. By signing that treaty, the United States hoped to bring a halt to the U.S.-Soviet arms competition. But today, given that Russia is strengthening democracy while struggling to prevent the further collapse of its emaciated military forces and to staunch the flight of capital, the risk that Russia would respond with a massive offensive arms buildup to U.S. deployment of modest missile defenses is not very credible. This is reinforced by the steadily improving cooperative relationship between the United States and Russia.

Just two weeks prior to the U.S. announcement of its decision to withdraw from the ABM Treaty, Russian officials were warning that such a step would force Russia to respond by substantially increasing its strategic offensive forces. Such blandishments were dismissed, however, by Russian President Vladimir Putin's statement following the U.S. announcement that, while Russia considered the decision a mistake, it would not pose a risk to Russia's security. President Putin thus made it clear that there would be no arms-race reaction from Russia.

Of course, some have speculated that Russia could reverse this calm reaction at any time in the future, especially if, for example, the United States proceeded to deploy a much more robust missile defense than currently contemplated. However, even if Russia mustered the political will to abruptly shift its current course toward greater integration with the West, and adopted a defiant and confrontational stance by renewing an arms race with the United States, the practical consequences of any action Russia could take are likely to be fairly limited for a number of reasons. START I reductions were achieved by the end of 2001, so a threat to suspend START eliminations and/or reductions has been rendered moot. Russian nuclear force levels are expected to decline with or without a START III agreement as a function of the shrinking Russian economy. The current slow pace of SS-27 production would mitigate the near-term military impact of adding additional warheads to SS-27 ICBMs, of which there are only about 20 deployed. Russia lacks the funds and the industrial infrastructure to undertake any major programmatic responses, such as accelerating the deployment of SS-27s, substantially extending the service life of SS-18 ICBMs, undertaking major countermeasure deployments, engaging in substantial modifications to entire classes of deployed missiles, or fielding entirely new strategic weapon systems.

Russia cannot afford to be perceived as promoting the proliferation of weapons of mass destruction, or as opposing or obstructing international nonproliferation efforts. Politically and economically, Russia needs cooperation with the West and closer ties to transatlantic and European institutions. These factors almost certainly figured prominently in President

Putin's decision to find some form of accommodation with the United States on missile defenses and to avoid reigniting an economically ruinous arms race it is in no position to win. Perhaps the most compelling reason for Russia's moderate reaction to the U.S. decision to withdraw from the ABM Treaty is to have some influence over setting the broader diplomatic constraints on whatever system the United States eventually deploys. An inflexible or intransigent stance would forfeit that opportunity.

Furthermore, the United States has made it clear that the kinds of missile defenses it intends to deploy are limited in scope and objective and are not intended to provide a hemispheric shield against large-scale attack—the hallmark goal of the 1980s Strategic Defense Initiative. Such a limited missile defense would in no way pose a threat to Russia's deterrent, setting aside the question of whether Russia continues to require such a deterrent. Moreover, the United States and Russia do not consider one another to be the implacably hostile opponent of a former era. As the U.S.-Russia cooperative relationship deepens and matures, there will be even less reason to consider the legitimate self-defense efforts of one as a provocation by the other. Thus, the third key assumption of the Cold War offense-defense relationship—that deploying ballistic missile defenses would spark a U.S.-Russia arms race—is no longer credible.

Missile Defense and Crisis Stability

The fourth central tenet of the traditional offense-defense relationship held that deploying missile defenses would create pressures or incentives for striking first in a crisis and were thus crisis-destabilizing. However, the classic desiderata of first-strike calculations under conditions of acute political crisis may no longer apply to the U.S.-Russia relationship. Given that the United States and the Russian Federation are developing a deeply constructive and increasingly cooperative relationship, and the absence of any substantial Russian global ambitions, it is highly unlikely that the United States and Russia would find their supreme national interests in conflict. Of course, U.S. and Russian national interests do not coincide perfectly, and the United States and Russia will no doubt find themselves on opposite sides of periodic crises in world politics. Nevertheless, it is difficult to conceive of any geopolitical crisis in which one side or the other would consider resorting to nuclear use, or even nuclear coercion, in order to affect the outcome or the course of the crisis. Structural asymmetries in their offensive and defensive force postures would therefore have no bearing whatsoever.

Furthermore, the limited missile defenses the United States government believes are necessary to address the emerging threat of rogue state missile programs will not threaten Russia's deterrent posture. This condition should be reinforced by the transparency and confidence-building measures Russian and American officials are putting into place with respect to U.S. missile defense efforts. These measures will further enhance crisis stability between the United States and Russia by reassuring Russia of the limited nature of U.S. missile defenses, improving communications between the two powers, and enhancing confidence in each other's respective declared missile defense plans. They may also contribute to more robust crisis management options to ensure that a crisis involving U.S. and Russian interests does not devolve into a U.S.-Russia nuclear confrontation.

Beyond the U.S.-Russia dynamic, missile defenses may strengthen crisis stability by expanding the options for responding to the escalation of a crisis. Their presence may buy time for political leaders to resolve a crisis short of either preemption or retaliation. Thus, the assumption that deploying missile defenses is crisis-destabilizing as another reason for maintaining or perpetuating an offense-dominant military posture is also subject to reexamination.

Arms Control and the
New Offense-Defense Relationship

The fifth key assumption of the existing Cold War offense-defense relationship is that strict limits on missile defenses are a necessary precondition to progress in offensive arms limitation and reduction agreements. Yet the United States and Russia are currently engaged in an arms control process likely to result in further reductions in strategic offensive weapons despite the U.S. intention to leave the ABM Treaty and deploy missile defenses. Furthermore, current arms control priorities have shifted from controlling the Cold War–era arms competition to addressing issues of nonproliferation throughout the world. Missile defenses are increasingly recognized as an important element in that global nonproliferation effort. Even Russia has proposed a pan-European theater missile defense system as a response to the threat of ballistic missile proliferation.

It is possible to conceptualize several ways that arms control could help in defining and establishing a new offense-defense relationship. Strategic arms control consultation, negotiations, and agreements could function as a "bridge" to help manage the transition to a more balanced offense-defense relationship, including deployed missile defenses. The purpose of such a bridge would be to help U.S. allies and erstwhile adversaries adjust their own national thinking to account for the new threats, new possibilities for missile defense, and new ways that missile defenses might be integrated into broader nonproliferation and counterproliferation strategies and regimes at the national and international levels. Arms control arrangements could help facilitate a stable transition to a more diversified approach to deterrence by mitigating arms race pressures and providing an agreed framework and timetable for sustained strategic offensive force reductions. They could promote transparency and predictability through agreed verification measures. Arms control agreements could encourage the continued nonuse of nuclear weapons. Many nations of the world, including our European and Asian allies, count heavily on the United States to exercise a critical leadership role in advancing a shared agenda composed of nonproliferation, regional security, and global stability objectives. Arms control negotiations and agreements are one accepted and expected means of achieving those goals. Thus, U.S. arms control initiatives can help sustain the legitimacy of America's leadership role among these nations.

Nevertheless, in order to promote a new relationship with Russia, and to further U.S. and allied nonproliferation objectives by proceeding with the deployment of missile defenses and introducing fundamental changes in the traditional offense-defense relationship, the U.S. administration concluded that it would be necessary to "move beyond" the ABM Treaty. In announcing the U.S. decision to withdraw from the ABM Treaty, President Bush said, "I have concluded the ABM Treaty hinders our government's ability to develop ways to protect our people from future terrorist or rogue state missile attacks."[8]

The Bush administration, rather than dwell on specific aspects of the ABM Treaty that would block developing and deploying highly effective and affordable missile defenses, had taken a different view that the treaty as a whole is fundamentally incompatible with the need to deploy missile defenses; also, it needlessly perpetuated a conflictual relationship with Russia based on the politically corrosive doctrine of mutual assured destruction (MAD). Moreover, as Secretary of Defense Donald Rumsfeld said in a *Wall Street Journal* op-ed piece: "The U.S. intends to build defenses to protect our people from ballistic missile attack—and the ABM Treaty's very purpose is to prevent us from doing so. That Treaty, a product of the Cold War, is no longer relevant to the security challenges of the new century."[9]

In programmatic terms the treaty promoted an artificial distinction between theater and national missile defense. Agreements associated with the treaty prohibited the concurrent operation of ABM systems and air defense systems. The trend in U.S. ABM Treaty implementation has been to avoid concurrent testing or operation of ABM systems and theater missile defense systems as well. Although theater programs were not specifically banned by the treaty, if the Bush administration had adopted an approach that used theater missile defense programs as stepping-stones to deploying more robust strategic missile defense systems, it would have no doubt run afoul of these constraints unless they were removed or modified. Therefore, unwilling to be in a position of violating a standing treaty, and unable to convince the Russians to go along with the necessary revisions, the administration took the extraordinary step on 13 December 2001 of invoking the U.S. right under article 15 to withdraw from the treaty.

Alternative Models

Withdrawal from the ABM Treaty will have important ramifications for the future of the offense-defense arms control relationship. There have been several public proposals for linking offensive and defensive forces in an arms control relationship, for example, by creating a single aggregate limit that incorporated both defensive missile interceptors and offensive ICBMs and SLBMs. General Vladimir Yakovlev, then head of Russia's strategic missile forces, proposed "an invariable aggregate index of strategic armaments to be made up of nuclear attack and missile defense means. . . . A country that wishes to enlarge one of the components will have to cut the other."[10] Such proposals would allow both sides freedom to mix offensive and defensive forces under a single aggregated ceiling. Some studies have examined alternative quantitative relationships and trade-offs between offenses and defenses that assigned fixed or sliding-scale ratios, such as permitting two or more offensive missiles for every interceptor. Many of these proposals have assumed the preeminence of offensive weapons as well as a need to retain MAD capabilities on the part of the United States and Russia. Classic first- and second-strike exchange models still dominate many conferences on strategic stability.

The exact nature of the new offense-defense relationship is not yet clear, and may not be for several more years. A deliberate process of consultation between the United States and its allies and between the United States and Russia will almost certainly be necessary to completely flesh it out and integrate its main themes and precepts into U.S. strategic and operational doctrine, into NATO's strategic concepts, and into the institutional framework of U.S./allied–Russia relations, including future arms control initiatives. For now, it is only possible to identify a number of alternative models regarding this nascent relationship.

Model 1:
No Change in the Cold War Offense-Defense Relationship

According to this model, there is not likely to be any change in the primacy of offensive strategic forces for some time to come. Given the endurance of this primacy, the deployment of ballistic missile defenses would represent a highly destabilizing development, despite dramatic advances in weapons technology and changes in the global security environment. This model presumes that offensive weapons will continue to have a decisive advantage over defensive weapons, that they are cheaper and easier to build, and that defenses can be relatively easily overcome through advanced countermeasures and penetration aids. Given this lingering offensive primacy, deploying robust missile defenses could lead to the collapse of international arms control and nonproliferation regimes. China and other countries would be less prone to cooperate in global nonproliferation efforts and may undertake to expand or accelerate their own deployment of offensive long-range ballistic missiles. Put simply, deploying missile defenses would result in a net loss to U.S. security. Therefore, the existing offense-defense relationship enshrining the primacy of the offensive, and its codification in existing strategic arms control agreements, should be preserved and perpetuated.

Model 2:
No Relationship Between Offensive and Defensive Forces

Some believe that the deployment of modest missile defenses will not appreciably affect the strategic balance between U.S. and Russian strategic offensive forces and will not force Russia to begin building up its ballistic missile arsenal. Countervailing factors, extraneous to the offense-defense relationship, have worked to eliminate or reduce arms race pressures on U.S. and Russian strategic offensive arsenals, such as the decimated condition of Russia's economy and the improving political atmosphere between the two countries. Because there is no longer any threat of precipitating an arms race by deploying missile defenses, and because missile defenses will not replace offensive forces for some time to come, there is no intrinsic offense-defense relationship. Missile defenses will be of such modest capability that they will not threaten Russia's strategic deterrent or substitute for reductions in strategic offensive forces. Because there is no inherent relationship, there is no rationale for formulating or fashioning a trade-off between offensive and defensive forces in an arms control context. Consequently, according to this model, offensive and defensive arms control measures should proceed on separate tracks.

A fundamental tenet of this model is that until the technology for missile defenses matures more substantially, offensive and defensive weapons will play separate and unrelated roles in U.S. national security. Therefore, it would be premature and even counterproductive for arms control to establish or define any specific relationship or to place restrictions on defenses in relation to offenses. Nevertheless, proponents of this model would not necessarily rule out codifying some relationship in the future as policies and missile defense technologies matured. Perhaps when missile defenses reach the point where it becomes necessary to include them in the U.S. nuclear targeting plan, and to integrate and deconflict offensive and defensive force operations, this relationship could be reassessed and some numerical trade-off could be established for purposes of arms control. In the meantime, according to this model, missile defenses and strategic offensive forces will make separate and distinct contributions to U.S. security policy. Missile defenses will contribute to deterring rogue states, promoting nonproliferation, and providing insurance against accidental and unauthorized ballistic missile launches, whereas strategic offensive forces will continue to underwrite "central deterrence" in the U.S.-Russia context. These forces may also provide the ultimate deterrent role in regional conflicts where the United States perceives substantial stakes.

Model 3:
Strategic Offensive Weapons as Bargaining Chips

According to this model, there is no intrinsic relationship between strategic offensive weapons and strategic defensive weapons, but a relationship is created for political, diplomatic, or arms control reasons. Such a relationship would be, by definition, a matter of expediency, and it likely would be temporary or provisional in nature. For purposes of this discussion, it assumes that offensive weapons become bargaining chips (either explicitly or tacitly) to trade away for Russian agreement or acquiescence in greater U.S. freedom to develop, test, and deploy ballistic missile defenses.

For example, some have made the case for a so-called new grand compromise whereby the United States would agree to deep cuts in offensive forces in return for Russia's agreement to deploy more robust missile defenses than permitted under the ABM Treaty. This approach assumes that offensive and defensive weapons have reversed roles in an arms control context. ABM systems played the role of bargaining chips to be negotiated away in the 1969–1972 SALT negotiations, where offensive weapons were the assets to be protected. In this sense, the ABM Treaty was considered the original grand compromise. According to this ad hoc model, the role and relevance of offensive weapons are declining due to a number of factors. Hence, the most constructive potential contribution of such weapons could be exchanging them for revised rights to deploy missile defenses in the process of negotiating a new offense-defense relationship. The increased security provided by deploying missile defenses might compensate for reducing the role of strategic forces in U.S. national security strategy, allowing for some offense-defense tradeoffs in a new strategic arms control regime.

Model 4: Defensive Weapons Operationally Dominant, Offensive Weapons Diminished

This is the so-called defense-dominance model because it assumes defenses overtake offenses in terms of cost, affordability, technological reliability, and military effectiveness, as well as in sheer deployed numbers. According to this model, the scope of offensive strategic nuclear deterrence has been reduced to a very narrow range of increasingly inconceivable contingencies. In other words, strategic offensive nuclear weapons would be used only as a last resort, and only if the very survival of the United States itself was at stake. Many believe that such weapons would be used only if U.S. national territory were directly attacked with nuclear weapons. Some even question the prudence of applying strategic offensive nuclear deterrence to deterring attacks by chemical or biological weapons. Moreover, according to this view, the credibility of U.S. willingness to employ strategic offensive nuclear weapons has steadily eroded over time, to the point that their relevance to underwriting U.S. security is seriously limited.

Over time, if the technology for missile defenses matured to the point that missile defenses were capable of fulfilling damage limitation roles currently assigned to strategic offensive weapons, it may be possible to contemplate a transition to a defense-dominant form of deterrence with missile defenses facilitating the phasing out of strategic offensive weapons.

These four models are not necessarily mutually exclusive. Over the course of time, the technology and politics of missile defenses may result in an evolution of the offense-defense relationship that passes through phases consisting of two or more of these models.

Conclusion

There is emerging recognition that the primary assumptions of the MAD framework that prevailed during much of the Cold War have been rendered obsolete, irrelevant, and perhaps even counterproductive by new, dangerous, and unpredictable threats. Surprise nuclear attack between the United States and Russia is no longer the primary threat. The driving threat scenario today is the proliferation of weapons of mass destruction and their ballistic missile means of delivery. A policy of promoting and institutionalizing deliberate nationwide vulnerability to ballistic missile attack may have been considered appropriate to the circumstances of a different era, but today many see it as promoting proliferation by offering a free ride to rogue-state ballistic missile programs. Moreover, it is not an appropriate basis for a long-term cooperative relationship with Russia.

The key arms control premise of the MAD framework was that deploying ABM systems would provoke an action-reaction arms race with Russia, obligating Russia to respond by deploying additional offensive weapons. This premise is now open to question. This is not to say that there are no lingering sentiments of distrust or any legitimate security issues between the two countries. Where those do exist—such as in cooperation on dismantling the countries' respective Cold War nuclear arsenals, securing and accounting for nuclear materials, and combating the proliferation of weapons of mass destruction—progress is being made. Russia does not have the resources to undertake a militarily meaningful arms race response to U.S. deployment of limited missile defenses. Both face threats from rogue-state ballistic missile programs, and both have recognized the fundamental importance of missile defenses in responding to such threats.

Other tenets of the MAD framework are also being revised. Due to advances in a variety of technical fields, theater and strategic ABM systems are increasingly becoming technologically feasible and economically affordable. The threat of a devastating retaliation by offensive forces is no longer sufficient as the sole basis of deterrence. Many now believe that deterrence must be based on a mix of offensive and defensive strategies and forces, posing both assured destruction and damage limitation–type deterrent threats.

These are the reasons, in summary, for the prospective passing of the old offense-defense relationship. The new offense-defense relationship at this stage could be considered primarily a policy initiative. But it is a policy initiative that takes into account political and technical realities. The new offense-defense relationship has not been fully elaborated, and it may not be for several years. The basic elements of the new offense-defense relationship do not necessarily represent a mature consensus, but the trend is toward fundamental reconsideration of the basic tenets, structures, and institutions of the Cold War and their relevance to today's challenges, as well as the recognition that we live in a new era with its own threats to global peace, security, and stability.

The United States has not abandoned deterrence as a general objective. What is changing is the way that the United States defines and implements deterrence. U.S. policymakers are developing new answers to the questions of *who* it is the United States wants to deter, *what* it is the United States wants to deter them from doing, and *how* U.S. forces and diplomacy can best do that.

The next several years will constitute a transitional period for this new offense-defense relationship and the revised approach to offensive and defensive arms control that it represents. The United States is still in the process of elaborating its missile defense plans and architecture. The desired direction of evolution in offensive and defensive forces will follow from these decisions once they are made. Specific arms control approaches will be based on this framework and will need to take into account a process of consultation with U.S. allies and friends, including Russia. U.S.-Russia relations are also in transition. And there is a dynamic threat environment that can change radically from one moment to the next. The United States will need to retain considerable freedom to adjust its force structure decisions to respond in a timely manner to such fluctuations. For these reasons, the United States must approach any new arms control initiatives with healthy caution and retain considerable flexibility.

The offense-defense relationship, when viewed over the course of recorded history, is fundamentally cyclical. There is no immutable law of physics conferring eternal ascendancy to offensive strategies and forces. The offense-defense relationship prevailing in any given era is a function of technology, strategy, and politics. The United States and the Soviet Union could just as easily have agreed in 1972 to banning offensive weapons and permitting only defensive ones, and each country could have devoted its considerable resources to developing and deploying missile defenses rather than the offensive nuclear triad. In this respect, the offense-defense relationship may be much more a matter of policy choice than has heretofore been appreciated. As such, the United States can, through its policies and initiatives, influence and guide the direction of its development.

The role of arms control in bridging the transition from the old offense-defense relationship to a new one is also being reconsidered. Arms control derives its legitimacy from the degree to which it contributes to broader U.S. national security objectives. Arms control derives its effectiveness from the extent to which policymakers and negotiators successfully integrate diplomatic and military initiatives, as well as the degree to which these initiatives are backed up by political willingness to undertake military actions in support of national security objectives. New approaches to strategic arms control—based on a new or evolving offense-defense relationship and backed up by such political will and appropriate military initiatives—can contribute to underwriting the new requirements of stability and deterrence.

Notes

The views and analysis contained herein are those of the author and should not be construed as necessarily representing those of the U.S. Department of State or any other U.S. government agency.

1. *Strategic offensive weapons* consist of long-range bombers, sea-launched ballistic missiles and the submarines they are launched from, as well as intercontinental-range ballistic missiles launched from land-based silos. These are the weapons used to attack distant targets across intercontinental ranges. *Strategic defensive weapons* or assets may consist of antiballistic missiles and or other missile defenses, antisubmarine warfare forces (air-, land-, or sea-based), antiaircraft defenses, civil defenses, anti–cruise missile defenses, and any other weapon and asset devoted to defense of the national territory. In the past, the term *missile defenses* sometimes referred to ABM defense of missile silos, versus ABM defense of other assets, such as leadership centers and populations. In contemporary discussions the term is used to encompass any ballistic missile weapon used to defend against offensive ballistic missile attacks.

2. President George W. Bush, Remarks to Students and Faculty at National Defense University, Fort McNair, Washington, DC, reprinted in *New York Times*, 1 May 2001.

3. Fareed Zakaria, "Misapprehensions About Missile Defense," *Washington Post*, 7 May 2001, p. A19.

4. Barry Wolf, *When the Weak Attack the Strong: Failures of Deterrence* (Santa Monica, CA: RAND, 1991), p. 5.

5. For a coherent argument regarding the technological hurdles still facing missile defenses, see Forrest E. Morgan, "Ballistic Missile Defense: Flying in the Face of Offensive Technological Dominance," paper presented at the annual convention of the International Studies Association, New Orleans, LA, 27 March 2002.

6. Ballistic Missile Defense Organization, *Harnessing the Power of Technology: The Road to Ballistic Missile Defense from 1983 to 2007* (Washington, DC: U.S. Department of Defense, September 2000). This report cites the miniaturization of advanced inertial measurement units as a key example. "What had been a state-of-the-art, lightweight ring laser gyro unit in the 1980s (replacing the earlier mechanical gimbaled gyro), evolved into a solid-state fiber-optic gyro, then to a quartz tuning fork gyro, to a micro-mechanical gyro. By the mid-1990s, the instrument's size had shrunk from 0.47 to 0.17 cubic inches and its weight had dropped from about 4 ounces to less than half an ounce—about the size of a grain of rice." Also see Dennis M. Ward, "The Changing Technological Environment," in James J. Wirtz and Jeffrey A. Larsen, eds., *Rockets' Red Glare: Missile Defenses and the Future of World Politics* (Boulder: Westview, 2001).

7. House Armed Services Committee, U.S. National Missile Defense Policy and the Anti-Ballistic Missile Treaty, Hearing Before the Committee on Armed Services, House of Representatives, One Hundred Sixth Congress, First Session, 13 October 1999.

8. "Remarks by the President on National Missile Defense," The White House, Office of the Press Secretary, 13 December 2001, accessed at www.whitehouse.gov/news/releases/2001/12/print/20011213-4.html.

9. Donald H. Rumsfeld, "Toward 21st-Century Deterrence," *Wall Street Journal*, 27 June 2001.

10. Martin Nesirky, "Missile Chief Shifts on ABM," *Washington Times*, 14 November 2000; and Reuters, "Russian Missile Chief Proposes ABM Index," 13 November 2000.

Suggested Readings

Harknet, Richard J., T. V. Paul, and James J. Wirtz. *The Absolute Weapon Revisited: Nuclear Arms and the Emerging International Order*. Ann Arbor: University of Michigan Press, 1998.

Lin, Herbert. *New Weapons Technologies and the ABM Treaty*. McLean, VA: Pergamon-Brassey's, 1988.

Lodal, Jan. *The Price of Dominance: The New Weapons of Mass Destruction and Their Challenge to American Leadership*. New York: Council on Foreign Relations, 2001.

National Institute for Public Policy. *Rationale and Requirements for U.S. Nuclear Forces and Arms Control*. Fairfax, VA: National Institute for Public Policy, 2001.

Payne, Keith B. *Deterrence in the Second Nuclear Age*. Lexington, KY: University Press of Kentucky, 1996.

Quester, George H. *Deterrence Before Hiroshima: The Airpower Background of Modern Strategy*. New York: John Wiley and Sons, 1966.

Smith, James M., ed. *Nuclear Deterrence and Defense: Strategic Considerations*. Colorado Springs, CO: USAF Institute for National Security Studies, February 2001.

———. *Searching for National Security in an NBC World*. Colorado Springs, CO: USAF Institute for National Security Studies, July 2000.

U.S. Senate. Committee on Governmental Affairs. *Stubborn Things: A Decade of Facts About Ballistic Missile Defense*. Washington, DC: U.S. Government Printing Office, September 2000.

Wirtz, James J., and Jeffrey A. Larsen, eds. *Rockets' Red Glare: Missile Defenses and the Future of World Politics*. Boulder: Westview, 2001.

17

Arms Control in Outer Space

Patricia A. McFate

In January 2001 the commissioners of the U.S. Space Commission stated that they "believe the U.S. Government should vigorously pursue the capabilities called for in the National Space Policy to ensure that the President will have the option to deploy weapons in space to deter threats to and, if necessary, defend against attacks on U.S. interests."[1] In contrast, a Canadian-government document released four years earlier made it clear that "Canadian policy . . . remains the promotion and maintenance of outer space for peaceful purposes, with the rule of law and multilateral agreements constituting the basis for such pursuits."[2] These statements present markedly different views on the conduct of nations in outer space. The space commissioners argued that if required for national security purposes, the United States will deploy space weapons unilaterally. The Canadian government relies upon cooperative security to maintain peace. Many countries have joined with Canada in its efforts to negotiate an international ban on all weapons for use in outer space.[3] The United States remains consistently opposed to such a ban.

Policies concerning outer space must be placed in context. The multilateral agreements cited in the Canadian statement refer to space treaties negotiated in the 1960s and 1970s, periods in which only the United States and the Soviet Union (now the Russian Federation) had military and civil space assets. A vast global economy based in space was inconceivable. Forty years later the United States dominates space. Approximately 300 of the 600 operational satellites in orbit are U.S. satellites.[4]

The once clear-cut distinctions about space systems—civilian, military, commercial, and intelligence—have disappeared. Weather satellites, for example, are significant force-enhancers when used for military purposes. In 2002, an orbiting NASA satellite provided the U.S. Air Force with before-and-after hyperspectral imagery of bombed targets in Afghanistan. The

U.S. Global Positioning System (GPS) provides the standard for accurate location and timing data needed for precision navigation to users worldwide. Although the intentional degradation of its signals available to the public (so-called selective availability) was stopped in May 2000, the United States has demonstrated its ability to deny signals on a regional basis when U.S. national security is threatened. Coalition troops relied upon GPS capabilities for navigational purposes during the 1991 Gulf War, but at the same time both coalition and Iraqi forces used channels for communication on ARABSAT, a satellite dedicated to Middle East communications and run by the Arab Satellite Communications Organization, raising questions concerning the usefulness of designations such as "friendly" and "enemy" satellites. GPS-guided bombs such as the Joint Direct Attack Munition were used during the 1999 air war over Serbia and in Operation ENDURING FREEDOM in Afghanistan.

The lines between open and secret space technology blurred when commercial ventures entered into the field of satellite reconnaissance. Formerly classified Russian military satellite systems are now making imagery available through the SPIN-2 satellite. On 1 May 2000 *Aviation Week and Space Technology* published 2 meter–resolution images of the U.S. government's highly classified Groom Lake, Nevada, test base taken in 1998 by SPIN-2. Photos of the base taken in April 2000 by the U.S. IKONOS satellite, the first commercial satellite with 1-meter resolution, were also published. In late 2001 the U.S. government purchased exclusive rights to color images of Afghanistan from the IKONOS satellite.

The chances of achieving a multilateral treaty banning space weapons appeared unlikely following the U.S. elections in 2000. Initial actions of the George W. Bush administration—such as unwillingness to promote ratification of the Comprehensive Test Ban Treaty (CTBT) and refusal to implement the Kyoto agreement on global warming—nettled the international arms control community. President Bush's announced intention to make a unilateral reduction of U.S. nuclear weapons suggested that he favored an abandonment of strategic offensive arms negotiations. His statements on deployment of a ballistic missile defense system placed the 1972 Anti-Ballistic Missile (ABM) Treaty in jeopardy. His concept of a new relationship with Russia emphasized understandings and discussions, not negotiations and treaties. The Space Commission report quoted above raised the prospect of space-based interceptors and antisatellite (ASAT) weapons when it advocated deployment of "the means to deter and defend against hostile acts directed at U.S. space assets and against the uses of space hostile to U.S. interests."[5]

In this chapter I examine two themes associated with space arms control. The first is the tension inherent in reconciling unilateral actions and multilateral goals, in this case, protection of the overwhelming U.S. lead in outer space and adherence to the provisions found in international treaties that the United States has signed. The second theme is the contrast between the vastly different space worlds of the 1960s—the beginning of the space age—and the present day. I also examine congressional- and military-driven activities related to space, as well as the impact of the U.S. war against terrorism launched after the events of 11 September 2001. Finally, I propose several concepts for multilateral space agreements.

Space arms control is a unique and important field. Outer space remains the only environment in which weapons have not been deployed. Decisions made by the United States concerning the last frontier could affect the international community for generations to come.

The Existing Space Arms Control Framework

The laws governing activities in space are found in a variety of multilateral agreements negotiated during the height of the Cold War at the very beginning of the space age.[6] Given the dominance of the superpowers in the international arena, it was inevitable that these space treaties were linked to bilateral negotiations on strategic weapons.

During a speech in June 1963 President John F. Kennedy announced an end to U.S. nuclear tests in the atmosphere as long as the Soviets followed suit; he also called for negotiation of a comprehensive test ban or, if that were not possible, a ban on all but underground tests. His speech was followed by a pause in Soviet testing. Negotiation of the Limited Test Ban Treaty (LTBT)—the first global multilateral treaty regulating military activities of states in outer space—followed soon after. The LTBT, signed in August 1963, bans nuclear weapons tests in the atmosphere, in outer space, and under water.

Subsequent to unilateral but identical declarations in support of a 1963 United Nations (UN) General Assembly resolution calling upon all states to refrain from introducing weapons of mass destruction (WMD) into space, the United States and Soviet Union negotiated and signed the Outer Space Treaty on 27 January 1967.

Considered to be the cornerstone of the outer space regime, the Outer Space Treaty, like its predecessor, the Antarctic Treaty, is a so-called non-armament agreement. In Outer Space Treaty article 4, state parties agree "not to place in orbit around the Earth any objects carrying nuclear weapons or any other kinds of weapons of mass destruction, install such weapons on celestial bodies, or station such weapons in outer space in any other manner."[7] Article 4 also limits the use of the moon and other celestial bodies exclusively to "peaceful purposes." Under article 6, state parties bear international responsibility for "national activities" in outer space regardless of whether they are conducted by government agencies or by nongovernmental entities.

The 1979 Moon Agreement reiterates the Outer Space Treaty's statement that the moon shall be used exclusively for peaceful purposes. The 1968 Rescue Agreement requires nations to render all necessary assistance to astronauts if they have "suffered accident, or are experiencing conditions of distress or have made an emergency or unintended landing" in the territory of another state.[8] That agreement accords astronauts a diplomatic immunity not afforded military pilots captured as a result of straying into another nation's sovereign airspace. The Liability Convention (1972) requires prompt and equitable compensation for victims of damage caused by space objects. It reinforces the view that states are legally responsible for their activities in outer space.[9] The Registration Convention (1975) establishes a mandatory and uniform registration system for objects launched into outer space.[10] The central registry is kept by the UN Secretary-General and is publicly accessible. Although the latter convention requires the submission of data, each nation can determine the content of its registry, and notice need not be given in advance of the launch.

The most recent multilateral space agreement, the 1996 Comprehensive Test Ban Treaty, bans nuclear weapons testing in all environments. The U.S. Senate rejected the CTBT on 13 October 1999, a reflection of partisanship and long-held convictions concerning the verifiability and enforceability of the treaty's provisions. The Bush administration has announced that it will not seek Senate approval for U.S. ratification.

Space law also includes bilateral agreements. In the U.S.-Soviet Agreement on Measures to Reduce the Risk of Outbreak of Nuclear War (1971), the parties legitimized the existence and the use of certain satellite systems for military purposes. The Hot Line Modernization Agreement (1971) provided for the establishment of two satellite communications circuits between the two countries in the interest of mutual security.

The 1972 ABM Treaty limited the deployment of ABM systems and components to agreed levels and regions.[11] The treaty prohibited, inter alia, the testing, development, and deployment of space-based ABM systems or components. The first agreements under the Strategic Arms Limitation Talks (SALT I—the ABM Treaty and the Interim Agreement on the Limitation of Strategic Offensive Arms) were the first accords to refer to verification by *national technical means* (NTM).[12] The concept of noninterference with NTM, stipulated in article 12 of the ABM Treaty and article 5 of the Interim Agreement, was far-ranging because NTM includes both ground- and space-based systems. Whether noninterference implies protection from *any* form of interference, such as temporary blinding or jamming, is a matter of debate.

The 1988 Agreement on Notification of Launches of Intercontinental Ballistic Missiles and Submarine-Launched Ballistic Missiles (ICBMs and

SLBMs, respectively) stipulates that each party shall provide notification, no less than 24 hours in advance, of the planned date, launch area, and area of impact for any launch of an ICBM or SLBM. A subsequent memorandum of understanding (2000) expanded the agreement to include shorter-range ballistic missiles, sounding and research rockets, and most space launch vehicles.

Efforts to Internationalize and Institutionalize Space

For years, while most of the world's familiarity with satellite reconnaissance was limited to nightly weather forecasts from meteorological satellite images, the two superpowers maintained a monopoly on a vastly superior technology. Despite the fact that Cold War–era space technology was developed competitively and in the national interests of each country, the satellites served to support international stability. Many believe that the superpowers might not have been able to overcome persistent suspicion and enter into negotiations for bilateral arms control without the development of NTM. It is no surprise, then, that some countries have made proposals to widen access to this technology in order to enhance international security.

The best known of these proposals was the French recommendation for the International Satellite Monitoring Agency (ISMA), presented at the UN Special Session on Disarmament in 1978. The ISMA proposal was neither the first nor the last recommendation to envision the use of satellite reconnaissance for multilateral arms control verification and crisis management. A direct precursor to the idea can be found in President Dwight D. Eisenhower's Open Skies proposal. On 21 July 1955 President Eisenhower proposed the Open Skies Treaty at a summit conference in Geneva, Switzerland. Eisenhower reasoned that getting permission to overfly Soviet military facilities while granting permission to the Soviets to overfly U.S. military installations would greatly ease tensions between the two superpowers. Though it occurred prior to the space age, the Open Skies proposal incorporated the assumption that greater transparency leads to greater stability. The Soviets rejected the proposal, fearing that the United States intended to trick the Soviet Union into a disadvantageous position.

ISMA and a number of other formal and informal proposals for an UN-based monitoring agency foundered because the two superpowers were firmly opposed. They were keenly aware of the leverage and power conferred by high-resolution satellite reconnaissance, and neither country would easily give up that privilege. U.S. and Soviet military and intelligence satellite systems remained highly classified during the Cold War.

In 1988 the Soviet Union reversed its opposition to an international role in verification as well as international satellite reconnaissance capabilities. It proposed the creation of the World Space Organization with responsibilities including "verification of compliance with agreements to prevent the extension of an arms race into outer space."[13] The Russian Global Control System for Non-Proliferation of Missiles and Missile Technology, a proposal made in 2000, included a missile launch transparency regime, a mechanism to guarantee the security of participating states that renounced the possession of missile delivery vehicles for WMD, and an international implementing body.[14] Thus far the U.S. government has shown little interest in the development of this regime, preferring instead to continue along its own course of verifying arms control compliance.

In 1982 the international community agreed that the UN Conference on Disarmament would address all future issues of outer space related to international security. The Conference on Disarmament has not been able to agree on the formation of an ad hoc committee with a mandate for outer space. Although in earlier periods its discussions revolved around negotiation of a ban on the deployment of weapons other than WMD in outer space, the issue has more recently become linked to U.S. development of missile defenses. Because the Conference on Disarmament works by consensus, the United States has been able to block formation of a mandate for treaty negotiation.

Efforts to negotiate a bilateral agreement on ASAT systems have also been unsuccessful. In the United States ASAT policy has been intertwined with policy on ballistic missile defense since the days of President Eisenhower. The U.S. Army proposed utilizing Nike Zeus antiballistic missiles in an ASAT role in 1957. It is axiomatic that a weapon system capable of defeating a ballistic missile reentry vehicle is more than capable of defeating a satellite, given the relative hardness of the reentry vehicle versus that of a satellite. Satellites are also easier targets than are ballistic missiles because, generally, they are in immutable orbits and their future position in space and time is highly predictable.

Formal negotiations between the United States and the Soviet Union on ASAT control were proposed in 1977, begun in 1978, and broken off in 1980 by the United States in response to the Soviet invasion of Afghanistan. Despite occasional efforts on an international basis, ASAT treaty discussions have never achieved any momentum because the United States has not believed that an ASAT treaty would be in its national security interest. In mid-September 1997 Russian President Boris Yeltsin wrote to U.S. President Bill Clinton, condemning U.S. efforts to build ASAT weapons and revealing that Moscow already had weapons capable of destroying satellites in space. President Yeltsin proposed "in-depth and open dialogue" aimed at curbing ASAT weapons; "the immediate goal is to agree on the ban on any systems destroying strategic warning satellites."[15] If President Clinton did in fact reply, his answer remains unknown. In October 1997 the Clinton administration authorized an experimental laser-beam attack against a U.S. satellite, arguing the purpose was solely defensive—to see whether the satellite was vulnerable to such an attack while in orbit.

Shortly thereafter it was widely reported that discussions took place with Russia on a multilateral accord among countries that operated ground lasers aimed above the horizon. Under the proposal, U.S. Space Command would have informed laser operators whether the use of laser illumination in a particular area of space at a specific time might inadvertently hit an orbiting object such as a nation's satellite, space shuttle, or space station. No agreement was reached, however.

The ABM Treaty and Ballistic Missile Defense

Once a subject for occasional, arcane disputes between its parties, the ABM Treaty became a topic invoking pronouncements and compliance judgments by nonsignatories in the early twenty-first century.[16] Homeland defense has always been the province of a country's national security policy. Nevertheless, in 2001 the international community appeared reluctant to accept the announced U.S. intention to deploy a ballistic missile defense system if it led to withdrawal from the ABM Treaty. This concern was exacerbated when, in a speech on 1 May 2001, President Bush stated, "We need a new framework that allows us to build missile defenses to counter the different threats of today's world. To do so, we must move beyond the constraints of the thirty-year-old ABM Treaty."[17]

In response, China tabled a draft treaty banning weapons in outer space at the Conference on Disarmament on 7 June 2001. China's ambassador, though not naming the United States, cited the "danger" to outer space created by the development of a missile defense program. China viewed the proposed U.S. missile defense system as an attempt to negate China's small nuclear forces (fewer than 200 strategic nuclear warheads, of which about 20 are deployed).[18] Beijing had also apparently concluded that deployment of missile defenses was a manifestation of the U.S. determination to be a global hegemon.[19]

Although missile defense was hardly a new subject, the enthusiasm for the concept exhibited by the Bush administration stemmed from developments taking place in 1998. On 15 July 1998 the congressionally mandated Commission to Assess the Ballistic Missile Threat to the United States (the Rumsfeld Commission, named after its chairman, Donald Rumsfeld, who in 2001 became secretary of defense under the Bush administration) reported its findings. The commission warned that:

Concerted efforts by a number of overtly or potentially hostile nations to acquire ballistic missiles with biological or nuclear payloads pose a growing threat to the United States, its deployed forces and its friends and allies. These newer, developing threats in North Korea, Iran and Iraq are, in addition to those still posed by the existing ballistic missile arsenals of Russia and China, nations with which the United States is not now in conflict, but which remain in uncertain transitions.[20]

As if on cue, one month after the release of this report North Korea attempted to launch what it described as a satellite on a TAEPO DONG-1 rocket. Although the attempt failed, the launch demonstrated several of the key technologies required for an ICBM, most notably multiple-stage separation. Although the U.S. intelligence community had expected a TAEPO DONG-1 test for some time, the National Intelligence Estimate (NIE) released in September 1999 admitted that it had not known in advance that North Korea had acquired a third stage for the missile or that it would attempt to launch a satellite.

In testimony on 9 February 2000 Robert Walpole, the national intelligence officer for strategic and nuclear programs, stated that the intelligence community "continues to judge that we may not be able to provide much warning if a country purchased an ICBM or if a country already had a space launch capability." Acquiring long-range ballistic missiles armed with a weapon of mass destruction would probably enable weaker countries to "deter, constrain, and harm the United States." The NIE projected that "during the next 15 years the United States most likely will face ICBM threats from Russia, China and North Korea, probably from Iran, and possibly from Iraq. . . . North Korea, Iran, and Iraq would view their ICBMs more as strategic weapons of deterrence and coercive diplomacy than as weapons of war."[21]

In a speech at the Munich Conference on European Security Policy in February 2001, Secretary of Defense Rumsfeld laid out the Bush administration rationale for missile defense:

> No U.S. President can responsibly say that his defense policy is calculated and designed to leave the American people undefended against threats that are known to exist. And they are there, the threats. Let there be no doubt: a system of defense need not be perfect; but the American people must not be left completely defenseless.[22]

Secretary Rumsfeld, who described a missile defense as nothing less than a moral imperative, announced that the United States was prepared to assist "friends and allies threatened by missile attack" in deploying defenses.

On 16 June 2001 President Vladimir Putin of Russia and President Bush met for the first time in Slovenia. President Putin called the ABM Treaty "the cornerstone of the modern architecture of international security." Two days later he was more specific. He told reporters that Russia would view START I and II as "negated" if the United States decided to unilaterally build missile defenses in violation of the ABM Treaty. However, on 22 July 2001, during the G8 summit (G8 being the seven leading industrialized nations, or G7, plus Russia), Presidents Bush and Putin announced that they would begin intensive consultations leading to a "strategic framework" that would reduce both sides' nuclear weapons while allowing the United States to build a missile defense.[23]

President Bush's concept of a less formal arrangement—a framework agreement that would be signed by Russia and the United States but would not require Senate ratification—raised broader questions about his views on arms control. A new strategic arrangement with Russia involving deeper cuts in the nuclear arms arsenal and a limited missile defense system would be a desirable achievement, but the question remained: Must the ABM Treaty be discarded?

By 2001 U.S. policymakers faced a difficult dilemma. Countries that previously were unable to threaten the United States with ballistic missiles and WMD were acquiring the means to do so. Ballistic missiles were certainly not the only national security challenge the United States faced, but they represented a class of threat that could deliver widespread destructive force directly on U.S. soil. In addition, a rogue state's threat of an attack could hold hostage U.S. regional policy and treaty pledges. There was a real obligation to avoid this scenario and to protect the U.S. populace. At the same time, confidence in the delicate balance between the U.S. and Russian strategic arsenals, and efforts to reduce those arsenals, could not be undermined.

On 11 September 2001, terrorists hijacked four U.S. commercial jets and in a coordinated attack hit the World Trade Center and the Pentagon. Thousands died in this surprise attack on the U.S. homeland. The trauma caused by the events of 11 September pushed into the background some of the issues that had troubled the U.S.-Russia relationship. President Bush's stated intention to build a missile defense plan was still on the table but no longer the centerpiece of his agenda. Although Russian President Putin ruled out any "haggling" with the United States over Russia's cooperation in the war on terrorism, saying support for retaliatory strikes was not contingent on the United States backing away from its planned missile defense system, he reiterated his opposition to President Bush's stated intention to withdraw from the ABM Treaty. He also noted that the proposed missile defense system would not have protected the United States from the terrorist attacks. Nevertheless, on 13 December 2001 President Bush announced that he had given formal notice to Russia that the United States would withdraw from the ABM Treaty in six months.

The Space Commission and Space War Games

The congressionally mandated U.S. Space Commission reported its findings on 11 January 2001.[24] Two passages from that report are directly relevant to space arms control:

> The present extent of U.S. dependence on space, the rapid pace at which this dependence is increasing and the vulnerabilities it creates, all demand that U.S. national security space interests be recognized as a top national security priority. . . .
>
> We know from history that every medium—air, land and sea—has seen conflict. Reality indicates that space will be no different. Given this virtual reality, the U.S. must develop the means both to deter and to defend against hostile acts in and from space.[25]

On 8 May 2001 Secretary of Defense Rumsfeld, citing the dependence of the United States on space "for its security and well-being," announced initiatives that would improve the leadership, management, and organization of the nation's defense and intelligence space programs.[26] The U.S. Air Force (USAF) was named the executive agent for space, in charge of all military space operations, including the use of space in intelligence, communications, and warfare. The selection of USAF General Richard Myers as chairman of the joint chiefs of staff underlined the role space was expected to play in transforming U.S. military services. General Myers, while serving as the head of the U.S. Space Command in 1999, had declared that the United States must develop a "space control mission" that would "ensure use of space on our terms."[27]

Starting in 1999, war games allowed the U.S. military to examine a number of complexities associated with space policy, strategy, and operations. Command and Control Simulation 99 used a computer simulation tool (Wargame 2000) to examine scenarios that reflected a spectrum of potential missile threats the United States might face in 2006, as well as the effectiveness of a land-based national missile defense system. Schriever 2001 was the first war game designed to examine several key space issues in greater depth, including space control, force enhancement, and force application in the context of combat operations in a major theater war against a near-peer competitor. The scenario, set in 2017, required the players to apportion their space and terrestrial assets. In the war game players discovered that space resources helped shape, deter, and halt aggressive actions. The scenario of the U.S. Army's 2001 Space and Missile Defense Wargame involved a conflict in the Middle East in 2015 in which rogue nations acquired missiles similar to the TAEPO-DONG with a 4,000-kilometer range and various WMD warheads.[28] This war game underlined the notion that what might be termed a *theater* ballistic missile (because it is incapable of reaching the

United States) might be considered a *national* ballistic missile to Western European allies whose population centers and capitals were at risk.[29]

The scenarios of the war games and the conclusions of the Space Commission report inevitably raised questions about weapons in space. When asked in June 2001 if he predicted the country would deploy space weapons, Secretary Rumsfeld quoted the following from the National Space Policy dated 19 September 1996, saying that it is "the policy today":

> DoD [the U.S. Department of Defense] shall maintain the capability to execute the mission, areas of space support, force enhancement, space control and force application. Consistent with treaty obligations, the United States will develop, operate and maintain space control capabilities to ensure freedom of action in space, and if directed, deny such freedom of action to adversaries. These capabilities may also be enhanced by diplomatic, legal and military measures to preclude an adversary's hostile use of space systems and services.[30]

Dating from the Clinton administration, this directive attempts to balance space control and space treaty obligations. Although the concept of space control is currently under review by the Bush administration, it is a recurrent theme in many military documents. As defined in the DoD's Space Policy Directive 3100.10 dated 9 July 1999, the space control mission area includes "negation of space systems and services used for purposes hostile to U.S. national security interests."[31]

On 17 July 2001, the Bush administration announced that it planned to test a space-based laser interceptor as early as 2005 as part of its study of missile defense technologies.[32] If deployed, a space-based laser would have both ASAT and ballistic missile defense capabilities. The Quadrennial Defense Review released on 30 September 2001 stated that a key objective for military transformation would "ensure the U.S. ability to exploit space for military purposes, but also as required to deny an adversary's ability to do so."[33]

Future Arms Control Challenges

The Soviet Union launched the first man-made satellite, SPUTNIK 1, on 4 October 1957; on 15 May 1958 it launched the first automatic scientific lab aboard SPUTNIK 3, proving that satellites could have important military uses. EXPLORER 1, the first U.S. satellite, was launched on 31 January 1958. China orbited reconnaissance satellites in the 1970s, although little was known of their capabilities. These and other dates in the history of spacefaring nations point to the reality that the space arms control agreements were negotiated and signed during a period in which the vast majority of the parties to those treaties were unable to undertake space activities.[34]

Space systems and technologies have grown so powerful that the concepts underlying the older treaties may no longer apply. The space agreements have loopholes and definitional problems. No single treaty fully specifies which activities are permitted and which activities are prohibited in outer space. Other than WMD, the current space law regime does not preclude the stationing or use of weapons in outer space; therefore conventional and/or exotic weapons are permissible in space.

The Outer Space and Moon Treaties stipulate that outer space, celestial bodies, and the moon must be used for "peaceful purposes," a phrase that has not been universally understood. Some nations hold that military use of outer space must be restricted to "nonaggressive" use such as reconnaissance, communications, navigation, and early warning missions. They argue that "aggressive" missions, such as the stationing of weapons in outer space, are prohibited by the prohibition in the United Nations Charter on the threat or use of force against the territorial integrity of any UN member state. Other nations believe that even military use is prohibited and that there should be an immediate demilitarization of outer space. Still other nations argue that the Outer Space Treaty's reference to the UN Charter's right of self-defense permits uses of outer space deemed necessary for national security. Thus, not only military force support missions are permitted; potentially military force application missions, such as stationing of weapons in outer space, are permitted as well. As defined in the U.S. National Space Policy, *peaceful purposes* allow defense- and intelligence-related activities in pursuit of national security and other goals.[35]

Many countries delineate between airspace, which is subject to claims of national sovereignty, and outer space, which is not subject to such claims. Advances in technology have blurred the distinction between airplanes and rockets, and future aerospace objects will pose additional challenges to space law. The Russian BAIKAL-1, for example, a reusable rocket concept, is half-missile and half-aircraft.

Definitional issues could form the basis of an argument in favor of a new space treaty that would clarify ambiguities; or, it could be argued, negotiation of such a treaty would be impossible when even the most fundamental concepts defy universally accepted definition. The most complex definition may be that of *space* itself. Is it a medium no different than land, sea, and air? Or is it a sanctuary to be preserved?

Apart from definitional issues, there are other challenges to the development and negotiation of space arms control agreements. No space war has taken place, but because space assets provide many forms of information for the military, it is possible to envision attacks on satellites in scenarios where there is little danger of a strategic exchange.

The U.S. military, in accordance with DoD 3100.10, *Joint Vision 2010,* and other documents, has focused on technological advances for space capabilities.[36] Military leaders are concerned that an adversary might elect to attack U.S. information processes, including space systems and technologies, because the adversary would know it could not match the United States on the level of other military equipment. This concern was reflected in the repeated warning of the Space Commission that the United States would be an attractive candidate for a "space Pearl Harbor." The National Space Policy declares: "The United States considers the space systems of any nation to be national property with the right of passage through and operations in space without interference. Purposeful interference with space systems shall be viewed as an infringement on sovereign rights."[37]

Many countries believe that a multilateral convention for the non-weaponization of space is needed before the last frontier is invaded. Yet the fact that the U.S. military has the highest reliance on satellites of any force in the world could lead to the conclusion that it should not sign treaties that ban the weaponization of space. The Space Commission argued that the United States must be cautious of "agreements intended for one purpose that, when added to a larger web of treaties or regulations, may have the unintended consequences of restricting future activities in space."[38]

U.S. satellites might make an attractive—and possibly asymmetric—target for potential adversaries. Although mutual forbearance has kept the United States and Russia from exercising ASAT capabilities against one another, other countries might not be of like mind. Satellites are easy to locate, and interference with their operation does not require nuclear weapons. Rogue nations such as North Korea and Iran could readily acquire the technology to destroy the operation of U.S. satellites. Ground stations are also vulnerable to sabotage and direct attack by states and terrorist groups that would be unlikely to sign an agreement banning ASATs.

Verifying compliance with an ASAT treaty would be daunting. Potential adversaries are researching or developing parasite ASAT satellites, ground-based lasers to blind or "dazzle" the optical arrays of reconnaissance satellites, satellite-frequency jammers, and experimental electromagnetic pulse weapons to destroy satellite circuitry.

Adversaries could also target commercial satellites—U.S. assets worth billions of dollars—which have not been protected under space arms control treaties. In addition to their contribution to the economy, commercial satellites played a role during the Afghan campaign in the U.S. war on terrorism as intelligence officers provided the military with the most critical weapon: information.

In the Afghan campaign the United States did not face an adversary with space assets. The next conflict might not be as asymmetrical. Players in the Schriever 2001 war game discovered that space has a great power to deter because spacefaring nations carefully guard and highly value their space assets; a direct threat to those assets can be a powerful deterrent. If forces are robust, a little pressure applied in space can potentially control the escalation of a conflict. Enemies are less inclined to launch a surprise attack if they know their military movements can be seen. Furthermore, pressure applied in space can be dramatic to an aggressor but invisible to other nations, thus allowing the former to withdraw without having to consider the latter's reaction to his response.

Negotiation of a ban on weaponization of space might lock in U.S. superiority in space. However, such a ban, like an ASAT ban, has opponents who say that threats to space assets will be nontraditional and difficult to monitor. In testimony before Congress in February 2001, the director of the Defense Intelligence Agency, Vice Admiral Thomas Wilson, said that "a number of countries are interested in or experimenting with a variety of technologies that could be used to develop counterspace capabilities" against the United States.[39] Director of Central Intelligence George Tenet, in a briefing the same day, reinforced this testimony by stating that "operations to disrupt, degrade, or defeat U.S. space assets will be attractive options for those seeking to counter U.S. strategic military superiority."[40] Nonstate actors that might wish to threaten these assets will not be parties to a space arms control agreements among nations. Rogue nations might not sign an agreement, or they might sign and clandestinely violate its provisions. But if the United States places the reconnaissance satellites of other nations at risk by building ASATs, Russia, China, and other countries could respond in kind.

Conclusion

Although prospects for multilateral arms control negotiations remain dim at the moment, and the glacial pace of multilateral negotiations in the Conference on Disarmament is hardly an inviting prospect, there are other cooperative arrangements that would enhance international security in space. On a bilateral level, targeted technical and financial assistance could be given to Russia to improve its deteriorating early warning systems.

A bilateral memorandum of agreement in 2000 established a Joint Data Exchange Center in Moscow for the exchange of data from U.S. and Russian early warning systems. The center will allow timely sharing of information on ballistic missile launches and space launch vehicles detected by each side's early warning systems. The center still needs to be funded and staffed. Another bilateral project, the Russian-American Observation Satellite (RAMOS), also needs additional support. An innovative two-satellite program, RAMOS engages Russian developers of early warning satellites in the development and testing of space-based surveillance technologies.

Multilateral agreements might be reached on transparency arrangements that would not limit space technologies or systems. For example, space powers could share more information with the international community on their current and prospective nonmilitary activities in space. A multilateral agreement outlining an outer space code of conduct could stipulate rules of behavior that would provide a means of distinguishing an incident of accidental origin from an act of intentional aggression. Another accord might define rules of the road, modeled on agreements that prevent dangerous practices at sea.[41] Allies and friends could be invited to participate in war games so that they would have a better understanding of the critical role played by U.S. space assets in times of regional conflicts.

Negotiation of an international convention prohibiting interference with national technical means of verification would greatly enhance national and international security. A crisis is less likely to escalate out of control if each adversary is confident, through data gathered from NTM, that the other side is not making preparations for a first strike.

Space arms control agreements should not be viewed as icons or impediments. They neither guarantee good behavior nor promote a false sense of security. The world has already learned that rogue nations do not comply with arms control treaties. However, strengthening the legal framework involving space could be to the benefit of the United States and other space-faring nations. Ultimately, decisions regarding space arms control will come down to the answer to one question: Does the United States stand to gain or lose by restraining the growth of weapons in space?

Notes

General (USAF ret.) John Piotrowski, VADM (USN Ret.) Lyle Bien, VADM (USN Ret.) David Frost, and Dr. Matthew Nichols (U.S. Army Space and Missile Defense Command) provided substantive comments to a draft of this chapter, for which I am grateful.

1. Commission to Assess United States National Security Space Management and Organization, *Report of the Commission to Assess United States National Security Space Management and Organization: Executive Summary.* Washington, DC, 11 January 2001, p. 12. Hereafter cited as *The Space Commission Report.*

2. "Canada, Outer Space, and 'The Existing Legal Framework,'" Canadian government white paper, 16 January 1998. Canada has continued to reiterate its opposition to the weaponization of space.

3. Canada's views are important because the United States and Canada share a binational command, the North American Aerospace Defense Command (NORAD). In the proposed missile defense system, the commander in chief (CINC) NORAD, double-hatted as CINCSPACE, is envisioned to be the operational decision authority regarding engagement of threat missiles.

4. Data change weekly as new satellites are launched and others are decommissioned or malfunction; thus it is difficult to provide a specific number of currently operational satellites. Various public sources yield the following approximate numbers for midyear 2001: United States, 350; Russia, 75; rest of the world, 200.

5. *The Space Commission Report,* p. 7.

6. See Appendix 2 in this volume for a survey of the agreements, as well as descriptions thereof, cited in this section.

7. The language permitted the two superpowers to continue to develop ballistic missiles because they do not go into orbit.

8. Article 1 of the treaty.

9. When the Soviet KOSMOS-954 nuclear-powered satellite fell on Canada in 1978, Canada billed the Soviet Union for expenses associated with the cleanup. Moscow paid Canada a portion of its claim.

10. The Space Control Center of the U.S. Space Command tracks more than 8,000 man-made objects, softball-sized and larger, orbiting earth. Approximately 7 percent of these objects are operational satellites.

11. For an analysis of the ABM Treaty, see Sidney N. Graybeal and Patricia A. McFate, "Strategic Defensive Arms Control," in Jeffrey A. Larsen and Gregory J. Rattray, eds., *Arms Control Toward the 21st Century* (Boulder: Lynne Rienner Publishers, 1996), pp. 119–137.

12. The interim agreement was the first step toward placing limits on U.S. and Soviet land- and submarine-based offensive nuclear weapons. NTM includes reconnaissance satellite systems using photographic, infrared, radar and electronic sensors, ground- and sea-based radars, seismographs, communications collection stations, and underwater acoustic systems.

13. United Nations, *Study on the Role of the United Nations in the Field of Verification* (New York: United Nations, 1991), p. 26.

14. An unofficial translation of the proposal, made at an International Global Control Systems Experts meeting in Moscow on 16 March 2000, may be accessed at www.fas.org/nuk.

15. Bill Gertz, "Yeltsin Letter Reveals Anti-Satellite Weapons," *Washington Times*, 7 November 1997.

16. In August 2001 the Department of Defense announced that its differentiation between theater and national missile defense programs no longer existed; a single integrated ballistic missile defense system would be developed.

17. President George W. Bush, Remarks at National Defense University, Fort McNair, Washington, DC, reprinted in *New York Times*, 1 May 2001.

18. Robert S. Norris, William M. Markin, Hans F. Kristensen, and Joshua Handler, "National Resources Defense Council Nuclear Notebook: Chinese Nuclear Forces, 1999," *Bulletin of Atomic Scientists* (May/June 1999); also *Foreign Missile Developments and the Ballistic Missile Threat to the United States Through 2015* (Washington, DC: National Intelligence Council, September 1999).

19. For further information on this subject, see *BMD and Northeast Asian Security: Views from Washington, Beijing, and Tokyo*, Report of the Monterey Institute of International Studies, 18 April 2001.

20. Commission to Assess the Ballistic Missile Threat to the United States, *Report of the Commission to Assess the Ballistic Missile Threat to the United States: Executive Summary* (the Rumsfeld Commission), 15 July 1998, p. 5.

21. Quotations are taken from Robert D. Walpole, National Intelligence Officer for Strategic and Nuclear Programs, Statement for the Record to the Senate Subcommittee on International Security, Proliferation, and Federal Services on the Ballistic Missile Threat to the United States, 9 February 2000.

22. Department of Defense, *Remarks as Delivered by Secretary of Defense Donald H. Rumsfeld, Munich, Germany, 3 February 2001*. United States Department of Defense Speeches, www.defenselink.mil/speeches.

23. Mike Allen, "Bush, Putin Agree to Arms Dialogue," *Washington Post*, 23 July 2001.

24. Donald Rumsfeld was chairman of the Space Commission but resigned when he was appointed secretary of defense.

25. *The Space Commission Report,* pp. 9–10.

26. U.S. Department of Defense News Transcript, 8 May 2001.

27. As quoted in "Space, the Frontier," editorial, *Washington Times,* 28 August 2001.

28. It has been reported that Pakistan's Shaheen-II missile range has been increased substantially. "Pakistan Shaheen-II Missile Range Increased to 4,000 KM, India's 'Unreliable,'" Foreign Broadcast Information Service, FBIS Document ID: SAP20010402000032, 2 April 2001.

29. The classified war games were played at the Joint National Intelligence Center, Schriever Air Force Base, Colorado. The first game was cosponsored by USSPACECOM and the Joint Program Office, National Missile Defense. The second and third games were part of the Department of Defense's Title X service-specific war games.

30. The White House, *National Space Policy,* Presidential Decision Directive (Washington, DC: National Science and Technology Council), 19 September 1996, www.ostp.gov/NSTC/html/fs/fs-5.html.

31. Ibid.

32. Vernon Loeb, "U.S. Plans to Test Space-Based Laser to Intercept Missiles," *Washington Post,* 18 July 2001, p. 10.

33. *Final Report of the Quadrennial Defense Review,* Washington, DC, 30 September 2001.

34. As of May 2001 there were 91 signatories to the Outer Space Treaty. The United States, Russia, China, Japan, India, Israel, and Ukraine are spacefaring nations, that is, countries able to launch satellites. The European Space Agency, consisting of 15 countries, also launches satellites.

35. "Introduction," *National Space Policy,* 19 September 1996.

36. *Joint Vision 2010* is the conceptual template for the U.S. armed forces. This document emphasizes information superiority and innovation to meet asymmetric threats and operate across the full spectrum of military operations.

37. "Introduction," *National Space Policy,* 19 September 1996.

38. The *Space Commission Report,* pp. 17–18.

39. This memorandum was accessed at www.web7.whs.osd.mil/text/d310010p.txt.

40. Both quotations from Bill Gertz, "Space Seen as Battlefield of Future," *Washington Times,* 8 February 2001.

41. On 25 May 1972, the U.S.-Soviet Agreement on the Prevention of Incidents on and over the High Seas was signed. The agreement followed several incidents between forces of the U.S. Navy and the Soviet navy involving planes passing near one another, ships bumping one another, and both ships and aircraft making threatening movements against those of the other side.

Suggested Readings

Bunn, George, and David Holloway. *Arms Control Without Treaties? Rethinking U.S.-Russian Strategic Negotiations in Light of the Duma-Senate Slowdown in Treaty Approval.* Stanford: Stanford University Center for International Security and Arms Control, 1998.

Carter, Ashton B. "Satellites and Anti-Satellites: The Limits of the Possible." *International Security* (Spring 1986): 46–98.

Chayes, Antonia H., and Paul Doty, eds. *Defending Deterrence: Managing the ABM Treaty Regime into the 21st Century*. Washington, DC: Pergamon-Brassey's, 1989.

Commission to Assess the Ballistic Missile Threat to the United States. *Executive Summary of the Report of the Commission to Assess the Ballistic Missile Threat to the United States*. Washington, DC, 15 July 1998.

Commission to Assess United States National Security Space Management and Organization. *The Report of the Commission to Assess United States National Security Space Management and Organization*, Washington, DC, 11 January 2001.

Krauthammer, Charles. "The New Unilateralism." *Washington Post,* 8 June 2001, p. A29.

Krepon, Michael. "Lost in Space: The Misguided Drive Toward Anti-satellite Weapons." *Foreign Affairs* (May/June 2001): 2–8.

McFate, Patricia. "Is the World Too Much with Us? The Impact of a National Missile Defense System and the ABM Treaty on International Security." In James Brown, ed. *Conundrums in Arms Control: The New Millennium*. Albuquerque, NM: Sandia National Laboratories, 2000.

Nolan, Janne. *Trappings of Power: Ballistic Missiles in the Third World*. Washington, DC: Brookings Institution, 1991.

Richelson, Jeffrey T. *America's Space Sentinels: DSP Satellites and National Security*. Lawrence: University Press of Kansas, 2001.

Stares, Paul B. *Space and National Security*. Washington, DC: Brookings Institution, 1987.

Wilson, Tom. *Threats to United States Space Capabilities*. Undated report prepared for the U.S. Space Commission. This and other background papers written for the Space Commission may be found on the website of the Federation of American Scientists, www.fas.org.

18

Security in Cyberspace

Gregory J. Rattray

The United States is leading the world into the information age. Developments such as cellular and satellite communications, personal computers, and high-speed access to the Internet, accompanied by rapid development of new applications for their uses, have made the world a much more interconnected place. However, a realization has also dawned that this information age will have a dramatic impact on security affairs. Successful integration of information systems enabling sophisticated employment of conventional strike forces proved decisive during the Gulf War, the Kosovo conflict, and in Afghanistan. U.S. military involvement in Somalia, the Balkans, and the global war on terrorism also demonstrated the influence of increasingly global media. At home, activities of hackers and systems failures affecting critical institutions such as air traffic control, banks, and the Department of Defense have increased worries that a whole new type of security threat may be emerging. Information systems may now serve as both weapons and targets.

Little consensus yet exists regarding what constitutes the full scope of information operations or information warfare.[1] Topics discussed range from the improved use of electronic means to achieve advantage on conventional battlefields to very broad conceptions of the capacity to affect the decision-making of adversaries in peacetime and wartime. Yet despite the lack of conceptual clarity, concern over the challenges presented by information warfare and cyberterrorism have risen dramatically. The possibility for digital conflict in cyberspace has achieved a prominent place in these discussions.[2]

Pursuing arms limitations and international agreements provide a means for states and other international actors to help manage their security concerns arising from the threats posed by digital attacks. In this chapter I analyze possibilities for applying frameworks for international cooperation to the emerging challenges posed by information warfare.

Rising Concern over Information Operations

The U.S. government has placed increasing emphasis on information warfare and protecting itself against digital attack.[3] Prompted by Congress and elements within the executive branch, President Bill Clinton formed the Commission on Critical Infrastructure Protection in 1996. As worries rose over hacker incidents and system failures, the ability to protect the nation's information systems, networks, and their operations (collectively, the *information infrastructure*) against disruption became a new focus of national security concerns. Based on the commission's report, President Clinton put out Presidential Decision Directive 63 to help to protect the United States against digital attacks.[4] A national plan, *Defending America's Cyberspace: Version 1.0,* was issued in January 2000, creating a number of governmental initiatives designed to address challenges in establishing digital defenses.[5]

As early as 1996 the U.S. national security strategy also recognized the significance of information warfare.[6] According to the national strategy document, within the broader rubric of information operations and information warfare cyberspace provides a new realm that the United States should seek to dominate. Control of this realm would enable U.S. forces to use computer and communications systems freely to conduct all types of military operations while providing the opportunity to disrupt enemy operations and supporting activities. The president also assigned U.S. Space Command the responsibility under the Unified Command Plan for conducting computer network defense and attack as part of U.S. military operations.[7]

Other states and international actors also recognize the emergence of a new realm for competition and conflict. The Russian Federation has an expansive approach to understanding information warfare and weapons. Russian think tanks, internal security institutions, and military organizations are engaged in analyzing the concept of information warfare and the implications for security and deterrence. The Russian Academy of Natural Sciences defines information weapons as

> the sum total of information technology (the organized sum of processes, elements, equipment and methods used for processing information), and the means and methods of information influence (the sum total of linguistic, software, technical and other methods designed to extract, distort, or destroy information resources of the state) designed for waging an information war.[8]

The People's Republic of China is also engaged in understanding how information warfare will impact its security and military strategy. Wei Jincheng has called for a "people's war" in an information warfare context: "Carried out by hundreds of millions of people using open-type modern information systems . . . the chance of people taking the initiative and randomly participating in the war are increased."[9] Such an approach differs greatly from U.S. concepts for employing information warfare. Timothy Thomas has concluded that both Russia and China fear that U.S. leadership in information technology will enable that country to dominate conflicts in this new realm and that employment of digital attacks could destabilize existing deterrence dynamics.

Other political entities also understand the rising significance of cyberspace as a place for competition and conflict. Increasingly, groups ranging from Greenpeace, the Zapatista rebels, and the Irish Republican Army to Hamas use the Internet to publicize their cause and call for action. As an example, ethnic Tamil guerrillas are reported to have swamped the e-mail services of Sri Lankan embassies in 1998.[10] Often these activities emanate from multiple locations where sympathizers reside, including the United States and other Western nations.

Individuals and independent hacker groups have become active in politically motivated, disruptive digital attacks. As tensions have risen between Israel and the Palestine Authority, hackers sympathetic to one side or the other began widespread efforts to disrupt government and privately owned computer systems of the adversary.[11] The bombing of the Chinese embassy in Belgrade in May 1999 resulted in a spate of hacker activity against U.S. defense and other government computer systems.[12] Tensions that arose after China forced down a U.S. EP-3 reconnaissance aircraft in April 2001 resulted in even greater levels of activity as U.S. hacker groups defaced scores of Chinese websites and Chinese groups attempted denial-of-service attacks against the White House's public servers.[13]

Why Is Information Warfare a Concern?

Determining the significance of cyberwarfare also presents challenges. Much hype has attended the possibilities. The U.S. president, members of Congress, and senior defense leaders bemoan the vulnerability of critical U.S. infrastructures. The former director of the Central Intelligence Agency once stated that digital attacks could constitute the employment of weapons of mass disruption.[14] The Russians warned the United Nations (UN) Secretary-General about the possibility of information warfare and weapons "provoking a new spiral of the arms race . . . deviating vast resources much needed for development."[15] Others caution that cyberwar has yet to result in paralyzing military operations or inflict massive economic or social disruption. Most agree that the growing dependence of military operations, economic gain, and social activity on advanced information systems increases the imperative to understand the threats posed by cyberwar.

The rise of digital means of encoding and transferring information has created new ways to attack information systems. Impacts of digital attacks can range from total paralysis of networks to intermittent shutdown, random data errors, information theft, and data corruption. The tools and techniques for attacking information systems have received detailed attention.[16] Digital attacks can cause disruption, damage, and destruction through achieving unauthorized access and control over targeted information systems. Such attacks are enabled by a vast array of intrusive tools and techniques (hacking). If control over a targeted computer or network is achieved, digital attackers can inflict a wide range of effects. Possibilities range from changing the graphics on a website to corrupting the delivery schedules for medical supplies and military equipment, denying access to 911 services, and disrupting air traffic control data and telecommunications backbone networks. Malicious software code (viruses and worms) provides another potential means for cyberterrorist attack, as millions of e-mail users have discovered. The effects of viruses and malicious software range from benign messages displayed at system startup to code that can cause hardware failures and wide-area network overloads. Combining features of both intrusions and malicious code, digital attacks could also intentionally corrupt software programs in targeted information systems and infrastructures. A terrorist group or adversary nation may endeavor to corrupt software in the production process by emplacing backdoors for access or inserting so-called Trojan horses to cause desired effects at a predetermined time or upon a given command.

Setting Boundaries

Conceptual clarity must underpin any understanding of the potential for international agreements related to digital attacks. We begin by distinguishing between four categories of malicious activity that can be conducted in cyberspace: cyberwar, cyberterrorism, cybercrime, and cyberactivism. The matrix in Table 18.1 focuses on the type of actors, objectives, and activities that delineate these four categories.

Drawing boundaries between different sorts of activities in cyberspace is difficult. The matrix in Table 18.1 is not all-inclusive. For example, cyberespionage conducted by state and nonstate actors could constitute another category. However, we can also treat that type of activity as espionage, punishable by domestic laws but permissible under international law and not a fruitful subject for efforts at international cooperation.[17] Political activism in cyberspace (so-called hacktivism) already involves the use of disruptive means to garner attention. Yet if hacktivism causes widespread effects against information infrastructures, or if significant destruction or death typifying terrorist purposes result, we can treat it as cyberterrorism.[18] The types of malicious activity and actors who conduct it are likely to multiply over time, making distinctions even more blurred and rigorous analysis even more important. The matrix in Table 18.1 simply provides a framework for establishing broad categories and terms for discussion.

Additionally, efforts at cooperation in securing cyberspace must overcome difficulties in distinguishing who is involved and their intent when digital intrusions and attacks occur. The difficulty of discerning the relationship between governments and hacker groups involved in malicious activity in cyberspace makes it difficult to categorize specific events expeditiously. This difficulty will carry over into efforts to achieve cooperation and agreements. States and other actors use different terminology and have divergent priorities regarding the significance of digital intrusions and attacks. Therefore, any initiative to enhance security in cyberspace must begin with an understanding of the actors involved and the objectives of possible agreements.

Efforts at International Agreements and Cooperation

Rising concern over malicious activity in cyberspace has prompted a range of efforts to discern the applicability of international agreements and legal constructs. As the possibilities for cyberwar became clearer, specific analyses of the applicability of international laws were conducted.[19] The provisions of treaties and agreements, including the UN Convention on the Law of the Sea, the Outer Space Treaty, the International Telecommunication

Table 18.1 Four Types of Malicious Cyberactivities

Activity	Types of Actors	Objectives Pursued via Digital Attack	Likely Types of Digital Attack
Cyberwar	State	Political/military	Full range of widespread disruptive and focused intensive techniques
Cyberterror	Nonstate	Political (via disruption and/or fear)	Likely to involve widespread disruption and/or significant destruction or death
Cybercrime	Nonstate	Financial/ nonpolitical	Likely to involve focused intrusion and manipulation
Cyberactivism	Nonstate	Political (raising awareness)	Nondisruptive

Satellite and International Maritime Satellite Agreements, and the International Telecommunications Union Convention, have been analyzed. The general conclusion was that these agreements provide few constraints on states in the conduct of information warfare. Additionally, substantial legal attention has focused on the applicability of the United Nations Charter regarding the use of force and the applicability of the law of armed conflict to instances of digital attacks.[20] However, because these sources of international law are concerned with the obligations of state actors, they provide little help regarding ways to control the behavior of nonstate actors.

Law enforcement authorities have also endeavored to understand laws related to cybercrime, as well as to construct arrangements to deal with transnational criminal activity occurring in cyberspace. National laws governing what constitutes criminal activity in cyberspace vary widely.[21] Differing standards across states create an opportunity for so-called safe havens for malicious activity. Additionally, the ease of transiting political and jurisdictional borders while conducting digital attacks has been widely recognized, creating great difficulties in pursuing cybercriminals and, potentially, cyberterrorists. The relative stealthiness and anonymity of digital attack techniques make the problem worse.

Governments have recognized these problems and undertaken efforts to improve international responses to cybercrime. The United Nations has issued a manual on computer-related crimes, trying to establish awareness of the problems presented.[22] As early as 1983 the Organization for Economic Cooperation and Development (OECD), whose membership includes 29 economically advanced nations, established an effort to define computer crime. The OECD's Proposed List of Computer Crimes focuses on the use of computer systems to commit acts of illicit funds transfer, forgery, computer and telecommunications system disruption, copyright infringement, and unauthorized access.[23]

The Convention on Cybercrime

The Council of Europe (COE) has led the most significant of efforts so far in the realm of combating cybercrime. The COE began its initiative in 1989; since then the COE effort has come to encompass many nations outside Europe, including the United States and Japan. In November 2001 the COE adopted the Convention on Cybercrime.[24] Key provisions of the convention include establishing a clear list of definitions and offenses related to cybercrime; strong mechanisms for international cooperation in the pursuit of cybercriminals, including extradition requirements, obligations, and procedures for mutual assistance in investigation and for prosecution and preservation of evidence; and establishing a 24-hour network for all parties to the agreement. The convention is under consideration for adoption by a number of other states, including the United States.

The COE convention also includes provisions that may limit the number of parties who implement its provisions. The scope of what is defined as *cybercrime* is very broad. States must make criminal certain types of digital content and enforce international intellectual property conventions. Criminalizing certain offenses may conflict with U.S. First Amendment rights.[25] Other nations, such as China, may be leery of requirements to enforce intellectual property provisions. The COE draft also does not deal with large-scale disruptive activities against information infrastructures, leaving the potentially most significant cyberterrorist activities untouched.

The COE initiative prompted a group of academics at Stanford University to issue a proposal for the International Convention on Cyber Crime and Terrorism.[26] Directly addressing perceived weaknesses while building on the COE approach, the Stanford group has offered three major refinements: (1) more bounded provisions excluding content and intellectual property to cast a wider net over potential signatories and ensure the protection of privacy rights; (2) explicitly addressing the requirement to include protecting information infrastructure and combat cyberterrorism, including provisions that reinforce other international agreements such as the International Civil Aviation Organization and International Telecommunications Union; and (3) establishing an international agency for infrastructure protection that focuses on preventive action by developing standards and practices for cybersecurity. The future of the Stanford proposal remains an open question.[27] At a minimum, though, it demonstrates the possibility for involvement of nongovernmental organizations (NGOs) to foster and expand the dialogue over the role and nature of international agreements in this area.

UN Efforts

The United Nations has become a forum for discussion on limiting cyberwar. As early as 1994 the UN General Assembly passed a broad resolution on the role of science and technology that "invites Member states to widen international dialogue, seeking international norms and guidelines that would regulate international transfers of information technology with military applications."[28] Also, Russia has endeavored to motivate the UN to actively address national security concerns related to information warfare and weapons. The Russians have clearly stated concerns about the potentially destabilizing nature of cyberattacks against command-and-control systems and the growing dominance of that realm by the United States. The Russian government explicitly stated that it would consider the use of nuclear weapons in response to information attacks against Russian strategic command-and-control systems.[29]

UN Resolution 53/70, passed in January 1999, addresses "developments in the field of information and telecommunications in the context of information security" and focuses on the need to "prevent the misuse or exploitation of information resources or technologies for criminal or terrorist purposes."[30] The resolution calls on UN member states to engage in multilateral discussions of information security concerns and provide the Secretary-General their views on the "advisability of developing international principles that would enhance the security of global information and telecommunications systems and help combat information terrorism and criminality." The resolution makes no mention of information warfare or weapons.

The United States appears to have the most to gain from a globally networked society and therefore the most to potentially lose from cyberinsecurity. Yet the U.S. national security establishment also wants to preserve its flexibility to pursue a wide range of options in achieving information superiority and developing dominant information warfare forces for the future.[31] The Department of Defense offices of general counsel and public affairs have both issued statements that the department believes that its conduct of information operations will be governed by the principles of the law of armed conflict and that those constraints provide sufficient international controls over such capabilities.[32] The degree to which the United States uses multilateral and international approaches to controlling digital attacks will revolve around balancing these central concerns.

Learning from Past Efforts

States facing new security challenges such as the threat of digital attacks can respond in a number of ways. Often states unilaterally eliminate threats and create defenses that mitigate the risks posed by new adversaries and military developments. States have also sought to reduce the level of threat, risks of conflicts involving new military capabilities, and the cost of defending their interests through cooperation with other states. During the Cold War cooperation often took the form of bilateral formal arms control treaties such as the Strategic Arms Limitation and Strategic Arms Reduction Treaties, which limited the types and numbers of military systems that could be fielded. Other multilateral arms control agreements have endeavored to outlaw the existence and/or use of certain types of weapons (e.g., the Biological Weapons Convention), limit their spread (e.g., the Nuclear Non-Proliferation Treaty), or put regions off-limits for deployment (e.g., nuclear weapon–free zones). Lessons from these efforts may be drawn for international cooperation to reduce risks of cyberwar and cyberterrorism.

Although the tools and techniques used for digital attacks are generally not considered arms per se, they certainly create potential security challenges for states and other actors. Even though nonstate actors are less observable in terms of their intent and activities, states have long tried to deal with security challenges posed by terrorists and other groups. If nonstate actors use digital attacks, efforts to control the means for such attacks must deal with the adversaries.

Lessons and Limits of the
Cold War Arms Control Experience

During the Cold War, arms control efforts generally focused on lengthy formal negotiations to manage the strategic balance between the superpowers. Given the centrality of this balance to security, the parties required strict verification of compliance with agreements. A fundamental difference between Cold War arms control approaches and efforts to limit digital attacks on information infrastructures relates to the actual nature of the weapons involved and the ability to verify whether the other side is properly following the terms of the agreement. Cold War arms control stressed managing the types and numbers of weapon systems possessed by each superpower or allied bloc. The limited items were large observable systems such as strategic missiles, submarines, aircraft, and tanks. The presence of such systems was verified by large and expensive intelligence organizations in two primary ways: use of national technical means of collection (particularly satellite imagery), and on-site inspections conducted by the parties. These verification efforts endeavored to deter all but marginal, militarily insignificant cheating due to the observability of the systems and well-developed intelligence techniques for tracking these systems.

Regimes built around highly observable, tightly monitored objects will not work in controlling the tools necessary for strategic information attacks. Even if large-scale, highly intrusive on-site inspection procedures were implemented, the ubiquity of computer-processing capabilities today and the ease of transmitting and hiding electronic tools would make even discovering their existence nearly impossible. Agreements specifying "force levels" to limit the potential for cyberwarfare would prove futile.

The Cold War arms control experience does point to some general lessons applicable to establishing international cooperation for securing cyberspace. First, the Cold War demonstrated the utility of having adjudicating bodies set up to handle disputes arising from the implementation and monitoring of these arms control agreements. The Standing Consultative Commission for the ABM Treaty handled a large number of very contentious, often technical issues.[33] The presence of such mechanisms provided both a forum and a procedure for bringing problems out into the open, for requiring the possible transgressor to respond, for allowing international scrutiny of the claims, for delaying the parties from using other means to redress their grievances, and possibly for deterring further violations. Given the difficulties of determining the cause of information infrastructure disruptions and the need to identify the perpetrators of digital attacks, such mechanisms may prove particularly useful in fostering security in cyberspace.

Less tangible, but probably even more significant, was how the arms control process itself began to foster understanding of differing perspectives on weapons, military strategies, and doctrines regarding their use. Throughout the 1970s and 1980s Soviet intransigence about reducing land-based intercontinental ballistic missile forces came to be understood more thoroughly. The process of acknowledging a common concern and working together on securing cyberspace may have utility without reaching detailed, enforceable agreements. Understanding how other actors conceptualize digital attacks as a new means of threatening national security will be a crucial first step in controlling their effects.

Lessons and Limits of
Multilateral and Global Arms Control Approaches

Efforts to limit the spread and use of nuclear, chemical, and biological weapons (collectively, weapons of mass destruction, or WMD) involve technologies with dual military and commercial uses, similar to the challenges posed by digital warfare technologies. Dual-use technologies confront the global community with actors possessing tools useful for peaceful purposes that also have utility for harming others. The WMD regimes are aimed at limiting diffusion of such potentially harmful technology while generally allowing peaceful uses. In doing so those regimes strive for universal adherence to agreements among states and enforcement against nonstate actors.

Nonproliferation regimes attempt to control physical precursors in the weapons-creation process. The size and complexity of the technologies vary, but they are fairly tangible in nature and stress on-site inspection regimes. The nature of substances used to make biological weapons may provide the closest approximation to the tools and techniques for digital warfare. Hospital and research laboratories must have small quantities of deadly viruses to conduct disease research. Yet these small amounts can be rapidly grown into large quantities for use in weapons.[34] This situation is analogous to the requirement for network systems administrators to have tools, such as the systems analysis tool for network administrators, to identify their own vulnerabilities but that can also be used to identify weaknesses of other computer networks. Digital tools can also be easily replicated and dispersed. However, use of biological weapons to accomplish political objectives requires that they be put into a deliverable form and physically transported to the target. Such activities create another layer of observability, especially in dealing with particularly toxic materials.[35]

The electronically transferable codes in digital weapons make them nearly impossible to observe. A person carrying a disk in his pocket may well be equipped with a weapon of sorts capable of global reach when the disk is put into a computer with an Internet connection. An agreement listing prohibited types of malicious software tools, such as viruses, might be envisioned similar to the categories of chemicals identified in the Chemical Weapons Convention.[36] However, the ease of modifying digital code to create a new tool arguably not covered by the agreement would make such controls unworkable.[37]

Also, part of the effectiveness of WMD regimes revolves around outlawing weapons with clearly abhorrent effects.[38] Cyberwar and cyberterrorism discussions often involve notional attacks on control systems of key infrastructural systems. As yet, however, there have been no confirmed incidents of purposeful digital attacks causing widespread violence and destruction. A sense of moral outrage may never exist regarding tools for digital attacks.

Efforts to control the proliferation of WMD show that even though 100 percent compliance may prove impossible, such agreements can assist in creating international norms to deter cheating and punish violators.[39] Supporters of multinational WMD agreements argue that even though a single violation may not be critical to global peace or a nation's security, the goal of such regimes is to raise the chance of detection and deter actors from choosing to acquire and use these capabilities.[40] Moreover, simply becoming a holdout state from a treaty creates suspicion, causing states and other actors concerned to focus their intelligence efforts on the holdout. Formal conventions might provide a crucial legal and ethical basis for action for dealing with digital attacks where the origin and intent are unclear. Creating the conditions for retaliatory actions in the advent of digital attacks may provide a key rationale for cooperative efforts.

Other important lessons can be learned from the process of putting together and managing these regimes. The need for industry involvement in controlling dual-use technologies has been clearly recognized. Any efforts to control and monitor the spread of digital warfare technologies would require substantial private-sector involvement given commercial firms' role in constructing and governing the global information infrastructure.[41] The Council of Europe set a useful precedent by soliciting comments from nongovernmental organizations on drafts of the Convention on Cybercrime.[42]

The need to deal with dual-use technologies in arms control has also reinforced the value of creating transparency regarding the different actors possessing potentially threatening tools and techniques. Numerous organizations have created databases to track instances of both open and illicit trafficking in nuclear materials.[43] In a similar fashion, the international community of computer emergency/incident response teams (CERT/CIRTs), information security associations, and companies specializing in cyber-security all endeavor to track the emergence of new viruses and intrusion techniques. Simply requiring potential possessors of digital weapons to enter into arms control forums can provide information through analysis of issues that parties would not otherwise discuss.[44]

The gains from such transparency are determined in large part by the willingness of the parties to adhere to a principle of reciprocity. In trying to gain transparency regarding the development of capabilities for digital attacks, cooperative arrangements must strive to be as broadly inclusive as possible.

The need to deal with nonstate actors and individuals has also become an increasingly important part of the WMD regimes. Dealing with nonstate actors will prove crucial in securing the global information infrastructure given the difficulties in distinguishing between types of malicious activities and securing international prosecution of individuals and groups involved with disruptive computer network intrusions.[45]

These regimes provide useful examples of cooperative efforts to ensure security without expectations of complete compliance. The expectations, institutions, and mechanisms for verification and transparency must match the environment. In dealing with the environment for digital attacks, efforts to use national technical means and on-site inspections for creating any sort of confidence in verification will prove futile. International efforts would be better expended in creating dialogue, openness, and some degree of transparency among all parties involved with the development and security of the global information infrastructure. Past experience provides a useful basis for analyzing how parties involved with securing their information infrastructures may proceed in addressing potential cyberwarfare and cyber-terrorism threats created by a globally networked society.

Looking to the Future

In looking forward the United States and the international community as a whole must consider what paths to pursue in securing cyberspace. Not all paths will lead to useful destinations. Many could prove to be dead ends and exacerbate tensions between actors in the international community.

What Should Be Reinforced?

Limiting the ability of nonstate actors to use disruptive digital attacks to conduct cybercrime and cyberterrorism already has widespread support.

Improving harmonization across legal regimes within states to make clear the criminal nature of these activities and establish stiff penalties should be encouraged. Elimination of digital safe havens and cooperative international enforcement of cybercrime laws to rapidly identify and pursue those committing malicious attacks at the level of cyberterrorism are essential. The efforts of the COE have momentum. The Stanford proposal has a scope that is probably more acceptable to many states, but it lacks a sponsoring forum and the long-term consensus-building efforts that underpin COE's progress. The United States needs to lead efforts to reach an international agreement that helps combat nonstate actors using digital attacks.

What's Missing and Possible?

Although efforts to combat cybercrime and terrorism have started, no serious dialogue on securing the global information infrastructure as a whole has yet to seriously begin. Given the advantages held by digital attackers and the porous nature of cyberdefenses, international cooperation to strengthen information infrastructures may be the most useful path to pursue.

The dialogue on shoring up foundations and defenses needs to be inclusive. Appropriate players include the representatives of states (to include diplomats, arms control experts, regulators, and military and law enforcement officers), information-technology corporations and their industry associations, intergovernmental organizations (especially the International Telecommunications Union and the International Standards Organization), cyberlibertarians and privacy advocacy groups, and members of technology forums that shape standards for the global information infrastructure (such as the Internet Engineering Task Force and the World Wide Web Consortium).

Why is such a broad set of players necessary? All are influential stakeholders in establishing and modifying the global information infrastructure that requires improved protection. The commercial sector dominates the creation of information technologies, the development of physical pathways that allow digital communications to occur, and the establishment of standards that enable communication between devices. In reaching agreements involving significant sacrifices by private-sector stakeholders, nongovernmental players must be involved from the start.

Bringing such a large and diverse group of players together should build on existing forums that already contribute to global efforts to protect the information infrastructure. Much information exchange already occurs between private, academic, and government CERT/CIRTs to quickly identify security vulnerabilities, exchange information on disruptive and malicious activity, and cooperatively develop and implement technological fixes.[46] The Forum of International Response Teams sponsors awareness events. Information security forums and associations such as the Systems Administration,

Networking, and Security Institute have international reach in establishing and exchanging best practices on information security policies and to provide education and training. Efforts within the United States to establish public/private–sector cooperation under the presidentially directed critical infrastructure protection rubric include information-sharing, analysis centers, and the Federal Bureau of Investigation Infraguard program. The United Kingdom, Germany, Japan, and South Korea are also establishing efforts along these lines, often with U.S. assistance. Interpol is working to improve international law enforcement cooperation in pursuing cybercriminals.[47] Technology firms such as Microsoft and Cisco have become more actively engaged in government-sponsored security forums. Privacy groups have also begun to sit across the table from government representatives to wrestle with the relative importance of the interests involved.[48]

Expectations for reaching any type of consensus on how to combat cyberterrorism and limit security risks posed by the threat of cyberwar must remain modest over the short term. Governments as well as corporations will worry that information shared may move beyond the control of those involved in a productive dialogue to potential adversaries who would use it to exploit vulnerabilities. Corporations willing to cooperate on cybersecurity issues may seek quid pro quos from the government in other areas such as intellectual property protection and antitrust enforcement. The equities of law enforcement and intelligence communities will continue to clash with those concerned with protecting confidentiality and personal privacy over issues such as encryption technology and its control. The immediate goal must be to influence the decisions of the stakeholders involved by creating increased awareness and hoping for indirect effects in policy, legal, and technology forums.

Over time, this developing dialogue should enable governments and others concerned with global cybersecurity to build a more defensible information infrastructure. A key objective should be to shape the evolving technological foundations of cyberspace via forums such as the Internet Engineering Task Force.

Another major step forward would be to pursue an international agreement focused on combating large-scale cyberterrorism under the auspices of the United Nations. The United Nations could add protection of the global information infrastructure to the agenda of the Conference on Disarmament. Within that forum, an ad hoc committee could be set up to consider measures to foster a global agreement to combat digital attacks against information infrastructures. This step would implement the intent of UN Resolution 53/70 by providing a specific venue in which to discuss draft proposals for a treaty. The initial sessions would have to focus on definitions, the scope of an agreement, and its relationship to other efforts such as the draft COE convention.

The issuance of a no-first-use pledge by the United States and other nations has potentially great significance in creating an environment for productive discussions on global cybersecurity. Such a pledge might involve promising to refrain from large-scale digital attacks on information infrastructures while retaining the right to develop such capabilities as a deterrent and warfighting capability to respond in kind. Again, definitional issues would come to the fore in specifying exactly what would be off-limits. Another unilateral move might involve the United States explicitly adding cyberwar to its counterproliferation efforts. Such an effort would plausibly include efforts to limit the spread of digital attack means as well as a focus on defending and protecting U.S. forces and the U.S. homeland. Either move would be extremely controversial, but the costs and benefits of such initiatives should receive serious consideration.

What Should Be Delayed for Now?

Seeking agreements that prohibit the conduct of cyberwar or place specific limits on the development of cyberweapons does not seem likely to make useful progress and may even be counterproductive. The nature of digital weapons and the inability to discern their presence and point of release would make any agreement largely unenforceable. Concepts for agreements that prohibited the use of certain types of weapons that cause widespread disruption have surfaced.[49] The cybersecurity dialogue could include efforts to identify types of weapons with abhorrent effects in cyberspace, similar to previous bans on poison weapons and dum-dum bullets in the Hague convention.

However, as in the early twentieth century, efforts to limit specific weapons today will be undermined by the pace of technological change. The systems and networks that make up advanced information infrastructures, as well as the digital tools and techniques that disrupt them, change at an astonishing rate. Information-technology developers talk in terms of three-month "web years" and six-month "product cycles." Although portions of the infrastructures have a longer life, key components will continue to evolve quickly. The ability to launch malicious code from a hand-held wireless device into networks that currently have few mechanisms for identifying malicious activity illustrates the challenges of reaching broad agreement on what constitutes a technology tool or technique that might be controlled or banned. Commercial information-technology firms have made clear that government intervention could have negative impacts by limiting research and impeding the establishment of global markets for their products. Military and intelligence organizations are likely to be extremely leery of engaging in any specific discussions, let alone agreeing to cooperative measures on accounting for and inspecting digital weapons. Such discussions and measures might provide potential adversaries with insight into future capabilities and plans, destroying their value.

What Might Change the Landscape?

Changes in priority and expectations for reaching agreements could emerge from dramatic and catastrophic events resulting from a digital attack. A demonstrated ability to shut down trading on a major stock exchange for a prolonged period, or to cause airliner crashes by disrupting air traffic control systems, might engender a rapid groundswell of interest in global cooperation and agreements that help thwart such activity. State and nonstate actors may feel public pressure to agree to constrain the development of malicious software code and to improve the ability of the international community to identify and punish those whose digital attacks cause death and destruction. Even without precipitating events, the increasing success of NGOs in shaping the agenda for global cooperation (as was demonstrated in the development of the ban on landmines) may become a force for reaching agreements in this realm.

Finally, change in cyberspace itself could make certain types of agreements and controls more plausible. The pace of change may decline as technologies mature and economic activity slows. Governments, companies, and technologists could consciously and unconsciously make choices that increase transparency by implementing new standards for connecting and communicating in the digital realm. Finding out who commits malicious acts and how to undertake an appropriate response may become more feasible, increasing the importance and scope of international cooperation and agreements.

Conclusion

Governments have much to think about as they decide how to use international cooperation as a means for achieving security in cyberspace. The United States faces general as well as specific challenges in this regard. Within its own jurisdiction, domestic policy and legal concerns will be prominent. The advocates of privacy and private control of cyberspace will want to foster a more secure environment—but through decentralized implementation measures such as the use of public key encryption that makes cyberspace more opaque. The obligations of corporations to develop and implement technologies and infrastructures that impact national and global security have yet to be defined, and private firms will resist government mandates. Legal concerns over the role of military, intelligence, and law enforcement organizations must also be addressed.[50]

The United States leads the globe in the development and use of information technology, in the conceptualization of information operations as a new realm for conflict, and in the vulnerability of its economy and society to digital attack. The choice to use negotiations to improve security must be based on a deeper analysis of the trade-offs involved. The United States should foster the dialogue and explore opportunities for global cooperation. An effort to seek unilateral control and dominance in cyberspace may prove counterproductive and probably cannot be achieved.

The rise of cyberwar and cyberterrorism epitomizes many of the new concerns and challenges facing efforts to enhance cooperative international security at the start of the twenty-first century. In this new realm, forums for discussion have formed, negotiations have been instituted, and possible agreements are being formulated. Progress is likely to be slow. Today, however, improving our understanding of risks and opportunities seems most important.

Notes

1. Definitions differ for these terms both within U.S. military doctrine and among other nations. Martin Libicki provides a very good description of the conceptual debates within the United States in *What Is Information Warfare?* (Washington, DC: National Defense University Press, 1995).

2. *Cyberspace* is a physical domain resulting from the creation of information systems and networks that enable digital interactions to take place. Gregory J. Rattray, *Strategic Warfare in Cyberspace* (Cambridge: MIT Press, 2001), p. 17.

3. An extensive history of the development of U.S. policy, doctrine, and capabilities for information warfare is provided in ibid., pp. 309–460.

4. Information on the National Infrastructure Protection Center mission, organization, and activities is available at its website, www.fbi.nipc.gov.

5. The Defending America's Cyberspace plan is available on the Critical Infrastructure Assurance Office website, www.ciao.gov.

6. The White House, *National Security Strategy of Engagement and Enlargement* (Washington DC: U.S. Government Printing Office, February 1996), p. 13.

7. Department of Defense, Office of Public Affairs, "Public Affairs Guidance—Computer Network Attack," (Washington, DC: Office of the Secretary of Defense, 1 November 2000), p. 1.

8. As cited in Timothy Thomas, "The Death of Nuclear Deterrence," Foreign Military Studies Office, Fort Leavenworth, KS, October 2000, p. 17.

9. Wei Jincheng, "New Form of People's Warfare," *Jiefangjun Bao*, 11 June 1996, reprinted in Michael Pillsbury, ed., *Chinese Views of Future Warfare* (Washington, DC: National Defense University Press, 1997).

10. Dorothy Denning, "Activism, Hacktivism, and Cyberterrorism: The Internet as a Tool for Influencing Foreign Policy," *Computer Security Journal* 16, no. 3 (2000): 28.

11. See the article at *The Hacktivist* website, www.thehacktivist.com/zine/vol/html (accessed 7 July 2001).

12. Timothy Thomas, "Like Adding Wings to a Tiger: Chinese Information Warfare Theory and Practice," Foreign Military Studies Office, Fort Leavenworth, KS, August 2000, pp. 16–17.

13. See "U.S.-China Hacker War Looms," www.zdnet.com/zdnn/stories/news (accessed 7 July 2001).

14. Quoted in Michael Evans, "War Planners Warn of Digital Armageddon," *London Times*, 20 November 1999.

15. Letter from I. Ivanov to United Nations Secretary-General with attachment "The Russian Federation: Draft Resolution, Achievements in the Sphere of Information and Telecommunication in the Context of International Security," 1 October 1998.

16. A very good up-to-date reference of commonly known hacker tools and techniques and protective measures is provided by John Chrillo, *Hack Attacks Revealed* (New York: John Wiley and Sons, 2001).

17. On overview of international law and agreements relevant to cyberespionage is provided in Thomas C. Wingfield, *The Law of Information Conflict* (Falls Church, VA: Aegis Research, 2000), pp. 350–357.

18. Denning uses the same distinction in "Activism, Hacktivism, and Cyberterrorism," pp. 33–34.

19. Extensive analysis of these issues is provided by Richard W. Aldrich, *The International Legal Implications of Information Warfare,* INSS Occasional Paper No. 9 (Colorado Springs, CO: USAF Institute for National Security Studies, April 1996); and Wingfield, *The Law of Information Conflict,* especially chap. 9, "Effect of Hostilities on the Peacetime Regime of Sea, Air, Space, and Foreign Domestic Law," pp. 305–348.

20. See Department of Defense, Office of General Counsel, "Assessment of International Legal Issues in Information Operations," (Washington, DC: Office of Secretary of Defense, May 1999); and Gregory D. Grove, Seymour E. Goodman, and Stephan J. Lukasik, "Cyber-Attacks and International Law," *Survival* (Autumn 2000): 89–100.

21. For example, the National Infrastructure Protection Center website lists more than 40 statutes, regulations, and other binding directives that govern activity in cyberspace within U.S. borders. The scope of what should be defined as *computer crime* has also become a topic of discussion. Should definitions focus on the act committed, or does any criminal act involving a computer constitute a computer crime? See Richard W. Aldrich, *Cyberterrorism and Computer Crimes: Issues Surrounding the Establishment of an International Regime,* INSS Occasional Paper No. 32 (Colorado Springs, CO: USAF Institute for National Security Studies, April 2000), pp. 8–10.

22. Aldrich, *Cyberterrorism and Computer Crimes,* p. 10.

23. Organization for Economic Cooperation and Development, "Computer-Related Crime: Analysis of Legal Policy," no. 25 (1986).

24. See the Council of Europe's website on its conventions for the full text of the treaty and the accompanying COE report, www.conventions.coe.int.

25. Aldrich, *Cyberterrorism and Computer Crimes,* pp. 52–53.

26. Abraham D. Sofaer and Seymour E. Goodman, *A Proposal for an International Convention on Cyber Crime and Terrorism* (Stanford: Center for International Security and Cooperation, Stanford University, August 2000).

27. This proposal received significant attention at the national conference titled "Protecting Cyberspace: The International Dimension," cosponsored by the Center for International Security and Policy, Stanford University, and the Georgia Tech

Information Security Center, attended by the author in Washington, DC, 1 May 2001.

28. United Nations, *UN Disarmament Yearbook 1994,* vol. 19 (New York: United Nations Press, 1995), pp. 183–184.

29. Timothy L. Thomas, "Russian Views on Information-Based Warfare" *Airpower Journal* (Special Edition 1996), pp. 25–35.

30. "United Nations, Developments in the Field of Information and Telecommunications in the Context of Information Security," Resolution 53/70 (New York: UN, January 1999).

31. See, for example, Workshop Proceedings, "Cyberwarfare: What Role for Arms Control and International Negotiations," sponsored by the Air Force Deputy Chief of Staff for Operations and the Chemical and Biological Arms Control Institute, 20 March 2000.

32. See Department of Defense, Office of General Counsel, "Assessment of International Legal Issues in Information Operations," and Department of Defense, Office of Public Affairs, "Public Affairs Guidance—Computer Network Attack."

33. See Sidney N. Graybeal and Patrica A. McFate, "Strategic Defensive Arms Control" in Jeffrey A. Larsen and Gregory J. Rattray, eds., *Arms Control Toward the 21st Century* (Boulder: Lynne Rienner Publishers, 1996), pp. 128–129.

34. Stephen Rose, "Hard Choices About Chemical Weapons," in Thomas C. Gill, ed., *Essays on Strategy VII* (Washington, DC: National Defense University Press, 1990), pp. 3–5.

35. Marie I. Chevrier and Amy E. Smithson, "Preventing the Spread of Arms: Chemical and Biological Weapons," in Larsen and Rattray, eds., *Arms Control Toward the 21st Century,* p. 207.

36. For example, "Cyberwarfare: What Role for Arms Control and International Negotiations," supra, p. 16, suggests considering limitations on viruses based on their infection rates, as well as limits on network scanning systems based on the speed and comprehensiveness of their operating features.

37. The international diffusion of genetic engineering and other biotechnologies have made even strong proponents of a verification regime for the BWC shy away from the idea of lists of prohibited materials. See Johnathan B. Tucker, "Strengthening the Biological Weapons Convention," *Arms Control Today* (April 1995): 12.

38. Chevrier and Smithson, "Preventing the Spread of Arms," p. 202.

39. Guy B. Roberts, *Five Minutes Past Midnight: The Clear and Present Danger of Nuclear Weapons Grade Fissile Materials,* INSS Occasional Paper No. 8 (Colorado Springs, CO: USAF Institute of National Security Studies, February 1996), p. 51.

40. Michael Moodie, "Ratifying the Chemical Weapons Convention: Past Time for Action," *Arms Control Today* (February 1996): 4.

41. Rattray, *Strategic Warfare in Cyberspace,* provides an in-depth analysis of the role of the private sector in the establishment and operation of information infrastructures in chap. 1, pp. 31–46.

42. See the website of the Center for Democracy and Technology at www.cdt.org/international/cybercrime for examples of the type of comments offered by such groups.

43. Roberts, *Five Minutes Past Midnight,* pp. 11–12.

44. Moodie, "Ratifying the Chemical Weapons Convention," p. 5.

45. Cases that exemplify the difficulties of the international prosecution of computer intruders include tracking down West German hackers in the 1980s, described

in Clifford Stoll, *The Cuckoo's Egg* (New York: Simon and Schuster, 1989); the 1991 intrusion of Dutch hackers into U.S. Defense Department systems is documented in U.S. General Accounting Office, *Computer Security: Hackers Penetrate DOD Computer Systems*, GAO/T-IMTEC-92-5 (Washington, DC: U.S. General Accounting Office, 20 November 1991); and the 1994 case of a British hacker breaking into the U.S. Air Force's Rome labs is documented in *Information Security: Computer Attacks at Department of Defense Pose Increasing Risks*, GAO/AMID-96-84 (Washington, DC: U.S. General Accounting Office, May 1996).

46. For prime examples of the types of information exchanges and services provided by CERT/CIRT teams, see the websites of the National Computer Emergency Response Team at the Software Engineering Institute, Carnegie-Mellon University, www.sei.org, and the Forum of International Response Teams, www.first.org.

47. My assessment is based on the presentation by Mark Goodman, an Interpol official, at the "Protecting Cyberspace: The International Dimension" conference.

48. These groups were prominently represented at the "Protecting Cyberspace: The International Dimension" conference and the "The Challenges of Cyberwar for American Foreign Policy" panel at Harvard University's 2001 Colloquium on International Affairs.

49. "Cyberwarfare: What Role for Arms Control and International Negotiations," p. 16.

50. Excellent studies on these issues are Gregory D. Grove, *The U.S. Military and Civil Infrastructure Protection: Restrictions and Discretion Under the Posse Comitatus Act* (Stanford: Center for International Security and Cooperation, Stanford University, November 1999); and Ekaterina A. Drozdova, *Civil Liberties and Security in Cyberspace* (Stanford: Center for International Security and Cooperation, Stanford University, August 2000).

Suggested Readings

Aldrich, Richard W. *Cyberterrorism and Computer Crimes: Issues Surrounding the Establishment of an International Regime.* INSS Occasional Paper No. 32. Colorado Springs, CO: USAF Institute for National Security Studies, April 2000.

Denning, Dorothy E. *Information Warfare and Security.* Reading, MA: Addison-Wesley, 1999.

Landau, Susan, and Whitfield Diffie. *Privacy on the Line: The Politics of Wire Tapping and Encryption.* Cambridge: MIT Press, 1998.

Office of the White House. *Defending America's Cyberspace: Version 1.0.* Available on the Critical Infrastructure Assurance Office website, www.ciao.gov.

Rattray, Gregory J. *Strategic Warfare in Cyberspace.* Cambridge: MIT Press, 2001.

Sofaer, Abraham D., and Seymour E. Goodman. *A Proposal for an International Convention on Cyber Crime and Terrorism.* Stanford: Center for International Security and Cooperation, Stanford University, August 2000.

Wingfield, Thomas C. *The Law of Information Conflict.* Falls Church, VA: Aegis Research, 2000.

19

Arms Control in the Year 2025

John A. Nagl

The 1969 song "In the Year 2525 (Exordium & Terminus)" painted a picture of a bleak future in which technology changed human life for the worse until humankind ultimately destroyed life on Planet Earth.[1] At the beginning of the twenty-first century, the future looks much brighter than it did just a generation ago, largely because of the success of arms control during the Cold War. Changes in the international system and in the United States itself will necessitate a very different understanding of national security for the next quarter-century, and arms control—one of the key instruments of national security policy—also will be very different. In this chapter I examine some of the forces of change driving us toward the globalized world of 2025 and conclude with a vision of how arms control may increase peace and security as we move toward that future.

A World of Tiers

Arms control is only one element of a comprehensive national security policy. Arms control policy, like any other aspect of national security policy, does not function in isolation from the state of international relations extant at the time that it is implemented or enforced. In order to predict how arms control might serve to increase the security of the United States and the world in 2025, it is first essential to think about what the world will look like at that time. The global balance of power, the number of great powers in the world, and the state of relations among and between them will all play a significant role in how effective arms control will be in helping create a more stable and peaceful future. I therefore attempt to extrapolate from today's world to that of 2025, including the likely threats in that world and the ability of arms control to assist in the effort to ensure that humans are still alive in the year 2025.

First, we must understand the world of today. Many analysts believe there is but one superpower in the wake of the collapse of the Soviet Union, forming a unipolar world.[2] According to this argument, the United States has shaped much of the world in its own image through its economic hegemony and regime formation, helping to create what can be called the *first tier* of economically advanced liberal democracies.[3] Other authors refer to this same group of states as a *Zone of Peace* within which war is essentially inconceivable.[4]

It is difficult to overstate the importance of this development. For the first time in history, the great powers of the international order have essentially renounced the use of force against one another. Much of this change is based on the shared economic systems of the industrialized democracies. Francis Fukayama has described the triumph of liberal capitalist democracy as "the end of history," arguing that this system has proven so successful that there is simply no imaginable alternative to it.[5]

However, the first tier comprises only about one-seventh of the world's population. The rest of the globe—ruled by governments that are either not fully democratic, do not have industrialized capitalist economies, or both— does not enjoy the same freedom from concerns about warfare among states or inside their own borders. Instead traditional balance-of-power politics, mercantilism, and instrumental nationalism continue all too often to make life nasty, brutish, and short. The primary problem of international relations for the foreseeable future is how the states of the first tier will deal with those that languish in the second tier—a very different problem than that which drove the international system during the Cold War, a problem with huge implications for the future of arms control.

A Global World

The post–Cold War world can be described as a "globalizing" world.[6] *Globalization* is a pattern of relations among nations based on the free exchange of goods, ideas, and information that is dramatically affecting both the domestic and international behavior of states, because free markets generally produce free governments. The demands of competing in the global economy create compelling pressures for free transfers of information in the economic realm—and systems that transfer information on prices and economic demands also carry political demands. The trend toward democratization is also likely to continue. As one recent study has put it, "The resulting trend in the direction of democracy is undeniable: from almost zero several hundred years ago, the percentage of countries in the world that could roughly be described as democratic may exceed 80 percent by the year 2005."[7]

One primary driver of globalization is information technology. Alvin Toffler argues that the third great revolution of human existence is information technology and that it will transform human life as dramatically as did the invention of agriculture and the Industrial Revolution.[8] We are at a very early stage of the information revolution, and its impact on our lives during the coming decades can barely be imagined, but it is already opening up the world in many dramatic ways.

The United States is uniquely positioned to take advantage of the information revolution. For a number of reasons, ranging from labor mobility to tax structures to immigration policies, the United States is well out in front of the race for superiority in the information revolution—and its lead is increasing. The United States will set global standards for information technology, global taxation policies, financial accounting rules, and transparency in financial transactions. This so-called soft power will immensely broaden both the reach and the grasp of the United States in the world.[9] Michael Mazaar notes the effect of a world that increasingly follows the same economic rules: "It makes war less likely."[10]

The National Intelligence Council agrees. In December 2000 it released *Global Trends 2015: A Dialogue About the Future with Nongovernmental Experts.*[11] The report suggests that for at least the next 15 years "the risk of war among developed countries will be low." However, the developing world will see substantial conflict, ranging from "relatively frequent small-scale internal upheavals to less frequent regional interstate wars. . . . Internal conflicts stemming from religious, ethnic, economic or political disputes will remain at current levels or even increase."[12] Because of overwhelming U.S. military superiority over the developing world, most future adversaries "will try to circumvent or minimize U.S. strengths and exploit perceived weaknesses. . . . Such asymmetric approaches—whether undertaken by states or nonstate actors—will become the dominant characteristic of most threats to the U.S. homeland."[13]

The era of globalization has complicated the national security equation immensely. During the Cold War the focus of international relations was on the interactions between states—especially the military relations between the two superpowers—but today more actors play a role in the globalized system and must be considered in the formulations of security policy and arms control. In terms of interstate relations, the United States holds the greatest power differential since the Roman Empire—and that lead will increase in the next few decades.[14] The United States will continue to use its nuclear and conventional arsenal to deter attacks on its homeland and allies, and it will rely upon diplomacy and arms control to retain good relations and diminish threats internationally. But unlike recent U.S. history, interstate threats will not be the primary concern of U.S. policy.

Instead the focus will be on the second and third systemic "balances" of globalization.[15] The second balance, between nation-states and global markets, is also dominated by the United States, and this will be an increasingly effective arena of U.S. foreign policy. Instead of threatening to use nuclear or conventional forces to get other states to accede to U.S. wishes, carrots such as assistance from the International Monetary Fund will be used to convince other states to act in ways which will advance their interests as well as those of the United States.

The third balance of the globalized world is the one between nation-states and individuals and transnational actors. The very globalization of the system—its increasing interconnectedness—is a huge source of vulnerability. Individuals and small groups will increasingly be able to access the technology and information that holds the key to the entire system. Those with the desire to do so may attempt to turn that key and bring it all crashing down.

The Two-Tiered World of 2025

It appears likely that the division of the world into two tiers—one composed of democratic, industrialized countries with free markets, the other composed of countries that are neither liberal democracies nor industrialized capitalist states—will continue to describe the world of 2025.[16] If current trends continue, the first tier will be larger, with the current G7 states joined by South Korea (or a unified Korea), Australia, Brazil, South Africa, Argentina, Taiwan, and conceivably several others. The second tier will bifurcate, with a number of states attempting to climb into the first tier through the development of democratic governments and free-market economies, with others sinking farther behind.[17]

The global marketplace will both create and enforce regimes, not only governing international trade but also rules of economic governmental transparency. This development will be largely in the U.S. interest and will promote a more widespread acceptance of Western norms.[18]

Governments will increasingly rely upon the support of their citizens to govern. Those that do not may face riots in the streets or terrorist attacks, as empowered individuals who do not perceive their government as legitimate decide to take action against it. Already, terrorist assaults against the United States have been committed by those who felt that the United States was attacking their national identity, destroying the environment, or treating its own citizens unfairly. These attacks from without and within are likely to continue. Because of the proliferation of technology, these attackers may also have the ability to accomplish their desires to bring down the system that is providing health and wealth to an ever-increasing number of their peers around the world. They will present the most serious national security challenge to the United States in the year 2025, as many would argue they do today.[19]

The diminished incidence of war among states in the first tier, the increasing number of liberal democracies in the world, and the fact that the United States already maintains a substantial national security apparatus to deter and, if necessary, defeat state threats mean that substate threats will become relatively more important. The rising tide will not lift all boats. Those who do not want to join the globalized world, or who are unable to do so, will almost invariably blame the United States as the point of origin of much of the structure and content of the new world order. Those who are left behind will have a real desire to damage or destroy the system.[20] In the words of David Kay, "The United States has overwhelming power in the world and we're going to remain overwhelming. There is a body of resentment that is going to increase because of who we are. That resentment is a reservoir and breeding ground for terrorist organizations."[21]

Those organizations may use weapons of mass destruction (WMD) to further their goals. The high-level Deutch Commission, formed by the U.S. government to assess its ability to respond to the proliferation of WMD, stated in 1999 that WMD "pose a grave threat to the United States and to our military forces and our vital interests abroad." The most serious threats are:

- Terrorist use of weapons of mass destruction against the United States or its allies;
- Possession of, and the manufacturing infrastructure for, [WMD] by Iran, Iraq, North Korea, or other unfriendly states;
- Diversion of WMD-related weapons, technology, materials, and expertise from Russia;
- Transfer of nuclear, chemical, and biological weapons, delivery means, and technology by China; and
- Destabilizing consequences of WMD programs in the Middle East, South Asia, and East Asia.[22]

The globalized world makes this an even greater concern, as interconnected economies are more vulnerable to threats that begin in one area but quickly spread across continents. According to one study, "This increased vulnerability magnifies the power of nonstate actors, making cooperation among the core countries against potential threats more desirable than ever."[23]

One of the key threats will come from the nuclear, biological, and chemical weapons left over from the Cold War, particularly those in the uncertain hands of the Russian military. Lax Russian control over its weapons and the resulting fear of accidents and proliferation to third parties alarm many observers.[24] As one scholar notes, "The Cold War is over, but the triple threat of chemical, biological, and nuclear proliferation will be with us for a long time to come."[25] Another made the point even more starkly:

"The danger of weapons of mass destruction being used against America and its allies is greater now than at any time since the Cuban missile crisis of 1962."[26]

In addition to the threat of terrorist use of WMD, we must also be aware of terrorist attacks upon our information infrastructure, including offensive use of computers—so-called cyberwar. A recent RAND study noted that "unlike traditional weapons technologies, development of information-based techniques does not require sizable financial resources or state sponsorship. Information systems expertise and access to important networks may be the only prerequisites."[27]

Arms Control to 2025

The emerging international environment poses the increased danger that nonstate and substate actors may use new technologies to strike an increasingly vulnerable West.

The Expanding Threat

Table 19.1 summarizes the WMD threat for the foreseeable future and illustrates the difficulties of monitoring and controlling limits on testing, development, deployment, and employment of these weapons. Note that even though it is comparatively simple to control nuclear weapons, the problem

Table 19.1 WMD and Prospects for Arms Control in a Globalized World

	Nuclear	Chemical	Biological	Cyberspace
Number of participants	P5+3+?	100s	100s	10,000+?
Research and development limits	ABM Treaty, CTBT	No testing	Testing limits	None
Production/storage	Declarations, limits	Ban	Ban	None
Deployment	Launcher limits	None	None	None
Testing	Warhead limits	Ban	Ban	None
Use	Legal	1993 ban	1972 ban	Criminal law
Barriers to entry	High	Moderate	Low	Very low
Offense	Dominant	Limited	Dominant	Dynamic
Defense	Very difficult	Dominant	Difficult	Dynamic
Verification	Relatively easy	Difficult	More difficult	Very difficult
Dual purpose	Low	High	High	Very high
Role of nonstate actors	Low	Moderate	High	Very high

becomes exponentially more difficult with chemical, biological, and information weapons as the number of potential actors increases and the weapons and their production facilities become increasingly less tangible. It is well worth exploring the potential of arms control to limit these dangers—but it is also important to keep in mind the difficulties associated with controlling the more elusive weapons in a globalized world.

Arms control improved U.S. national security during the Cold War largely because of the bipolar nature of the international system. The threat was clear and relatively easy to monitor, and the two countries that really mattered in terms of international security recognized that each had a great deal to gain if arms control worked. Both also understood that they had much to lose if arms control failed. None of these facts remain true today. And in a globalized world of 2025 the number of threats and their variety, as well as the more difficult tasks involved in tracking more complicated WMD systems, will mean that arms control as it has traditionally been understood will be much less useful.

Broadening the definition of *arms control* could increase the relevance of the concept. Originally it was intended to include "all the forms of military cooperation between potential enemies in the interest of reducing the likelihood of war, its scope and violence if it occurs, and the political and economic costs of being prepared for it."[28] The definition became more constrained in practice during the Cold War to include only negotiated treaties between adversaries. Today it must be defined more broadly. Arms control in 2025 will have to focus more on confidence-building measures, cooperative threat reduction, nonproliferation, export controls, and conventional weapons, in addition to continuing its more traditional role in the strategic control of WMD.

In a world of tiers, security policy and arms control will have to be tailored to each of the tiers in the new world order. States within the first tier of liberal democracies—and, in the case of chemical and biological weapons, multinational companies within them—can be expected to set and enforce regimes that limit the proliferation and use of such weapons.[29] These states will also attempt to bring second-tier states into the first tier. Those second-tier states that refuse to adhere to arms control regimes must be deterred from using their weapons through more effective nonproliferation regimes as well as the old standby of deterrence. Although cheating is always a risk, the increasing marginalization of rogue states that fail to follow norms, and the guarantee of swift and severe punishment for violations, will make it increasingly less attractive for state actors to ignore the rules.

The real concerns, then, are nonstate actors. Their actions are impossible to control through either negotiations or deterrence as it has conventionally been known. Current efforts at arms control and threat reduction must be aimed more explicitly at tightening control over WMD and WMD technology to prevent their acquisition by substate actors, and states must be held accountable for terrorist actions committed with WMD acquired through their negligence.

Table 19.2 summarizes suggested uses of arms control, nonproliferation, and criminalization to enhance U.S. national security. It notes that nonproliferation is likely to be most successful in the case of nuclear weapons, as their production requires a substantial industrial base. In the case of chemical and biological weapons, however, production is much easier. Controlling those weapons will require not only governmental action but also help from multinational corporations that legally produce and distribute chemicals and biological organisms. They must work to ensure that the raw materials for weapons do not fall into the wrong hands. And in the case of information operations—because almost any computer can become a weapon of mass disruption—it makes more sense to proscribe the improper use of computers as weapons than it does to try to limit access to them.

Changes in Arms Control

In addition to this process of broadening regarding the nature and scope of arms control—a process that will continue for decades—it is possible to discern several other trends in the changing role of arms control.[30] These include a greater focus on morality and the role of moral example in furthering arms control; continued success in nuclear arms reductions; a shift in focus from deployed systems to control of the underlying technology, with a corresponding increase in the collaborative role of commercial enterprises in arms control efforts; growing difficulty confirming compliance with arms control regimes; a change in the enforcement mechanisms for arms control agreements; and increasing attention to regional rather than global arms control regimes.

Table 19.2 Approaches to Improving Security in a World with Weapons of Mass Destruction

	Nuclear	Chemical	Biological	Cyberspace
First tier	Arms control/ nonproliferation	Arms control/ nonproliferation (NGO help)	Arms control/ nonproliferation (NGO help)	Arms control/ criminal
Second tier	Nonproliferation/ deterrence	Nonproliferation/ deterrence	Nonproliferation/ deterrence	Criminal
Nonstate Actors	Nonproliferation/ criminal	Nonproliferation/ criminal	Nonproliferation/ criminal	Criminal

The role of moral example in furthering arms control. Unless the world's most powerful nations make real efforts at disarmament, they will be unable to convince the rest of the world to accede to their demands for stricter nonproliferation regimes. As generational change in political leadership occurs and the era of long peace continues, Western leaders may become more willing to make substantial reductions in their deployed arsenals. The increased role of nongovernmental organizations (NGOs) in supporting arms control regimes will lead to much more public attention on lower-level issues and to greater pressure on governments to respond to humanitarian and environmental concerns. Note, for example, the role of NGOs in creating and promoting the Ottawa Convention to ban antipersonnel landmines.[31]

Continued success in nuclear arms reductions. Reduction of nuclear arms was the most successful arena for arms control during the Cold War. Yet partly because of the relative difficulty of producing nuclear weapons and the relative ease of tracking them, there has been less interest in working to move agreements beyond START I and START II. Although START II remains in abeyance for the present time, some observers talk of bypassing it to move directly to START III. Once the number of warheads possessed by the United States and Russia has declined below approximately 1,000 each, it will be necessary to multilateralize negotiations, bringing in China, Britain, and France. Although this will complicate the process, it is not unreasonable to suppose that arms control in the nuclear arena could make further progress by 2025, leading to a verifiable level of perhaps 2,000 warheads in existence worldwide. Observers and other intrusive verification means could be designed not only to ensure that no state cheated on its numbers but also to reduce the chances of false alarms. This would represent a dramatic improvement in U.S. national security from the present day.[32]

Shift in focus from deployed systems to control of underlying technologies. Arms control may become an increasingly collaborative effort between governments and private industry, particularly in the areas of chemical, biological, and information warfare. Unlike nuclear weapons, which require a substantial and relatively easy-to-monitor infrastructure to develop and deploy, the creation of chemical, biological, and information warfare weapons requires only readily available commercial technology. Export controls will be an increasingly unreliable means of limiting proliferation of this technology. Instead the U.S. government will have to rely upon the assistance of multinational companies to police themselves, to report unusual users of their technology, and perhaps even to investigate and punish those who use or attempt to use such weapons.

One conclusion of those who study post–Cold War globalization is that the essential precursor to ensuring economic growth in a country is the existence of the rule of law to establish and enforce contracts. Governments that provide and enforce this rule of law enable economic progress by their citizens, and companies rely upon them to do so. The partnership will become ever closer in the industrialized world by 2025. Governments will increasingly rely upon makers of chemicals, biological products, and computer networks to safeguard their own technology—something that all of us will depend upon in the years to come. Export controls will also have to be carefully monitored as technology improves at an ever-faster rate.

Growing difficulty in confirming compliance with arms control regimes. Largely a bilateral exercise during the Cold War, arms control will increasingly become a multilateral effort. It will be essential that first-tier countries cooperate in the twin efforts to deny WMD capabilities to rogue states and to preempt them from using such weapons against civilian and military targets. Intelligence-sharing will have a large role to play in this effort, as states increasingly find that their security depends upon the willingness of other states to compromise their sovereignty in return for collaborative assistance against nonstate threats.

Change in enforcement mechanisms for arms control agreements. In addition to convincing prospective enemies to demobilize their weapon systems so that they cannot threaten international peace and stability by firing them directly at their enemies, future agreements must also convince them to demobilize their weapons so that they do not trickle into the hands of rogue states, individuals, or substate groups that would then fire them at first-tier states. Achieving this goal will demand increasing reliance upon economic and political means of persuasion. The globalized world economy should make this enforcement mechanism more powerful over time. As communications become more effective and available, enhanced transparency will allow national and international pressure on states that flaunt international arms control regimes. For example, though it is obviously difficult to enforce regimes against individuals, in the field of biology it can be imagined that someone involved in the production of a biological weapon could be held criminally liable and subject to prosecution anywhere in the world—as is currently the case for pirates and skyjackers. As the locus of warfare shifts from states to individuals, so too will the locus of reprisals shift: from holding governments responsible under international law, to holding individuals responsible by national criminal law.

Increasing attention to regional arms control regimes. Arms control policy is a subset of national security policy. As we turn away from the strategic U.S.-Soviet conflict, and as we achieve success in limiting the proliferation of nuclear/chemical/biological weapons, the next frontier will be regional conflicts that increase pressures to proliferate conventional weapons.

This increased focus on regional arms control does not mean that multilateral efforts to control or even eliminate arms will diminish; indeed we have already noted the important and increasing role that NGOs have played in current arms control agreements, and there are grounds for optimism about stricter controls on nuclear weapons in the future. However, there are limits to what can be accomplished, and the success of both the Chemical Weapons Convention and the Biological Weapons Convention— not only in controlling but also legally eliminating those two classes of weapons—is a dramatic achievement. Further progress in chemical weapons arms control is difficult to envision. Because it will be impossible to completely prevent the proliferation of chemical weapons, it will be essential to improve defenses against their use, as several secretaries of defense have recently argued.[33]

It is far more challenging to hope for much in the realm of biological weapons. Scientific progress is too rapid, verification too difficult, the dual uses of technology too vast to provide much hope for either traditional arms control or nonproliferation techniques to have much effect. And if it is difficult to conceive of arms control regimes regarding biological weapons, it is even harder to think of effective limits on information technology. Limitations on research and development, production, and deployment of computer network attack tools would be all but unverifiable. Trying to impose limits on tools for computer network attack would be akin to banning personal computers and the Internet. In fact, the United States itself might resist controls, as it is the clear leader in this area and is likely to remain so. U.S. superiority will allow it to impose its will at low cost, and the country will be unwilling to surrender its advantage without hope of reciprocal gain. Instead it is likely that the United States will adopt measures to increase public-private cooperation for national defense of cyberspace.[34] Rather than making unenforceable and unverifiable arms control agreements with other states, the United States must develop stronger systems and make attacking them more dangerous, not least by relying upon existing international law that classifies attacks on another nation's computer networks as hostile or criminal acts.[35]

Conclusion

Thomas Schelling and Morton Halperin noted some 40 years ago that they did not believe "the problems of war and peace and international conflict are susceptible of any once-for-all solution. Something like eternal vigilance and determination would be required to keep peace in the world at any stage of disarmament, even total disarmament."[36] Arms control is but one of many tools in that long struggle, one that must be evaluated carefully. As a senior official in the George W. Bush administration recently put it, "You have to look at each case and you have to look *closely* at each case. Arms control is not an easy solution. There *are* no easy solutions."[37]

We are not likely to hammer swords into plowshares by 2525. We may, however, with vigilance, determination, and a little luck, manage to create a world in which the likelihood of war is diminished, its scope and violence are limited, and the costs of preparing for it are minimized. If we manage to do so, an effective use of both formal and informal cooperative agreements with allies and enemies will have played a major role in achieving that fortunate outcome.

Notes

The views expressed in this chapter are those of the author and do not reflect the official policy or position of the Department of the Army, Department of Defense, or the U.S. government. This chapter builds upon John A. Nagl, "Defending Against New Dangers: Arms Control of Weapons of Mass Destruction in a Globalized World," *World Affairs* (Spring 2000): 158–173, and a chapter with the same title in James M. Smith, ed., *Searching for National Security in an NBC World* (Colorado Springs, CO: USAF Institute for National Security Studies, 2000), pp. 55–94.

1. Zager and Evans, "In the Year 2525 (Exordium & Terminus)," available on Billboard Top Ten Hits (1969).

2. Kenneth Waltz, *Theory of International Politics* (New York: McGraw-Hill, 1979).

3. The concept of a world of tiers is drawn from Donald M. Snow, *The Shape of the Future: The Post–Cold War World* (New York: M. E. Sharpe, 1995).

4. Michael Doyle, "Liberalism and World Politics," *American Political Science Review* 80, no. 4 (1986).

5. Francis Fukayama, *The End of History and the Last Man* (New York: Free Press, 1992).

6. The single best source on globalization is Thomas Friedman, *The Lexus and the Olive Tree: Understanding Globalization* (New York: Farrar, Straus, Giroux, 1999).

7. Michael J. Mazarr, *Global Trends 2005: The Challenge of a New Millennium* (Washington, DC: Center for Strategic and International Studies, 1997), pp. 13–14.

8. Alvin Toffler, *Powershift: Knowledge, Wealth, and Violence at the Edge of the 21st Century* (New York: Bantam Books, 1991). See also Jared Diamond, *Guns, Germs, and Steel: The Fates of Human Societies* (New York: W. W. Norton, 1998).

9. Robert Keohane and Joseph Nye, *Power and Interdependence* (New York: Addison-Wesley, 1989).

10. Mazaar, *Global Trends 2005*, p. 14.

11. National Intelligence Council, "Global Trends 2015: A Dialogue About the Future with Nongovernmental Experts," www.cia.gov (Publications and Reports), December 2000, p. 7.

12. Ibid.

13. Ibid., p. 22.

14. Carla Anne Robbins, "To All but Americans, Kosovo War Appears a Major U.S. Victory," *Wall Street Journal*, 6 July 1999, pp. A1, A8.

15. Friedman, *The Lexus and the Olive Tree*, pp. 11–12.

16. National Defense University, *Strategic Assessment 1998: Engaging Power for Peace*, www.ndu.edu/inss/sa98/sa98ch1.html.

17. Ibid.

18. Ibid.

19. This argument was conceived prior to the attacks of 11 September 2001. For suggestions as to how the national security establishment should respond to the sort of threats predicted in this chapter, see John A. Nagl, "Hitting Us Where We Don't Expect It: Asymmetric Threats to U.S. National Security," *National Security Studies Quarterly,* Autumn 2001, pp. 113–121.

20. Mazaar, *Global Trends 2005*, pp. 32–33.

21. Presentation by David A. Kay, SAIC Center for Counterterrorism and Analysis, at the USAF Institute for National Security Studies conference entitled "Terrorism and U.S. National Security," National Defense University, 28 July 1999.

22. *Report of the Commission to Assess the Organization of the Federal Government to Combat the Proliferation of Weapons of Mass Destruction* (Deutch Commission), 14 July 1999, www.senate.gov/~specter.

23. National Defense University, *Strategic Assessment 1998.*

24. Leon Sloss, "The Current Nuclear Dialogue," *Strategic Forum,* no. 156 (Washington, DC: National Defense University Institute for National Strategic Studies, January 1999), p. 4. See also Rensselaer W. Lee III, *Smuggling Armageddon: The Nuclear Black Market in the Former Soviet Union* (New York: St. Martin's, 1998); and William J. Broad, "Finding Penance in Going Public About Making Germs into Bullets," *New York Times Week in Review*, 27 June 1999, p. 7.

25. Allan S. Krass, *The United States and Arms Control: The Challenge of Leadership* (Westport, CT: Greenwood, 1997), p. 205.

26. Ashton Carter, John Deutch, and Philip Zelikow, "Catastrophic Terrorism: Tackling the New Danger," *Foreign Affairs* (November/December 1998): 81.

27. Roger C. Molander, Andrew S. Riddle, and Peter A. Wilson, *Strategic Information Warfare: A New Face of War* (Washington, DC: RAND, 1996), p. 15, www.rand.org/publications/MR/MR661/MR661.pdf.

28. Thomas C. Schelling and Morton C. Halperin, *Strategy and Arms Control* (New York: Pergamon-Brassey's, 1985), p. 2.

29. Zachary D. Davis, "The Convergence of Arms Control and Nonproliferation: *Vive La Difference,*" *Nonproliferation Review* (Spring-Summer 1999): 98–108.

30. Some of these ideas were influenced by Jeffrey A. Larsen's concluding chapter, "The Evolving Nature of Arms Control in the Post–Cold War World," in Larsen and Gregory J. Rattray, eds., *Arms Control Toward the 21st Century* (Boulder: Lynne Rienner Publishers, 1996), pp. 285–292.

31. See the *Safelane* website at www.mines.gc.ca/english/index.html, in particular Canadian Foreign Minister Axworthy's speech on humanitarian security at Harvard University on 25 April 1998.

32. See Gwendolyn M. Hall, John T. Cappello, and Stephen P. Lambert, *A Post–Cold War Nuclear Strategy Model*, INSS Occasional Paper No. 20 (Colorado Springs, CO: USAF Institute for National Security Studies, July 1998).

33. See Department of Defense, *Annual Report to the President and Congress by the Department of Defense, Volume I: Domestic Preparedness Program in the Defense Against Weapons of Mass Destruction* (Washington, DC: U.S. Government Printing Office, 1 May 1997), www.defenselink.mil/pubs/domestic/.

34. Carter et al., "Catastrophic Terrorism," pp. 87–88.

35. Rattray, *Strategic Warfare in Cyberspace* (Boston: MIT Press, 2001).

36. Schelling and Halperin, *Strategy and Arms Control,* p. 5.

37. Author interview with Robert Joseph, National Defense University Center for Counterproliferation Research, 28 July 1999.

Suggested Readings

Commission to Assess the Organization of the Federal Government to Combat the Proliferation of Weapons of Mass Destruction (the Deutch Commission). *Report of the Commission to Assess the Organization of the Federal Government to Combat the Proliferation of Weapons of Mass Destruction.* www.senate.gov/ ˉspecter. 14 July 1999.

Friedman, Thomas. *The Lexus and the Olive Tree: Understanding Globalization.* New York: Farrar, Straus, Giroux, 1999.

Fukayama, Francis. *The End of History and the Last Man.* New York: Free Press, 1992.

National Intelligence Council. "Global Trends 2015: A Dialogue About the Future with Nongovernmental Experts." www.cia.gov (Publications and Reports). December 2000.

Schwartz, Peter, Peter Leyden, and Joel Hyatt. *The Long Boom: A Vision for the Coming Age of Prosperity.* Cambridge: Perseus, 1999.

Snow, Donald M. *The Shape of the Future: The Post–Cold War World.* New York: M. E. Sharpe, 1995.

Toffler, Alvin. *Powershift: Knowledge, Wealth, and Violence at the Edge of the 21st Century.* New York: Bantam Books, 1991.

20

Conclusion:
The Future of Arms Control

James J. Wirtz

Much has changed in the world since 1994, the year that many of the contributors to this volume began work on the earlier book, *Arms Control Toward the 21st Century*.[1] Although that edition highlighted the relevance of the arms control theories, policies, and treaties that had been central features of Cold War politics, the authors in this volume note that we are at a crossroads regarding arms control and the nascent efforts toward cooperative security. Hindsight makes it clear that political and bureaucratic support for an extensive arms control agenda had peaked by the mid-1990s. Indeed, our previous expectations for a bright future for traditional arms control were based on post–Cold War exuberance, faith in existing international agreements and institutions, and an unspoken assumption that continuity would be reflected in the future strategic setting. As we confront today's evolving strategic landscape, however, those Cold War institutions and agreements are beginning to show signs of wear and tear. More than a decade after the end of the Soviet Empire, the Cold War arms control regime appears to be threatened by a creeping bloc obsolescence.

What has happened to reduce the relevance of the existing arms control regime? From a realist's perspective, the end of the Cold War minimized the need for traditional arms control as the Russian Federation and the United States reduced and even eliminated major portions of their nuclear arsenals. Confidence-building measures and cooperative efforts to deal with decaying and potentially deadly remnants of Russia's nuclear, chemical, and biological arsenals remain important, but the pace of such programs is influenced more by the funding supplied by the U.S. Congress than by any fundamental international political disagreement over their importance. By contrast, strategic arms control agreements seemed to be providing a floor, not a ceiling, for weapon deployment, slowing reductions and adjustments in Russian and U.S. long-range nuclear forces. Critics even noted that arms control itself was a greater source of acrimony between Russians and U.S. citizens than the military arsenals it was intended to control. But even before the attacks of 11 September 2001, slowly improving U.S.-Russia relations had taken much of the urgency out of arms control negotiations. Arms control is not necessary to stop an arms race between states that lack the political will and, in one case, the financial resources needed to engage in an arms competition in the first place. Kerry Kartchner makes this very point in Chapter 16: some critical arms control solutions to Cold War security threats have actually outlived the problems that they were meant to solve.

The erosion of a clear bipolar structure to international relations also reduced the de facto international management once supplied by the superpowers. Unconstrained by either a superpower patron or antagonist, many states used a newfound freedom of maneuver to make their preferences known, undertake regional initiatives, settle old scores, and even gamble on aggression. No longer constrained by the Cold War, the interests, objectives, and disputes of many states and nonstate actors began to emerge on international agendas and to dominate headlines. These disputes, once considered to be so-called lesser included threats when compared to the cataclysmic nuclear war that might have been unleashed by the superpowers, are now perceived as major challenges to global security. Many of the U.S.-Soviet agreements reached during the Cold War were never intended to apply to these emerging actors and issues. Of course, multilateralism and multilateral agreements existed during the Cold War, but those treaties, which were backed by the superpowers, were supported by the order and general restraint produced by bipolarity. Today multilateral treaties as well are under increasing pressure. Universal norms against the development and deployment of chemical or biological weapons, for instance, are threatened not only by nonconforming states but also the legitimate security concerns of countries that want to comply with treaty obligations but see reduced benefit from arms control agreements that fail to constrain a growing number of international bad apples.

Technology also has created new challenges. In the 1960s only the United States and the Soviet Union could deploy intercontinental ballistic missiles; today many states have long-range ballistic missiles. Instead of fading into Cold War history, weapons of mass destruction remain on center stage, as state and nonstate actors have either acquired or are making efforts to acquire nuclear, radiological, chemical, and biological weapons. Space surveillance is no longer controlled by two superpowers, creating a mixed blessing for the arms control community. On the one hand, increased transparency supplied by satellite reconnaissance can be used to verify treaty compliance and support confidence-building measures. On the other hand, space surveillance, combined with the revolution in precision guidance and real-time intelligence, could create windows of opportunity and incentives for preventive war and preemption. The information revolution also empowers everyone who can gain access to a computer and the Internet.

Technology poses a triple challenge to the arms control community. Its spread equips new actors with weapons that were once owned only by the Soviet Union and the United States. It creates new types of weapons, especially by upgrading existing systems with advanced computer and guidance technology. And as Schuyler Foerster notes (see Chapter 3), technology is empowering not only small states but also all types of nonstate actors and groups. Additionally, technology is creating super-empowered individuals—people who become international actors in their own right.

Domestic and bureaucratic politics also have contributed to a gap between arms control and emerging security challenges. In the United States the political standoff between those who believe arms control is obsolete and those who believe that maintaining and expanding the international arms control regime is in the U.S. interest has been broken. The U.S. Senate's rejection of the Comprehensive Test Ban Treaty in October 1999, as well as the George W. Bush administration's July 2001 rejection of the verification protocol to the Biological Weapons Convention and its December 2001 decision to withdraw from the Anti-Ballistic Missile (ABM) Treaty, have placed arms control advocates on the defensive, a situation that is not conducive to the development of new initiatives. In terms of bureaucratic impediments to innovation, the United States and other parties to existing agreements maintain significant government organizations with the express purpose of implementing current treaties, but little is heard from the bureaucracy about new types of cooperative security measures. The bureaucratic machinery behind arms control is clearly intended to maintain the status quo and to implement existing treaties.

By the end of President Bill Clinton's administration, the changes unleashed in the post–Cold War period began to overwhelm the forces that had preserved continuity in the international arms control regime. These events came as a shock to many in the arms control community. The Bush administration's decision to withdraw from the ABM Treaty, for example, is a sign of these changing times. Officials in the Bush administration want new cooperative initiatives to replace nuclear deterrence as the foundation of the U.S.-Russian strategic relationship. Because the ABM Treaty was intended to preserve a situation of mutual assured destruction, Bush officials believed that the treaty locked Russia and the United States into an adversarial strategic relationship that no longer reflected improving relations and political opportunities. They also noted that the spread of nuclear, chemical, and biological weapons to a variety of states and nonstate actors has raised doubts about the efficacy of deterrence. The ABM Treaty prevented the United States from developing missile defenses to protect itself in the event that religious fanatics, millenarians, or desperate leaders managed to gain control of long-range ballistic missiles armed with nuclear, chemical, or biological warheads—a possibility that appeared highly salient in the aftermath of 11 September. An arms control regime designed to deal with the Cold War was viewed by the administration as an impediment in responding to the emerging security threats faced by the United States.[2]

Emerging Roles for Arms Control

In assessing the prospects for arms control, it is important to recognize that current trends are not likely to apply universally or to continue indefinitely into the future. It also is important to remember the limits of arms control. Arms control will not prevent conflict if one or both of the parties involved actually believes that violence will improve their position or will help them to achieve some grand objective. Arms control will not prevent war if people really want war. Arms control, for example, would not have prevented al-Qaida's attack on the World Trade Center because the terrorists turned civilian airliners, not a weapon or device subject to arms control, into a precision-guided fuel-air explosive. Arms control also is unlikely to be employed if states believe they can satisfy their security concerns unilaterally.

Today critics of arms control would assert that these limitations always have bedeviled international agreements and are just more apparent today, despite the optimistic expectations of arms control advocates. But as Thomas Schelling noted in an address to our contributors, it would be a mistake to conclude that arms control during the Cold War was misguided or that arms control and confidence-building measures will never again be relevant to future security problems. The end of the ABM Treaty does not mean that the agreement was a bad idea or that it failed to serve a useful purpose. It only means that the treaty no longer addresses today's strategic situation.[3] The problem that we face might not be the obsolescence of arms control but rather a reluctance on the part of the arms control community to abandon a status quo based on past success in order to address emerging challenges to international security. Admittedly these problems would have appeared farfetched just a decade ago, but the idea of arms control itself also appeared revolutionary—or at least counterintuitive—in the early 1960s.[4]

Opportunities for arms control exist when parties come to believe that they might benefit from either unilateral or mutual restraint regarding the size of their forces, the kinds of weapons included in their arsenals, and the nature of their defense policies. Longtime critics of arms control have seized upon this necessary condition for constructive arms control to note that "arms control works best when least needed."[5] But dismissing arms control in this way ignores how agreements can save valuable resources and create constructive dialogues that calm unrealistic or imagined fears.

Indeed, the very act of talking about one's security concerns and plans with a potential opponent sends a strong signal that peace, not war, is possible. The fact that U.S. and Russian citizens today share a common language and history when it comes to their strategic policies might even be a sign that they have transcended the need for arms control. Instead of negotiating cuts to existing arsenals, they are coordinating their defense policies informally, deciding in advance what types of weapons they will develop and deploy.

Today arms control still makes an important contribution to international security. Asia is just one place where arms control has an important role to play. As Brad Roberts notes (see Chapter 15), the end of the Cold War has led to an increase in the importance of arms control in Asia. The U.S.–North Korea Agreed Framework, for example, has constrained North Korea's nuclear program, reducing pressures on Japan, Taiwan, and South Korea to develop their own nuclear programs. Nonproliferation agreements and cooperative security initiatives also have helped stem the flow of Soviet-era weapons, technologies, and expertise into the region. Roberts suggests that as China modernizes its nuclear forces, and as U.S. and Russian strategic forces continue to shrink in size, stability in the region might be enhanced if China could be brought into the strategic arms control process. Arms control thus has a potentially stabilizing effect in Asia by helping states in the region adjust to growing Chinese military capability. Arms control also helps to prevent political and military shocks that could destabilize the nuclear balance in the region.

Another region where arms control and confidence-building measures can contribute greatly to international security is South Asia. In the wake of the 1998 Indian and Pakistani nuclear tests, the ongoing dispute between those enduring rivals over Kashmir threatens to spark a nuclear war. Although, as Peter Lavoy notes (see Chapter 14), there is no consensus about the types of arms control agreements and confidence-building measures that might reduce the prospect of a nuclear exchange, it does appear that many Cold War arms control lessons are applicable to the India-Pakistan rivalry. Lavoy suggests that an important first confidence-building measure between New Delhi and Islamabad would be the initiation of an informal diplomatic or academic exchange of ideas to help create a culture of arms control and an arms control community in South Asia. The emergence of this epistemic community is important because it would allow for the creation of a common strategic language between India and Pakistan as both sides clarify their own and their rival's doctrines, security concerns, and procurement policies. Still, time might be running out for arms control and confidence-building measures in South Asia. It took at least a decade for the concept of arms control to build political and intellectual support on both sides of the Cold War divide. By contrast, in South Asia, where both sides appear interested in testing the leverage created by their nuclear capabilities, the time needed to cultivate a culture of arms control might be in short supply.

Technology, specifically the information revolution, has created theoretical and practical challenges and opportunities for the arms control community. The spread of information technologies across the globe increases government, business, and personal reliance on the Internet and computers, but it also creates opportunities for states, terrorist organizations, and individuals to conduct information warfare campaigns. As Greg Rattray notes (see Chapter 18), little international agreement exists about how to protect this extraordinarily important medium of international communication and commerce, even though there is a growing perception that regulation is needed to contain disruption caused by cyberattacks. But the regulation of cyberspace with an eye toward limiting cyberattacks and cyberterrorism is complicated by the fact that the information revolution involves new technologies and social and commercial interactions that are not well understood by experts in arms control or, for that matter, by most diplomats and elected officials.

Creating an arms control regime for cyberspace also presents challenges for theorists. For example, nonstate actors and transnational corporations have played a part in the creation and implementation of past arms control regimes. Nongovernmental organizations and interest groups might lobby for the inclusion of key provisions in a proposed agreement. Corporations involved in missile production also have found their activities at specific sites governed by international agreement. But today nonstate actors and corporations might play a dominant role in developing and implementing cooperative security measures designed to reduce the threats posed by increasing access to information systems. Another interesting challenge faced by theorists is the fact that regulating cyberspace would directly affect individuals. The state parties to an agreement might no longer be the primary target of an international regime governing cyberspace.

Arms control also has an increasing role to play in safeguarding communications and reconnaissance assets in outer space. The Outer Space Treaty, which entered into force in October 1967, still remains in effect. It bans placing nuclear weapons in orbit and on celestial bodies and calls for treaty parties to use space only for peaceful purposes. Little has been done since 1967, however, to help slow the militarization of space and to safeguard the billions of dollars' worth of national and commercial assets now in orbit. Like cyberspace, outer space is no longer just the realm of the United States and Russia. Many small states, nonstate actors, and businesses have a significant presence in earth orbit. And, like the effort to regulate cyberspace, the arms control community faces significant challenges when it comes to devising methods to slow the weaponization of space.

The Future of Arms Control

Today arms control theory, theorists, and institutions continue to reflect their Cold War origins. Bureaucratic inertia, a lack of theoretical innovation, and domestic political battles have been identified as possible sources of continuity in an arms control regime facing dramatic change. But this observation also raises several important questions for arms control theorists and practitioners alike. Was traditional arms control primarily a Cold War phenomenon? Did bipolarity make arms control possible because it simplified what is usually a highly complex strategic environment, allowing policymakers on both sides of the Cold War divide to focus on their primary security threat (i.e., the other superpower)?[6] Did the situation of mutual assured destruction that existed between the United States and the Soviet Union throughout the latter half of the Cold War eliminate any realistic opportunity for gaining a unilateral military advantage, thereby creating a necessary condition for arms control?[7] Indeed, cooperation might have been the only way for both the United States and the Soviet Union to obtain their primary security objective: avoiding nuclear armageddon.[8]

Viewed in this way, arms control is likely to make a significant contribution to international security only under a specific set of circumstances. The number of great powers at any one moment probably affects the prospects for successful arms control. In a world with only one great power, arms control might be unlikely because the great power would be able to achieve its security objectives unilaterally. In a world of many great powers or scores of interested actors, it might be difficult to negotiate arms control agreements that satisfy actors' specific security concerns or to generate a common political consensus necessary to undertake constructive negotiations. Indeed, as the number of parties to an agreement increases, issues of transparency, verification, and compliance become highly problematic. The probability of free riding (i.e., the effort of one party to exploit the cooperation of others by clandestinely violating the treaty) also increases as the number of parties to a treaty grows.

Because they empower individuals at the expense of bureaucracies and states, today's cultural, social, technological, and economic trends might undermine the ability of traditional parties to the international arms control regime to negotiate and implement arms control agreements. By lowering the costs of communications and organization, the information revolution can empower groups and individuals, creating the conditions for a clash of civilizations and even a general descent into chaos.[9] Under these circumstances, traditional arms control can make little contribution to international security.

Yet globalization optimists would suggest that the spread of free markets, democracy, and a democratic peace sets the stage for a renewed interest in arms control as states seek formal and informal ways to reduce military expenditures. In addition, there are geographic regions and new arenas of multinational concern that could be enhanced through cooperative security efforts. These could benefit from the lessons learned by arms control initiatives during the Cold War. From this perspective arms control is not dead; it just needs to be applied to the new fields that would benefit from it. This calls for a broader vision on the part of the traditional arms control community, as well as the willingness on its part to perform an educational role in these areas.

As we stand at a crossroads in the history of arms control and cooperative security, it is clear that the broad trends in global politics—not just the record of past arms control accomplishments—will shape future arms control regimes. The real contribution that today's arms control community can make to future security is not to simply preserve existing agreements but rather to apply the theories, concepts, and techniques that have helped to constrain past arms competitions to solve emerging problems. As technology proliferates and becomes more complex, and as the number of interested actors and issues multiply, the challenges faced by the academic and policy community are indeed profound. Yet the hardest challenge remains the one faced by Thomas Schelling and other intellectual pioneers more than 40 years ago: convincing all concerned that it is possible to collaborate with potential enemies and actually increase one's security.

Notes

1. Jeffrey A. Larsen and Gregory J. Rattray, eds., *Arms Control Toward the 21st Century* (Boulder: Lynne Rienner Publishers, 1996).

2. Leon Fuerth, "Return of the Nuclear Debate," *Washington Quarterly* 24, no. 4 (Autumn 2001): 97–108; and Robert Joseph, "The Changing Political-Military Environment," in James J. Wirtz and Jeffrey A. Larsen, eds., *Rockets' Red Glare: Missile Defenses and the Future of World Politics* (Boulder: Westview, 2001), pp. 55–77.

3. Thomas Schelling, Address to Workshop titled "Arms Control and Cooperative Security in a Changing Environment," Science Applications International Corporation, McLean, VA, 11–12 July 2001.

4. The counterintuitive notion embodied in arms control was best expressed by Thomas Schelling more than 40 years ago: "One can simultaneously think seriously and sympathetically about our military posture and collaborating with our enemies to improve it." Schelling, "Reciprocal Measures for Arms Stabilization," *Daedalus* (Fall 1960): 892.

5. Colin Gray, *House of Cards* (Ithaca: Cornell University Press, 1992).

6. Kenneth Waltz, *Theory of International Politics* (Reading, MA: Addison-Wesley, 1979).

7. Robert Jervis, *The Meaning of the Nuclear Revolution: Statecraft and the Prospect of Armageddon* (Ithaca: Cornell University Press, 1989).

8. Richard J. Harknett, "State Preferences, Systemic Constraints, and the Absolute Weapon," in T. V. Paul, Richard J. Harknett, and James J. Wirtz, eds., *The Absolute Weapon Revisited* (Ann Arbor: University of Michigan Press, 1998), pp. 47–72.

9. Samuel Huntington, *Clash of Civilizations and the Remaking of World Order* (New York: Touchstone, 1998); and Martin Van Creveld, *The Transformation of War* (New York: Free Press, 1991).

Acronyms

ABM	Anti-Ballistic Missile [Treaty]
ACDA	Arms Control and Disarmament Agency
ACRS	Arms Control and Regional Security
AF/XONP	U.S. Air Force National Security Policy Division
APL	antipersonnel landmines
ASAT	antisatellite
ATTU	Atlantic to the Urals
BWC	Biological and Toxin Weapons Convention
CANDU	Canadian deuterium uranium reactor
CBMs	confidence-building measures
CBW	chemical and biological weapon(s)
CCCW	Convention on Certain Conventional Weapons
CERT/CIRT	computer emergency/incident response team
CFE	Conventional Armed Forces in Europe [Treaty]
CINC	commander in chief
COE	Council of Europe
CSBM	confidence- and security-building measure
CSCE	Conference on Security and Cooperation in Europe
CTBT	Comprehensive Test Ban Treaty
CTR	Cooperative Threat Reduction
CWC	Chemical Weapons Convention
DoD	Department of Defense
DTRA	Defense Threat Reduction Agency
ECOWAS	Economic Community of West African States
ENDC	Eighteen-Nation Disarmament Conference
EU	European Union
EUCs	end-use certificates
FMCT	Fissile Material Cut-Off Treaty
FSC	Forum for Security Cooperation
GCC	Gulf Cooperation Council

GCD	general and complete disarmament
GLCM	ground-launched cruise missiles
GPS	Global Positioning System
HEU	highly enriched uranium
IAEA	International Atomic Energy Agency
ICBM	intercontinental ballistic missile
IGO	international governmental organization
INF	Intermediate-Range Nuclear Forces [Treaty]
INSS	Air Force Institute for National Security Studies
IPP	Initiatives for Proliferation Prevention
ISMA	International Satellite Monitoring Agency
ISTC	International Science and Technology Center
JCS	Joint Chiefs of Staff
KGB	Soviet intelligence agency
LEU	low-enriched uranium
LTBT	Limited Test Ban Treaty
MAD	mutual assured destruction
MBFR	Mutual and Balanced Force Reduction [Talks]
MINATOM	Russian Ministry of Atomic Energy
MIRV	multiple independently targetable reentry vehicle
MOX	mixed oxide
MPC&A	material protection, control, and accounting
MTCR	Missile Technology Control Regime
NATO	North Atlantic Treaty Organization
NBC	nuclear, biological, and chemical [weapons]
NCI	Nuclear Cities Initiative
NGO	nongovernmental organization
NIE	National Intelligence Estimate
NIS	newly independent states
NNSA	National Nuclear Safety Administration
NNWS	non–nuclear weapon state(s)
NORAD	North American Aerospace Defense Command
NPT	Nuclear Non-Proliferation Treaty
NSC	National Security Council
NTM	national technical means
NWS	nuclear weapon state(s)
OAS	Organization of American States
OECD	Organization for Economic Cooperation and Development
OPCW	Organization for the Prevention of Chemical Weapons
OSCE	Organization for Security and Cooperation in Europe
PACATOM	Pacific Atomic Energy Agency
PNET	Peaceful Nuclear Explosions Treaty
PNI	presidential nuclear initiative

Pu-239	Plutonium-239
RAMOS	Russian-American Observation Satellite
SALT	Strategic Arms Limitation Talks/Treaty
SLBM	submarine-launched ballistic missile
SLCM	sea-launched cruise missile
SSBN	nuclear ballistic missile submarine
START	Strategic Arms Reduction Talks/Treaty
TAE	Transformacao de Armas em Enxadas (Transforming Arms into Plowshares)
TLE	treaty-limited equipment
TTBT	Threshold Test Ban Treaty
U-235	Uranium-235
UN	United Nations
UNAEC	UN Atomic Energy Commission
UNCCA	UN Commission for Conventional Armaments
UNSCOM	UN Special Commission on Iraq
USAF	U.S. Air Force
WMD	weapon(s) of mass destruction

Appendix 1

Chronology of Arms Control Since 1945

Jeffrey A. Larsen

1945

26 June   United Nations Charter signed in San Francisco, California (entry into force 24 October 1945).

16 July   United States tests atomic bomb.

17 July–

2 August   Berlin (Potsdam) Protocol by United States, United Kingdom, France, USSR (dealt with Germany's disarmament and division into occupied zones).

1946

4 April   Atomic Energy Act (also known as the McMahon Act) passes, creates U.S. Atomic Energy Commission.

14 June   Baruch Plan presented by the United States to UN Atomic Energy Commission (also known as Dumbarton Oaks Plan) to place all global atomic material, weapons, and energy under UN control (vetoed by USSR in December 1946).

1947

UN Commission on Conventional Armaments established.

10 February   Italian Peace Treaty signed in Paris (limited Italy's military and removed fortifications along borders); also treaties for Bulgaria, Finland, Hungary, and Romania signed.

11 June   Soviet Proposals to United Nations for International Control of Atomic Energy.

26 July   U.S. National Security Act signed into law, creating Department of Defense, Central Intelligence Agency, and National Security Council.

1948

9 December   United Nations adopts Convention on the Prevention and Punishment of the Crime of Genocide.

1949

United States passes Export Control Act (to control dual-use items).

4 April	North Atlantic Treaty signed in Washington (leads to creation of North Atlantic Treaty Organization on 17 September 1949).
13 April	Agreement Between the Governments of the United States, France, and the United Kingdom on Prohibited and Limited Industries in the Western Zones of Germany.
12 August	Geneva Convention signed in four parts: I (Wounded and Sick Members of the Armed Forces in the Field); II (Amelioration of Wounded, Sick, and Shipwrecked Members of Armed Forces at Sea); III (Treatment of Prisoners of War); and IV (Protection of Civilians in Time of War).
29 August	USSR tests atomic bomb.
November	United States and six West European states create Coordinating Committee for Multilateral Export Controls (COCOM) to prevent transfer of militarily useful technology to communist countries.

1950

25 May	Tripartite Arms Declaration signed by United Kingdom, France, and the United States regarding security in the Near East.

1952

January	UN Disarmament Commission created.
3 October	United Kingdom tests atomic bomb.

1953

8 December	United States makes Atoms for Peace proposal to the UN General Assembly.

1954

	UN Disarmament Commission establishes the Subcommittee on Disarmament in London (for three years the primary international negotiating forum).
30 August	U.S. Congress enacts Atomic Energy Act, amending 1946 McMahon Act, allowing peaceful sharing of nuclear knowledge.
23 October	Protocol to the Brussels Treaty (West Germany pledges not to produce, procure, or possess weapons of mass destruction and is allowed to rearm conventionally).

1955

19 March	United States creates office of Special Assistant to the President for Disarmament.
10 May	USSR proposes atomic test ban.
14 May	Eastern Europe and USSR form Warsaw Treaty Organization (known as Warsaw Pact).
21 July	U.S. Open Skies proposal presented at Geneva Conference of Heads of Government (to allow aerial overflight and inspection of states parties).
8–20 August	First International Conference on Peaceful Uses of Atomic Energy held in Geneva.
4 November	Austrian State Treaty (prohibited Austria from possessing special weapons).

1956

12 July	Indian Proposal to the Disarmament Commission to end nuclear weapon tests.
18 July	The Law of Land Warfare published in U.S. Army Field Manual FM 27-10 (forbidding certain means of waging warfare).
26 October	International Atomic Energy Agency (IAEA) created, based in Vienna.

1957

2 October	Rapacki Proposal (by Poland) to establish a denuclearized zone in Central Europe (reiterated in 1958 and 1962).

1958

10 January	United States tests world's first intercontinental ballistic missile.
March–August	United States and USSR introduce unilateral reciprocal nuclear testing moratoriums (lasting through September 1961).
September–January 1959	Surprise Attack Conference.
October	Conference on the Discontinuation of Nuclear Weapons Tests formed in Geneva (through 1962 the primary forum for discussions on the partial test ban).

1959

January	United States proposes limited test ban for atmospheric testing.
1 December	Antarctic Treaty signed by 12 nations (demilitarized the continent); entry into force 23 June 1961.

1960

	UN Ten Nation Committee on Disarmament established in Geneva (the name of this ongoing forum changed to the Eighteen-Nation Committee on Disarmament in 1962, to the Conference of the Committee on Disarmament in 1969, and to the Conference on Disarmament in 1979).
13 February	France tests atomic bomb.

1961

26 September	United States passes Arms Control and Disarmament Act, assigning lead role for these activities to secretary of state and establishing U.S. Arms Control and Disarmament Agency (ACDA).
24 November	UN Resolution on Nuclear Weapons (General Assembly Resolution 1653).

1962

15 March	Soviet proposal for general and complete disarmament to the UN Eighteen-Nation Disarmament Committee.
18 April	U.S. proposal to the United Nations for General and Complete Disarmament.

1963

20 June	Hot Line Agreement signed by the United States and USSR in Geneva.

5 August	Limited Test Ban Treaty signed by United States, USSR, and United Kingdom in Moscow (banned nuclear weapon tests in the atmosphere, outer space, and underwater); 125 follow-on signatories; entry into force 10 October 1963.
7 August	UN arms embargo against South Africa enacted (Security Council Resolution 181); reiterated in Resolutions 182 (1963), 418 (1977), and 558 (1984).

1964

January	United States proposes program to UN Eighteen-Nation Disarmament Committee to halt nuclear arms race.
21 July	Declaration of the Denuclearization of Africa (by Organization of African Unity).
September	United States ceases production of highly enriched uranium for weapon purposes.
16 October	People's Republic of China tests atomic bomb.

1967

27 January	Outer Space Treaty signed by 67 countries (established principles regarding peaceful, nonmilitary exploration and use of outer space and celestial bodies); entry into force 10 October 1967.
14 February	Latin America Nuclear Weapon Free Zone (Treaty of Tlatelolco) signed by 20 nations in Mexico City; entry into force 22 April 1968.
23 June	Glassboro summit between the United States and USSR; began discussions leading to Anti-Ballistic Missile and Strategic Arms Limitation Treaties (SALT).
13 December	United States discloses it has tested multiple independently targetable reentry vehicles on an ICBM.

1968

1 July	Treaty on the Non-Proliferation of Nuclear Weapons signed by 73 countries in Washington, London, and Moscow (eventually 187 members); entry into force 5 March 1970.

1969

17 November	SALT talks begin in Helsinki, Vienna, and Geneva.
25 November	U.S. unilateral ban on biological weapons and biological weapon research and no-first use pledge regarding chemical weapons.
16 December	UN Resolution on Chemical and Bacteriological (Biological) Weapons.

1970

5 March	NPT entry into force.

1971

11 February	Seabed Treaty signed by 63 nations in Washington, London, and Moscow (prohibits placement of nuclear or other weapons of mass destruction on or under the seafloor); entry into force 18 May 1972.
30 September	Nuclear War Risk Reduction Agreement signed by United States and USSR in Washington (also called the Accidents Measures Agreement; enhanced transparency, early warning, openness).

| 30 September | Hot Line Agreement signed between the United States and USSR in Washington (modernized and expanded the 1963 agreement). |
| 16 December | India proposes Indian Ocean Zone of Peace to United Nations. |

1972

10 April	Biological Weapons Convention (BWC) signed by 139 parties in Washington, London, and Moscow; entry into force 26 March 1975.
25 May	Prevention of Incidents at Sea Treaty signed between the United States and USSR in Moscow.
26 May	Strategic Arms Limitation Treaty (SALT I) signed in Moscow by United States and USSR; includes Interim Agreement on Limiting Strategic Offensive Arms (limiting ballistic missile delivery vehicles and submarines) and Anti-Ballistic Missile Treaty, which limited strategic defenses (two sites, 100 interceptors each). Entry into force 3 October 1972. United States withdrew from ABM Treaty 13 June 2002.
26 May	Standing Consultative Commission created in Geneva to monitor SALT and ABM treaties.
22 November	Conference on Security and Cooperation in Europe (CSCE) talks begin in Geneva and Helsinki.

1973

| 31 January | Mutual and Balanced Force Reductions begin in Vienna (talks last through 1989). |
| 22 June | Prevention of Nuclear War Agreement signed by United States and USSR in Washington (agreement to consult in times of crisis). |

1974

3 September	NPT Exporters Committee (the Zangger Committee) founded (33-nation agreement to develop lists of nuclear equipment and material exports that trigger IAEA safeguards), based in Vienna.
18 May	India tests atomic "device."
3 July	Threshold Test Ban Treaty (TTBT) signed by United States and USSR in Moscow (limited size of underground nuclear weapons tests to yields of less than 150 kilotons); entry into force 11 December 1990 (though observed by both sides prior to that date).
3 July	Protocol to the ABM Treaty signed in Moscow by the United States and USSR; limited each side to one strategic defensive site; entry into force 24 May 1976.
24 November	Vladivostok Agreement between U.S. and USSR presidents; sets numerical limits and terms of reference for SALT II Treaty.

1975

22 January	United States ratifies 1925 Geneva Protocol outlawing use of poisonous gas and bacteriological warfare.
5–30 May	First NPT Review Conference held in Geneva.
1 August	Helsinki Accords (also known as Helsinki Final Act) signed by 35 states (created the CSCE).

1976

28 May   Peaceful Nuclear Explosions Treaty (PNET) signed between the
              United States and USSR; entry into force 11 December 1990.

1977

              Conventional Arms Transfer Talks (to limit Soviet arms sales) begin
              in Geneva and Mexico City (talks end in 1979).

18 May   Environmental Modification Treaty (or Convention) (prohibits
              military or other hostile use of environmental modification
              techniques); entry into force 5 October 1978.

June   Indian Ocean Arms Limitation talks begin in Moscow, Washington,
              and Bern (talks suspended in 1979).

21 September Nuclear Suppliers Group (also known as the London Club) agrees on
              principles and guidelines (to restrict exports of sensitive technology).

3 October   Trilateral negotiations on a comprehensive test ban begin between
              United States, United Kingdom, and USSR in Geneva (through
              1981).

10 October   UK-USSR Prevention of Accidental Nuclear War Agreement signed
              in Moscow.

18 November   U.S.-IAEA Safeguards Agreement signed in Vienna.

1978

              U.S.-Soviet antisatellite talks begin in Helsinki, Bern, and Vienna
              (talks suspended in 1979).

10 March   United States passes Nuclear Non-Proliferation Act.

12 June   United States announces negative security guarantee to NPT non-
              nuclear weapon states.

30 June   UN holds first General Assembly session on disarmament, establishes
              Disarmament Commission as subsidiary body to General Assembly.

1979

January   First meeting of UN Conference on Disarmament (formerly
              Conference of the Committee on Disarmament).

18 June   Strategic Arms Limitation Treaty (SALT II) signed between United
              States and USSR in Vienna (limited strategic delivery vehicles to
              2,400, with sublimits by category).

12 December   NATO agrees on Dual Track strategy; simultaneously deploying
              intermediate-range nuclear force missiles and negotiating INF arms
              control with USSR.

18 December   Agreement Governing the Activities of States on the Moon and Other
              Celestial Bodies signed by 16 countries (none of them current or
              potential spacefaring nations).

1980

4 January   President Carter withdraws SALT II Treaty from Senate consideration.

3 March   Convention on the Physical Protection of Nuclear Material opened for
              signature in New York (entry into force 8 February 1987).

17 March   UN Committee on Disarmament begins work on a chemical weapons
              convention.

2 July	United States ratifies 1977 agreement to adhere to IAEA safeguards.
11 August– 7 September	Second NPT Review Conference held in Geneva.

1981

10 April	UN Convention Restricting Excessively Injurious or Indiscriminate Conventional Weapons (or Inhumane Weapons Convention) opened for signature, entry into force 2 December 1983 (also called Convention on Certain Conventional Weapons).
22 September	USSR proposes "no-first-use" pledge by superpowers to United Nations.
18 November	United States proposes "zero option" for elimination of all INF weapons.
30 November	INF Negotiations begin in Geneva.

1982

9 May	United States proposes Strategic Arms Reduction Talks (START).
29 June	START negotiations begin in Geneva.
10 December	UN Convention on the Law of the Sea opened for signature.

1983

23 March	President Ronald Reagan announces U.S. plans to develop strategic missile defenses (Strategic Defense Initiative).
Spring– Summer	United States deploys INF missiles to Europe.
8 December	START talks adjourn indefinitely.
15 December	MBFR talks adjourn indefinitely.
December	Cameroon Initiative (UN effort to reenergize its disarmament efforts and extend arms control beyond the superpower competition).

1984

17 January	Stockholm Conference on Confidence- and Security-Building Measures in Europe begins.
17 July	Hot Line Memorandum of Understanding between the United States and USSR signed in Washington (updated 1963 and 1971 agreements).

1985

12 March	Nuclear and Space Talks begin in Geneva (United States and USSR); includes START, INF, and Defense and Space Talks.
June	First meeting of the Australia Group in Brussels (15-country effort to curb transfer of chemical weapon precursors and technologies to third world).
August	U.S. Congress passes Pressler Amendment (restricts military sales to Pakistan unless it can prove it is not pursuing nuclear weapons).
6 August	Treaty of Rarotonga signed, creating South Pacific Nuclear Free Zone; entry into force 12 December 1986.
27 August– 21 September	Third NPT Review Conference held in Geneva.

1986

15 January	USSR proposes complete elimination of nuclear weapons by year 2000.
22 September	Agreement on Confidence- and Security-Building Measures and Disarmament in Europe (also known as the Stockholm Agreement) signed by 35 states in Stockholm; entry into force January 1987.
26 September	Early Notification of a Nuclear Accident Agreement signed in Vienna.
11–12 October	Reykjavik summit between U.S. and Soviet presidents furthers progress toward strategic agreements.
17 November	Delhi Declaration urges comprehensive test ban treaty.
11 December	Brussels Declaration on Conventional Arms Control by NATO (which leads to the Conventional Armed Forces in Europe Treaty in 1990).

1987

16 April	Missile Technology Control Regime established to limit risks of proliferation by controlling technology transfers in multiple categories (25 members).
15 September	Nuclear Risk Reduction Centers Agreement signed between the United States and USSR in Washington (to provide advance warning of missile tests and establish centers in both countries with communications links); centers open 1 April 1988.
15 September	United States and USSR begin INF negotiations.
8 December	Intermediate- and Shorter Range Nuclear Forces Treaty signed in Washington between the United States and USSR (global elimination of missiles with ranges of 500–5,500 kilometers, with intrusive verification requirements); entry into force 1 June 1988.

1988

26 January	U.S. On-Site Inspection Agency (OSIA) created within Department of Defense to handle INF verification and compliance duties.
February	United States closes plutonium production facilities.
31 May	Ballistic Missile Launch Notification Agreement signed by United States and USSR in Moscow.
31 December	Indian-Pakistani Agreement Not to Attack Nuclear Installations signed in Islamabad.

1989

6 March	NATO and Warsaw Pact begin talks in Vienna on CFE Treaty.
12 May	United States renews and expands its 1955 Open Skies proposal.
12 June	Agreement on the Prevention of Dangerous Military Activities signed by the United States and USSR in Moscow.
23 September	Agreement on Notification of Strategic Exercises signed between the United States and USSR in Jackson Hole, Wyoming; entry into force 1 January 1990.
23 September	Memorandum of Understanding regarding data exchanges and inspections for Chemical Weapons Convention signed by the United States and USSR in Jackson Hole.
9–10 November	Berlin Wall falls.

1990

12 February   Open Skies negotiations begin between NATO and Warsaw Pact
members.

May   OSIA expands mandate to handle inspections for CFE, START,
TTBT, and PNET treaties and chemical weapons agreements
(and in July 1991, UNSCOM).

1 June   United States and USSR sign Bilateral Destruction Agreement for
chemical weapons, and verification protocols for TTBT and PNET.

20 August–
14 September   Fourth NPT Review Conference.

22 August   Joint Declaration of the Federal Republic of Germany and of the
German Democratic Republic on Non-Proliferation of Nuclear,
Chemical, and Biological Weapons (in association with the
reunification of Germany; this declaration was made at the 1990
NPT Review Conference).

12 September   German Unification Treaty (also known as the 4+2 Treaty) signed in
Moscow by United States, United Kingdom, France, USSR, and West
and East Germany (ending World War II).

17 November   Vienna Document 1990 agreed at CSCE summit in Paris.

19 November   Treaty on Conventional Armed Forces in Europe signed by 22
member nations of NATO and Warsaw Pact.

21 November   Charter of Paris for a New Europe signed to reflect end of the
Cold War.

28 November   Argentine-Brazilian Joint Declaration on Nuclear Policy issued at Foz
do Iguazú, Brazil (confidence-building and data-sharing).

1991

1 January   CSCE Vienna Document 1990 enters into force (strengthens CSBMs
in Europe and establishes Conflict Prevention Center in Vienna).

31 March   Warsaw Pact dissolved.

3 April   UN passes Resolution Prohibiting Iraqi Possession of Weapons of
Mass Destruction; also created UN Special Commission on Iraq
(UNSCOM) to verify compliance (UN Security Council Resolutions
687, 707, and 715).

29 May   Middle East Arms Control Initiative proposed by United States.

9 July   Big Five Initiative on Arms Transfer and Proliferation Restraints
signed in Paris by the United States, USSR, China, France, and the
United Kingdom (reiterated in communiqué issued in London
1 October 1991)

18 July   Argentine-Brazilian Bilateral Accord on Nuclear Energy signed (also
known as Guadalajara Agreement).

31 July   Treaty on the Reduction and Limitation of Strategic Offensive Arms
(START I) signed between United States and USSR in Moscow;
limits strategic delivery vehicles to 1,600 and warheads to 6,000 each.
Entry into force 5 December 1994.

27 September   U.S. Presidential Nuclear Initiative on nonstrategic nuclear weapons
reductions and dealerting (Soviet and Russian presidents respond with
parallel initiatives October 1991 and January 1992).

27 November   U.S. Congress passes Nuclear Threat Reduction Act to help the former USSR transport, store, safeguard, and destroy nuclear weapons (this act created the Cooperative Threat Reduction Program in 1993; also known as the Nunn-Lugar Program).

9 December   United Nations General Assembly Resolution 46/36L adopted, creates Transparency in Armaments regime, including annual UN Register of Conventional Arms.

25 December   Soviet Union formally dissolved.

1992

20 January   Joint Declaration on the Denuclearization of the Korean Peninsula.

27–28 January   U.S.-Russia joint understanding on further strategic nuclear reductions, call for START II negotiations.

29 February   Vienna Document 1992 signed.

24 March   Treaty on Open Skies signed in Helsinki (25-nation agreement to allow unarmed surveillance flights).

1 May   Vienna Document 1992 enters into force (European CSBMs).

23 May   Lisbon Protocol (to START I) signed; admits Soviet successor states (Ukraine, Belarus, and Kazakhstan) as nonnuclear state parties to START and NPT.

1 June   IAEA and UNSCOM complete destruction of Iraqi nuclear weapon development facilities.

9–10 July   Helsinki CSCE summit agrees to create Forum for Security Cooperation, based in Vienna.

17 July   CFE-1A Treaty signed in Vienna (limits personnel in Europe).

4 September   United States initiates unilateral moratorium on nuclear testing.

15 September   First meeting of United States, Russia, and Great Britain in Trilateral Working Group on biological weapons.

1993

3 January   START II Treaty (Treaty on Further Reduction and Limitation of Strategic Offensive Arms) between Russia and the United States signed in Moscow (limits strategic nuclear warheads to 3,000–3,500 each and eliminates MIRVed warheads and heavy ICBMs). Ratified by United States 26 January 1996 and by Russia 14 April 2000.

13 January   Chemical Weapons Convention signed in Paris by 130 countries (bans production, acquisition, stockpiling, and use of chemical weapons); entry into force 29 April 1997.

18 February   United States and Russia sign agreement to convert Russian highly enriched uranium to civil reactor use in the United States.

24 March   South Africa announces it had a clandestine nuclear weapon program since 1974 that built six nuclear devices.

27 September   United States announces that it will place excess fissile material under IAEA safeguards.

7 December   United States announces its new counterproliferation initiative.

16 December   United Nations passes resolution calling for negotiations leading to Fissile Materials Cutoff Treaty.

1994

	U.S. national laboratories begin lab-to-lab contacts with Russian and former Soviet laboratories to deal with fissile material protection, control, and accounting.
25 January	Negotiations begin on a CTBT in the Conference on Disarmament, Geneva.
March	United States and Russia agree to create regime of mutual reciprocal inspections of plutonium and highly enriched uranium inventories.
30 April	U.S. Arms Control and Nonproliferation Act instituted by Executive Order (continues key features of 1949 Export Control Act).
30 May	United States and Russia detarget strategic nuclear missiles.
23 June	United States and Russia sign agreement to shutdown Russian plutonium production reactors by 2000.
23 October	United States negotiates Agreed Framework with North Korea, promising economic aid and safe nuclear power in return for an end to Pyongyang's nuclear weapon program.
16 November	UN Convention on the Law of the Sea enters into force.
28 November	CSCE Vienna Document 1994 signed.
28 November	Global Exchange of Military Information Agreement adopted by CSCE Forum for Security Cooperation; entry into force 1 January 1995.
5 December	START I entry into force
6 December	CSCE changes its name to the Organization for Security and Cooperation in Europe; members agree to military code of conduct, abiding by principles of Helsinki Final Act.

1995

23 March	Fissile Material Cut-Off Talks begin in Conference on Disarmament, Geneva.
24 March	United States ratifies Convention on Certain Conventional Weapons.
17 April– 12 May	NPT Review and Extension Conference in New York reaches consensus agreement to extend treaty indefinitely.
9 December	Wassenaar Arrangement signed by 33 nations in the Netherlands (to control dual-use conventional exports); implementation date 1 November 1996.
15 December	Southeast Asia Nuclear Weapon Free Zone created via Bangkok Treaty; entry into force 27 March 1997.

1996

26 January	U.S. Senate ratifies START II Treaty.
11 April	Pelindaba Treaty signed by 43 nations in Cairo, Egypt, creating Africa Nuclear Weapon Free Zone.
8 July	International Court of Justice issues advisory opinion on the legality of the use of nuclear weapons.
14 August	Canberra Commission on the Elimination of Nuclear Weapons issues its report.

10 September   United Nations Passes Comprehensive Test Ban Treaty (eventually 161 signatories).

1997

21 March   At Helsinki summit U.S. and Russian presidents agree to begin START III talks once START II enters into force, with limits of 2,000–2,500 strategic warheads; protocol verifying agreement signed in New York 26 September 1997.

25 April   United States ratifies Chemical Weapons Convention.

23 September   United States and Russia sign Plutonium Production Reactor Agreement on closing or converting Russian plutonium production reactors.

26 September   United States and Russia sign memorandum of understanding in New York to amend START II and ABM Treaty.

3 December   Mine Ban Treaty (also known as the Ottawa Convention) opened for signature; entry into force 1 March 1999; more than 125 state parties.

1998

14 January   Iraq expels UNSCOM inspectors.

19 January   Military Maritime Consultation Agreement signed by United States and China in Beijing.

11–13 May   India tests atomic weapons.

28–30 May   Pakistan tests atomic weapons.

2 September   United States and Russia sign agreement on management and disposition of excess plutonium.

1 October   U.S. Defense Threat Reduction Agency created by combining On-Site Inspection Agency, Defense Special Weapons Agency, and Defense Technology Security Administration.

1999

6 January   United States passes National Missile Defense Act calling for missile defense deployment at earliest opportunity.

April   U.S. Arms Control and Disarmament Agency eliminated; functions absorbed by U.S. State Department.

13 October   U.S. Senate votes against ratifying Comprehensive Test Ban Treaty.

16 November   OSCE Vienna Document 1999 signed.

2000

14 April   Russian Duma ratifies START II Treaty

24 April–
19 May   Fifth NPT Review Conference in New York.

13 October   U.S. Senate refuses to ratify CTBT.

2001

25 July   United States rejects draft BWC Protocol.

11 September   Terrorist attacks strike U.S. World Trade Center and Pentagon; United States creates coalition to conduct global war on terrorism.

13 November   U.S. and Russian presidents agree to further unilateral cuts in strategic nuclear arsenal.

13 December   United States notifies Russia of intent to withdraw from ABM
              Treaty.

2002

1 January	Open Skies Treaty enters into force.
9 January	U.S. Nuclear Posture Review released.
24 May	United States and Russia sign treaty on strategic offensive reductions in Moscow.
13 June	United States withdraws from 1972 ABM Treaty.

Appendix 2

Treaties, Agreements, and Organizations of Particular Interest

Jeffrey A. Larsen & Kurt J. Klingenberger[1]

Agreed Framework with North Korea

The Agreed Framework with North Korea was signed in October 1994, ending a crisis that had been building for several years. This measure shored up stability on the Korean Peninsula at a time when the North was dangerously flaunting its responsibilities under International Atomic Energy Agency rules and was running the risk of war with the United States in so doing. The agreement offered proliferation-resistant nuclear reactors, food, and oil to North Korea in exchange for the exposure, deconstruction, and monitoring of its nuclear weapons infrastructure—particularly its plutonium reactors and reprocessing facilities. Although not a traditional arms control agreement per se, the Agreed Framework reduced a threatening military capability at reasonable political and economic cost. The Agreed Framework established a new international organization, the Korean Peninsula Energy Development Agency, to finance and construct the new nuclear power plants. There are 13 members of this organization, but Japan and South Korea will provide most of the funding.

Anti-Ballistic Missile Treaty

Signed on 20 May 1972, the Treaty Between the United States of America and the Union of Soviet Socialist Republics on the Limitation of Anti-Ballistic Missile Systems was one result of the initial Strategic Arms Limitation Talks (SALT I). It prohibited the deployment of an antiballistic missile (ABM) system for "the defense of the territory" and the provision of "a base for such a defense." The former prohibition included a nationwide defense, whether on land, sea, air, or space; the latter encompassed items such as large phased-array radars, which are the long–lead-time items of a deployed land-based ABM system. An *ABM system* was defined as a system "to counter strategic ballistic missiles or their elements in flight trajectory" and consisted of three components:

371

launchers, interceptor missiles, and radars. The ABM Treaty encompassed all ABM systems, whether based on current or future technology. It prohibited the testing in an ABM mode of non-ABM systems such as surface-to-air missile systems. The ban covered development and testing as well as deployment.

The ABM Treaty limited each side to two ABM deployment sites (later reduced to one site by a 1974 protocol). The United States chose to locate its site at the Grand Forks, North Dakota, intercontinental ballistic missile fields, whereas the Soviet Union chose to defend Moscow. The treaty imposed a ceiling of 100 ABM launchers and 100 ABM missiles at launch sites in the ABM deployment area.

Provisions of the treaty were to be verified solely by national technical means (NTM); each party agreed not to interfere with the other's NTM and not to use deliberate concealment measures that would impede verification by NTM.

The treaty was of unlimited duration, with review conferences every five years. A party could withdraw from the treaty with six months' notice. The Standing Consultative Commission served as the forum that addressed compliance issues and ongoing problems and challenges. It met in Geneva, Switzerland.

The United States and the Russian Federation signed a series of agreements on 27 September 1997 regarding demarcation between theater and national ballistic missile defenses, as well as to allow Belarus, Kazakhstan, Russia, and Ukraine to succeed the Soviet Union as state parties to the treaty.

The ABM Treaty came under increasing scrutiny and reconsideration in the late 1990s as the United States began seriously considering the deployment of a national missile defense system. The Bill Clinton administration hoped that Russia would be willing to renegotiate or modify the treaty to allow for modest defenses against rogue states, theater protection, and accidental launch, but Russia (indeed, most of the world community) opposed that idea. Many arms control advocates called the ABM Treaty "the cornerstone of strategic stability" in the international system. In May 2001 President George W. Bush announced that the United States would not be constrained by an outdated treaty that did not reflect the political realities of a world with new threats posed by rogue states armed with weapons of mass destruction and the means to deliver them against U.S. territory and interests. On 13 December 2001 the United States informed Russia that it would withdraw from the ABM Treaty in six months in order to develop a missile defense system. The treaty expired on 13 June 2002.

Australia Group

The Australia Group was formed in June 1985 in response to the use of chemical weapons during the Iran-Iraq War. Its purpose was to control the export of materials used in the manufacture of chemical and biological weapons. It created a control list of dual-use chemicals, facilities, equipment, and related technology that could have both commercial and military application. The Group of 30 industrialized nations (with the European Commission) meets annually in Paris to exchange data and coordinate actions. The group has no charter; it operates by consensus.

Biological and Toxin Weapons Convention

Building on the Geneva protocol of 1925, which bans the use of chemical and biological weapons in war, the Convention on the Prohibition of the Development, Production, and Stockpiling of Bacteriological (Biological) and Toxin Weapons and on Their Destruction (commonly cited as the Biological Weapons Convention, or BWC) bans the development, production, stockpiling, and acquisition of biological weapons. It was opened for signature on 10 April 1972 and entered into force on 26 March 1975. As of January 2002 there were 145 state parties to the convention.

In September 1992 trilateral negotiations between the United States, the United Kingdom, and the Russian Federation began in an effort to resolve compliance concerns and improve verification methods. These talks became multinational in 1995, and an ad hoc group began using a rolling text draft protocol in the summer of 1997. In March 2001 the BWC chairman released his own draft verification protocol, which was circulated for comment and consideration. In July 2001 a U.S. interagency review under the George W. Bush administration determined that the United States could not accept the current draft, and the BWC review conference that followed in November ended in disarray.

Certain Conventional Weapons Convention

The Convention on Prohibitions or Restrictions on Use of Certain Conventional Weapons Which May Be Deemed to Be Excessively Injurious or to Have Indiscriminate Effects (known as the Inhumane Weapons Convention, or the Convention on Certain Conventional Weapons) was opened for signature in 1981 and entered into force on 2 December 1983. The convention's purpose is to regulate conventional weapons that risk indiscriminate damage and injury to civilians or can cause unnecessary suffering. There are currently 88 state parties who have agreed to one or more of the four protocols involving restrictions on the manufacture, stockpiling, and use of certain conventional weapons. The first three protocols cover nondetectable fragmentation weapons; mines, booby traps, and other devices; and incendiary weapons. During the 1995–1996 review conference, a fourth protocol was added regarding blinding laser weapons. A review conference in December 2001 considered other weapons of war and also discussed the possibility of expanding the convention to internal conflicts rather than its current focus on international conflicts. The review conference also examined inspection, compliance, and enforcement measures.

Chemical Weapons Convention

The Convention on the Prohibition of the Development, Production, Stockpiling, and Use of Chemical Weapons and on Their Destruction (commonly cited as the Chemical Weapons Convention, or CWC) bans the development, production, stockpiling, transfer, acquisition, and both retaliatory and first use of chemical weapons. It prohibits a state from aiding any other state, even if not a party to the convention, in the pursuit of treaty-banned activities. Parties were required to declare all chemical weapons and facilities and to destroy all chemical weapons within 10 years of entry into force. The convention requires declarations on the production of precursor and dual-purpose chemicals.

It took 12 years of negotiations before the CWC was opened for signature on 13 January 1993. It entered into force on 29 April 1997 and currently has 178 signatories (of which, as of November 2001, 144 had ratified the convention). Its duration is unlimited.

The verification regime includes routine intrusive on-site inspections of declared government chemical weapon facilities as well as civilian facilities that use certain chemicals that could be used or converted to make weapons. When necessary it allows for short-notice inspections as well. The CWC is implemented by the Organization for the Prohibition of Chemical Weapons, located in The Hague, Netherlands.

The United States and the Soviet Union entered into two bilateral agreements regarding chemical weapons in order to facilitate the CWC. A memorandum of understanding signed in 1989 called for two phases of data exchanges and inspections of facilities. Phase 1 was completed in December 1989, when the United States and the Soviet Union declared that they had 29,000 and 40,000 agent metric tons, respectively. Phase 2 called for more detailed exchange of information and more thorough inspections; a series of presidential summits extended the Phase 2 deadline to 2007. A bilateral destruction agreement was signed in Washington, D.C., on 1 June 1990. This agreement bans chemical weapon production, provides a schedule for the destruction of all chemical weapons, and allows for on-site inspections. Financial assistance to help Russia meet these deadlines was provided by the Nunn-Lugar Act, which created the U.S. Cooperative Threat Reduction program.

Comprehensive Test Ban Treaty

The concept of a comprehensive test ban can be found in the preamble to the Limited Test Ban Treaty, signed in 1963. Negotiations on a comprehensive ban between the United States, the United Kingdom, and the Soviet Union from 1977 to 1980 ended without result. Nonetheless, the original five nuclear powers have enacted unilateral testing moratoriums. The U.S. moratorium was initiated by Congress on 4 September 1992 and was extended through 2001 by President Bill Clinton. President George W. Bush has urged all states to continue existing testing moratoria.

After initial consultation between the five nuclear powers, on 19 November 1993 the First Committee of the United Nations (UN) General Assembly approved a resolution by consensus that advocated a global treaty to ban all nuclear weapon tests. As urged by the UN resolution, the Conference on Disarmament created the Nuclear Test Ban Ad Hoc Committee of the Conference on Disarmament, which held several negotiating rounds beginning in 1994. The result was a treaty opened for signature on 24 September 1996. Although 161 states have signed the treaty, it cannot enter into force without 44 states having ratified it, including 13 key states. As of early 2002 only 41 had done so. The group of key states includes the United States and China as well as India, Pakistan, and Israel. The United States was the first country to sign the CTBT; however, citing concerns with verifiability, the U.S. Senate voted against ratification on 13 October 1999.

Although it has yet to enter into force, the CTBT verification regime has moved forward with concrete steps. It now includes a global network of hydroacoustic and seismic stations, infrared and radionucleide sensors, and the right to conduct on-site inspections. The treaty established a new international organization in Vienna, the Comprehensive Test Ban Treaty Organization, to implement the treaty and oversee compliance.

Conference on Disarmament

The Conference on Disarmament is the independent negotiating body of the United Nations (UN) for arms control treaties. Established in 1979, it succeeded other negotiating forums dating back to 1960. It is one of three international disarmament forums (with the UN Disarmament Commission and the UN General Assembly First Committee), but it is the only body that negotiates treaties. The conference consists of 66 members, including the five original nuclear weapon states. Additional states are allowed to participate as nonmembers. Although they maintain an open agenda, participants normally discuss weapons of mass destruction, conventional weapons, reduction of military budgets and armed forces, and confidence-building measures. Most of the work on these topics is accomplished in ad hoc committees. The Conference on Disarmament is located in Geneva, Switzerland.

Confidence- and Security-Building Measures

Confidence- and security-building measures (CSBMs) are intended to foster transparency and trust through purposely designed cooperative measures. They help clarify states' military intentions, reduce uncertainties about potentially threatening military activities, and constrain opportunities for surprise attack or coercion. As one example of a CSBM in the European context, the Conference on Security and Cooperation in Europe (CSCE, the forerunner of the Organization for Security and Cooperation in Europe, or OSCE) established a series of agreements and procedures designed to increase the security of members through increased military transparency and cooperation. The Helsinki Final Act, signed in 1975, was the first of these measures.

A CSCE subcommittee, the Conference on Disarmament in Europe, met from 1984 to 1986. One of the results of this conference was the Stockholm document, which entered into force in January 1987, expanding the requirements for notification and providing for observation of military activities. Members of the CSCE met in 1989 and 1990 to strengthen existing CSBMs. The result was Vienna Document 1990, which entered into force on 1 January 1991. Vienna Document 1992 supplemented these measures and entered into force on 1 May 1992. Vienna Document 1994 was signed 28 November 1994. Vienna Document 1999 entered into force 1 January 2000. Each of the Vienna documents updated and expanded the previous constraints on the 54 OSCE participants, including restrictions on the size and notification procedures for large-scale military activities in Europe. The member states further agreed to a Military Code of Conduct that is designed to describe how they agreed military operations should be conducted to safeguard the rights and property of civilians. Vienna Document 1999 also provides for the evaluation and inspection of OSCE members' military facilities.

Conventional Armed Forces in Europe Treaty

The Treaty on Conventional Armed Forces in Europe (CFE) was signed by the 16 members of the North Atlantic Treaty Organization (NATO) and the eight former Warsaw Pact states on 19 November 1990. There are now 30 state parties to the CFE Treaty. The area of application for the treaty is commonly referred to as the Atlantic to the Urals (ATTU). For those countries that either do not fall within this area, such as the United States and Canada, or those that have territory extending outside of the area, such as Russia, Turkey, and Kazakhstan, the treaty's limits apply only to forces stationed in the ATTU zone.

The CFE Treaty divides Europe into two groups: NATO, and members of the former Warsaw Treaty Organization, limiting conventional arms equally in both. Each group's holdings are limited in five major categories: tanks, artillery, armored combat vehicles, combat aircraft, and attack helicopters.

Four nested zones were created with specific limits on the ground equipment allowed in each zone. These zones were designed to reduce the large troop concentrations in Central Europe, thus decreasing the threat of a surprise attack. There were limits put on the number of forces that could be stationed in the so-called flank zone. This was an area that included both the Leningrad and North Caucasus military districts of the USSR. This was done to prevent the Soviet Union (now the Russian Federation) from repositioning its forces previously located in Central Europe to the borders of Turkey and Norway, forcing them instead to be moved deep within Russia.

The treaty established limits in all categories of military equipment for both NATO and the Warsaw Pact. The members of these two groups then negotiated their respective national totals within those limitations. The resulting national limits were designed to stress the importance that no one nation dominate the continent. Additionally, restrictions were placed on the amount of equipment that one state could station on the territory of another. Personnel limits were addressed in the Concluding Act of the Negotiation on Personnel Strength of Conventional Armed Forces in Europe (the so-called CFE-1A Treaty), signed in Vienna on 9 July 1992. This was a political agreement that allowed each state to set its own manpower limits. The levels are subject to discussion but not negotiation.

The CFE Treaty allows for several methods of ensuring compliance, including national and multinational technical means, information exchanges, and on-site inspections, all of which are supervised by the Joint Consultative Group in Vienna.

In May 1992 the members of the Commonwealth of Independent States that had territory within the area of application met in Tashkent to divide the former Soviet Union's allotment of equipment.

At the 1 December 1996 Organization for Security and Cooperation in Europe heads of state summit in Lisbon, state parties to the CFE agreed to revise the treaty. On 24 July 1997 a plan was devised to set national maximum force levels for each signator rather than keeping collective limits on the original groups of states. A document revising the treaty in this manner was signed at the OSCE summit in Istanbul in November 1999. Entry into force for a "new" CFE Treaty will take place following ratification by all 30 state parties.

Cooperative Threat Reduction Program

In the fall of 1991 conditions in the disintegrating Soviet Union created a global threat to nuclear safety and stability. The U.S. Congress, recognizing a window of opportunity to materially reduce the threat from nuclear weapons in the former Soviet Union and the proliferation potential they represented, enacted the Soviet Nuclear Threat Reduction Act—also called the Nunn-Lugar Act for its primary sponsors. Subsequently the program has expanded to include all weapons of mass destruction (WMD), assistance for defense conversion, and military-to-military contacts.

The Cooperative Threat Reduction program provides assistance to reduce or eliminate the threat posed by the thousands of existing WMD and associated infrastructure remaining in the former Soviet Union. Through the program, Kazakhstan, Ukraine, and Belarus are now nuclear weapon–free. In Russia primary program objectives include accelerating WMD dismantlement and destruction while ensuring a strong chain of custody for fissile material transport and storage. These objectives also foster compliance with the Strategic Arms Reduction Treaties, the Lisbon protocol, the Nuclear Non-Proliferation Treaty, the Chemical Weapons Convention, and a 1994 trilateral statement on biological weapons. As of 2000 more than $3 billion had been spent on the program. In June 1999 the United States and the Russian Federation extended the program seven more years.

Environmental Modification Convention

On 18 May 1977 34 nations signed the Convention on the Prohibition of Military or Any Other Hostile Use of Environmental Modification Techniques in Geneva. It entered into force on 5 October 1978. Although the use of environmental modification techniques was not considered likely in military planning when the convention was signed, this treaty reflected an attempt to preempt the consideration of such techniques in the future. The convention includes a prohibition against the deliberate manipulation of natural processes of the earth, the atmosphere, and outer space, including changes in the weather, the ozone layer, and the ionosphere, and upsetting the ecological balance of a region. As of January 2002, 51 states had signed the convention.

Fissile Material Cut-Off Treaty

The idea of a fissile material production cutoff gained prominence from 1956 through 1969. Limited success was realized in 1964 when the United States, the United Kingdom, and the Soviet Union announced reductions in the production of weapon-grade fissionable materials. The success of superpower arms control initiatives, a U.S. halt in production of fissile material, and President Bill Clinton's speech to the United Nations in September 1993 all provided renewed impetus for a cutoff convention.

The Conference on Disarmament began preliminary discussions on a fissile material cutoff convention during its 1994 session. In tandem with these negotiations, technical discussions were held in Vienna, with assistance from the International Atomic Energy Association, to address technical and verification issues. Among the more prominent obstacles to serious negotiations were differing views on whether the talks would cover only future production or also encompass existing stocks of weapon-grade nuclear material. Once the Indian and Pakistani nuclear programs became public knowledge in 1998, both dropped their resistance to a fissile material production ban, which served as another obstacle. The Conference on Disarmament reached consensus on a negotiating mandate in 1998. Today, however, some delegations want the Fissile Material Cutoff Treaty to be negotiated only in parallel with other discussions on nuclear disarmament and preventing the weaponization of outer space. Such perspectives have prevented the development of a consensus on the treaty within the Conference on Disarmament.

Forum for Security Cooperation

At the July 1992 Helsinki summit of the Conference on Security and Cooperation in Europe, a decision was made to form the 54-nation Forum for Security Cooperation (FSC). This organization, which meets weekly in Vienna, is tasked with carrying out follow-on negotiations to the Conventional Forces in Europe Treaty, the CFE-1A Treaty, and the confidence- and security-building measures (CSBMs) included in the Vienna documents. Additionally, this body oversees implementation, implementation assessment, discussion, and clarification of existing CSBMs.

The purpose of the FSC is to implement a work program to address concerns regarding arms control, disarmament, and confidence- and security-building measures; enhance regular consultation and cooperation among participating states relating to security matters; and further the process of reducing the risk of conflict.

Geneva Convention

The Geneva Convention is really four separate conventions, all of which were signed on 12 August 1949. Geneva Convention I (Amelioration of the Condition of the Wounded and Sick in Armed Forces in the Field) builds upon the Red Cross convention, signed in Geneva on 27 July 1929. It states that persons taking no part in hostilities, and those placed hors de combat by sickness, wounds, or detention, shall be treated humanely. It lists prohibited actions by a belligerent. It also describes appropriate actions for caring for the wounded and sick of either side in a conflict. For example, the winner of a battle agrees to search the field for wounded and dead and show them all courtesy. Belligerents agree to forward to each other the names of wounded, sick, and dead taken or discovered by them, as well as personal effects found on the battlefield. They shall also honorably inter or cremate all bodies after determining their identities. Geneva Convention II (Amelioration of Wounded, Sick, and Shipwrecked Members of Armed Forces at Sea) lays out similar rules. Geneva Convention III (Treatment of Prisoners of War) describes who can be a prisoner, outlines general protections for prisoners, and describes requirements for their humane treatment, including rules regarding quarters, food, clothing, and hygiene and medical attention. Geneva Convention IV (Protection of Civilian Persons in Time of War) deals with identifying protected civilians, as well as detailing protections to be provided, including sanctuary for hospitals.

The Geneva conventions were buttressed by United Nations General Assembly Resolution 2675 (Protection of Civilians), passed 9 December 1970.

Geneva Protocol

The Protocol for the Prohibition of the Use in War of Asphyxiating, Poisonous, or Other Gases, and of Bacteriological Methods of Warfare (the Geneva protocol) was an attempt by the victorious powers of World War I to ensure that chemical weapons were never again used on the field of battle. The restrictions imposed on Germany, Austria, Bulgaria, and Hungary in their peace treaties, including the Versailles Treaty, were codified in the Washington Naval Treaty of 1922 and, three years later, in the Geneva protocol. The protocol was signed on 17 June 1925 and entered into force on 8 February 1928. The protocol was honored by most parties during World War II, but violations by Iran and Iraq in the 1980s led to an international conference in Paris in 1989 that resulted in the

Chemical Weapons Convention. The United States did not ratify the protocol until 22 January 1975. The protocol has been signed by 135 nations.

The Hague Conventions

The Hague conventions were adopted in the Netherlands at the turn of the twentieth century and represented one of the earliest multinational attempts at regulating war. Hague Convention II (1899) limited sieges and bombardments and pronounced that the right of belligerents to adopt means of injuring the enemy is not unlimited. Specifically, the convention restricted several aspects of warfare: the use of poisoned arms, to kill or wound "treacherously," to kill or wound soldiers who are surrendering, to declare that no quarter will be given, to employ weapons that cause superfluous injury, to misuse a flag of truce or the uniform of an enemy, to wantonly destroy property, to attack an undefended city, to attack without warning, and to pillage a city. Before sieges and bombardments all opportunities should be taken to warn the besieged authorities and to protect cultural and scientific sites and hospitals. Hague Convention IV (1907) reiterated those rules and added new restrictions, including the abolishment or suspension of laws relating to the citizens of a belligerent country. It also outlawed forcing the nationals of a hostile country to take part in the operations of war directed against their own country.

Helsinki Agreements

U.S. President Bill Clinton and Russian Federation President Boris Yeltsin agreed to the Joint Statement on Parameters on Future Reductions in Nuclear Forces at their meeting in Helsinki, Finland, in March 1997. This statement underscored the requirement for ratification of the second Strategic Arms Reduction Treaty (START II) by both countries, as well as an agreement to begin negotiations on START III once START II entered into force. The goal of START III negotiations was to be a ceiling of 2,000–2,500 strategic warheads by 31 December 2007. That date is also the extended deadline for START II eliminations. In order to ensure the irreversibility of these reductions, the new treaty will include inventory transparency provisions and call for the destruction of nuclear warheads. The two sides also agreed to discuss nonstrategic nuclear weapons (tactical weapons and sea-launched cruise missiles) in a separate but parallel forum, and they agreed to the goal of making all START treaties unlimited in duration. The March agreement was codified in memorandums of understanding signed in New York on 26 September 1997.

Helsinki Final Act

Signed in 1975, the Helsinki Final Act was the first of a series of agreements and procedures designed to increase the security of the members of the Conference on Security and Cooperation in Europe (later the Organization for Security and Cooperation in Europe). It was signed by the United States, Canada, and all European nations except Albania. In addition to recognizing existing borders and the need for economic cooperation, the act required advance notification of military maneuvers involving more than 25,000 troops. This agreement set the foundations for the complicated and increasingly intrusive measures that followed in the realm of confidence- and security-building measures.

Hot Line Agreements

In order to minimize the chances of miscommunication leading to miscalculation during times of emergency, the first of three so-called hot line agreements between Washington and Moscow was signed in Geneva on 20 June 1963. Both sides agreed to a direct communications link between their capitals using telegraph-teleprinter terminals, duplex wire telegraph circuits, and radiotelegraph circuits, as well as procedures for sending nearly instantaneous messages in both languages. In a revised treaty signed in Washington on 30 September 1971, the two countries agreed to a direct communications link encompassing satellite communications systems and teleprinter terminals. Another memorandum of understanding was signed by both parties on 17 July 1984 in Washington, in which they agreed to improve direct communications by establishing links employing INTELSAT satellites and modems, facsimile machines, and computers.

Incidents at Sea Agreement

The U.S.-Soviet Agreement on the Prevention of Incidents on and over the High Seas was signed in Moscow on 25 May 1972. The agreement was a confidence-building measure designed to reduce the frequency and severity of incidents of ships and aircraft interfering with one another at sea, thereby increasing stability and reducing the possibility of conflict by accident, miscalculation, and failure of communication. It established steps to avoid collision, safe distances to remain from the other sides' formations, standard international signals when maneuvering near one another, and similar measures.

Intermediate-Range Nuclear Forces Treaty

The U.S.-Soviet Treaty on the Elimination of Their Intermediate-Range and Shorter-Range Missiles (INF) provided for the complete elimination of all U.S. and Soviet intermediate-range (1,000–5,500 kilometers) and shorter-range (500–1,000 kilometers) ground-launched ballistic and cruise missiles. The INF Treaty was signed on 8 December 1987 and entered into force on 1 June 1988. The treaty is of unlimited duration; the inspection regime lasted 13 years, ending on 31 December 2001. The INF treaty was marked by the unprecedented use of intrusive inspections.

Despite the fact that the final elimination of missiles was completed by 1 June 1991, the on-site inspection regime continued until 2001 to ensure compliance. This included continuous monitoring of the ground-launched cruise missile final assembly facility at Magna, Utah, and the SS-20 missile facility at Votkinsk, Russia. Additionally, on-site inspections of former missile operating bases and missile support facilities were allowed until 31 May 2001. Some of these facilities were located in successor states other than the Russian Federation. The Special Verification Commission was the body tasked with overseeing verification and compliance; it was based in Geneva.

Law of the Sea

The United Nations Convention on the Law of the Sea was opened for signature in December 1982 and entered into force on 16 November 1994. U.S. reluctance to sign the Law of the Sea convention was based on its potential restriction on possible future entrepreneurial deep-sea mining ventures by itself and other industrialized states. Most countries of the world are signatories to the Law of the Sea. In addition to defining rights and obligations with regard to mining the ocean floor, the Law of the Sea also guarantees freedom of navigation and overflight.

The Law of the Sea established several specific zones with corresponding rights. Within these zones a coastal state can exercise limited control as necessary to prevent and punish infringement of its customs, immigration, and sanitary laws and regulations that occur within its territory or territorial sea. Exclusive Economic Zones, which can extend out 200 nautical miles, are areas beyond and adjacent to the territorial sea. The convention elaborates the principles of freedom of the high seas that have developed over many centuries. However, the right to fish has been made subject to additional requirements. The continental shelf is the seabed and subsoil beyond a state's territorial seas (but not the water and airspace above), which may extend out to 200 nautical miles from the baseline over which a state can exercise sovereign control.

The convention's major provisions on navigation and overflight include the right of innocent passage (not including the right of submerged passage). Freedom of navigation and overflight through international straits is guaranteed for merchant ships, cargo ships, naval ships and task forces, submarines, and military aircraft. International airspace begins at the outer limit of the territorial seas. Hence, sovereignty extends over territorial seas, as well as over all inland waters and land territory.

The convention does not recognize the right to establish military security zones. The convention protects and strengthens the principle of sovereign immunity for warships and military aircraft. Convention provisions on the protection and preservation of the marine environment do not apply to warships and military aircraft.

Limited Test Ban Treaty

The Treaty Banning Nuclear Weapon Tests in Atmosphere, in Outer Space, and Under Water (known as the Partial Test Ban Treaty or the Limited Test Ban Treaty [LTBT]) was signed on 5 August 1963 by the United States, the United Kingdom, and the Soviet Union and entered into force on 10 October 1963. The signatories agreed not to carry out any nuclear weapon test explosion in the atmosphere, in outer space, underwater, or in any other environment that would cause radioactive debris to spread outside the territorial limits of the state that conducted the test. There are currently 125 parties to the treaty.

Mine Ban Convention

The Convention on the Prohibition of the Use, Stockpiling, Production, and Transfer of Anti-Personnel Mines and on Their Destruction was opened for signature on 3 December 1997 and entered into force on 1 March 1999 following ratification by 40 states. The initial campaign that led to the convention was begun by a group of nongovernmental organizations, largely humanitarian groups who saw their work impeded by the indiscriminate use of mines. A significant number of nations came to support a ban, which was negotiated in Ottawa, Canada. After initial support and involvement in the negotiations, the United States refused to sign the treaty in order to preserve its ability to use mines to defend the border between North and South Korea. Several other key mine-producing nations, including Russia and China, have refused to sign the treaty. Almost all members of NATO are signatories.

The United States has been a leader in other efforts to reduce or redress the effects of antipersonnel mines. In 1992, the United States announced a moratorium on exports of antipersonnel landmines and in 1996 unilaterally ended its use of non–self-destructing antipersonnel landmines except in marked and monitored areas on the Korean Peninsula. The United States has sought to pursue improvements in the Certain Conventional Weapons Convention and through the Conference on Disarmament.

Missile Technology Control Regime

In April 1987 the United States, Canada, France, West Germany, Italy, Japan, and the United Kingdom created the Missile Technology Control Regime (MTCR) to restrict the proliferation of missiles and missile technology. The MTCR is the only multilateral missile nonproliferation regime. It is a voluntary arrangement, not an international agreement or treaty, among countries with an interest in stopping the proliferation of missile technology. The regime develops export guidelines that are applied to a list of controlled items and implemented according to each nation's procedures. In January 1993 the guidelines were expanded to restrict the spread of missiles and unmanned aerial vehicles with a range of at least 300 kilometers capable of delivering a 500-kilogram payload or a weapon of mass destruction. The guidelines are designed not to impede a nation's space program as long as it does not contribute to the delivery of weapons of mass destruction. Membership in the MTCR is open to any country that commits to the principles of nonproliferation and has a record of effective export controls. The MTCR regime currently has 33 members.

Nuclear Non-Proliferation Treaty

The Treaty on the Non-Proliferation of Nuclear Weapons (NPT) obligates nuclear weapon state parties (NWS) to the treaty (the United States, Russia, United Kingdom, France, and China) to three main principles: not to transfer nuclear weapons or control over such weapons to any recipient, directly or indirectly; not to assist, encourage, or induce any non–nuclear weapon states (NNWS) to manufacture or otherwise acquire such weapons or seek control over them; and to actively work toward complete nuclear disarmament. Additionally, the NWS are required to assist NNWS in the use of nuclear energy for peaceful purposes, including the benefits of peaceful nuclear explosions.

NNWS may not receive the transfer of nuclear weapons or control over them. They are also prohibited from manufacturing, seeking help in manufacturing, or otherwise obtaining nuclear weapons. Although they are known or suspected of having nuclear weapons, India, Pakistan, and Israel are officially NNWS, according to the treaty.

All states must accept safeguards negotiated with the International Atomic Energy Agency (IAEA) to prevent the diversion of nuclear energy from peaceful purposes to nuclear weapons. The IAEA is the treaty's implementation and compliance body and meets in Vienna. The NPT is also reinforced by two multilateral nuclear export control organizations: the NPT Exporters Committee (also known as the Zangger Committee) and the Nuclear Suppliers Group.

The NPT was signed on 1 July 1968 and entered into force on 5 March 1970. The original duration called for a review after 25 years. At the 1995 treaty review conference the state parties agreed to an indefinite extension of the regime. The parties agreed to principles and objectives for nuclear nonproliferation and disarmament, including the goal of achieving a comprehensive nuclear test ban. The conference called upon the states in the Middle East to agree to the creation of a zone free of weapons of mass destruction. Review conferences will continue to take place every five years.

At the 2000 review conference in New York the NWSs agreed to unequivocally seek "the total elimination of their nuclear arsenals, leading to nuclear disarmament," but no time line for doing so was agreed upon.

Nuclear Suppliers Group

The founding members of the Nuclear Suppliers Group and the Zangger Committee began meeting in April 1975 to help implement the export control restrictions of the Nuclear Non-Proliferation Treaty (NPT). They were motivated by India's explosion of a nuclear device in May 1974. Like the Zangger Committee (see entry below), the Nuclear Suppliers Group (also known as the London Club) adopted a "trigger list" of items related to nuclear weapon production. These guidelines were published by the IAEA in February 1978. The 39 members of the Nuclear Suppliers Group have agreed to restrict exports of sensitive technology, including uranium enrichment and reprocessing equipment. In 1992 the Nuclear Suppliers Group adopted the rule that members would make nuclear exports to non–nuclear weapon states only if the recipient had accepted International Atomic Energy Agency inspections on all of its nuclear facilities— a situation known as "full scope safeguards." This rule has banned exports to Israel, India, and Pakistan. China is the only nuclear weapon state that is not a member of this group.

Nuclear Weapon–Free Zones

There have been several efforts by international and regional organizations to ban or limit the use of nuclear materials in specific regions of the world. In addition, three separate treaties, which have been signed by almost all the nations of the world, prohibit nuclear materials from being stored and tested in outer space, on the seabed floor, and in Antarctica.

Five regional nuclear-free zones have been established through treaties, effectively making most of the Southern Hemisphere nuclear free. The South Pacific Nuclear Free Zone, created on 6 August 1985 with the signing of the Treaty of Rarotonga, entered into force on 11 December 1986. It is a multilateral treaty that bans the stationing, manufacturing, testing, and dumping of nuclear weapons and nuclear waste within the zone. The issue of ship and aircraft traffic is left up to individual countries. There are 11 parties to the treaty, including Australia and New Zealand. The Latin America Nuclear Weapon Free Zone was formalized in the Treaty of Tlatelolco, signed in Mexico City on 14 February 1967 with entry into force 25 April 1968. The treaty bans the storage and testing of nuclear weapons within the signatory countries but does allow for the peaceful use of nuclear material. All Latin American states except Cuba have ratified the treaty. The Treaty of Pelindaba was signed on 11 April 1996 in Cairo, Egypt, to create the Africa Nuclear Weapon Free Zone. Entry into force awaits ratification by 28 African states. The Treaty of Bangkok, signed 15 December 1995, established the Southeast Asia Nuclear Weapon Free Zone. Seven of the ten regional states had to ratify the treaty before entry into force, which occurred on 28 March 1997. Its provisions cover foreign ships and aircraft transiting the region, but the United States has not recognized this treaty. The Antarctic Treaty was signed on 1 December 1959 in Washington, D.C., and entered into force on 23 June 1961. One of the first international arms control treaties, it demilitarized the continent, ensuring its use for peaceful purposes and scientific exploration.

Efforts are currently under way to establish additional nuclear- or nuclear-weapon–free zones in the Middle East, South Asia, and the South Atlantic.

Open Skies Treaty

The Treaty on Open Skies was signed in Helsinki on 24 March 1992 by members of the North Atlantic Treaty Organization and the former Warsaw Pact. The United States ratified it on 3 November 1993. Each participating state has the right to conduct, and the obligation to receive, overhead flights by unarmed fixed-wing observation aircraft; the aircraft can carry a variety of sensors. Normally the inspecting party will provide the aircraft used in the overflight, but the host nation may require that one of its aircraft be used. The number of flights each country can conduct and must receive is limited to negotiated annual quotas. Any state may acquire the data from any overflight.

On 2 November 2001 Russia and Belarus deposited their instruments of ratification. The treaty entered into force on 1 January 2002. It is of unlimited duration with an initial review after three years and at five-year intervals thereafter.

Outer Space Treaty

The Treaty on the Principles Governing the Activities of States in the Exploration and Use of Outer Space Including the Moon and Other Celestial Bodies was negotiated primarily between the United States and Soviet Union. There are currently 113 states parties to the treaty. It serves to limit the militarization of outer space. Signed on 27 January 1967, the treaty prohibits any state from placing weapons of mass destruction in outer space and deploying them on celestial bodies. In addition, all celestial bodies are to be used solely for peaceful purposes and may not be used for military bases, fortifications, and weapon-testing of any kind.

Peaceful Nuclear Explosions Treaty

The U.S.-Soviet Treaty on Underground Nuclear Explosions for Peaceful Purposes (PNET) was signed on 28 May 1976, but its protocol on the verification of compliance was not completed until 1 June 1990. It allows peaceful nuclear explosions outside declared testing sites but prohibits any individual explosion exceeding a yield of 150 kilotons. Group explosions are limited to a yield of 1.5 megatons, provided that each individual explosion's yield can be verified and does not exceed 150 kilotons. The protocol for PNET requires notification of explosions and allows for on-site inspections and other methods of measuring the yield of the detonation.

Presidential Nuclear Initiatives

Between September 1991 and January 1992 a series of initiatives by the presidents of the United States and Russia significantly affected the nuclear force structure. Some measures simply accelerated measures mandated by the first Strategic Arms Reduction Treaty (START I), whereas others were incorporated into START II. In addition, there were binding actions not addressed in either treaty. In late 2001 the U.S. and Russian presidents agreed to additional unilateral but reciprocated reductions.

On 27 September 1991 President George Bush announced that the United States would remove all U.S. strategic bombers and 450 Minuteman II intercontinental ballistic missiles (ICBMs) from day-to-day alert; remove all tactical nuclear weapons on surface ships, attack submarines, and land-based naval aircraft; and cancel plans to develop a nuclear short-range attack missile, the Peacekeeper Rail Garrison ICBM, and the mobile version of the Small ICBM. He also proposed eliminating all U.S. and Soviet ICBMs containing multiple independently targetable reentry vehicles (MIRVs).

On 5 October 1991 Soviet President Mikhail Gorbachev responded by declaring similar reductions. He also suggested reducing each side's nuclear arsenal to 5,000 warheads (below the START I limit of 6,000) and reducing strategic offensive arms by approximately 50 percent. He suggested discussions on nonnuclear ABM systems and a one-year moratorium on nuclear testing.

In his State of the Union address to the U.S. Congress on 28 January 1992, President Bush announced further reductions in the U.S. strategic force to include limiting B-2 bomber production to 20 planes; limiting advanced cruise missile production to 640; and canceling the Small ICBM and Peacekeeper missiles and the W-88 warhead for Trident missiles. Additionally, he stated that if Russia were to eliminate all MIRVed ICBMs, the United States would take the following actions to cut strategic nuclear warheads to approximately 4,700: eliminate Peacekeeper missiles; reduce Minuteman III missiles to one warhead per missile; reduce the number of Trident submarine warheads by a third; and convert a large number of strategic bombers to conventional use.

Russian Federation President Boris Yeltsin responded on 29 January 1992 by stating Russia's intention to abide by all arms control agreements signed by the Soviet Union, as well as his support for the Nuclear Non-Proliferation Treaty, the Missile Technology Control Regime, the Comprehensive Test Ban Treaty, and the Fissile Material Cut-Off Treaty. He made public additional reductions in strategic offensive forces and proposed several new U.S.-Russia reciprocal actions.

In January 1994 Presidents Bill Clinton and Boris Yeltsin agreed at the Moscow summit that strategic forces under their control would be detargeted (no longer aimed at each other) by 30 May of that year. The United Kingdom took a similar initiative.

In November 2001 Russian President Vladimir Putin met with President George W. Bush in Washington, D.C., and Crawford, Texas, where they agreed to further reductions in each side's nuclear arsenal. Attempting to overcome the stalemate in strategic negotiations, the two leaders established a goal of 1,700–2,200 long-range warheads on each side. Russia expressed its desire to eventually have the deal formalized in a treaty, which was signed by both presidents on 24 May 2002 in Moscow.

Seabed Treaty

The U.S.-Soviet Treaty on the Prohibition of the Emplacement of Nuclear Weapons and Other Weapons of Mass Destruction on the Seabed and the Ocean Floor and in the Subsoil Thereof was signed by the parties on 11 February 1971 and entered into force on 18 May 1982. Like the Antarctic Treaty, the Outer Space Treaty, and the various nuclear weapon–free zones, the Seabed Treaty seeks to prevent the introduction of international conflict and nuclear weapons into an area previously free of them. Negotiations over the treaty, however, took several years, as interest in the seafloor was growing among many nations as the science of oceanography advanced. The treaty outlaws a party placing weapons of mass destruction on or in the seabed beyond a 12-mile coastal zone. Review conferences have been held every five to seven years.

Strategic Arms Limitation Treaty (SALT I)

SALT I included both the Anti-Ballistic Missile Treaty as well as the U.S.-Soviet Interim Agreement on Certain Measures with Respect to the Limitation of Strategic Offensive Arms. Both were signed on 26 May 1972 and were the result of the first series of Strategic Arms Limitation Talks, which had begun in November 1969. The interim agreement froze the number of strategic ballistic missile launchers at existing levels (1,054 for the United States, 1,618 for the Soviet Union) and prohibited the conversion of older launchers to accommodate modern heavy intercontinental ballistic missiles (ICBMs). An increase in submarine-launched ballistic missiles (SLBMs) was allowed provided an equal number of land-based launchers were destroyed. The United States was authorized up to 710 SLBMs, the Soviet Union 950. Mobile ICBMs were not covered by the agreement.

The agreement was perceived as a holding action, and its duration was limited to five years in the hope that a more comprehensive agreement would be reached. The U.S. Congress passed a joint resolution supporting the agreement, and it entered into force on 3 October 1972.

Strategic Arms Limitation Treaty (SALT II)

The U.S.-Soviet Treaty on the Limitation of Strategic Offensive Arms resulted from talks lasting from November 1972 until 18 June 1979, when the treaty was signed in Vienna. The treaty placed limits on ballistic missiles and their launchers but did not require the reduction of such items. Each country was limited to 2,250 launchers, with a sublimit of 1,320 launchers for missiles with multiple independently targetable reentry vehicles (MIRVs). MIRVed ballistic missiles were limited to 1,200, of which only 820 could be intercontinental ballistic missiles (ICBMs). In addition, new ICBMs were limited to ten warheads, whereas submarine-launched ballistic missiles were allowed to carry up to 14 warheads. Last, the treaty prohibited spaced-based nuclear weapons, fractional orbital missiles, and rapid-reload missile launchers.

A protocol to the treaty was signed at the same time and was to remain in effect until 31 December 1981. The protocol prohibited the deployment of ground-launched cruise missiles (GLCMs) and sea-launched cruise missiles (SLCMs) with a range of over 600 kilometers, as well as mobile ICBMs. Additionally, MIRVs, GLCMs, and SLCMs with a range over 600 kilometers could not be tested.

President Jimmy Carter submitted the treaty to the U.S. Senate immediately following the signing, but due to political considerations and the Soviet invasion of Afghanistan, he was forced to remove it from congressional review in January 1980. Because the treaty was never ratified, it became a politically, not legally, binding agreement. On 27 May 1986 President Ronald Reagan, after citing Soviet violations, declared that the United States would no longer abide by the limits of the SALT agreements; the United States exceeded those limits on 28 November 1986.

Strategic Arms Reduction Treaty (START I)

The U.S.-Soviet Treaty on the Reduction and Limitation of Strategic Offensive Arms, which was signed on 31 July 1991, reduced U.S. and former Soviet strategic offensive arms—intercontinental ballistic missiles (ICBMs), submarine-launched ballistic missiles (SLBMs), and heavy bombers—to 1,600 and attributed warheads—an agreed-upon number of warheads that are associated with each weapon system—to 6,000. There were additional sublimits for attributed warheads: 4,900 warheads on deployed ballistic missiles, and 1,100 warheads on deployed mobile ICBMs. The former Soviet Union was also limited to 154 deployed heavy ICBMs (down from 308 before the treaty), each carrying 10 warheads.

Warheads carried by heavy bombers, including those in long-range nuclear air-launched cruise missiles, were counted at a discount rate. Especially significant was the discount rate for penetrating bombers, which counted as only one warhead regardless of how many missiles they were capable of carrying. Politically binding side agreements also limited the number of deployed nuclear sea-launched cruise missiles and Soviet Backfire bombers.

An extensive series of on-site inspections and an exchange of geographical and technical data for all systems, with regular updates, complemented each party's national technical means to monitor compliance with the treaty. The two sides agreed to exchange telemetric information from all test flights of ICBMs and SLBMs. The Joint Compliance and Inspection Commission is tasked with monitoring compliance with the treaty and has been meeting in Geneva since 1991.

On 23 May 1992 a protocol was signed in Lisbon that made START I a five-nation, multiparty treaty. The protocol and appended presidential letters obligated Belarus, Kazakhstan, and Ukraine to become nonnuclear state parties to the Nuclear Non-Proliferation Treaty (NPT). On 14 January 1994 in Moscow, the presidents of Ukraine, Russia, and the United States signed the Trilateral Agreement, which promised Ukraine financial and security assistance as a means of persuading Kiev to ratify START I and the NPT. On 5 December 1994 Ukraine deposited its instruments of ratification for the NPT, allowing START I to enter into force. Its duration is 15 years, with an option to extend at five-year intervals. Treaty limits were officially reached by 5 December 2001.

Strategic Arms Reduction Treaty (START II)

The 1991–1992 Presidential Nuclear Initiatives (see entry above) set the foundation for the signing of a joint understanding at the June 1992 summit between President George Bush and Russian Federation President Boris Yeltsin in Washington, D.C. The joint understanding called for the elimination of all intercontinental ballistic missiles (ICBMs) with multiple independently targetable reentry vehicles (MIRVs) and deep cuts in submarine-launched ballistic missiles (SLBMs), forming the basis of the U.S.-Russia Treaty on Further Reduction and Limitation of Strategic Offensive Arms, or START II. This treaty was signed at the 3 January 1993 Moscow summit by Presidents Bush and Yeltsin. It relied heavily on START I for definitions, procedures, and verification. The U.S. Senate ratified START II on 26 January 1996, and the Russian Duma did so on 14 April 2000.

The eliminations are to take place pursuant to a two-phase process. Within seven years of the treaty's entry into force, each side must reduce its deployed strategic forces to 3,800–4,250 attributed warheads, within which the following sublimits apply: 1,200 warheads for MIRVed ICBMs, 650 warheads for heavy ICBMs, and 2,160 warheads for SLBMs. Phase 2 limits must be reached by 2003. At that time each party must have reduced its deployed strategic forces to 3,000–3,500 attributed warheads, within which the following sublimits apply: zero warheads for MIRVed ICBMs, 1,700–1,750 total warheads for SLBMs, and elimination of all heavy ICBMs. At the March 1997 Helsinki summit Presidents Bill Clinton and Boris Yeltsin agreed to extend the time for START II implementation and reductions to 31 December 2007. Systems to be eliminated under this treaty must be deactivated, however, by removing their warheads by December 2003. Because the treaty did not enter into force until April 2000, both phases must now be completed simultaneously.

In order to reach the lower warhead ceilings, the Russian Federation is allowed to download 105 SS-19 ICBMs by five warheads, leaving only one warhead per missile. Additionally, any missile that was previously equipped with six warheads or more, except for the SS-19s, must be destroyed, whereas those equipped with five or less may be retained provided they are downloaded to only one warhead.

START II also has several provisions regarding bombers. The B-2 must now be exhibited and is inspectable. A one-time reorientation of up to 100 nuclear heavy bombers to a conventional role is allowed without adhering to the START I conversion procedures as long as they were never accountable as long-range nuclear heavy bombers. The United States chose this option for its B-1 fleet. Additionally, conventional and nuclear bombers must be based separately and crews separately trained and have differences observable by national technical means and visible during inspection. START II also provides the right to change the number of nuclear warheads attributed to a bomber if there is a visible change in the plane's configuration. Approximately 1,300 warheads may be attributed to bombers in each country, depending on the number of ICBMs and SLBMs retained by each party.

Although this treaty builds on START I, some additional verification measures are included. START II significantly increases the number of on-site inspections, mostly relating to the retention of converted Russian heavy ICBM (SS-18) silos and the conversion of heavy bombers. Compliance is governed by the Bilateral Implementation Commission in Geneva.

Threshold Test Ban Treaty

The U.S.-Soviet Treaty on the Limitation of Underground Nuclear Weapons Tests was signed by the parties on 3 July 1974. It prohibits parties from the underground testing of nuclear weapons with a yield greater than 150 kilotons at declared testing sites. A subsequent protocol requires notification of explosions and provides various options for measuring the yield of the explosions, including on-site inspection for tests with a planned yield above 35 kilotons.

The United States has only one declared testing site, located in Nevada. The former Soviet Union maintained two testing sites, one within the Russian Federation, the other in Kazakhstan.

UN Register of Conventional Arms

The United Nations General Assembly adopted resolution 46/36L on 9 December 1991 entitled Transparency in Armaments. This resolution established an annual Register of Conventional Arms. UN member states were requested to provide data every calendar year on imports and exports in seven categories. These included the five categories found in the CFE Treaty (tanks, armored combat vehicles, artillery, attack helicopters, and combat aircraft) plus warships and missiles/missile launchers. No verification provisions accompanied the resolution, but its sponsors hoped that increased transparency would encourage restraint by both buyers and sellers, and would lead to public pressure on those states who supported irresponsible or destabilizing arms transfers.

Wassenaar Arrangement

On 18 December 1995, 28 nations meeting in Wassenaar, Netherlands, agreed to set up an export control organization. The Wassenaar Arrangement on Export

Controls for Conventional Arms and Dual-Use Goods and Technologies calls upon states parties to exchange data, notify other parties of violations of the controlled items list, and coordinate export licenses. Participation is voluntary. There is no enforcement mechanism, but a secretariat is located in Vienna, and a plenary session is held at least annually.

The participants agree to implement controls on a list of technologies and conventional weapons systems, known as the List of Dual-Use Goods and Technologies and the Munitions List. The latest updates to this list were approved at the plenary session held on 1 December 2000. As of January 2002 there were 44 member states.

Zangger Committee

The Zangger Committee was formed in 1974 to establish guidelines for implementing the export control provisions of the Non-Proliferation Treaty. Its official name is the NPT Exporters Committee. The committee developed a so-called trigger list of materials and equipment that triggers safeguards by the International Atomic Energy Agency, items that might otherwise be used to develop a nuclear explosive, including plutonium, highly enriched uranium, reactors, reprocessing and enrichment facilities, and associated equipment and supplies. The list is updated regularly. There are 34 states in the Zangger Committee, all of which (with the exception of China) are also members of the Nuclear Suppliers Group (see entry above).

Note

1. Appendixes complied from Jeffrey A. Larsen and Gregory J. Rattray, *Arms Control Toward the 21st Century* (Boulder: Lynne Rienner Publishers, 1996), pp. 296–328; Jeffrey A. Larsen and James M. Smith, *Historical Dictionary of Arms Control and Disarmament* (Lanham, MD: Scarecrow Press, forthcoming); *The Arms Control Reporter* (Cambridge: Institute for Defense and Disarmament Studies, annual); Richard Dean Burns, *Encyclopedia of Arms Control and Disarmament* (New York: Charles Scribner's Sons, 1993); and websites of the U.S. State Department (www.state.gov/t/ac/trty/index.cfm), the Federation of American Scientists (www.fas.org), and the U.S. Air Force National Security Policy Division (www.sunman1.saic.com:8002/xon/xonpu/armsctrl/profile_summary/index.shtml).

The Contributors

Christopher Carr is professor at Air War College in Montgomery, AL. He holds a Ph.D. from the London School of Economics.

Marie Isabelle Chevrier is associate professor at the University of Texas–Dallas. She earned her Ph.D. at Harvard University.

Schuyler Foerster is president of the Pittsburgh, PA, World Affairs Council. He earned a D.Phil. at Oxford University.

Jo L. Husbands is a senior program officer and director of the Committee on International Security and Arms Control at the National Academy of Sciences, Washington, DC. Her Ph.D. is from the University of Minnesota.

Kerry M. Kartchner is a member of the U.S. delegation to the Special Consultative Commission and serves in the U.S. State Department. Kerry's Ph.D. is from the University of Southern California.

Kurt J. Klingenberger, colonel, U.S. Air Force, is inspector general of the 5th Bomb Wing, Minot AFB, ND. He holds an M.A. from the Johns Hopkins University School of Advanced International Studies.

Jeffrey A. Larsen is a senior policy analyst with Science Applications International Corporation in Colorado Springs, CO. He earned his Ph.D. from Princeton University.

Peter R. Lavoy is assistant professor of national security affairs and director of the Center for Contemporary Conflict at the Naval Postgraduate School, Monterey, CA. He holds a Ph.D. from the University of California–Berkeley.

Jeffrey D. McCausland holds the class of 1961 Chair of Leadership, U.S. Naval Academy, Annapolis, MD. His Ph.D. is from the Fletcher School, Tufts University.

Patricia A. McFate lives in Santa Fe, NM, and served on the U.S. State Department's Arms Control and Nonproliferation Advisory Board from 1995 to 2001. Her Ph.D. is from Northwestern University.

John A. Nagl, major, U.S. Army, is an armor officer at Fort Riley, KS. He earned a D.Phil. at Oxford University.

Joseph F. Pilat is a senior analyst at Los Alamos National Laboratory, Los Alamos, NM. He holds a Ph.D. from Georgetown University.

Gregory J. Rattray, lieutenant colonel, U.S. Air Force, is commander of the 23rd Information Operations Squadron, San Antonio, TX. He holds a Ph.D. from the Fletcher School, Tufts University.

Brad Roberts, member of the research staff at the Institute for Defense Analyses in Alexandria, VA, earned his doctorate at Erasmus University, Rotterdam, Netherlands.

Guy B. Roberts is associate counsel (arms control) in the Office of Navy Strategic Systems Programs, Washington, DC. He holds a J.D. from the University of Denver and an L.L.M. from Georgetown University.

Thomas C. Schelling is distinguished university professor at the University of Maryland, College Park. He earned his Ph.D. at Harvard University.

Glen M. Segell, the Lord of Deadington, is director of the Institute of Security Policy. He holds a Ph.D. from the University of London.

Jennifer E. Sims is a professorial lecturer at the Johns Hopkins University School of Advanced International Studies in Washington, where she also earned a Ph.D.

Leonard (Sandy) Spector is deputy director of the Center for Nonproliferation Studies, Monterey Institute of International Studies, in Washington, DC. He holds a J.D. from Yale Law School.

Forrest E. Waller Jr. is vice president and senior scientist with Science Applications International Corporation in Arlington, VA. He holds an M.P.A. from the Woodrow Wilson School, Princeton University.

Michael O. Wheeler is senior defense analyst with Science Applications International Corporation in McLean, VA. He earned his Ph.D. at the University of Arizona.

James J. Wirtz is professor and chairman of the National Security Affairs Department, Naval Postgraduate School, Monterey, CA. He earned his Ph.D. at Columbia University.

Index

ABM Treaty. *See* Anti-Ballistic Missile (ABM) Treaty
Accidental launch, leading to retaliation, 275
Accidents Measures Agreement (1971), 30, 34, 104
Acheson, Dean, 67
ACRS. *See* Arms control and regional security (ACRS) working group
Additional Model Protocol, 95(n9)
Aerial reconnaissance programs, 25, 27, 87, 94(n6), 95(n9)
Afghanistan, Soviet invasion of, 32, 105
Africa: arms trade into, 232–234; arms trade within, 234–238; small arms proliferation, 229–230; WMD development, 230–231
Africa Nuclear Weapon Free Zone, 387
Agreed Framework with North Korea, 36, 50, 75(n1), 129, 134, 139(n36), 371
Agreements. *See* Treaties and agreements
Alamogordo, New Mexico, 101
Albania, 209, 211
Algeria, 139(n40), 219
Alliance-formation, in strategic nuclear arms control, 103–104
Al-Qaida extremists, 247–249
American Academy of Arts and Sciences, 63
American University speech, 27
Ancient warfare, 19
Andropov, Yuri, 33
Angola, arms trade into, 231
Antarctic Treaty (1959), 26, 102–103, 256, 387
Anthrax, 152, 231
Anti-Ballistic Missile (ABM) Treaty, 371–372; alternatives to, 282; ballistic missile defense systems, 297–299; Bush's (George W.) promise to withdraw from, 35; Bush's space weapons policy, 292; Cold War era, 317–318; negotiation of, 105; offense-defense relationship of the U.S. and Soviet Union, 271–272; outer space systems, 294; potential arms race with Russian Federation, 278; result of SALT, 29; as stabilizing force in international political relations, 56–57; START II conditions, 108; U.S. withdrawal from, 37, 116(n27), 281–282. *See also* Strategic Arms Limitation Talks
Anti-ballistic missile systems, 271, 372
Antipersonnel land mines. *See* Ottawa Convention
Antisatellite weapons, 292
ARABSAT, 292
Argentina: CTBT ratification, 139(n40); member of Korean Peninsula Energy Development Agency, 139(n36); renouncing nuclear weapons, 122
Armenia, 211
Arms Control and Disarmament Agency, 27, 65–66, 77(n19), 116(n34)
Arms control and regional security (ACRS) working group, 217–218, 225(n16)
Arms Control Export Act, 138(n33)
Arms control theory, 1–2, 6–7, 335
Arms race: future arms race with Russia, 277–279; military security dilemma leading to, 2
Arms reduction: Bush's (George W.) goal of, 35–36; Cold War conventional and nuclear reductions attempts, 25–26;

About the Book

More than a decade after the end of the Cold War, the need to control the spread of arms remains clear even as the usefulness of traditional paradigms is increasingly called into question. The authors of *Arms Control* thoroughly review this complex topic, exploring differing approaches to arms control, successes and failures thus far, and the likelihood of future agreements. With topics ranging from the United States and Europe to Africa, Asia, and the Middle East, from conventional weapons to potential threats from outer space—and cyberspace—the book is designed to serve as an accessible introduction to the subject of arms control, as well as a convenient, comprehensive resource for any student of international affairs.

Jeffrey A. Larsen is a senior policy analyst in the Strategies Group of Science Applications International Corporation (Colorado Springs) and president of Larsen Consulting.